P9-BJP-166

# ART
# AND THE SPIRIT
# OF MAN

# ART
# AND THE SPIRIT
# OF MAN

### RENE HUYGHE

*of the Académie Française*

HARRY N. ABRAMS, INC., *Publishers*

NEW YORK

This book is dedicated to the memory of Raymond Koechlin and
to my friend Jean-Louis Vaudoyer—both equally dear to me.

RENE HUYGHE

"The wisdom of the gods and of the blessed immortals cannot
be expressed in words but only by beautiful images."

PLOTINUS

Library of Congress Catalog Card Number: 62-11622
MILTON S. FOX, Editor
Translated from the French by Norbert Guterman
Published in the United States of America, 1962
All rights reserved. No part of the contents of this book may be reproduced without the written
permission of the publishers, Harry N. Abrams, Inc., New York
Illustrations printed in France
Text printed and bound in The Netherlands

# TABLE OF CONTENTS

## PART I

# THE MEANS OF EXPRESSION

### CHAPTER I

### CHAPTER II

### CHAPTER III

# LIST OF COLORPLATES

de
ha
gi
li
in
cl
o

r

*Paintings have a life of their own that derives*
*entirely from the painter's soul.*
*Van Gogh (Letter 439 to Theo)*

# FOREWORD

MODERN man was dazzled to discover—or rediscover—that art does not need to imitate nature. Since then, he has re-examined, justified, and discussed the antithesis between so-called figurative and so-called abstract art; and his preference for the newer, latter variety is plain. To show its existence, its legitimacy, and its range of possibilities seems now the only task of aesthetics, to reveal its antecedents the only justification for art history. Are we condemned forever to keep circling round the single ring of this fashionable circus? The obsession might well turn into a limitation, and even into a hardening of the intellectual arteries—one of those premature "fossilizations" of culture that render the thought of an epoch obsolete before its time, already dead in the eyes of the next generation. The purpose of this book is to help us escape such a fate.

Art, thank God, raises other problems, both bigger and more serious. Its essential, unvarying role, from the very beginning, has been to serve as one of mankind's modes of expression. In a hundred years, the problem of abstract art may be interesting mainly for the light it sheds on present-day man—who, let us not forget, will not then be "modern."

For this reason, it is time to raise the question of art and the spirit of man, of art as the language of the human spirit. This is not to ignore or neglect the problem of art as construction, as plastic form, whether in terms of an elaborated geometry or unpremeditated spots of color. But let us bear in mind that art would be no more than an idle pastime, were concern for art as expression ever to disappear.

Our purpose is not to disavow modern art, but we must not get bogged down in it. We are urging art to transcend itself in accordance with the law that governs all life.

It is rare today (though it might be healthy) to find anyone who states publicly the point that Rodin made: "There is perhaps no single work of art whose charm rests solely on the balance of lines and tones, and whose appeal is solely to the eye." The work must also be created by and for the human spirit—must express it, nourish it, enrich it.

There exists a language of the intelligence, which has come down to us as the language of the word. Art, however, is a language of the spirit, of our feeling as well as our thinking nature, our nature as a whole in all its complexity. Such a definition will seem restrictive or inadequate only to those who cling to outmoded, exclusively rational conceptions of language, and only if they disregard the concepts of modern psychology.

11

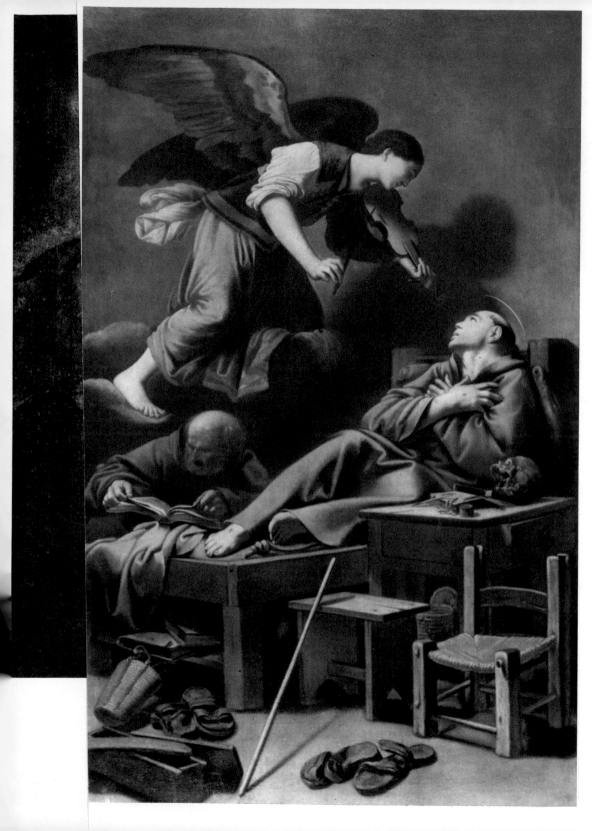

*Art,*
*language*
*of the*
*ineffable....*

**2. -** *CARLO*
*SARACENI.*
THE ECSTASY
OF
ST. FRANCIS.
Il Redentore,
Venice

3. - *REMBRANDT. OLD MAN READING (detail). The Louvre, Paris*

# INTRODUCTION: ART AS LANGUAGE

*To rely solely on sight, neglecting the mind, is
to confine oneself to seeing and painting only the
superficial aspect of form. To acquire true knowledge of form, we must illumine all things with the
rays of our soul and be ready to receive the light
that emanates from things visible and invisible.*
Rabindranath Tagore

M ANY sterile quarrels about aesthetics, many misunderstandings and one-sided views
that obstruct full comprehension of art would be avoided if, instead of looking for
some single principle or key to art, we grant that its nature is complex—complex to the
point of seeming contradictory.

THE TWOFOLD NATURE OF THE WORK OF ART. Is the work of art a plastic
object, and does it, by the combination of its resources—line and form, materials and colors
—provide our vision with a specific pleasure, such as Classical authors called "beauty"? The
modern abstract artists seek to eliminate all ambiguity from the work of art by banishing
the simple evocation of nature or of a subject. Actually, both the Classics and the moderns
start from the same guiding principle, though they apply it in different ways.

Or, should we say, with painting especially, but also with sculpture—the expressive

15

means of architecture are less obvious—that the work of art is a psychological confession? Does it enable the artist to communicate his way of seeing, feeling, and being, to use it as language, by investing these same lines and colors with emotional force? This conception is vouched for by a long line of artists, from Giorgione to Rembrandt, from the Romantics down through the Fauves, the Expressionists, and the Surrealists.

A judgment that aims at completeness cannot choose between these alternatives; it must adopt both. It must recognize that art has twin missions and that its richness is increased thereby. To be sure, art is capable of pure creation, purged of all contingency and pursuing, as Kant observed, its "end in itself." But even as he devotes himself to this aim and imagines that it is his only aim, the artist is quenching his thirst for expression; thanks to art, he can break out of his silence, his incommunicability, project himself outside. If it is true that every one of us has at some time dreamed of sharing with his fellow men the life that is inclosed within him—otherwise doomed to disappear with him, like the moment of existence just now forever past—of leaving the mark of his spirit on some communication capable of defying time, then some exploration of the human spirit deserves to be, indeed, must be attempted.

Today, concern for balance makes it important to stress the psychological aspect of things. Since the beginning of this century, we have been concerned, fruitfully, but too exclusively, with the formal, plastic aspect. We should not turn our backs upon recent indispensable achievements, but the time has perhaps come for us to throw all our weight on the other side of a dangerously listing boat. It may be high time to break the monotonous round traced by so many feet all moving in the same direction, as though in lock step. This must be done if we are ever to arrive at that still largely unexplored territory where the spiritual secrets of the great artists await us.

For the danger is pressing. Whereas the art of the ancients was a willing vehicle for any and every sort of message—ideas, beliefs, religious dogmas, even narratives—today's art, in its eagerness to purify itself, has banished everything that can be expressed by means other than its own. Whatever can be narrated is dismissed as anecdotal; whatever can be translated into words is rejected as literary. The nineteenth century began this trend when it limited art to the expression of nonrational states or states inaccessible to analytical approach, when it exalted the restless, ever-changing sphere of the emotions, of what is felt rather than what is thought. The twentieth century, going even further in this direction, has made a clean sweep. Fauvism and Expressionism lingered in a world of feeling, but feeling reduced to its crudest, rawest state. Surrealism went down into the cellars and subcellars of the unconscious, bringing back a human stuff that was murky and absurd, but that could still produce shock. Abstract art demanded thoroughgoing asepsis: every element capable of evoking an appearance of reality was excluded. In the end, lines and colors were turned away even from the formal constructions the predecessors of the Abstractionists had cherished since Cubism. Technique has been reduced to the recording of quasi-organic impulses, which translate the obscure sense of life that links man to matter. Thus, by a steady, relentless process of cutting down—today carried to its furthest extreme—art seems to have got rid of every vestige of what used to be called "content," to have broken every last link with thought, even with conscious life. It remains to be seen whether this negation of consciousness in the most unorganized forms of painting anticipates a new consciousness of the world. But that is not a question that concerns us here.

And yet, for all this progressive "reduction" of the intelligible (or merely signifying) part of art, a twofold tendency seems still to be at work, whether with respect to form or to content. To Classicism—to the Classicism of Ingres, for example, oriented toward formal beauty—the nineteenth century opposed the Romanticism of Delacroix, loud in its claims for an art expressive of the world of passion. Similarly, the twentieth century opposed Fauvism and Expressionism to Cubism. More recently, the kind of abstract art concerned for geometry and skillful color harmonies has been opposed by an art which is called nonformal and which, appropriately, is reduced to a set of intense spots.

This duality of art—which is not contradictory, as mediocre minds imagine, but complementary, as superior artists have always known—began to be perceived as such lucidly only with Poussin, it would seem: he was enamored of both ideal beauty and expression. His theory of the modes, to which we will come back again (cf. Part II, Ch. IV, 2), aimed at endowing the painter with "the power to arouse a variety of passions in the soul of the viewer." This surely means that he expected paintings to contain a communicable burden of feeling. Paillot de Montalembert, who was also a Classicist and even one of the theoreticians of Neo-Classicism, formulated similar thoughts in his *Traité complet de la peinture* early in the nineteenth century. This follower of David seems to have been paving the way for Romanticism when he observed, with rare penetration, that aesthetics "has merely confined itself to distinguishing between greater and lesser visual pleasure." This, he says, is a serious oversight, for this approach has led us "too often to forget… the metaphysical pleasure[1] in harmony, arrived at through suitability, through unity or accord between the subject and the optical combination that portrays it." He is saying, in the clumsy language of his day, that, in his opinion, painting does not merely aim at a harmony devised for the pleasure of the eye, but that it has an expressive mission. Being of his time, he confines this expressive content to the subject, since then banished by the moderns. But no matter: he realizes that the painting is charged with emotion that its task is to transmit to "the soul of him who looks at the painting" (as he adds, very nearly in Poussin's words).

Art, then, appears as a language the precise definition of which does away with the ambiguities that might mislead us. A language must be more than a mere vehicle of communication; to fulfill its task, it must be capable of extracting harmony and beauty from the *means* available to it. When, in literature, words attain the level of poetry, a certain magic is given off by the very rhythm and sonority, but the great writer knows how to make use of this seemingly gratuitous felicity the better to pass on his deeper message.

ART, THE "OTHER" LANGUAGE. In art, too, the flattest language is the descriptive: recounting what the artist has seen or conceived, it is limited to realism. However, it can become poetic and it can make use of resources of suggestion exclusively, so as to reveal the treasures of the inner life. At the furthest extreme, it is transmuted into pure poetry, and then the architecture of its lines and colors must suffice to delight the viewer. But this is the extremest case, where art deliberately—and may I add, pointlessly—sacrifices a major part of its power, perhaps even its duty. Except in theory, however, does art ever really do this? Who can prevent lines and colors from awakening in the viewer echoes of the psychic forces that presided over their disposition and arrangement?

[1] This phrase must be understood in the strict etymological sense of pleasure that transcends material aspects.

*The artistic image can be a descriptive language, exact and prosaic, built on a rigorous syntax.*

**4. - *CARPACCIO*. ST. URSULA AND FIANCÉ TAKING LEAVE OF THEIR PARENTS (detail).**
Accademia, Venice

For all their affected anonymousness, the colored squares assembled by Van Lint and following the same principles as Mondrian reveal a sensibility more delicate and refined than Mondrian's; we recognize in them the man whose presence we divined in the silhouettes of peasants he used to paint. Just possibly, two craftsmen, could they succeed in attaining mechanical perfection—which is very doubtful—might produce identical works. Two artists, never. The irrepressible human presence asserts itself even in the intonation—

impossible to gauge—with which straight lines are made to intersect at right angles, with which the most elementary daubs of color are set down. All this goes to prove that art is forever language.

We are often unwilling to admit this because our conception of language, because it has not evolved as rapidly as our ideas of art, is out-of-date. We imagine that an art language would inevitably serve to render, in images, ideas as distinct as those expressed by words— a sort of visual literal translation.

To begin, the language of art need not in the least be a duplication of verbal language. Actually, art often serves to make up for gaps or weaknesses in writing. The language of art can never again be that "book speaking on the walls" which the Fathers of the Church wanted it to be. We are no longer suffering from the confusion that dominated Classical culture from the time of Cicero, when in the *Ad Herennium* this misleading formula was first given currency: *Poema loquens pictura; pictura tacitum poema.* "A poem is a speaking picture; a picture is a silent poem." Nine centuries later, the Council of Constantinople took over this false view of art and gave it the added sanction of Christian tradition: "What the Bible tells us in the Word, the icon discloses to us in color and renders it present to us." This confusion, so harmful to recognition of the true role of art, led our own epoch to react strongly and banish all significant content from the plastic image.

Furthermore, so false a view of art overlooks the fact that our knowledge of language, of both its nature and its potentialities, has greatly evolved. In his *Essai sur les données immédiates de la conscience,* Bergson formulated very clearly the limitations of verbal language, hitherto looked upon as the only one, in which "words with clearly marked contours... serve as a storehouse of all that is most stable, common, and, hence, impersonal in mankind's impressions." As a result, "Only those ideas that are least truly ours can be adequately expressed in words." The word corresponds to the idea, which in turn corresponds to "a clear and distinct notion"; and the latter is obtained by a process of depersonalization that makes it suitable for collective circulation. To be sure, words can overcome these limitations, but what we have then is poetry. Words have changed sides and gone over to the domain that is precisely that of art. Now, just what is this domain?

Whereas the well-defined, neutral idea calls for a word created for the express purpose of serving as its unambiguous sign, the more fluid substance of lived experience slips through the net of language, capable of catching only the most solid, consistent elements of life in its meshes. But what Baudelaire called *l'intime du cerveau* (the innermost part of the brain) also cries out for expression. The fact is that the most Classical of French centuries, the seventeenth, was not wholly unaware that its intellectual rigor was letting a good deal escape it: it detected the presence, which it still regarded as mysterious, of the *je-ne-sais-quoi* (the indefinable), and an essayist, Father Bouhours, devoted a whole chapter to it in his *Entretiens d'Ariste et d'Eugène.* Published in 1671, this book went through several editions within a few years.

In the eighteenth century, the Scottish psychologists were the first to question the resources of the language of words. David Hume denounced its limitations on the grounds that it could record and translate only socially significant ideas. This was the period when the individual soul was beginning to be concerned about its own existence and rights, and Hume doubted the ability of language to reveal its true nature. For language, he says, measures everything by the same standard: it would be impossible for us to communicate our feelings to one another if we did not correct the momentary appearances of things—

*By virtue of its restless imprecision, the artistic image is, above all, poetic. Such an image serves as a vehicle for impulses and aspirations, for the obscure and ardent powers that stir within the painter.*

**5. - TURNER.** SNOWSTORM AT SEA. National Gallery, London

that is, if we did not strip them of their uniqueness at the moment we perceive them, and if we did not ignore our present situation, that is, our own individual way of experiencing them.

The nineteenth century discovered that this language of the soul, in which Hume did not believe, was the legitimate domain of art. No need to wait till 1928 for Benedetto Croce's *Estetica come scienza dell'espressione e linguistica generale;* Croce was not the first to point out that art, because its approach is more vital than intellectual and because it is capable of intuitive expression, marks a return to the most direct form of human language. Successor to the eighteenth century and to Jean-Jacques Rousseau, thanks to whom man's natural, spontaneous, noneducated, and noncivilized sensibility was restored to its rightful place, the nineteenth century became aware that every individual's uniqueness was walled up in silence. Delacroix called attention to the opposition between two languages. On the one hand, there are in us "the ideas that words can express," and, on the other hand, there is all that goes to make up "the soul," something distinct from and vaster than the intellect. The soul, too, "will create a language for itself." Thus the theory is launched; there are two languages, and the language of art has a mission of its own. "Woe to him who sees only a *precise idea* in a good picture, and woe to the picture that shows nothing beyond the finite." For "what makes the value of the painting is what is indefinable in it: the very thing that eludes precision." Its domain is the still undetermined stuff of the inner life. Analytical methods cannot apprehend it; what is needed is an expressive magic. Such will be the language suitable for art, and for poetry, too (provided the latter transmutes words and invests them with the power of images).

Far from being obsolete today, this theory has made possible the whole development of modern art. Compare with it this statement made by a contemporary artist whom no one will suspect of clinging to outmoded conventions. It was Dubuffet who said that "painting is language, and a language far richer than that of words."

In the twentieth century, when psychology became more demanding and flexible, a broader and subtler definition of language encompasses artistic reality in its entirety. Phenomenology, especially, from Husserl to Merleau-Ponty, has revealed striking coincidences. According to Merleau-Ponty, language is "the operation as a result of which thoughts that, without it, would remain private phenomena take on intersubjective value and, in the end, ideal existence." Is this not the very mission we recognize as that of art? Where customary language has, for social convenience, reduced this "intersubjectivity" to the intercommunication of collective concepts, art, no matter how contaminated it may have been, has, for several centuries, steadily resisted being so "reduced." Art alone has been able to provide a direct link between the artist's subjectivity and the viewer's. Analysis of language restored to its original truth, such as Merleau-Ponty's, even seems to apply essentially to art, as though art alone had retained its fundamental powers. What the artist first feels stirring within himself are the still indistinct impulses of his inner life, seeking expression. He is well acquainted with the "vague signifying intention" which aspires "to be given body." However, he would not dream of trying to outfit it in some ready-made form, in any "already available significations" such as customary language provides. This unwillingness becomes more and more marked the closer we come to the art of our own day, which emphatically rejects all that is ready-made. Modern art could take Merleau-Ponty's lucid definition for its own: "The signifying intention is always... the overflow of what I want to say over that which has already been said." In looking for a language, its first act is "to know itself for what it is." "Indeed, to express something... is to become aware of" and "to take possession of" something that, without this effort, would remain vague within us. For, as our philosopher profoundly observes, "Self-possession, a kind of perfect inner congruity, is not the definition of thought; on the contrary, thought results from expression." How true this is of the artist, who knows his work and himself only after the work has been completed!

THE DUTY TO COMMUNICATE.   Modern art has been so struck by this "taking over" of the self, in which the work is for its creator, that it has been severely tempted to stop right there and not even try to go further. Its reason is that, as yet, it has an insufficiently clear conception of itself as a language. For language involves a second stage—the act of communication. Now, ever since Symbolism, a penchant for the nonexpressed, indeed for what is reputed inexpressible, has endowed obscurity with strange prestige, with a kind of value in itself. Long since, the poet Verhaeren wrote to René Ghil, "I shall assert that you have the right to remain obscure, for, in my opinion, it is sufficient that one understands oneself. One writes for oneself alone." Would it be unkind to note in this connection that, all too often, this utterly unwarranted respect for incomprehensibility has passed from art to critics and aestheticians, and that this is not the least of our present-day sins and shortcomings? *What has not yet been expressed should indeed be a temptation to the mind, for, without it, thought would cease to progress, but on condition that the mind make it clear and perceptible to others.* In no other connection is our need for an exact conception of language more apparent.

To go too far on the road of obscurity, to forget that art is one kind of language—however irrational—is to commit the disgraceful error of assimilating the artist to a schizophrenic. As everyone knows, the latter shuts himself away from the world to the point where he lives an exclusively inner life, neither communicating nor being communicated with, and finally falls into aphasia. Imprisoned in his autism, he not only repudiates the outside world as nourishment for thought, but also his fellow men as its object. This leads readily enough to the conclusion that the inclination of certain artists to elevate these two tendencies into dogma is a morbid symptom of the psychosis of our time as we undergo a painful crisis of civilization.

Art, like language, must counter this autism with its fundamental altruism. The artist, too, takes over what is his own in order to transmit it to his fellow men, to give it to them. But his ways are special: his innate solitude, instead of cutting him off from people, gives him special access to their inner depths. Karl Jaspers has shown that only the man who succeeds in finding himself in his solitude is capable of reaching another solitary man. Needless to say, he will succeed in doing this, not by resorting to the language of habitual ideas and phrases, known to everyone in advance, but by means of an act of communication that is at the same time a creative act.

It is a contemporary mistake that the artist need make no particular effort to reach others, that it is enough for him to exist and to create for himself, that it is up to the spectator to bridge the distance between them, no matter how far he has gone. Louis Lavelle, a philosopher who died before his time, called this "Narcissus' mistake." The very opposite is true, he wrote. "It is the most self-absorbed, the most solitary man who is capable of performing the most disinterested, purest act of communion." For what he encounters in his retreat, deep within himself, is his own heart and soul. There he finds the aspiration to break out of his own limitations and rediscover his fellow men. It is the descent into the self that creates the need to communicate, the need to give. What is involved is not some desire to explain things lucidly, but a deep impulse of solidarity with other human beings. It requires a pure language worthy of it, a language that does not distort or deaden the impulse but is shaped by its living energy.

Merleau-Ponty's theory of language also applies here. Although for convenience or facility "instituted significations" may be used as ready-made vehicles, nonetheless, by "arranging the signifying instruments" it is possible to provoke in others "the feeling of a new and different signification." This end is achieved in the attempt to create novel forms. Only abuse of this poorly understood but necessary method could lead the artist to be content with incomprehensibility. Our epoch may be proud of feeling very keenly an

Sometimes the language of art can go beyond the domain of sensations, ideas, and emotions, a domain that is itself beyond what words can express, whether poetry or prose. For the very reason that art uses neither words nor grammar, that its images can be an embodiment and, occasionally, a condensation of lived experience, that it brings us face to face with such experiences instead of organizing them and making them intelligible, it can express the ineffable. It is not a transcription in prefabricated signs coined by collective usage, as words are; it makes possible manifestation and communication of the inner life, even of its unconscious states.

**6. -** *REDON. PHANTASMAGORIAS*

23

obligation not to stagnate in well-tried formulas, which with wear and tear can only dry up expression and lead to mere repetition. This tendency is wholesome, the more so since ours is an epoch in which a new civilization is struggling to be born inside an inadequate, disintegrating civilization surviving on sheer inertia. But, far from justifying the impenetrability of art, this state of affairs implies an urgent imperative. Since art, by definition, is the language of that which is not yet expressed, codified in stagnant, oft-reproduced formulas, and since it is, par excellence, an attempt to discover form, an inner impulse directed "toward a specific void to be filled," as Merleau-Ponty puts it—then it is above all the task of art to forge means of expressing that which aspires to exist. No doubt this is why the public, guided by a deep instinct, assigns it so prominent a place today. Modern art, therefore, must not be confined within the limitations of artists playing private games of self-gratification. It is art, more than anything, that possesses the power of initiative, of giving visible form in the public world to the undreamed-of reality that every artist worthy of the name carries potentially within him. An artist must be an innovator, certainly, but a telling one: that is, he must carry out his linguistic mission all the way.

Charles Etienne, one of the most farsighted of modern critics, was well aware of this when he wrote, "The idea of breaking the sound barrier has never been clearer than it is today.... The impossible is the very purpose of art: the purpose of art is to say what has never been said, to give the inexpressible the plastic form its very nature rules out." But to *say* it! really to have something *to* say! Complacent repetition of sterile formulas is no more admirable when carried out by the snobbish few than when perpetrated by academism. In either case, language is not performing its functions; we only have the chattering of parrots.

What but just this did the masters of the past do—even when they believed they must at all costs perpetuate established usages? Their instinct—that is, their genius—forced them to say *more* than had already been said and to create expressive forms *unknown* before them.

To quote Delacroix once again: "What the genius realizes in art is some conception that has long been *dreamed of*. He clothes in graspable sensory form a fantasy previously invisible, merely immanent in the human mind." Whether the form be pictorial, poetic, or musical, "the idea has passed from the world of the spirit to the world of art and form." Odilon Redon, moreover, said, "To fashion somehow or other, as well as I could and in line with my inner dictates, things into which I have put myself entirely...."

How this miraculous mutation takes place, and how it has taken place in the course of the history of art, the development of human knowledge today permits us to grasp somewhat better than in earlier ages.

# PART I

# THE MEANS OF EXPRESSION

*A painting is the best hidden
image of the man who painted it.*
Picasso

*Nowhere are the powers of painting manifested more effectively than in portraiture. Actually, every painting presents us with individual features, those of a mind. Like these eyes looking out at us, it makes us sense a living man.*

**7.** - *VITTORE GHISLANDI (FRA GALGARIO)*. SELF-PORTRAIT. Accademia Carrare, Bergamo

# HOW ART TRANSLATES THE SPIRIT
# OF MAN

*Things look at us as we look at them. They seem
indifferent to us only because we look at them with
indifference. But to a clear eye all things are mirrors,
and to a sincere and serious eye everything is depth.*
      *Gaston Bachelard*

WE are poor judges of the revolutions we have been passing through; we keep
thinking ourselves contemporary with developments long since finished and past,
and we remain unconscious of what is really new in the present. We have to keep reminding
ourselves that over the past century our knowledge of man has gone through an upheaval
such as has perhaps not occurred since the appearance of Christianity or the birth of Greek
civilization. Our knowledge of art has necessarily been affected by it.

Body and soul, material life and the inner life, physiology and psychology—for a long
time these divisions were all that anyone needed. These were the bricks and mortar, while
much higher up there glowed a single beacon, all the light there was to illuminate the
enveloping darkness. Then one day somebody noticed that this light was somehow tied
up with obscure mechanical processes. Somehow, the inner life is not, after all, confined
to the glass-walled, well-lit cell at the top, from which everything is seen and understood.
Rather, it extends in depth endlessly inside the gloomy, concealed body; its source lies
within. The life of the mind does not comprise the whole of the inner life; this life is
bigger, heavier, and stranger, for it contains the whole immense domain of the unconscious.

The change has had consequences still impossible to calculate. Prior to it, the life of the
conscious mind seemed an adequate enough cause of all our reflections and actions; suddenly, this was no more than an end result, a reaction, or even a simple effect. The study
of the individual is not all that has been transformed; art history has been, too. Hitherto,
the former had been based on the study of great men, intellectual agents in history
guiding events. Now an unconscious was discovered at work in history too: even the
anonymous masses were guided blindly by hidden motives. Art history, meanwhile, had
consisted of "Lives" of a succession of famous masters who, by deliberate research, had
created the visible forms of beauty. Now everything—theories and facts alike—was seen
to be passively subjected to an inevitable material evolution and to obey only unconscious
collective dictates. Taine accounted for art in terms of environmental conditions, much as
Marx accounted for social life by dialectical materialism. A wave of determinism at the
close of the nineteenth century swept all before it, and to many, consciousness became
no more than an epiphenomenon, a recording apparatus.

Since then attempts have been made to restore the balance. Thought has reacted against
the limitless world of the unconscious, alien to it by its very nature, yet upon which it
nonetheless closely depends. Nothing, by definition, being irreducible to thought—not

even what is most opposed to thought—the generation of Bergson and Proust attempted to make its methods more flexible, so as to analyze, rather than just to negate, the inherited antinomy.

Paul Valéry carried the discussion a step further: in him, thought attempted the total reconquest of responsibility and freedom. More acrobatic and lucid than ever before, subtle enough to take the full measure of the unconscious and penetrate it with comprehension, thought threw off the alien tutelage, going so far as to repudiate inspiration as too obscure a source, the better to establish perpetual control over itself. This may define Valéry's true position in the history of thought; in this sense he perhaps continued Bergson as well as reacted to him.

Be that as it may, for the past fifty years man has adapted to a double understanding of himself—one reading being in plain language, the other in cipher. The former is based on conscious, explicit ideas, on the course of reflective thought and the goals it assigns: this is the traditional method of the old moralists. The latter explores the signs and involuntary clues that unconscious, spontaneous activity leaves as record of itself, and tries to discover to what they correspond in the individual's hidden nature; systematized, this method has become psychoanalysis.

Art history could not ignore this development, and it has now become dependent on it. Three modes of investigation have become available to us. The reading "in clear" consists of studying the conscious goals stated by the artist, his aesthetic program, and ascertaining to what extent his work achieves them. But the historian who follows the teachings of Taine—still valid within certain limits—must go beyond this conscious zone. He must specify the environmental conditions, both social and historical, to which the work of art is inevitably subjected and which all but mold it. This is not all, however. He must go on to decipher the work, to carry out a kind of psychoanalysis in the broadest sense of the term, by getting inside the work through the back door of the unconscious. Every line, every form, every brush stroke must be regarded at least as much an instinctive as a deliberate gesture; in them the artist expresses conscious intentions, but he also records his deeper, essential nature. Without being aware of it, he endows the work with the features of his innermost being, features he himself does not notice at the moment he sets them down, any more than he notices his own physiognomy, his own gait, gestures, tics, or other aspects of his spontaneous behavior. He is whole and entire in his work, at once concealed and yet irrefutably present with all the evidence of his being. Thus, the work of art is a text to be read, revealing its author's character by its content (which needs only to be understood) and simultaneously by its graphism (which must be interpreted). It is a text that, to be grasped fully, requires both a reader and a graphologist.

No art, perhaps no mode of expression, lends itself to such exploration more readily than painting. In other arts, the work is the result of a slow elaboration, and the writer, composer, or architect gives us the fruit alone, torn from the branch that gave it life. In any painting, the record of its elaboration is present very nearly in its entirety along with the result intended, inseparable from it. The painter was concerned with giving us an image, but the image inevitably, at the same time, in every line and brush stroke, records the very motions of the hand that constructed it. More accurately, the image is nothing but the permanent record of all the creative acts that went into its making—and, as such a record, painting possesses a clarity and suggestive force that cannot be paralleled in any other art.

**8. -** *VASARI.* ALLEGORY OF PAINTING. Drawing. Uffizi Gallery, Florence

CHAPTER I

# DRAWING AND THE HAND

O<small>F</small> all the creative acts performed by the artist, the most directly legible is drawing. Drawing is also the first to which the artist resorts when he sketches the future form of what is still a mere feeling within himself. Finally, it is the act that is most directly and spontaneously governed by his nervous and muscular system. It is gesture even when it wants to be thought. As gesture, it is inseparable from, and hence expressive of, the organism that made it, both in its physical and its psychological structure. Graphologists long ago began to study handwriting for what it might be able to tell us, although it consists of letters whose forms are imposed in advance. More recently, psychologists have looked for similar clues in seemingly elementary gestures like those performed by a man using a tool without any special intervention of intelligence, will, or even consciousness. The manipulator of a blowtorch "never makes a straight line in the metal,"[1] for in handling this tool his purpose is purely practical and he does not follow any line traced in

---

[1] I want to thank M. Eugène Sorez, an engineer with the I.D.N., for having called my attention to the article in *Science et Vie* (May 30, 1949) dealing with safecracking and the identification of burglars. My quotations above are from this article.

advance. He produces a wavy line. "Now, engineers specialized in the manufacture of oxyhydrogen and acetylene torches take it as established fact that a metallic surface cut by a blowtorch shows incised lines characteristic of the worker who handles it. That is, every man who operates a blowtorch... performs a gesture that is both peculiar to him and unvarying, so that it is always possible to identify a given worker and distinguish him from all others." This can be done with such accuracy that it has been possible to identify safecrackers by this means. Before World War I, on the occasion of the notorious Bonnot affair in France, one of the burglaries perpetrated by this gang was traced to it in this way.

It will be readily admitted that if a seemingly mechanical gesture or—for that matter— the form of a given letter of the alphabet in careful imitation of a conventionally prescribed form can be so intensely personal, so expressive of the man who made it, then the graphism of an artist engaged in asserting his innermost gifts must be loaded with still more meaning. And the fact is that such graphisms do give away personal characteristics of the artist, and it is possible from them to distinguish definite types and temperaments.

# I. THE HUMAN TYPES

FIGURATION.    Often—and this is the most natural attitude—the draftsman believes himself to be no more than a spectator and his task merely to record the scene before his eyes. He is then called a "realist." But to reproduce a scene is to transcribe the sensation one has of it. Clearly, these very sensations and the record of them involve the man who has them and transcribes them, disclosing his *manner* of experiencing and expressing them, and thus give us access to his inner, invisible being, his individuality, his personality.

Let us, then, assume that we are dealing with a draftsman who is unaware or scornful of this inescapable capacity for transposition, even eager to minimize it in order to be wholly objective, utterly faithful to what he sees. Let us assume that he wants to restrict *his* role to his choice of subject, and, once he has made this choice, to devote himself exclusively to recording its impersonal appearance. In this case, he will have to mistrust and reject both the steady line, on the ground that it interprets reality too deliberately and intellectually, and the arabesque or expressive spot, on the ground that it interprets reality too freely and too impulsively. His aim is to make us forget, to conjure away, as it were, the artifices of his trade, so he falls back on the simple line, modest and anonymous in its unpretentious brevity. He reduces his drawing to the exactest possible notation, and worries solely about fidelity to his model. However, if the form, by its divisions, suggests a contour, he follows its successive directions with little strokes of pen and pencil—short, straight lines that form brisk angles and are discontinuous with respect to any preconceived idea of harmony.

Fifteenth-century Flemish drawing, with its angular, broken, jumbled, but close and faithful use of line, is an excellent example of this kind of self-restraint. It is in sharp contrast with the ductile French arabesque and with Italian drawing of the same period, more condensed in line and so elaborate as to suggest geometric patterns.

Although form, to all these artists, is the beginning of conception, it counts for less than appearance—that is, than the impression. By means of tiny lines as flexible as brush strokes,

*Figuration: this drawing seeks to be the equivalent of what it represents to the point of illusion; it tries to make us forget that it is a drawing.*

**9. -** *THÉODORE ROUSSEAU.* FOREST OF FONTAINEBLEAU. Drawing. Private collection, Paris

they try to "represent" the visual impression they receive. The dots, scratches, and cross-hatchings are adapted to every sort of requirement, so as to render tangled foliage, a rumpled head of hair, the folds, shadows, and texture of drapery. The Northern Primitives are expert draftsmen in this flexible manner. Modestly, they attempt no other; and their successive refinements of the manner pave the way for the consummate art of the seventeenth-century Dutch landscape painters.

In the nineteenth century, Théodore Rousseau brought this technique of direct transposition to an almost fabulous degree of virtuosity. His line, both with pen and pencil, can give body to any subject: with complete self-abnegation, it adapts to render irregularities of grass, straw, leaves, rocks, the bark of trees, the falling rain, clouds in the sky. Submitting to every conceivable kind of metamorphosis, his line mimics not only appearances, but movements: it supports, swells, and gathers itself together to detail the way a branch is gnarled and twisted; it flutters tremulously to render a mass of delicate leaves; it ripples with water, soars with clouds, and comes back to earth again with stones. It shoots up in the sweep of a tree; it becomes delicate and impalpable in brittle twigs or in sky lines bulging with fresh air; and it becomes robust and emphatic in the presence of a boulder or the face of a cliff. It is a virtuoso performance, where one actor keeps changing his voice and adjusting his make-up and gestures to play every part in some "vast comedy in a hundred different acts" (Fig. 9).

The draftsman who is faithful to this tradition, keeping himself in the background, is,

31

all the same, anything but neutral. He must have a great deal of intelligence, feeling, and loving experience of things to be able to adapt to so many modulations, as endless in their variety as the dizzying variety of creation itself. However self-restrained, he cannot help putting something of his secret being into the invention, the fever, and the passion that animate his line.

SUGGESTION.   In the type of drawing discussed above, the artist confines himself—or means to confine himself—to his immediate sensations, set down as faithfully as possible. He relies solely on the accuracy of his transcription to convey the echoes that, from time to time, they awaken in his emotional depths. Such art is, or means to be, an art of the senses—more exactly, an optical art.

We can readily believe, however, that as practiced by the greatest artists, the type of drawing just described goes beyond sensory limitations. Who can tell where the senses stop and the sensibility begins, or for that matter, who can separate sensation from emotion, the initial shock from the echoes it arouses in us? For there are artists who cross the boundary between the outside world and the inner world (Fig. 246).

The latter is a strange world made up of vibrations, palpitations, and intensities, a world hitherto reserved to individual experience. Drawing can serve as a graph of the inner world—much as a recording apparatus traces variations in an electrical current, without directing it. The draftsman of the inner world is not trying to represent it, but to evoke or suggest it. He is no longer the servant of nature; rather, he makes use of nature and phenomena to gain access to what cannot be seen or said, to what can only be lived.

The new approach presents a new difficulty. The artist now must find, beside equivalents for the material world—the drawing belongs to this world by its physical nature—equivalents also for the nonmaterial world, to which the drawing does not belong by nature. From figuration we have passed to suggestion—from the domain of real space and objects to that of life itself, life in the sense of "intensity." At his disposal, however, in pursuing his new ambition, the draftsman has only the same vocabulary of visible things with which to communicate to us the invisible!

The search for graphic equivalents to the visible model had led the artist, for example, to render a lock of hair with curving lines, the sharp edges of metal by incisiveness of line, the texture of flesh by delicate shadings. So concrete and instinctive a symbolism of technique will now be more subtly adapted to new meanings. To begin with, the artist will stress and underline only what strikes him as important in the model; he will omit what holds no interest for him. With a violent partiality in itself expressive, he will choose among the multiplicity of things only what affects his own sensibility.

Nor is this enough. He must also give his drawing the precise character of his own feelings, the reaction aroused in him by the model. This requirement is not so farfetched as it might seem. After all, our bodies give us many examples of the conversion of spiritual impulses into muscular movements. If the arm or hand can model itself on a sudden emotion and imitate in a gesture, tensing or relaxing as rapidly as facial expression changes, why should it not in the line that it traces convey characteristics derived from the soul? Here is the fundamental miracle without which there would be no art. Muscular pressure produces the insistent downstroke, and lessening of that pressure the throbbing upstroke. Nervous or calm, powerful or jerky, it is this movement that generates line, and, whether

*Suggestion: in this drawing every line serves to evoke more than to represent.*

**10. -** *REMBRANDT.* SATAN SHOWING CHRIST THE KINGDOMS OF THE WORLD. Drawing.
Kupferstichkabinett, Berlin

33

*Whereas representational drawings seemingly efface themselves before the model, suggestive drawings take the model's place and even invest it with their own life. In the work shown here, the spirited action of the human figure and the horse has been rendered in accordance with the lightning speed with which the artist's hand dashed off the line. Like a snapshot, this speedy sketch records, for all time, the nervous passion characteristic of the artist's temperament and inspiration. The line is like the recorded graph of a dynamometer or an encephalogram.*

**11.** - *GROS. BUCEPHALUS TAMED BY ALEXANDER. c. 1798. Drawing. G. Delestre Collection, Paris* frozen or fulgurating, produces a code for the transcription of inner life—a code recognized instinctively by a sharp eye, as in all the other forms of mimesis.

Thus, Michelangelo's line swells and rolls like muscles rippling; implacably the pressure of the hand conveys the assurance of a titan. Rubens' line, more fleshly than sinewy, animated by carnal stirrings and throbbing pulses, moves more swiftly and directly than Michelangelo's. Dürer's line, burdened with the complexities and jagged edges of the Germanic soul, is all coils and twists; its profusion and teeming details make his drawings harsh, concentrated, and incisive to a painful degree. Tiepolo's line is more darting, shifting direction frequently and soaring again like the swift flight of a songbird; his line is in accord with his sensibility, which is energetic and so excessively refined as almost to be fatigued. But Rembrandt was the most prodigious of all these recorders of the invisible. Rembrandt dazzles: his every line leaps and strikes at the heart with electric energy, light suddenly piercing darkness. It can be emaciated from excess of spirituality, from the artist's zeal to render light and movement in all their purity, out of fear of betraying their links with matter.

This natural symbolism is unequivocally expressed in our language. We use the same words to describe lines and feelings: *biting, powerful, hard, gentle*, etc. (Figs. 10 and 227).

SPEED AND SONORITY.   Our task of determining where the visible and the immaterial meet may be aided by introducing into art history a notion that has been completely neglected, though it plays an essential role—speed. We are too prone to dwell on the immobility, the fixity of the work of art, and we naturally tend to overlook the elements of time and rhythm, associating these more readily with music. Yet these very elements may help account for certain suggestive powers inherent in the visual arts, and especially in drawing (where we are closest to the creative impulse itself). In drawing, we have a record of characteristics inherent in time, rendered in spatial terms. The completed work of art is immobile forever; nothing in it can be changed around without degrading it. But this appearance of death has, nonetheless, been generated by a living movement of which the work preserves the imprint. The speed and intensity of the creative gesture remain visible in it. Who has not observed that a painting by Tintoretto or El Greco is more dynamic than a painting by Raphael? Every work has a certain coefficient of speed and a certain modulation of this speed, as significant elements of its character and suggestive power. This is perceptible even in paintings where the initial gesture has been quite submerged by the overpainting—how much more perceptible, then, in drawings! What is drawing, in the most literal sense, if not the visible record of the motion of the hand that traced it? The drawing is nothing but a map of the hand's travel in space, now made permanent; it is but the graph of a movement, which it preserves, capturing it as it took place and freezing it thus for all time, as visible as the recording of a seismograph and just as easy to read.

Drawing is, thus, essentially movement, as much as it is the intensity of something dark on something light. The way in which a black is set off against a white, the modulation of the transitions from one to the other or the fixedness of the contrasts between them, all contribute to suggest a specific rate of speed. A spot in a drawing is as much regulated as is a sound. Save when these elements are deliberately neutralized (for reasons we shall shortly discuss), the drawing is nothing but an imprint—a secretion, as it were—of characteristics

released—all this Delacroix's line conveys with an implacable sureness that reveals execution and perception to be, in this artist, of lightning-like rapidity (Figs. 11 and 250).

The sensibility has not only its "voltage," so to speak, but also what I shall call its *sonority*. Beside a certain rhythm, we must also become aware of a certain tonality. In music, the same theme will affect us differently according to whether it is played in a major or a minor key.

Can a drawing communicate the depth of sensibility as well as its intensity? Its intensity is expressed essentially in the greater or lesser rapidity of the line, but what is the equivalent of depth of sensibility in perceptual terms? It exists—atmosphere, penumbra, luminosity. This is the domain of the spot, which generates imprecision, which blurs, which produces darkness, and hence mystery. Herein is the dreamlike power of drawing. In flat whiteness, when an expressive line is set down, the realm of depth—an obscure hollow in which dwell silence and the ineffable—is suddenly pierced (Fig. 12).

The sense of the enigmatic was introduced into painting by Leonardo's *sfumato*; of meditation and dream by Rembrandt's *chiaroscuro*. But in a technique that shows everything clearly—whether because of the whiteness of the sheet of paper or the course of the line—this spreading out into boundless shadow is even more striking. We are suddenly made aware of the presence of a background receding to infinity. Victor Hugo was familiar with the secrets of *la bouche d'ombre* (mouth of darkness): the vague, the ineffable, can only come to the surface under cover of darkness and obscurity. These qualities flee clarity as they flee precision: only the spot and the wash make it possible to give them expression in graphic art (Figs. 48 and 13).

Without invoking the supreme example of Rembrandt, we may follow the mounting poetic quality of paintings by Poussin and Claude Lorrain as they made more and more use of shadow. In the nineteenth century, poetic power can be measured by Corot's and Delacroix's use of shadows (and can be seen also in the drawings of a poet like Hugo). Corot wraps himself in shadow as in a gentle twilight, imperceptibly deepening into the mystery of night. Like Hugo, Delacroix opens up vistas into the unknown and invisible, the realm where the imagination takes flight and soars (Figs. 61 and 249).

By these means, sensibility has gradually found expression, transcending the domain of the visible, transcending every notion of a graphic handwriting, going beyond both the model and the means of execution—introducing into both harmonies derived from the artist's own inner lyricism. By intuitively grasping equivalences and correspondences between the qualities of graphic art and the inner life of man, by projecting intensity into line, by opening up the new and evocative dimension of depth with the aid of the spot, the draftsman has endowed his means of expression with boundless powers of suggestion.

CONSTRUCTION. However, when he is face to face with nature, the artist is not merely a sensibility, a bundle of feelings bubbling up and attaining expression. He also stands for another reality, another autonomous realm—that of the intellect and its power of abstraction. This brings us to a third attitude the draftsman may take with reference to model and technique. Face to face with reality, he constructs his own intellectual system. To find his way in the infinite and changing complexity of the real world, man must fit the latter into a precisely subdivided and articulated framework of idea and belief. The artist treats the visible world in much the same way, imposing, on ever-changing, fleeting,

*Construction: space and forms are subjected to a geometric order and to harmonies dictated by the intellect.*
**14.** - *RAPHAEL.* THE ANNUNCIATION. Drawing. The Louvre, Paris

random appearances, a discipline, order, logic, and harmony inherent not in them but in his own mind. He brings nature into conformity with his own mental constitution. An Italian, Bellori, has given a profound formulation of this fact: "We must draw things in such a way that they express our ideas of them."

The transmutation so effected is not at all the same as that discussed above. Here, the draftsman no longer impresses his individual sensibility upon nature, but a universal intellectuality, i.e., the fundamental principles that enable the mind of our species, by logical means common to all, "to see clearly" through the stormy proliferation of the phenomena. De Piles, the seventeenth-century author of a *Cours de Peinture*, formulated this strikingly: "Drawing [i.e., Classical drawing] is the organ of our thoughts, the instrument of our demonstrations, the light of our understanding!" What the artist perceives is a colored image, but his mind *knows* that the palpitating blur of his perception is the optical message through which solid objects, which his hands and habits have taught him to discern and isolate, manifest themselves to the eye. Just as he separates them in his mind and thinks of them as distinct entities, so now he restores them to autonomy in his own vision, reconstituting them by giving them individual outlines. By means of arbitrary lines—the more arbitrary because they are continuous and disregard the breaks actually created by the play of shadows and reflections—he traces the boundaries of forms as only the hand can verify them. He unravels the chaos of brute perception, much as the geographer by mental artifice establishes demarcation lines on a map without actual equivalents in the meadows or forests through which they pass. Just such an artifice is involved when the artist lets his contour "think" the forms in order to clarify human vision. As Théophile Gautier said, it is "an abstract and purely conventional matter" (Fig. 31).

Once the intellect has clearly delimited a field of vision, it undertakes a further operation. To secure full possession of the "subject," it attempts to reduce the unknown to the known, to identify and appropriate everything that seems new to it. To this end, it detects relationships and similarities with already familiar elements. The draftsman obeys similar laws: thanks to his intellect, he knows certain fundamental forms that constitute elements of geometry—the angle, the square, the circle, the oval, the ellipse, etc. Having established his own demarcation line in the original chaotic tangle of perception, he will instinctively try to relate it to these geometric elements. He reduces it to them, simplifies it the better to control it, the better to "understand" and possess it mentally with greater certainty and ease. Such a line, in itself an intellectual convention so far as visual reality is concerned, will now be tacitly reduced to the most habitual, conventional forms. In this way, the artist takes fuller possession of it, not affectively but intellectually. No other temptation has appealed more to the Mediterranean mind, obsessed as it is with clarity and order and bent upon extending the sway of mind over the nature that surrounds us on every side.

Does not the child, too, instinctively assert something very similar in the way of taking possession of the world, when, holding his pencil in hesitant fingers, he maltreats his model by reducing it to a few familiar geometric forms—the "stick," i.e., the straight line, the circle, and the square, with the help of which he will represent a torso, a head, arms, and legs? When Raphael deploys his sublime arabesque, he uses an infinitely more flexible and richer repertory of forms, but he is motivated by the same need to subdue the outside world, to subject it to the law of the mind. He merely carries this out at a more refined level than the child: the principle is essentially the same. His firm caress reduces everything to variously open or closed curves, countercurves, the circle, and the oval (Fig. 14).

Geometricization tends gradually to the curve and its variants. An ever more rigorous law will subject nature to the ever more exacting constraint of line, enclosing it ever more tightly in the net of lines. For the human mind seeks not only to clarify and order things, rounding them up like so many wild beasts that must be driven, separated, and penned up individually in the pre-existent restraints of mind and hand; in all this the mind merely gratifies its most immediate need and performs a utilitarian, practical function. Over and beyond matters of convenience, the mind is also aspiring to pleasure, to the special pleasure it finds in an ever-smoother play of its faculties. Where it can develop without encountering obstacles or surprises beyond the need to renew itself, where there is room to bring to bear the innermost laws of its own inner constitution, it attains the pleasure that is called "harmony."

Under such circumstances, form has not merely been made clear; it has become an object of delight. Among its parts, a proportion tends to be established, exact enough not to distract by sudden breakings-off, and distinct enough to renew the flavor of a taste that might otherwise become stale. A curve that would be wearying if too emphatic and

*Geometric form finds its perfect expression in flexible, sinuous curves where essential rigor and clarity are refined with elegance.*

**15. -** *PISANELLO.* FOUR NUDES with an ANNUNCIATION. Drawing.
Boymans-Van Beuningen Museum, Rotterdam

*At the end of the Middle Ages, the so-called International Style, which could be more correctly designated as the "Chivalric Style," popularized the aristocratic arabesque throughout Europe.*

**16. -** *STEFANO DA ZEVIO*. THE ANGEL OF THE ANNUNCIATION. Drawing. The Albertina, Vienna

demanding of attention will be succeeded by an inverse curve that relaxes, just as a new and contrary motion relaxes muscles tired out by the same repeated activity. In this way, drawing can give pleasure both to the mind and to the hand, which find their gratification in similar rules for exactly the same reasons. Both naturally find relaxation and pleasure in easy exercises that do not tire, and both induce the draftsman to make use of the wavy line that Hogarth favored above all others, to the point that he made it the foundation of the art of drawing and called it "the line of beauty" (Fig. 15).

The pre-eminence of the curve is merely one, but an essential, example of the pursuit of harmony through inflections, modulations, and other relationships introduced among various parts of a drawing. Thus, the type of drawing we shall call "intellectual" not only meets the obligations of clarity and abstractness, but crowns them with a pleasure that is also inherent in man's deepest nature.

It would serve no purpose to enroll artists exclusively under one or another of our categories. Similarly, it would be pointless to reduce inner life to some one "faculty." We are merely inventing categories for linguistic convenience. The human psyche is a living thing; all we can do is isolate its dominant features. It eludes intellectual simplification and classification, just as appearances refuse to let themselves be entirely enclosed in pure line. We cannot do without nuances, shadows, and transitions of one kind and another.

## 2. RELATIONSHIP TO LIFE

Is that all a drawing tells us about a man? Nothing but his type, as it were, his aptitudes, the orientation of his talent? But this is only a potential man, a theoretical model. Life throws the real man into the real world: he acts and reacts. The self that defines him and is revealed in his graphism is never solitary, though abstract definition makes him seem so. In actual fact he is continually confronting "the other"—whatever it is that surprises, threatens, or attracts him—the world of his fellow men. It is by continuous confrontations that he shows what he truly is, that he asserts himself. Conceived purely in terms of potentialities and aptitudes, he was merely a hypothesis. Life alone gives him reality, a reality conveyed also in his drawings, and just as clearly visible as in his life.

This problem of the self's confrontation with the world—is this not the essential problem posed by the arts, and above all, by the figurative arts?

*Ego* and *Alter*. What is an artist but a strongly defined self that posits itself, so to speak, by opposing itself to the outside world, as well as by acting upon and within it?

Sensibility is first and foremost reaction to whatever is outside, external to itself. Trust or fear? Attraction or repulsion? Love or aggressivity? It is these that determine the nature of a being.

LOVE, POSSESSION, AGGRESSIVITY. Love, like art, is but one way in which the equation between the self and the other is worked out. It is born of the ego's desperate effort to free itself from itself, to transcend itself, to overcome its limitations and selfishness by subordinating itself to something that is not itself. It abolishes itself and unites with God or with nature or with another being. The great artist exalts the powers of his self the better to love or admire, the better to communicate the fire that illuminates as it consumes. Divine love or human love, this is the light that transfigures the Christ of Rembrandt in the *Pilgrims at Emmaus* and the humble body and gentle face of Hendrickje in *Bathsheba*, just as it transfigures Corot's landscapes throbbing with feeling (Figs. 181 and 228).

At a lower level, this warmth and energy are neutralized; from love we descend to knowledge, from divine to human, from art to science. Between the self and the other there is

43

now only straightforward communication. Some painters resemble scientists in the way in which they observe and study the object; their sole concern is to take possession of it, to master it by discovering the secrets of its appearance, just as scientists attempt to discover the secrets of its structure. This is the level of possession in life, of understanding in the mind, of realism in art. Love, which is a giving, yields to avidity, which is a taking (Fig. 123).

In art, as elsewhere, love is made up of sacrifices of the kind stressed by Delacroix as a human need. But realism is insatiable—it wants everything, pursues everything. Compare Delacroix—an artist who is, if not love, then at least passion—with an artist like Ingres, all of whose spiritual ardor is reduced to sensuality, and you will see the real gulf between the two. Ingres' eye takes in everything and worships detail; that of Delacroix takes in only what moves him and nourishes him with its fervor. Delacroix's color exalts the secret harmonies and affinities he perceives between tones and subordinates them to an over-all harmony (thereby often disappointing neophytes who imagine "the great colorist" to be something else entirely). Ingres extracts maximum brilliance from every tone, often at the price of discordance; his strongest emotion is sensual avidity, where that of Delacroix is compassion. What is expressed in these two masters is less the opposition between two schools of art than that between two degrees in the scale of values we are outlining (Colorplate XIV).

With their relentless skill and rectitude, the realists take possession of things, but they do not give themselves to them. In these painters, line and color are precise; they define more than they evoke. They are a long way from the soft, quavering voices of artists raised in love, from Rembrandt's intimate, magical *chiaroscuro* in which they envelop their universe of discourse, from the deep feeling which gives Corot's color its gentle restraint and which makes his hand literally tremble with piety. Realistic painting is no more than a cage in which the painter exhibits the wild life that he captured on his latest expedition and subsequently tamed. He celebrates the defeat of nature, but, as with defeated people, he has only captured her body, not her soul. The soul is elsewhere and belongs to those who love nature, not to those who would keep her in bondage. Realism is like science: their nets have about the same-sized openings; while they manage to bag a good many things, just as many, more elusive, slip through.

At this level, however, one very great artist, Leonardo da Vinci, transcended the limitations of his heart by sheer genius. He was one of those who never know or experience love. The man of knowledge par excellence, he was as passionately interested in science as in art, and his whole career was one continuous striving for knowledge and power. Not just love but even affection was alien to him. To be sure, he was infinitely more subtle than latter-day realistic painters, rapacious of appearances in all their detail. Leonardo scorned inventories and proved himself adept at analysis; he is not collecting facts so much as penetrating secrets. The very grandeur of his ambition and the arid passion that animated him invest his art with a poetry as intense as that of artists whose creations are inspired by love. But how different he is from them! Unlike Rembrandt's, his *chiaroscuro* owes nothing to the imprecision of the dream; it derives from the insatiable pursuit of modeling. The soul is not for him a deeply moving mystery into the depths of which one plunges, but an irritating riddle which he is determined to account for and explain. In him, curiosity takes the place of ardor. He does not penetrate by force of feeling, but by dint of probing. Rembrandt, like all artists animated by love, brings to mind the mystic; Leonardo, like all those who are devoured by avidity, brings to mind the scientist (Figs. 110–24 and 222–30).

Beyond the neutral dividing line of objective knowledge there exists a sort of negative of the positive force of love, namely, aggression. With it, we reach a third stage, and step down into a dark subterranean zone that extends as far below as love extends upward to the heavenly realms of light. The one is as remote from the flat middle ground of realism as the other. In this third stage, the relations between the self and the other are reversed: the self feels the need to assert itself through cruel or destructive possession of the other. The self is not content with providing an equivalent for the other through knowledge where intellectual works are concerned, or through reproduction where artistic works are concerned. Now the compulsion is to subject, to exploit, to degrade, to annihilate. The self is interested in the outside world only insofar as the latter nourishes and justifies its hypertrophy; proud where it alone is concerned, it is cruel where the other is concerned.

Do we not find something very much like this in Picasso? At the risk of disagreeing with Maurice Thorez, who on one occasion called him a master of "tenderness," I suspect that Picasso is animated by Luciferian desires, is interested in creation only so as to undo it as it is and to remake it along the lines of plastic investigations. Thus we distinguish three major degrees in artistic aspiration—the Divine, the Human, and the Demonic. To them, in the domain of relationships among living beings, correspond the categories of Love, Possession, and Sadism.

The very first gesture that the artist makes as he addresses himself to a creative task involves an option that will carry him along one of these three paths.

The "possessive" drawing is the one we have just defined: it wants to be neutral, its only inspiration is avidity. This is what realistic drawing at its best achieves: it captures reality and does not so much assert its own nature, as lend itself—thanks to its docility and personal inconsistencies—to every sort of external situation.


"AFFECTIONATE" GRAPHISM.   Tenderness has a language all its own, as spontaneous in the modulation of light as in the harmonization of colors or the inflections of a continuous, wavy line. In the last, every change of direction gives rise to a curve, which never imposes itself as such but follows and softens the features of the model.

This type of drawing was developed as early as the twelfth century, at the time of a great upsurge of faith and love that was to send the mighty spires of the cathedrals soaring into the sky and to implant the rituals of chivalric love among a society still crude and warlike in its manners. On the one hand, St. Bernard and the Cistercian monks were promoting "the tender sentiments of the Word and the soul," further exalted in an affectionate cult of the Virgin. This cult was later adopted by Siena—Siena, *civitas Virginis*. The way was being prepared for St. Francis who, by the end of the century, became the bard of divine love. On the other hand, secular life was now passing under the influence of courtly love, of the worship of woman and the art of loving, whose source was being sought by Chrétien de Troyes, during this period, in his Breton lays (Fig. 17).

In this climate of fervor, of which France was the center, appeared an elegant, gentle graphism, first formulated in its perfection by Jean Pucelle. It came to full bloom at the same time as that School of Paris whose European influence was abruptly halted in 1415 by the disaster of Agincourt. A new era was beginning, more positivist in spirit and rougher in its manners. However, before giving way to the rule of bourgeois materialism, one last nostalgic surge of knightly culture spread from court to court, from London to Prague, the vogue of a so-called International Style. With it spread the new gentle graphism, which

*Jacques Daliwe left behind only one book of models, such as traveling painters used to carry. His affinities with Pisanello have often been pointed out, and they prove to what extent the Chivalric Style was international.*

**18. -** *JACQUES DALIWE. THREE HEADS.* Early fifteenth century. Franco-Flemish School.
Staatsbibliothek, Berlin

had been on the verge of disappearing. Just as in Flamboyant Gothic decoration, curve echoes countercurve and balances it in a gentle pervasive rhythm as uncomplex as life itself. The eye glides over occasional asperities or angularities of the drawing without being wounded; occasionally it meets the caressing line of a spiral or an elegant, refined loop such as a figure skater traces on the ice. Already tainted with Mannerism, this arabesque is found wherever an aristocratic medieval society enjoyed one last moment of brilliance. In a somewhat more acid form it turns up in English art, with a trifle more mellowness in Rhenish art; it passes across the Po Valley where the first princely courts of Italy were flourishing and pushes eastward into Bohemia. Only rarely, however, in the course of these peregrinations, does it keep the airy, limpid grace with which the School of Paris had invested it (Figs. 16 and 18).

*The gentle, delicate Chivalric Style, by contrast with the virile Classical forms, is characterized by a feminine quality in keeping with the subjects treated—leisurely activities in which graceful women play a leading part.*

**17. -** *Opposite page: FRENCH SCHOOL* (about 1408–10). LADY WITH DOG AND FALCON.
Watercolor study for an Arras tapestry. The Louvre, Paris

47

The Renaissance subsequently geometrized and intellectualized this fluid style of drawing, animated with the very breath of sensibility, and introduced into it a reflective rigor, concerned for the rules which a new idol shortly decreed: Beauty.

Wherever the example of Paris had not penetrated, or where that of the Italian Renaissance came much later, a primitive, angular, far from elaborate graphism proved more suitable for middle-class realism. What we call "affectionate graphism" disappeared along with the chivalric society that had created it; it survived only in a few princely milieus—in Florentine Mannerism, for instance, as Botticelli foreshadowed it. Classical drawing alone clung to the cursive outline, but now it became more austere. Elsewhere, in such Northern schools as those of Flanders and Germany, and wherever their influence spread, jagged angularity produced a more direct realism. It is instructive to compare the stiff, broken lines of a Flemish drawing (c. 1500) with the fuller, more flexible line of an Italian drawing of the same period; instructive also is the persistence of the angular line in seventeenth-century Dutch drawing, where it attains its peak with Rembrandt, all flashing animation. Among the more Italianized Flemish artists there appears a wavy linearity, luxuriant to the point of redundancy, of which Rubens is the greatest single exponent. And yet, often enough, naturalness reappears in a sketch, as a sort of native accent which the artists could not wholly lose; in certain pen drawings by Rubens or Van Dyck we find a fully Rembrandtesque exploration of the broken line (Fig. 19).

CRUEL GRAPHISM.   The rise of a diametrically opposed kind of sensibility can be traced in German drawing (Fig. 20).

Flemish drawings can be rough and unadorned, even brutal, seemingly uncontrolled. In them, line changes direction abruptly, jerkily; it is neutral, unconcerned for the subtleties of feeling. German drawing, which historically derives from the Flemish, outdoes it in these respects and becomes openly aggressive; there is an instinctive feeling for the visual equivalents to cruelty. Here line is no longer adherent, caressing, but abrupt, mischievous, hostile; it imitates everything that cuts, claws, pierces, or tears. Every stroke of the pencil terminates in a little hook, whether there seems to be justification for it or not. Sharp points are angrily set down one next to the other, suggesting feverish haste; jagged saw teeth evoke cutting blades, beaks, and talons in a murky symbolism expressing obsessions of feeling such as latter-day psychoanalysis has exploited and oversystematized (Fig. 21).

How it is that the artist's eye is drawn to this choice of objects, rather than that, is nothing if not plain to see. Fifteenth-century Parisian drawings were animated by noble draperies falling in waves and loops, with banderoles undulating at the slightest breath of air, and clouds that curl like angels' hair. Sixteenth-century German drawings are very different from fifteenth-century Flemish drawings, which are merely dry: they show a fondness of rags and tatters, breaks and indentations, bristling feathers, spiky vegetation. To imagine that the natural environment imposes such forms on the artist would be to take insufficient account of dark appetites ready to go far afield for their gratification— why, for example, does Grünewald make use of the palm tree, a foreign plant, unless it is because its foliage is like a panoply of bristling bayonets? Dürer, yes, even Dürer who like Goethe was seduced by the Latin love of serenity—a Faust whose heart softened whenever he looked upon Helen and who sought a key to harmony in the theory of the Golden Section taught him by Pacioli and Leonardo—even Dürer felt the stirrings of an inner demon and exposed a cloven hoof under his scholar's cloak. The self-portrait in the Louvre is especially revealing on this score. Is it not an act of love, having been painted for his fiancée? Has he not made a real effort to bring purity to his emaciated features, to record a state of mind and feeling well-nigh romantic? But what is the flower he is holding, in pledge of fidelity to his love? Not the shy, discreet forget-me-not, but—and as a German equivalent to the forget-me-not, Dürer's choice is most expressive—a thistle fairly bristling with spikes. And what a bony hand is holding it up, thin fingers arched, almost clenched! We cannot fail to see the affinity with Grünewald's treatment of hands as contracted claws (Fig. 24).

Ravens, eagles, black birds with hard feathers that evoke the bristling crest of a helmet or the pikestaffs of armored soldiers—these are the only birds that fly over these blue-green landscapes or alight within the unreal frames of heraldic drawings.

Investigation of the sources of this angular drawing characteristic of Germanism, which asserts itself as early as the Ottonian epoch—in some thirteenth-century miniatures, for example—might lead us to one of the essential causes of the opposition between the German and the Latin spirit. The civilizations which developed around the shores of the Mediterranean in a sunny climate, in a setting of constant travel and commerce, mastered the forces of nature at an early date, and for this reason display deep confidence in the power of the human mind and in the balance that rational laws can attain.

Central Europe was arrested at the prehistoric stage much longer; it owes its advances far more to the discovery of metals than to the pursuit of agriculture. There, nature inadequately brought under control and bristling with dark forests of the kind wherein the legions of Varus were destroyed is at once more profuse and less clear-cut (the climate is damper) than around the Mediterranean. Nature presents more of a threat, and life is more precarious. Only partly liberated from the fears his condition inspired, German man remained closer to the instinctual levels of life; the serenity of the logical mind was alien to him, and, without it, he was all the more directly at the mercy of unknown powers, both of the inner and the outer world. Resort to brute force, reactions of fear and self-defense, such as easily give rise to a combative reflex, shape a different psychology. In the fifteenth and sixteenth centuries, when the collapse of the medieval culture and the instability of a dying civilization spread everywhere an obsession with death and the Devil, German art gave more intense expression to these developments and clung to it longer than did the art of other countries. The saturnine spirit exalted in Dürer's *Melancolia*, to give only one example, has often been pointed out. The graphism of the epoch exhibits every symptom of aggressiveness and reflects a preoccupation with cruelty both as suffered and as inflicted upon others.

At the beginning of the fifteenth century, this spirit had hardly made its way to the Hanseatic School which, being close to "the Mediterranean of the North" and enjoying prosperity in trade, escaped the ascendancy of fear. Nor did it penetrate the Rhenish School in that period. The Rhine, known then as "the street of the clerics," was a great European waterway that served to convey spiritual as well as material goods. The homeland of Meister Eckhart, of Tauler, and of Suso had gone through an especially pronounced surge of mystic love; situated on the frontier of Germanism, it was open to outside influences. And, true enough, art, faithful to the correspondences we are discussing, responded to this effusion in every one of its plastic characteristics, most notably by a linear gentleness related to the School of Paris.

**19. -** *Opposite page:*
Attributed to
*VAN DER GOES.*
ST. GEORGE
AND THE
DRAGON.
Drawing. National
Gallery of Art,
Washington, D.C.

*In Flemish
drawings the
graceful nuances of
the Chivalric Style
give way
to the meticulous
observation
characteristic of the
middle classes.
Pursuit of realism
results in a graphic
treatment
employing
sweeping line and,
often, angular
forms. The German
drawing deriving
from it introduces a
complicated,
twisted, almost
tormented quality,
and the engraver's
technique expresses
a harsh, restless,
and sometimes
almost aggressive
psyche.*

**20. -** *DÜRER.*
DEATH
SLAYING
A JUMPING
RIDER.
Pen drawing.
Städelsche
Kunstinstitut,
Frankfort

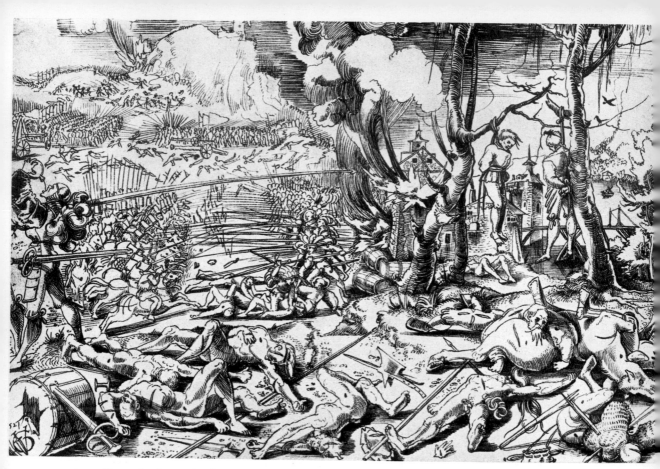

*German drawing occasionally attains a pitch of paroxysm, in which the painfulness of the subjects is matched by the convulsive nervousness of jagged, broken lines.*

**21. -** *URS GRAF.* BATTLEFIELD. 1521. Kupferstichkabinett, Basel

With the Reformation and the general break with Latin Catholicism, the special characterics of Germanic art were exacerbated, and German painting was transformed. Now all is paroxysm, tenseness, cruelty. Color becomes intense to the point of stridency and takes on an acid brilliance unknown in the other schools. Line, as we have seen, never ceases to search out analogies with aggressive forms, with whatever stabs, hooks, cuts, rends. The choice of subjects discloses a similar obsession. As was long since pointed out, there is a caricatural bestiality in the types, particularly those of Christ's executioners. The painters enjoy describing the ferocity of the latter with a realism we find in no other school, and the Crucifixion of Christ as well as scenes of saintly martyrdom provide them with images of atrocity, blood, and suffering. Manuel Deutsch needs no fewer than ten thousand impaled, dislocated, dismembered martyrs' bodies. And are there any nightmares more terrifying than those which obsessed Grünewald? Around his St. Anthony he groups pustulous putrefying monsters; his crucified Christ is a celebration of the ignominiousness of the dead human body, bruised from the blows of the soldiers, pierced with the crown of thorns, dripping with blood, and convulsed with the extremest suffering—face swollen and lower lip pendant. The hands, drawn back and curled like claws, make a haunting leitmotiv against the background of an opaque, hopeless night sky.

VARIATIONS ON A THEME.   To compare different treatments of the same theme is the best way to grasp the expressive language of forms. To place side by side a *Crucifixion* by a French miniaturist and a *Crucifixion* by a tormented German genius is to feel at once the antagonism between the spirit of love and the spirit of cruelty. It may be, with Grünewald, that the spirit of cruelty represents a painful detour in an unconscious search for love through the shock of pity and horror; still, the work has a specific quality and a specific idiom (Figs. 22 and 24).

Between these two extremes there is a *Crucifixion* by Antonello da Messina so objective in treatment that, by contrast, it seems more impassive than it may actually be. The firm, almost geometric line, the full, simple, well-defined volumes, the forms solidly based in a space where the light is even and seemingly indifferent—everything bespeaks the absence of "pathos" and passion alike. Intelligence, observation, and knowledge play a greater part in this work than feeling, or than any current of the soul, whether divine or merely unconscious (Fig. 23).

A fourth *Crucifixion* brings us back to our own day; it is by an eminent contemporary painter, André Marchand. It casts a great deal of light on ourselves. Before the war, Marchand had been fond of calm, blurry forms, crude volumes, subdued and meditative colors; he could then have been viewed as a descendant of the Romanesque artists and Le Nain, as assimilated through Cézanne. Then came the war. Marchand's painting underwent a prodigious mutation of all its external features. Color suddenly became strident and unrestrained in its violence; line broke up, became fragmented, jagged, and split off into bristling, discontinuous splinters; his somewhat hieratic impassivity was transformed into ardent eloquence. Now, this surprising change was not unique with Marchand. It was Grüber—a native, incidentally, of the eastern provinces of France—who seems to have inspired this taste for an angular, pointed graphism, which marks a complete break with the whole tradition of French, and even Latin, drawing. The art of this generation of painters, who came to maturity in the war years, could well be described as "a cruel art."

Indeed, the spirit of aggression has ever since dwelt in their works. Is this to say that cruelty is in their soul? No; but it has touched them. Its presence—throughout the war, the defeat, the occupation years—has become an obsession with them. Like some shrieking noise that we cannot protect our ears from, the painfulness of that unutterable period has left its mark on their inner life, affected their least glimpses around them and the least of their reflections. It is hardly surprising that the evolution of their style was sharply interrupted. In them, the spirit of love is struggling with the spirit of aggression—perhaps maimed and overcome, so that, for the first time in its history, French art reflects the cruel.

One more *Crucifixion*, this one by Buffet, owes so much to Grüber that it is perhaps little more than a vulgarization of Grüber's work, suitable to a public eager to find its own anxieties reflected in art. It suggests how deeply the French soul has been damaged by two world wars in as many generations (Fig. 25).

# 3 · THE INDIVIDUAL

WHEN we first took a look at drawing, we found in it a basis for making psychological distinctions between artists, and now we see that it takes us still farther: it also discloses the mental attitudes with which man confronts the world around him and his own fate in it. All that is left for the human soul to be fully realized in drawing is for it to transcribe expressively the individual's particular nature and the problems into which life plunges him. Now, drawing can do this to the extent that it is not envisaged in terms of a clockworks, to the extent that the artist's whole being is committed in the confrontation of what he is, what he wants to create, and what he is able to create. "What is drawing?" Van Gogh wrote to Theo. "It is the action of clearing a way for oneself through an invisible pile of iron that seems to lie between what one *wants* to do and what one *can* do." It is therefore in terms of Van Gogh's short career that we shall address ourselves to the question of how the way is cleared and how the drawing preserves a record of that "action." Such an investigation is necessarily complex, for we are dealing less with positive facts than with elusive mental realities.

It is not enough to analyze the features which give a work of art its particular quality, its particular individuality. First of all, we must isolate those which derive from outside influences (although we must not forget that to accept influence amounts to a choice that discloses the artist's individual predisposition). Only after the effects of external pressures have been delimited do the inner motives become discernible; here, again, it is important to separate those which reflect a collective reality—called the human type or the intellectual family—from those which derive from the innermost individual reality. This last is the nucleus, the center of gravity, of the exceptional man who imposes his revelation on us and overwhelms us with it.


VAN GOGH'S GRAPHOLOGY. Van Gogh's career as a painter was extraordinarily short—it extended over ten years only. In March, 1884, he was at Nuenen: there he made a drawing of the garden of the vicarage (Fig. 26), and, as in other drawings of his Dutch period, we are first struck by his obsession with the infinite: the horizon and the sky, the exaggerated speed of the perspective into the distance, toward which the figure is shown walking. It is no accident that the lines of perspective end in the church, which is framed and set off by arched branches. Son of a Protestant minister, Van Gogh had barely got over the crisis that led him to preach the gospel in the Borinage, cutting a sorry figure (his own church had just disowned him). His intoxication with the horizon, his taste for the infinite, are directly inspired by the Dutch landscape and pictorial tradition; but it takes on such bitter sense with Van Gogh because it reflects his own dramatic destiny. Although even a first impression is striking, we must not fail to go and analyze humbly the handwriting of the drawing. We see again an angular, stiff line that excludes all curves and consists entirely of discontinuous strokes—the same style of drawing that has, since the fifteenth century, been typical of the Low Countries and, as we have seen, as remote from the intellectuality of Italian geometry as from the French arabesque. Is this merely a matter of Van Gogh's inheritance from a particular school of art? Not entirely; it has something which is his alone—the hurriedness of his line, seemingly panting for breath, whose basic elements

*Different graphic interpretations of one and the same subject reveal to what extent artists may differ psychologically.*

**22.** - Pages from the MISSAL OF SENLIS. French manuscript, late fourteenth century.
Bibliothèque Ste-Geneviève, Paris

**23.** - *ANTONELLO DA MESSINA.* THE CRUCIFIXION. Royal Museum of Fine Arts, Antwerp

**24.** - *GRÜNEWALD.* THE CRUCIFIXION (center panel of the ISENHEIM ALTARPIECE). Museum, Colmar

**25.** - *BERNARD BUFFET.* THE CRUCIFIXION. 1946

*This early drawing by Van Gogh, with its meticulous, rigid, broken hatchings, seems to belong to the Northern tradition.*

**26. -** *VAN GOGH.* THE RECTORY GARDEN IN WINTER. March, 1884. Pen and pencil drawing.
Stedelijk Museum, Amsterdam

—hatchings and dots—take on a mechanical, tireless regularity under his stubborn hand. This feature points to obsessiveness, to mania, the graphologists would say, and could, in the case of psychological disturbances, lead to hallucinations. It cannot be repeated often enough that Van Gogh's madness does not account for his genius, but is one of the elements of his nature which he is compelled to make use of; thus it helps to determine his art, much as a geographical obstacle determines the course of a river though it has not created the river. Flight to the infinite and obsession—these two basic features explain why Van Gogh's subsequent graphism discloses certain affinities with the drawings of delirious mystics— leaving out qualitative considerations.

Four years later, in 1888, after a stay in Paris where his rapid, abrupt hatchings were shown to be admirably consistent with the discontinuous brush strokes of the Impressionists, Van Gogh arrived in Provence (Fig. 27). His fundamental characteristics now become more pronounced, and his dynamism increases and, as the artist gains experience, is liberated, leading to ever more rapid and passionate simplifications, ever more impulsive

*After Van Gogh went to southern France, his handwriting lost its stiffness and the hatchings gave way to dots.*

**27.** - *VAN GOGH.* VIEW OF LA CRAU FROM MONTMAJOUR. May, 1888. Pen drawing.
Stedelijk Museum, Amsterdam

gestures. The dynamism of line is communicated to the over-all vision in the movements that run across the ground and the foliage, like the wheat fields in the wind or ripples and eddies in water. But while the simplification becomes more synthetic, the rapid parallel hatchings become more profuse, and a pigmentation that crackles like hailstones becomes more obsessive. Like clouds of insects, the hatchings accumulate in the far distance of the landscapes where the horizon line is as imperious as before, and also in the backgrounds of the portraits. However, the graphic form has evolved: a more continuous, more *sustained* line rounds off the angular breaks in continuity and even blossoms out into curves, rudimentary arabesques. Influences? One may speak here of an assimilation of the French style, of the effect of Gauguin and Japanese prints. These are important elements, to be sure, but there is also an increasing reliance upon gestures of impulse, as the hand is flung at the canvas more and more impetuously.

The borrowed elements of style were quickly assimilated by the artist and internalized. Now arabesques and accumulating broken lines find a point of juncture, combine to

*At Saint-Rémy, the artist's line developed into a fragmented, throbbing, frantic arabesque.*

**28.** - *VAN GOGH.* WHEAT FIELD WITH CYPRESSES. 1888/89. Ink and pencil drawing.
Stedelijk Museum, Amsterdam

express jointly the obsessive thrust of lyricism, suggesting a language adaptable to its exalted rhythm. We are in the year 1889 (Fig. 28). Now the arabesque, obedient to deeper necessities, is incorporated in the artist's central obsession, his major symbol: fire. What he gains by this is nothing more or less than a flamboyant, i.e., a flaming style, which transforms trees into rivers and bushes into blazing fires, which turns the universe into molten lava, a white-hot sputtering crucible.

One more year goes by, and the artist is at Auvers, where he will shortly die. Van Gogh's original vision is accentuated; it has overcome every resistance, but at the same time it is showing signs of hardening into formula (Fig. 29). Earlier, at Saint-Rémy, his line had shown signs of a symptomatic muddiness, becoming stereotyped in the forms, sticky and heavy in the handwriting. The more massive, less fluid splashes were getting hard; it was as though the molten lava had flowed as far as it could, shuddering and shaking as it cooled. This antagonism between an ever more exacting desire for clear statement and a hand that sickness was making clumsy and unreliable may be the key to the artist's

*In Van Gogh's last drawings, the continuous line traces an arabesque with vehement but uncertain and chaotic curves.*

**29.** - *VAN GOGH.* HOUSE AMID TREES. 1890. Charcoal and blue wash drawing. Stedelijk Museum, Amsterdam

despair and dramatic end. "Once back here, I set to work again—though the brush almost slipped from my fingers," he wrote to his brother Theo shortly before his death (Letter 649), and just a little later (Letter 652) he even says that his "reason has half foundered." Nothing is more poignant than this contradiction between Van Gogh's sense of hopeless failure and the viewer's conviction of the artist's heightened powers.

Thus, only a few drawings serve to reveal Van Gogh's inner fatality, the influences he assimilated, how he fed the inner fires that finally consumed him. We would need more space to show how the graphism reflects the general features and the hidden truth of the man. In the beginning we witness the transition from an inherited Northern handwriting to the arabesque borrowed from the Japanese print, but in a short while Van Gogh's unrestrained flamboyant style reflects traits of his inner nature, though still in a general way. On the artistic plane, it is related to the eternal Baroque as on the pathological plane to the drawings of the insane, with its profusion of signs, its mounting frenzy, its feverish ascending movement. Van Gogh himself refers to "oleanders, raving mad" (Letter 541). If we penetrate deeper into this style of drawing, we nonetheless discover, over and above all ordinary expectations, that Van Gogh succeeded in transcribing the individual portion of his nature, the very hallmark of his uniqueness. So true it is that the artistic image, like all man's spontaneous symbols of himself, is multivalent and has many meanings.

However, it is the self that secures its superior unity, its final synthesis. For, if we turn away from Van Gogh's drawings and study the other aspects of his art, we find in them the same deep meaning, which the artist *lived*, though he was unaware of this in his lucid statements of intention. "To feel the stars and the infinite high and clear above you" (Letter 520), "the existence of something on high" (Letter 548), "aspirations toward this infinite..." (to Bernard), the inability "to do without something which is greater than I" (Letter 531). It is always the same appeal: the need to escape from his own nature, carried to the point of obsession ("This lives on, and it searches and searches forever!"), the need to soar toward the infinite. He had a physical foreboding of the infinite, but groped toward it with every fiber of his being. He sensed it at a great distance from himself—remember how the horizon haunted him—or at a very great height, for the sky, too, haunted him.

Along with a graphology of handwriting, we now have the beginnings of a far richer graphology, that of drawings. The way certain features of line are distributed over time and space, in confrontation with historical data, together with the fact that an exceptional individual is capable of inventing a new line—all this confirms that art is one of the most striking testimonies that man has ever given of himself.

**30. -** *LUCIANO LAURANA.* ARCHITECTURAL VIEW. Staatliche Museen, Berlin

CHAPTER II

# FORM AND INTELLECT

DRAWING is capable of recording our innermost nature and deepest instincts. In the preceding chapter we saw that its tendency to achieve a regular organization also expresses the operation of the intellect, which subjects the initial impulse to its own discipline. Drawing outlines and later clarifies form; with the help of drawing form, which the mind uses to unravel and understand the confused aspects of reality, to synthesize and unify it, is brought to its perfection in geometric order.

It remains to ask how man acquired his power to master the tumultuous and changing appearance of things, thus acceding to a realm situated outside time, to a space which is immune to the erosive action of time and which assumes definite forms governed by immutable laws; how this transcription of the changing universe into fixed forms has progressively asserted itself, and how it was modified over the ages. History tells us little about the origins and earliest phases of the conquest; it does not throw light on the very beginning.

61

Psychology, which deals with the human brain as we find it today, after long evolution, can reconstruct primitive mentality only hypothetically. But we do have the testimony of art. From prehistoric epochs, it has faithfully recorded the epic of the mind in its assault on the appearances of reality and the subjection of them to its own decrees. Indeed, we must recognize that art has been one of the major instruments in our mental domestication of the outside world.

Form is a reflection of intellectual life; unlike color, it does not lend itself easily to expression of the emotional life, save perhaps indirectly—through deformation. It is a clear structure imposed upon the turmoil of sensations, upon their ever-changing mirages. To be more precise, form projects onto sensations structures appropriate to thought. The Greeks were well aware of this: they designated both Form and Idea by the same word—*eidos*. We have as yet to study the close relationship between forms and ideas at any given time and place in some detail (cf. Part II, Ch. I). The link between them is a common disposition, in terms of which the corresponding states of mind are determined. They translate, the former in visual terms, the latter in intellectual terms, man's attempt to grasp the mass of his experiences in some straightforward fashion. There is thus an inevitable analogy between the logic that governs intellectual representations and the logic that orders visual representations. Both serve to liberate knowledge from the uncertainties and change inherent in human experience, and to isolate constants that can serve as foundation for reliable, lasting concepts. Bergson was struck by this, observing that the intellect is adjusted to stability and to clear-cut divisions in space, and yet rebels against mobile, continuous transformations in time. The affinity between mental forms and visual forms ought not to surprise us, since both are born of the same will to provide solid foundations for the eye that observes no less than for the mind that thinks.

MAKING THINGS OUT: CONTOUR. Originally, the problem was to determine such fixed elements as could be isolated in the immense, crowded field of perception. Clearly, these could be provided only by objects and bodies endowed with unity so manifest as to be distinguishable within the torrential flux, solid outcroppings of rock in the swirling currents of a fast-moving stream. Man needs a guide post, a firm footing.

This faculty of distinguishing a term as valid in the mental as in the visual domain is taken for granted. And yet it marks an advanced level of intelligence. Animal psychologists have shown that even highly evolved animals are not easily capable of making distinctions. For instance, someone had the idea of putting a monkey in a room with two doors. The doors were at opposite ends of the room and marked very plainly and differently—a red cross inside a circle on one, a green triangle inside a square on the other. There was food behind the first door. There was nothing behind the second door. It takes a few trials and errors, but the monkey quickly learns which door is which. It seems that the animal is guided by the signs. In fact, when the red sign is removed, the monkey loses its bearings. More than that: when the green triangle on the door that does not give access to food is removed, the monkey becomes just as confused. Obviously, the animal has a hard time finding its way among the totality of perceptions; all it can do is observe the whole within which it finds itself, orienting itself more or less intuitively,

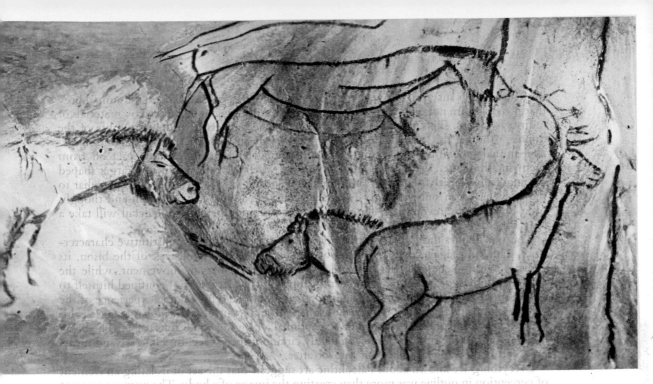

*The art of the prehistoric hunter expresses his optics: he sees the animal as a target defined in outline.*

**31.** - *PREHISTORIC ART.* HORSES AND DEER. Magdalenian period. Cave of Niaux (Ariège)

It cannot seize on any single element sufficiently reliable in itself to serve as invariable guidance.

At the other extreme, the very earliest works left behind by prehistoric man, even as far back as the Paleolithic age, prove that he had already acquired the power to analyze his vision as a whole and to reconstitute separately perceived forms within it. We should try to imagine this remote ancestor of ours, though a mere child in comparison with the maturer artists whom the species will produce later—that is, if we are indeed maturer than he. To say the least, this early artist was nothing if not a man: confronted with the fullness of optical sensations, much as the newborn infant still is, he did not find it easy to make sense of them. He had to introduce order into chaos, isolate objects, perceive their distance from himself; a particular moving spot means a specific object or body and must be separated from another moving spot, which represents another object or body.... An enormous education is implied; the first labor of the prehistoric artist must have been to make out specific things in the given confusion, among the constantly changing vibrations of light that the Impressionists much later had to reconstruct scientifically. That civilizations, like old men, are fond of going back to their childhoods seems an inescapable truism!

Thus, in the beginning, the artist concentrated on an effort to *distinguish*, to discriminate, which was still is the primary effort of the intellect (Fig. 31).

From all he perceives, man must pick out the elements of vision indispensable for his and

63

his fellow men's survival. Now, he is first a hunter, his life centered around the animal prey that provides him not only with food but also with clothing and the other raw materials of industry—bones, skins, sinews, etc. Nascent art hence sets itself to define the life of the hunter. And in this instance, "to define" is meant in the strict sense of "outlining." The animal—a mammoth, a bison—is set off from its surroundings and is set off from them in silhouette. We do no differently today when we raise a gun to a target shaped schematically, clearly a man or an animal, to show our skill. A bit of space peculiar to the prey has been unhesitatingly isolated in line; the animal has been seen and thought of as distinct from everything else. Concern for volume, for relief, for detail will take a long time.

Contour defines the animal in still another way: by showing its constitutive characteristics. Thinking, again, operates at one with vision: the powerful neck of the bison, its enormous hump, bespeak the tremendous weight of its mass in movement, while the extreme thinness of its legs expresses nervous speed. The artist has not confined himself to observation of an individual model, has not been dominated by a single experience of the model. He wants to make a universal, permanent statement of what he has seen. It is his way of escaping from the momentary, exceptional, changing conditions of life. The bison is taken out of time; it now occupies a firmly circumscribed space, for all to see and measure. This is the way we will see it forever after.

Everything we known about Paleolithic art suggests that the act of isolating an element of perception in outline was more than creating the image of a body. The purpose was not just visual, but magic. The image is not so remote from reality; it is meant as a double; to extract a contour from chaotic nothingness is to create a second order of reality. The prehistoric artist, less concerned with apparent results than with the *act* that generates the form thus created—and working, moreover, most often in the darkness of a deep cave, a darkness only momentarily dispelled by scanty lighting—does not hesitate to draw figures on top of other figures, so that they pile up over the course of generations. The result is an illegible jumble, what the Abbé Breuil expressively called a "macaroni" of lines, requiring enormous effort on our part to make anything out. In other words, the essential thing to the prehistoric artist was the act of separating some one thing by a line, "definition" in the strictest sense of the term, bringing a form into being. The visual result, the illusion provided to the eye—what we would call today "the figuration"—was of secondary importance.

Paleolithic art reflects the mental conditions of that epoch, the conquests effected by the human intellect in those times. Above all, it was the ability to abstract things both from the surroundings and from individual particularities that this art reflects, though we can also discern shortcomings in what is still a very limited undertaking.

What Paleolithic man did not know how to represent, what seems to have as yet mattered little to him, is not so much the relations between bodies in space (for several rudimentary battle scenes prove that he could group several figures in a common action, if only adversaries in a fight), as the relations of bodies to their surroundings. Proud of having been able to set up fixed points, he makes no effort to go further and establish a complex coherent relational system, a true order. The human intellect will not for long be content to define the elements of its vocabulary of thoughts and images by analytic means; if it is to develop, it must combine them in an ever vaster synthesis, co-ordinate them, and constantly extend the network of relationships. Once it had created separate and distinct figures, grouping them only in the sense of throwing them together pell-mell (as in the ceiling of Altamira), it was the task of art to arrive at the notion of a common environment in which the figures are linked and which itself can be organized in turn. There is no landscape in Paleolithic art, not even décor. When, occasionally, nature is evoked—at Lascaux, for instance, there is a scene of reindeer swimming across a river—the prehistoric artist confines himself to confronting the animal with an element (in this case, water) indispensable for portraying it in action. Similarly, in the fighting scenes just mentioned, he made the animal face an adversary.

THE BIRTH OF GEOMETRY.   The beginnings of Neolithic art open a different era. Its manifestations are found in the most various regions, from the Iberian Levant to the Sahara and Rhodesia: from now on, relationships are multiplied, the activities evoked are more complex, and numerous characters are brought into play. Communal life develops; as social life is constituted, interpersonal relations take precedence over relations between men and animals. Collective actions—battles, ritual dances—begin to play an increasing role. Individual elements no longer have the same importance: they are lost in the crowd. As a result, they are not so strongly and definitely characterized as before; they are reduced to spots, which, for a long time, remain evocative through their instantaneous rightness. As conventions become established, however, they end up as no more than a kind of numerical punctuation.

Composition makes its appearance. The stage in which bisons are placed, incoherently, one next to another, as at Altamira, is left behind. But spatial connections remain very uncertain; the figures do not rest upon a common foundation, the ground; they do not have the same axis of stability; they hover alongside each other, rather like debris tossed about on the surface of water.

Only with the beginnings of rural society, such as was organized in the second half of the fourth millennium B.C., and systematic cultivation of the soil (appearing simultaneously in Egypt and in Mesopotamia) did there arise a conception of form and of its installation in space that has largely remained valid down to our own day, at least for the arts of the Mediterranean tradition. The prehistoric artists at first represented individual animals, aiming above all at exact definition. Later they represented social activities such as hunts, feasts, combats; in such group pictures, the elements were reduced to their simplest expression, and only the collective action served as an organizing principle. In the Neolithic epoch, farming took precedence over hunting, and the artists realized the importance of the plane on which all human activities take place: the surface of the earth, the ground. In order to avoid disputes over land boundaries, it became necessary to divide the land into lots whose shapes are regular and easily juxtaposed. Reflecting these developments, prehistoric art for the first time felt the need to impose limits upon the field of vision (this term "field," of country origin, is itself significant). They did so with a simple, clear frame modeled on the parallelogram, which is the most convenient basis for dividing up land. In art, from that moment on, figures were no longer distributed more or less at random, like balloons tossed about by every breath of air; they were subjected to the strict discipline of the frame and arranged along lines parallel to its sides. The horizontal provided the rectilinear base of the ground where each body, each object now rose along an exact vertical. The sur-

**32.** - WAR CHARIOT AND CAVALRY (detail from an Assyrian relief). Seventh century B.C. The Louvre, Paris

face on which a mural representation was executed became of primordial importance to the artist, and determined the treatment of figures. For many centuries, the law of frontality was to reign supreme, right down to Classical Greece. The place occupied by the figure was no longer determined by its individual logic and structure, but subjected, at the price of arbitrary distortions, to the picture plane. Each part of the body—eye, head, torso, legs, feet—was represented flatly, in a position where it could be shown as completely as possible (Fig. 32).

It was then that geometry made its appearance in civilization. Born of the needs of ownership of the land, it was soon applied in city planning (as cities made their appearance), giving rise to a pattern of rectangular intersections within a regular-shaped fortified enclosure. It fully asserted itself in architecture, whose stability is based on the same fundamental forms; it gained such dominance in the human mind that now living beings were no longer rendered as "impressionistic" spots, but fitted into regular patterns, an earlier realistic vividness being replaced with rigid primary forms. Drawing and sculpture were governed by the geometric principles of symmetry,

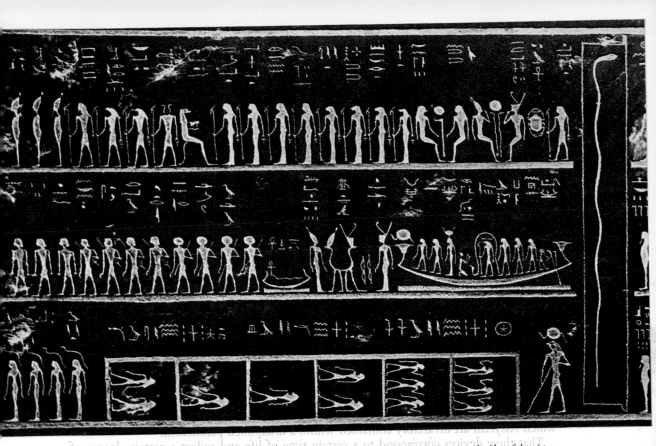

...*at the same time, the practice of the land survey, i.e., the organized division of the land, determines the idea of the picture frame and the division of picture space into quadrangles.*

**33. -** SARCOPHAGUS OF THE PRIEST T'AHO (detail). Egypt. Saïte period. The Louvre, Paris

repetition of identical elements, and simplification and systematization of contours (Figs. 33 and 34).

The art of the early agricultural and city civilizations thus came under the sway of form; it makes use of color to a limited degree and, apparently, only to secure a better design, a more accurate definition of the surface area. Space is victorious, now, and time seems to have been banished; even when an Egyptian low relief captures a movement, it is only to freeze it forever. Separated from what comes before and goes after, it is as immobile as dried plants precisely arrayed between the pages of an herbal. Like the mummies rendered motionless for their immutable journeyings after death, the figures are fitted into the forms, which play the part of mummy wrappings and, similarly, set the seal of eternity upon them. In many a statue, the contrast is all the stronger between lifelike eyes of enamel or lapis lazuli, seemingly about to flicker, and the rigid, logical solid masses that have escaped the irresistible course of time and stand there with a hypnotic, unfeeling stiffness. The full weight of form crushes every hint of flight from this petrified world and suggests a determination to

67

ignore "the current of life." For us, Egyptian art remains magically welded with death. The art of Mesopotamia obeys the same law; in this frozen universe, Gudea is situated next to Amenhotep.

AGRARIAN CIVILIZATION AND ITS ART.   But does this totalitarian rule of form exclude every stirring of life? However strongly these vast agrarian empires may be attached to their dream of immobility, of exemption from the degradation of change (in Plato, the Greeks still share this dream, which Herodotus had observed in Egypt), they are not unaware of the cycles of time. The peasant sees day follow day, season after season, year after year. The alternation may be intangible, but it draws him into it and carries him with it. As a matter of fact, the art of agrarian civilizations animated form by means of rhythms: repetition is the most usual, whether an enumeration of figures succeeding one another identically in somnambulistic procession, or distributed symmetrically so as to freeze visual appearance in a heraldic order. Whereas Mesopotamia was fond of both methods, it never found the other solution that the Egyptians, with their keener genius, discovered after many centuries—the rhythm of growth. And yet, in its eternal recurrence, it constitutes one of the fundamental experiences of country life; it is the law of the plant, of the tree. It also turns up in architecture with the device of boxes nesting within boxes, and, hence, with successively ampler door and window openings. It will turn up in the figurative arts, in the rendering of drapery, whose movement progressively modifies the folds and makes them pass, like an ebbing wave, from emphatic to more relaxed or even inverted curves. Similar effects will be found in arrangements of wing feathers, which Assyrian art invariably contained within a disciplined parallelism.

That these devices correspond to a certain type of life and reflect a certain degree of knowledge achieved, a certain mode of understanding, does not preclude the action of narrower, more material, more direct factors, which originate in visual memory. It is likely that the reason Mesopotamia exploited so persistently the rhythms of repetition and symmetry is that they were suggested by the widespread use of cylindrical seals. The craftsmen who produced these endlessly aligned identical figures on clay were familiar with the symmetrical combinations between the engraving on the matrix and its necessarily inverted impression. On the other hand, the Egyptians discovered the rhythm of growth, which is absent in Mesopotamian art, probably because, unlike the Mesopotamians, they made abundant use of wood and, especially, of hard woods. Now, on the smooth curved surface of a statue carved out of a tree trunk, the annual rings of growth are plainly visible, and, in taking on the shape of convex volumes, these give rise to catenary patterns that elongate successive arcs. The first sculptors could not fail to observe the harmonious linear combinations born of chance, nor could they fail to be inspired by them. We can see these rhythms of growth applied to drapery in two schools of sculpture that made particular use of hard woods—first, the Egyptian, and, then, the Japanese. The latter rediscovered the secret of rendering falling veils, the folds spread liquidly over ever wider surfaces.

The same mechanism of inspiration can be recognized in the angular decorative themes that, throughout world art, systematize accidental combinations derived from weaving and imposed by the practice of it. (See my *L'Art et l'Homme*, Vol. I, p. 14.)

*Classical architecture stays within the repertory of forms generated by the parallelogram and the triangle, as first formulated in Egypt.*

**34. -** DORIC TEMPLE AT SEGESTA, SICILY. Fifth century B.C.

Thus, the way of life of a given civilization determines the forms it invents, both materially, through accidental combinations suggested by particular techniques, and intellectually, through the specific structures it imposes on mental conceptions.

The agrarian civilizations, which were born on the eastern shores of the Mediterranean and later spread all around it, were thus instinctively guided to the problems and combinations of geometric form. They created an immense repertory of forms, which has had currency in the West down to our own epoch. These forms were only gradually modified, and only with the slow development of a tendency to realism, to imitation of visual appearances. In emancipating itself from the imperious conventions of its earliest days, such as the law of frontality, and in concentrating, from the Greeks onward, on aesthetic goals, on the pursuit of harmony and beauty, art nonetheless has not escaped a certain fatality that condemns it, again and again, to have recourse to geometry, to rely upon the order and regularity geometry imposes on line and on forms, however much more skillful and subtle techniques may become. What was called the "idealization" of reality consisted essentially in subordinating the latter to the intellectual principles that preside over geometric creations, and which became more flexible with the development of arithmetic and increasingly accurate measurement and observation. What but this is the sense of the "canons" of art, the basis of the proportions used both in the figurative arts and in architecture? In this way, art was reduced to a division of space—two-dimensional in painting, three-dimensional in sculpture and architecture. Later, painting too made use of three dimensions, suggesting depth by means of illusionistic devices. But perspective soon subjected illusionary depth to the rule of geometry, to authoritarian principles and measurements (Fig. 30).

Having thus been conceived more than any other art in terms of space and the laws peculiar to it, the art of the agrarian civilizations is averse to everything that suggests time, and the disturbances that time introduces into a regular arrangement of elements (Fig. 32).

This is an art deliberately situated in eternity, from the powerful architecture of Egypt to the unmodifiable balance and harmony of the Greeks. To be sure, movement is occasionally represented—for instance, on Greek vases. But it is not more than an instantaneous view, perceived with acuity, but isolated, extracted from life as a typical element. It is as though, after the attempts at expressiveness in early Neolithic art, all activity, all dynamism, had been regarded as disturbing and renounced as such.

DYNAMIC FORMS.   Were we to carry farther this essay in the social psychology of art, it could be shown (as I showed in *L'Art et l'Homme*, Vol. I, p. 174 f.) that, whenever he escaped from the discipline of country life, man was liberated from the domination of space, otherwise so uncompromising that his work was reduced to mere spatial arrangement. When metal came into use, man had a new experience—that of the transformation of matter. Fire, the energy which presides over these transformations and which itself suggests intensity by its brilliance and heat, came to be regarded as sacred. The use of flexible, malleable substances favored wavy, threadlike forms, in particular, terminal volutes. As a result, the eye and the mind were weaned away from the angularity of straight lines and plane surfaces, while at the same time these new experiences were enriching the plastic repertory of the imagination. Artists who had previously been engrossed in the problems of static space, now became interested in those of the continuous mutations effected by mechanical forces, and they were thus led back to the domain in which alone forces work —the domain of time.

Furthermore, the new ways of life created by the development of navigation, the adventures of seafarers and the unforeseen results of their voyages, opened vistas into an unknown and changing future, markedly in contrast with the life of the sedentary farmer, inexorably the same in recurring cycles. The flat, closed, fixed space of the farmer was now bursting open, as man learned to escape from it into the new dimension opened by time, as he learned to live in time, with all its surprises and ceaseless creations. Dry land yielded to the shifting, rocking motions of the sea, and to its terrible outbursts of fury. The eye learned to dance with it, was impregnated with sinuosities and windings, which were eventually integrated into a new decorative art.

In the fifteenth century, a French Primitive from Provence—a region more Latinized than others—was influenced by the revival of Classical form known as the Renaissance. Parallelograms and triangles hold reality captive in a tight grid; they extend their sway to the changing play of lights and shadows, though French painting took it over from the Flemish School, disclosing a purely sensuous vision liberated from preconceived formalism. We are witnessing here the last gasp of the medieval Gothic spirit, which is being subjected to the revival of geometric art, already triumphant in Italy, with Piero della Francesca, for instance, in his St. Francis Receiving the Stigmata (cf. Fig. 54).

**35.** - *NICOLAS DIPRE.* THE PRESENTATION OF THE VIRGIN (detail). Late fifteenth century.
Private collection, Paris

Viking art, last heir to the art of the steppes, shows how, under the twin stimulus of metalworking and seafaring, a type of continuous, wavy, dynamic form was created.

**36. -** *VIKING ART.* BRONZE ENSIGN FOR A VIKING SHIP NOW IN A CHURCH AT HALSINGLAND. About 1025. Statens Historiska Museum, Stockholm

In the Southern Hemisphere, the Polynesian navigators reinvented an art of uninterrupted tracery, of dizzily dynamic swirling lines.

**38. -** *Opposite page:* POLYNESIAN ART. PROW OF A MAORI CANOE. New Zealand. University Museum, Philadelphia

The resulting transformations of vision are particularly striking in the art that combined the influences of metallurgy and seafaring—the art of Crete. But the Cretans, like the Greeks in a later period, did not so much turn their backs on country life to pursue a radically new mode of existence as merely to broaden the former. Ultimately, the new conquests of form were always integrated within the rigid over-all patterns peculiar to agricultural societies, merely giving them new flexibility. The Greeks developed a varied serpentine line, for example, that softened the geometrism of their predecessors, but they did not break with any of its founding principles.

By contrast, in the civilizations of the Eurasian plain, whose growth was also due to advances in metalworking, life was radically different. There space never appeared as the

*Among nomadic peoples, the Scythians excelled in an art that used animal shapes and movements as a pretext for bending metal into endlessly winding curves and spirals.*

**37. -** *ART OF THE KUBAN NOMADS.* BUCKLE or HARNESS PIECE. Fourth or fifth century B.C. The Hermitage, Leningrad

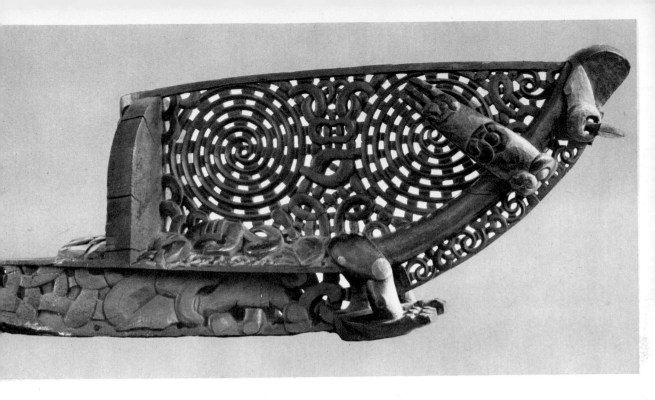

symbol of the finite, but as the symbol of the infinite. To the nomad, space does not suggest a segmentation such as generates forms, but the possibility of galloping on for hours, for whole days on end. The expanse of space here becomes the image of a boundless time. In the course of the centuries, the nomadic peoples of the steppes carried their grammar of forms from the frontiers of China, Mongolia, as far west as the Black Sea, where they made contact with the Greeks, and whence they made further inroads westward. One result of their invasions was the settling of the Celts to the northwest—in the last analysis, the birth of a European civilization vastly different in its origins from Mediterranean civilization. From its earliest to its final stage, from the La Tène to the Gallic period, this art displayed identical features sharply contrasting with the art of farming regions. The predominant, most influential art was that of the goldsmith, a refinement of earlier work in metals. Its influence is found in Irish illuminations (eighth century A.D.) and in the art of the Vikings. In popular survivals of the latter, we find paintings and wood carvings in which the forms are the same as those introduced in work with bronze: the same wavy contours and sinuosity of decoration, whether incised or filigreed. The surface is not treated as a space to be divided up into geometric fields; rather, the artist is attracted and even intoxicated by the prospect of a space to be traversed; line serves less to define areas in contour than to trace curves, spirals, interlacing lines that twist and twine and endlessly return to their origins. The absolute evoked by this art is the infinite, which absorbs and abolishes space. The case in agrarian art is very different: in it a perfection is set down for eternity, which absorbs and abolishes time. The art of the steppes and the arts which derived from it waver between schematic figuration and abstract ornamentation, but the figuration is almost exclusively animal, as it was in Paleolithic art, for the nomadic way of life had no place for agriculture and the hunt was all-important. However, these artists

*The ship raises the problem of a form in motion in a resistant milieu. Its architecture is conceived entirely in terms of dynamic curves. The Viking ships provide us with daring examples of these.*

**39. -** VIKING SHIP OF OSEBERG. About 850 A.D. Norway. Museum, Oslo

saw animals only from the point of view of their suppleness, the in-and-out dodging and interlacing of adversaries, for example, in conformity with the "spirit" of metal. As for abstract ornamentation, lines swirl and dart off without respite, in a kind of dizzy mobility. Sometimes, and especially in its medieval phase, this art combines the two solutions, and, intoxicated with instability, it passes without transition from an unrolled ribbon to a clutching paw or a devouring animal mouth, so that the inconstancy of metamorphosis is combined with that of mobility (Figs. 36 and 37).

The spread of agrarian civilization in its Greco-Roman form to the rest of Europe pushed back this art to its northernmost retreats, and, eventually, it became extinct. A curiously analogous art has been discovered among the Polynesians—nomads not of the plain, but of the ocean (Fig. 38).

74

A NEW CONCEPT: ENERGY.   Thus, the West saw the triumph of Greco-Roman aesthetics, remote descendant of the ancient agrarian civilizations whose economy and way of life Europeans merely extended. According to many observers, folk holidays and the symbolism they incorporate—still to be witnessed at the beginning of this century—go back to the Neolithic era. It must have seemed that nothing could possibly interrupt this continuity.

The conditions of human life, however, are always subject to upheavals that reshape them. We are, no doubt, witnessing such an upheaval in our own time: only thus can we account for the radical mutations to be observed in our daily life as well as in our thinking and our art. The visible sign is the restlessness and anxiety so characteristic of our epoch, which senses to what extent its stability and its traditions are threatened, perhaps doomed (cf. Part II, Ch. V).

In the seventeenth and eighteenth centuries, from the Renaissance to Classicism, the principles of Mediterranean aesthetics were formulated and developed; and Europe seemed bent solely upon refining the forms that it had perfected. In the eighteenth century, a new and disturbing principle began to assert itself. Although the farmer of that time—for that matter, the farmer of the early twentieth century—continued to cultivate his land and to exploit its resources on pretty much the same principles and with the same regularity as the farmer of the third millennium B.C., now a principle previously unknown made its appearance—the exploitation of energy. Our ancestors had known only of fire, to generate heat and to serve as basis for the first rudiments of industry—the early work with metals. Scarcely any real new developments had occurred for thousands of years. The pursuit of speed had been confined to exploitation of the swiftest runner found in nature —the horse.

In the eighteenth century, the exploitation of the energy of fire took a tremendous step forward with the discovery of the steam engine. Development of the machine led to indus-trialization and profound social changes, the emergence of an economy based on capital and a new class—proletarian workers now replaced craftsmen. Very soon, more new sources of energy were developed still more sweeping in their effects—electricity, petroleum prod-ucts, and, finally, the fission of matter to release atomic energy. At the same time, industry was invading agriculture, introducing new methods and doing away with traditional techniques. The scale of life was profoundly altered for everyone. The features inherent in the old agrarian civilization grew fainter and vanished, giving way to those of the new industrial era. The psychology of modern man has evolved as his life has been altered; inevitably the forms of art reflect this transformation.[1]

No one will deny that, in the twentieth century, Western art has been revolutionized from top to bottom, even where it was held to be most secure. However, in painting, which has come to be the art that receives most public attention, there is still a great deal of confusion. Aesthetic theories are applied unrestrainedly in this field, often before they have been properly digested, let alone assimilated. Hampered by this curtain of doctrines, painting does not easily make contact with the actual foundations of modern sensibility. The latter seems to be taking shape, slowly and still crudely, in the experiments of the

---

[1] I discussed the diversity and the features of these forms in *Dialogue avec le visible* (Ch. III). But there the point of view was different: my aim was to investigate the persistence and historical course of the tendencies to figuration and abstraction.

nongeometric abstract school. Although its "Classical" predecessors, particularly the De Stijl group in Holland, dominated by the austere rigor of Mondrian, believed that the purity required by art could be found only in a geometry reduced to its simplest traditional elements—and, especially, to the parallelepiped—the new school represented by the American avant-garde after Pollock conceived of painting in terms of pure intensity, freed from all intellectual constraint and even from voluntary control. Accident generates spots and thick layers of paint, wildly assorted in color, flung at the canvas and splashed onto it in a frenzied conglomeration that, in comparison with the old lyric harmonies, suggests a prolonged howl rather than a song. Others, less brutal, mostly to be found in France—men like Mathieu, Hartung, and Soulages—project their impulses onto the canvas, recording the gesture of the hand holding the brush. In both cases, models slowly elaborated over thousands of years are abandoned, as is all sense of a structure underlying form; and we find the same eagerness to capture the primordial impulse of life in terms of essential energy. The spot has become a blow with a fist, the brush stroke a stab of a knife; paint is laid on with a trowel. These artists make the canvas ring like a gong, and it is by means of such spontaneous vibrations that they seek to put themselves in tune with universal life, with the "cosmos," as they occasionally term it (Figs. 267 and 276).

FORMS AT THE SERVICE OF FORCES.   The utilitarian arts of architecture and furniture design reflect the dictates of modern life most directly and without doctrinaire distortions. Now, what do we find in these arts? A revolution in form without precedent for thousands of years. The forms of what we may call, in the broadest sense, the agrarian age—extending from the first Egyptian dynasties down to 1914, when the old world collapsed—expressed the deepest characteristic of that age: stability. Architecture was based upon a static balance of heavy masses: the pyramid was its most primitive expression (and reappeared later in the triangular pediment). The horizontal lintel on two piers, on two vertical legs, is its most essential and enduring structure (Fig. 34).

Architecture today, aware of the importance of energy, has given up the fundamental forms of the old geometry and seeks instead to achieve a balance of forces in action. Moreover, architects must be assisted by engineers capable of computing these forces with the utmost precision. We have to keep in mind that the first innovators in these fields were engineers like Eiffel, who built a tower and a bridge of steel, and Freyssinet, who constructed the concrete hangars at Orly. Plane geometry is no longer adequate to our ideas of how an area is delimited; the first books of Euclid with their regular parallelograms, triangles, and circles no longer apply. Rather, the concept is now one of lines of force, which only make their appearance with conic sections, in solid geometry. The traditional rectangle has given way to parabolas, hyperbolas, and other curves representative of bodies in motion and capable of variation, since they are employed to represent functions (Fig. 40).

*Modern architecture, breaking away from the Greco-Roman tradition of statically balanced and joined forms, uses metal to launch into space taut and flexible curves such as were used before only in Gothic art (cf. Fig. 89).*

**40. -** *EIFFEL.* VIADUCT OF GARABIT. 1884

Modern architects seek to reduce the number of supports and hence of foundations. Here again nineteenth-century steel architecture was the precursor; it had already learned—in the great halls of railway stations, for instance—to concentrate the load on points so accurately calculated that they were insignificantly small in relation to the masses they supported. But modern architects also seek to economize on matter, i.e., on building materials. The thick wall, its stability assured by its weight, has been abandoned for the wall that is merely a curtain. At the same time, there is a tendency to drop the principle of elevation in favor of that of suspension. A great architect like Perret still belongs to the past, despite the fact that he makes use of concrete, because he uses it in designs that could, just as well, be built of stone or brick. The same is true of architects who only a few years ago were regarded as modern, such as Mies van der Rohe, champion of the De Stijl group before he became a builder along the shore of Lake Michigan. He remains curiously attached to a structural system that is rational as well as economical, but resolutely static, and thereby associated with the traditional system. Le Corbusier has clearly seen what is at stake; as he put it himself, he tries to alternate "the right-angle poem" with curvatures "developed with the flexibility and freedom of living organisms." In his chapel at Ronchamp, especially, the dividing walls are no longer planes. They communicate curvatures, and the edges of their intersections suggest the streamlined prows of oceanliners rather than the traditional straight corners of edifices (Fig. 41).

Indeed, it is in ship construction that we might find the first anticipations of dynamic structure developed for bodies moving at great speed—racing cars, airplanes—against the resistance of air. The ship, too, was a moving body, and it, too, had to move in a shifting, fluid medium—water—and raised similar problems of construction. The builder has to conceive the ship in action, armed for struggle against the elements. For this reason, from the outset he employed the curves that architecture had resolutely ignored down to our own day, and it is interesting to note that the most daring examples of such curves occur in the boats of the Vikings and the Polynesians, who, moreover (as we have seen), were fond of ornamentation in dynamic lines (Fig. 39).

However, one type of architecture in the older Europe curiously anticipated the modern experiments—namely, Gothic architecture. Writers have always recognized the presence of the Nordic spirit in Gothic structures, and noted how they are opposed to the geometric Classicism of the Romanesque style preceding the Gothic and the Renaissance style following it. Now, the novelty of the Gothic structures consists precisely in this, that it substitutes the engineering for the architectural spirit: it is less concerned with observing traditional forms than with balancing and channeling the forces of load, no matter how far this preoccupation removes the structures from patterns securely established since antiquity. The curvature of the ogee arch, the nervous soaring of the flying buttress—even prior to Flamboyant Gothic, when the decorative, vibrant play of wavy lines and curves dear to the Celtic genius reappears—mark the emergence of dynamic architecture. Strzygowski, for all the exaggerations into which he was led by specious theorizing, was well aware of this when he established a correlation between this revolutionary style and the Scandinavian wooden structures that owe so much to the tradition of the Viking shipbuilders.

Stone, because it is heavy and because it consists of units that must be assembled, obstructs free transmission of energy; the Gothic masters nevertheless succeeded in transmitting energy through stone like an electric current through a wire. The combination of

*The pliability of concrete recalls the curves of a ship's bow.*

**41. -** *LE CORBUSIER.* CHURCH AT RONCHAMP (Haute-Saône). 1951–55

metal and concrete provides the architect of today with still more suitable means. There have been some perfect successes in this field already: we owe the principal successes to Guillaume Gillet, whom I regard as one of the greatest contemporary architects. His church at Royan, and, above all, his French Pavilion at the Brussels World's Fair of 1958, have gradually brought the new structural system to its highest peak: a metallic armature insures the tension of a thin wall, usually made of concrete, which, as he puts it himself, is like the fabric of an umbrella stretched tightly on its steel ribs. At the same time, a single point of support, as reduced in size as possible, is realized by recourse to the hyperbolic paraboloid—sometimes called, because of its appearance, "the horse saddle"—which, though it rests upon a very small base, gives a very broad covering surface (Fig. 42).

A similar evolution has been going on in furniture design. The old parallelepipedal chair owes its stability to the principle of the lintel, represented by the seat resting upon poles, i.e., legs. For several years now, we have witnessed the emergence of a formula which combines canvas and metal and which makes full use of their flexibility. The canvas bends, adjusting itself to the weight and curves of the body, and the metal, arched in a transverse direction, opposes to it its flexibility and tensile strength. A few years ago, at a congress where I advanced this idea, someone objected that one cannot speak of dynamism in relation to a chair, since a seated man is motionless by definition. The same criticism would apply to a monument, which is even more frozen by nature than a seated figure! But in either case, the concept of static balance obtained by forms at rest and by weight alone is replaced with the concept of dynamic balance, where apparent immobility is obtained only by the reciprocal neutralization of antithetical forces.

*The hyperbolid, which Gillet used here twice, is one of the warped surfaces, familiar to modern architects, marking a break with the cubes and planes of yesterday.*

**42.** - *GUILLAUME GILLET.* FRENCH PAVILION, WORLD'S FAIR, BRUSSELS. 1958.
Maquette by Roger Alfonsi

THE FUTURE TAKES SHAPE.   The evolution of forms is as apparent in the purely aesthetic domain as in the domain of industrial arts, where it is sufficiently accounted for by practical considerations. We are witnessing the emergence of a style and, hence, of a taste that makes us readier to accept what was at first a purely functional development. Even when it serves no practical function, the curve is today regarded as preferable, more pleasant to the modern eye and sensibility than rigid straight lines and plane surfaces. Not to mention the perambulators with paradoxically streamlined shapes, which were fashionable for a time, we are seeing an increasing tendency to get rid of angles and regular circles alike in the forms of table tops. We have even seen paper labels, which the manufacturer supplies in rectangular shape for convenience in handling, printed with colored designs contoured like conical sections. In this case, the aesthetic intention is clearly asserted, since it conflicts with utilitarian considerations.

Whereas the rectilinear style dominated even so modern a movement as Cubism, contemporary abstract art is developing entirely new forms. Just as America, a new nation less bound by a sense of the past than Europe, initiated many new forms in furniture—the creations of Knoll, especially, must be cited—so it seems also to have been prompt to evidence in its sculpture, though it is a disinterested, not a functional art, a gradual shift toward forms very different from the traditional. As early as the beginning of the twentieth century, Lachaise, as well as the Polish-American sculptor Nadelman, renounced spherical and cylindrical volumes such as were still used by Maillol and introduced profiles resembling ellipses or parabolas. But we must not forget that these timid

80

experiments, which were incidentally combined with realistic rendering, had their counterparts in Europe with the first great realizations of Brancusi: *Maiastra* and *Bird in Space* compel the torpedo- or rocket-shaped volumes to express the idea of a leap, a projection into space (Fig. 44).

It is true that space ceased to be conceived independently of time the day Descartes drew up the trajectories described by moving bodies. Its jealously preserved autonomy was a thing of the past; it was now put to the service of movements generated in time, which it served to transcribe. Descartes planted the first seeds of all that has led to the modern conception of space and time as merged, inseparable, and seemingly unified. Since Einstein, the Olympian dream of a theoretical space that owes nothing to time and even vaunts its serene immutability to time has collapsed. Collusion between the new artistic spirit and the new scientific spirit is manifest in the work of Pevsner, who transformed sculpture into an abstract art and thus brought it closer to solids embodying mathematical conceptions. Incidentally, his brother is a mathematician. Since the works of these precursors, the domain of the new visual repertory has extended its boundaries, and one need only walk through the rooms of the latest Biennale in Venice to verify its spread to international sculpture (Fig. 43).

The new style is favored by another factor, which is independent of social and technological evolution: among the Slavs, the Germanic peoples, and the Americans who seem to have contributed most to its rapid progress,

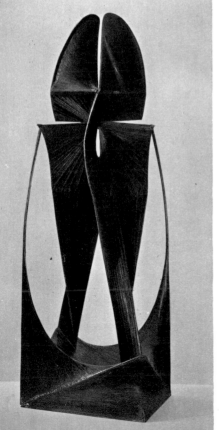

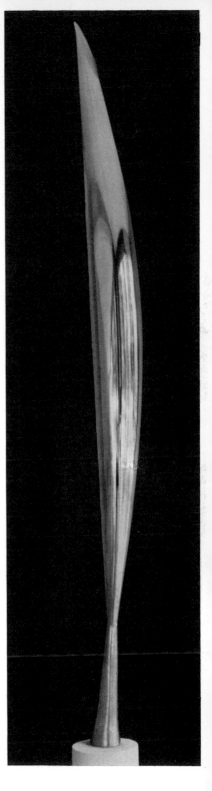

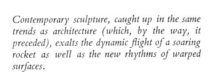

*Contemporary sculpture, caught up in the same trends as architecture (which, by the way, it preceded), exalts the dynamic flight of a soaring rocket as well as the new rhythms of warped surfaces.*

**43.** - *PEVSNER.* TWIN COLUMN. 1947. Bronze. The Museum of Modern Art, New York

**44.** - *BRANCUSI.* BIRD IN SPACE. 1919. The Museum of Modern Art, New York it reflects a kind of reaction against the centuries of uncontested Greco-Roman cultural domination. It is linked with the dislocation and rejection, observable everywhere, of moral and practical standards regarded as rational since Greek antiquity. It would seem that the anti-Latin spirit—after its one last effort during the Age of the Enlightenment to classicize itself—has been concerned for nothing but regaining its freedom, its dynamic anarchism, rather, and asserts itself best when it is most negative. Le Corbusier's exclamation, *Et-Vignole-enfin-est-foutu* (So Vignola [Giacomo Barozzi da Vignola, sixteenth-century Italian architect and theoretician, whose *Traité des cinq ordres d'architecture* was a standard textbook in the course of architecture at the Ecole des Beaux-Arts. Transl.] is at last done for) seems to be more than a harmless sally: it is profoundly significant.

We should, at this point, go on to show how the attempt to supplant the elementary Euclidean forms is often associated with a taste for nongeometric abstraction, for a pure, concrete "painting" that eludes the discipline of conceptual form and is one of the more important aspects of the latest abstract explorations. But to do this would involve us too deeply in the study of the problems raised by modern art. We shall limit ourselves to stressing the fact that once again—and in accord with the constant law we have tried to formulate—the renewal of forms runs parallel with upheavals in our civilization, and that it has been governed by the same guiding principles.

If drawing revealed the close ties that link graphism, not just to the temperament of every individual but also to the deep moral dispositions of human groups, to such a degree that we can read them as we read the curve of a graph, this rapid review of the evolution of forms under various regimes confirms the belief that man's plastic creations, even the most abstract, reflect the experiences and operations of his psychic life.

CHAPTER III

# LIGHT AND LIFE

For the human eye to be assailed and troubled by the multiplicity of sensations, for the mind behind the eye to apply itself to the visible chaos and seek to order it, endowing things with form, nature in her darkness has to be set off by light. Nature has always been there, but invisible, unknown, until, thanks to light, discovered and recognized. With light, nature becomes appearance.

For a long time, light was taken for granted, the humble servant of mankind. No one could see without it, yet it was nothing to think about; it was indispensable to life, yet it was not singled out for respectful attention. Only little by little did this servant of mankind come into her own—eventually, like Cinderella, to be recognized and given titles of nobility. Indeed, in time, her lovers—the painters—were to be so dazzled by her powers as to single her out for exclusive homage. A time would come, after many centuries—in the epoch of Impressionism—when painting would become so entranced with the powers and potentialities of light as to be consumed at the latter's shrine. In consequence of this immolation, a wholly new kind of painting has had to be devised.

*Definition of form by volume rather than by contour was made possible by the use of shadow in modeling.*

**46. -** WOMAN PICKING FLOWERS. Painting from Stabiae. Museum, Naples

**47. -** THE THREE GRACES. Painting from Pompeii. Museum, Naples

THE MEANING OF LIGHT. Our simplest notion of light derives from its contrast with darkness. You cannot have the one without the other, as the primitive imagination recognized when it elaborated a set of symbolic oppositions: white and black, day and night, life and death. On the moral plane, these were extended to include the positive and the negative, the good and the evil.

The alternation between light, which gives life, and darkness, which plunges us into apparent nothingness, made a strong impression on early man. It contributed to his religious beliefs, most notably in the Persian conception of an eternal antagonism between Ormazd and Ahriman. Indeed, the contrast between light and dark seems to be at the bottom of every dialectical pairing of opposites.

With light we associate empty space, air, the intangible; darkness summons up opacity, the mass and density of matter. Art arrived at this distinction at the end of the Paleolithic era, when it ceased to rely upon contour lines to isolate a body from its context, and the silhouette became a blacked-in spot. Later, when compositions containing more than one figure made their appearance and artists were in danger of losing their way amid the proliferation of phenomena, the pure concept of form was arrived at. By such means, it became possible to give shape to things as separate and distinct from their surroundings. The decorators of early Greek vases—the so-called black figured vases—employed this means. Opacity, which is the negation of light, was indicative of real things in all their

84

**48.** - *LEONARDO DA VINCI.* HEAD OF ST. ANNE (detail of THE VIRGIN AND ST. ANNE). Charcoal. Royal Academy of Arts, London

*Modeling adds to painting the illusion of form in relief. Leonardo's sfumato was an especially subtle approach to the problem. Instead of stressing, it dissolves form in the surrounding atmosphere. The skillful proportion of lights and darks results in a previously unknown vividness. The above drawing and the X-ray photograph (at the right) show how Leonardo obtained his sfumato.*

**49.** - *LEONARDO DA VINCI.* PORTRAIT OF A LADY (LA BELLE FERRONNIÈRE). X-ray photograph. The Louvre, Paris

mass and compactness. Already we may detect the germ of moral significance later to be attributed to light—which, being immaterial, is the sign of spirituality, of the soul, of God. At first instinctive, the contrast eventually gave rise to a symbolism capable of inspiring reflection, though not invariably. To some extent, the contrast has remained a mere stimulus to unconscious contents of the human soul. When we analyze—or psychoanalyze—the part played by shadows, and by the human shadow especially, we seem to find a recurrent memory of mankind given repeated expression. Many legends, as well as literary works, attest to this, the most famous being Chamisso's *The Man Who Lost His Shadow.*

To produce an opaque silhouette set off against a pale ground (instead of defining shapes, as had been done earlier, solely by outlining them) presupposes a clear conception of the contrasting effects of light and shadow. For some time, this still comparatively crude type of representation gratified the need for clarity and simplicity characteristic of the intellect. However, it could not forever conceal the existence of infinite transitions in nature between white and black, between day and night. Just as the slow agony of dusk brings about the death of daylight, experienced as a progressive decline, the differentiated scale of grays provides imperceptible transitions between the extremes of light and dark. Ranging from blatant, total brightness to no less concentrated shadow, these transitions supply the artist with what he calls his scale of "values."

Values! This kind of awareness reflects an experience very different from that provided by the division of space or the constitution of forms. In art, form serves to order the chaos of appearances; by means of form, human thought takes possession of them. Form corresponds to the mind's search for clarity and precision, its preoccupation with quantities and measurement. Only thanks to form

*The development of* sfumato *in the art of Correggio endows the evanescent forms with a new poetic quality.*

**50.** - *CORREGGIO.* EVE. Museum of Decorative Arts, Barcelona (Cambo Collection)

86

can the understanding operate surely and with a broad scope. Hence, the formal aspect of art relates art to logic and scientific method. Moreover, being born of the union between arithmetic and elementary geometry, form can solve the relational problems posed by surfaces.

Nonetheless, the scale of values from dark to light is not identical with the problem of form. We feel them, as well as see them, but it is difficult to reduce them to quantitative terms. In the simplest case (and for long only the simplest cases were considered), values serve to facilitate the modeling of volumes, and, so, are an indispensable supplement to definition of the figure by means of contour alone. Indeed, the latter type of definition ignores effects of relief so completely that Paleolithic artists often obtained such effects only by utilizing bulges in the walls on which they painted. When values are freely brought into play, however, the viewer perceives degrees of strength or weakness, and, as a result, a new kind of awareness of expression given to quantity—awareness of intensity. With this awareness, the problems of space and form are transcended. Form remains within purely intellectual limits, whereas intensity breaks through them. Of course, intensity can be measured—though less directly than form—but, beside being perceived, intensity must be felt. Although there can always be "more" or "less" of it, so that it seems to belong to the realm of quantity, still, intensity can be truly known only by those who have experienced it, by those who have lived it.

It follows that variations in light, to be rendered in terms of values, give rise to an entirely different mode of calculation, even of perception—one that the artist can be expected to assimilate only gradually. It did not occur to ancient artists to depict light itself and its nuances. What they did was to calculate the effect of light on form. Relief provides a gamut of values that differ according to the angle at which light falls upon it. The eye recognizes this, thanks to imperceptible changes in the modeling, as at once a modulation of natural light and a parallel modulation of values by the painter. Art has made use of such modulations since antiquity. In the fourteenth century, Cennino Cennini, a follower of Giotto and author of a famous treatise on painting, explained the technique as follows: "When you draw, place yourself in a temperate light. Following the light, from whatever side it may come, set shadows off against the relief.... You will need to come back to the extremities, which you will make darker [i.e., to reinforce the shading] more often than to the relief, so as not to subdue the highlights." At the time, the sole purpose of this technique was to produce a realistic illusion of form; nevertheless its use marks a first victory of light. Cennini recognized this: "As your guide and compass take the light of the sun, that of your eye, and that of your hand" (Figs. 46 and 47).

What had been no more than a technical device became an end in itself when Leonardo da Vinci invented *sfumato*. This marked a great step forward. Light and the modeling of light, although they supplemented the austerity of contour, had hitherto served only to enhance the forms, to increase their precision by seeming to provide them with relief. It was a great pleasure to the intellect thus to envisage order triumphing over the chaos of nature, but the sensibility remained ungratified. Not that it was completely kept out of things—for it was involved in the measurement of space, and pleasure in the play of relationships and proportions, which gives rise to harmony, is a basic element in aesthetics. However, there is more to sensibility than intellectual pleasure—however influential and significant the latter may be, and however great its role in the history of painting. There is a deeper reach of sensibility, at once profoundly linked with the particular nature of every individual and remote from such intellectual considerations as space and the measurement of objects in space. This deeper fund of sensibility is self-sufficient—it feeds on itself, caught up exclusively with its own enthusiasms and echoes. In the dimension of time it recognizes itself and develops. Frustrated—indeed, seemingly neutralized by formal considerations— it shuns excessive accuracy, excessive universality. To the deeper sensibility, formal considerations often seem to produce an essentially frozen, cold and rigid, kind of beauty.

THE DECLINE OF FORM. The Renaissance artists thought they had achieved a definitive aesthetics of formal harmony, in the period of rich development that came after the appearance of Giotto and Masaccio and culminated in Raphael. However, in a very few years a certain weariness became apparent, not without analogies to the weariness displayed by Hellenistic art once it attempted to go beyond the limits of Classical Greek art. The first great artist to break away from this aesthetics appeared as early as the sixteenth century. Michelangelo was his name. Heroic as his effort was, it came too soon to effect a complete break, or even to aim at a complete break. He was aware of his own inner turmoil, he was conscious of inner conflict. His traditional faith in form—which for all the indubitable richness of his gifts made him more a sculptor than a painter—inspired his devotion to the human form and made him contemptuous of landscape. At the same time, however, he felt uneasy about form, and there was an element of exaggeration, of overinflation, in his worship of it. He kept introducing the very opposite of form: the element of strength, of unleashed power. Michelangelo's formal discipline is constantly reminding us that the strength of his figures cannot truly ever be unleashed. He can only rebel against form as against a prison—yet unconsciously, unaware of the antagonism he is caught up in, and unwilling to recognize it as such. One objective expression of his unconscious struggle is his fascination with the theme of slaves in chains—seemingly, a new version of the struggle of Laocoön and his sons in the serpents' coils. There is the same emphasis upon muscles as creators of movement threatening to burst the bonds of form. Michelangelo's slaves are straining every limb against the bonds confining and, as it were, paralyzing them. The general effect is of human bodies struggling to free themselves from the stone matrix that immobilizes them, from which the sculptor's chisel has not completely delivered them. Similarly, Michelangelo's painted figures are stretched taut within the frames that confine them all too narrowly. They are a dramatic expression of Michelangelo's inner conflict, that conflict which, at a deeper level, characterized his attitude toward religion. Contemporary with the Reformation, ill at ease within the limits of a Catholicism to which he remained faithful, he seems to be trying desperately to expand these limits. A new world is emerging in him, testing its strength, trying to push back the walls surrounding it. With Michelangelo, the Renaissance spirit attains a kind of last gasp, and fails desperately to carry its creative powers forward to realization (Fig. 51).

As early as the beginning of the sixteenth century, the Renaissance achievement was beginning to flag. The total, absolute triumph of form it aimed at actually hastened reaction against it. Signs of imminent change were everywhere manifest: while Michelangelo was trying to animate form, Correggio—following the example of Mantegna (Fig. 53)—was trying to animate space. In his ceiling paintings at Parma, there are projections of swirling clouds and flying figures that anticipate and prepare the coming of the Baroque. Eventually,

The crisis of form at the climax of the Renaissance is reflected in Michelangelo's sculpture, where form seems to be struggling against a stifling pressure. This is true of his figures of slaves, which are all the more expressive for not being completed. The darker and more fluid modeling characteristic of the technique used here is in striking contrast with the clearer definition in the fifteenth century.

**51.** - *MICHELANGELO.*
UNFINISHED SLAVE
for the tomb of Julius II.
Accademia, Florence

*By its distortions, Mannerism intensified the attack on form. Here further distortion is obtained by imitating the image in a convex mirror, which also accounts for the shape of the picture.*

**52.** - *PARMIGIANINO.* SELF-PORTRAIT: THE YOUNG ARTIST IN A CONVEX MIRROR. 1524.
Kunsthistorisches Museum, Vienna

of course, the Baroque secured the victory of life (in its hitherto unrealized qualitative aspects) over form—form subjected to the discipline of space. But, before it, there was a transitional movement, of which Michelangelo and Correggio were early instances, that marked the rise of a new conception—Mannerism. The Mannerists turned openly against the rigorous immobilization of form in volumes. However, they were incapable of inventing any radically new conception, and their formal innovations have the character of distortions. They tampered with the accepted canons of form by means of elongations and displacements. A work by Parmigianino is especially revealing of the fever that was then undermining the world of forms. As a young man he painted his self-portrait using a convex—i.e., a distorting—mirror to bring out anomalies of structure and appearance on which he could later exercise his imagination (Fig. 52).

*The void, domain in which light supplants form, made its appearance in the decorations of ceilings. Here, the effect is of gazing into the sky.*

**53. -** *MANTEGNA.* CUPOLA, CAMERA DEGLI SPOSI. Ducal Palace, Mantua

Mannerism made use of still another device: it broke the centuries-old link between drawing and form, the notion of drawing as an outlining of forms. It separated the two, thereby giving back its graphic destiny to line, its own freedom to live and develop in the endless course of gentle undulations. This development had been anticipated in the fifteenth century by the restless, tormented, well-nigh morbid genius of Botticelli, and he was imitated by those of his contemporaries who had come under the influence of a style developed by goldsmiths. We have already stressed the importance of work with metals from the earliest epochs; its role is to introduce and reintroduce the dynamism of line into the static arts of form. In Botticelli's day, engraving on silver as well as filigreework restored to line the function of a rambling thread all but unrelated to strict expression of volumes.

91

LIGHT AS THE DISSOLVANT OF FORM: LEONARDO DA VINCI.  All such reactions were merely episodic, peripheral to the problem of form, although indubitably concerned with it, or with loosely related problems. Their general effect was necessarily limited.

To attack prevailing conceptions of form, the rules of form, with truly subversive efficiency, it was necessary to approach the task in an altogether different spirit. Long before there were other attempts to shake off a yoke sensed as too heavy, Leonardo da Vinci had come to realize that the play of values was opening a new and different field for the artistic imagination, wholly new possibilities in the use of light. Treating values in the same way as the Mannerists were later to treat drawing (though without achieving lasting results), he divorced values from the forms that they had hitherto served merely to model, to define more accurately thereby. Leonardo took the diametrically opposite tack: he utilized values to weaken and wear away form. If he did not quite destroy it, at least he distorted customary appearances. He no longer saw in values a means of modeling, but a means of dissolving lines and planes, sufficient to divorce the latter from the purely intellectual conception of plastic form. With Leonardo, the forms are invaded with imprecision and mystery, converted into objects of sensibility (Figs. 48 and 49).

Study of Leonardo's technique with the help of modern methods of investigation, such as have been applied in the laboratory of the Louvre,[1] has shown that to achieve his purpose, Leonardo effected a revolution even more crucial than may hitherto have been realized. The better to eliminate form, he reduced to almost nothing the drawing that painters had from time immemorial employed as a preliminary to the application of color. Renouncing the firm support of contour, he did not begin by defining forms; rather he built up his forms gradually, varying the degrees of condensation of values, regulating the density of a fluid mass of color.

Certain Gothic frescoes, when the top layers of paint peel off, disclose the original schema on which they were based. For instance, in the *Danse des morts* at La Chaise-Dieu, there is no careful, continuous underdrawing. The Northern artist was always less fond of this device than the Italian. However, we do find a vigorous, though rough "outline" made with the brush—something like a quick sketch—to make up for the absence of drawing. The undermost layers of Leonardo's canvas do not contain even so simplified a suggestion of form as this. We must recognize that his technique not only repudiates any such guarantee of solidity but relies deliberately on the fluid element alone, on liquid layers of paint, both tinted and transparent, superimposed upon one another in progressive definition of the initial mistiness. He assembles and intensifies the vapors and shadows that make up what he calls his *sfumato*, and he himself observed that "these shadows do not stand out in a hard and dry manner, but are imperceptibly submerged." The very term "submerged" suggests a liquid, fluid world in which form leads no more than a ghostly existence.

Such a revolution was made possible technically by the Northern artists' unexpected discovery of the possibilities of oil. This alone freed artists from the circumscribed flat areas of the miniaturists, and made possible effects of transparency that were perhaps suggested partly in emulation of stained glass. The pigment was no longer applied evenly

[1] A description of these investigations by Madame Hours, director of the laboratory, and M. Rudel can be found in a special issue of *L'Amour de l'Art: Connaissance de Léonard de Vinci* (March, 1953).

over a flat surface within the boundaries of a given area; it was held in a state of suspension in the medium within which it bathes. Thanks to transparent glazes—indeed reminiscent of stained-glass windows—its strength can be variously modulated and thinned. Color no longer spreads flat; it vibrates. Leonardo made use of all the new possibilities that had become familiar to the eye since Van Eyck, but he was on guard against the seductions of color, just as he was armed against those of form. Unlike the Flemish Primitives, he dedicated the new powers made available to the painter wholly to the service of values. With him, color and form are held in a state of indecision, the one no less than the other, and the world he imagines remains on the threshold of the reality that we experience with our senses.

Thus, in opposition to harmony, which the other Renaissance masters regarded as the crowning glory of an art conceived architecturally, Leonardo began to emphasize poetry —which is at the heart of the vague reveries of sensibility. He notes: "A body that bathes in a weak light will show little difference between its shadows and its lights. This occurs at nightfall when the sky is overcast; such works are impregnated with suavity, and every face is adorned with charm." The transitions between light and dark—Leonardo's *sfumato* —by creating indecision banished the visual dictatorship of form. Henceforward, images will no longer be conceived in intellectual terms; rather, the soul will learn to pour itself into them. While Leonardo did not go quite this far—this was not done until Giorgione— he put an end to the hegemony of form, which, since antiquity, had limited and formularized art. However, his contemporaries did not in the least suspect what a revolution had got under way: in their eyes he had merely found a new and caressing method of enveloping form, of adorning it with unprecedented charm.

His mind discloses the same bent in all its manifestations: infatuated with Aristotle, as we shall see later (Part II, Ch. I), rather than with Plato, as were the other Renaissance masters and theorists, he was opposed to every sort of intellectual formalism, to all a priori conceptions that freeze the mind. He turned to observation because it opens up new vistas, and, being an engineer more than a philosopher, he felt that the essential riddle of life lies in movement, in the forces that cause it, in the universal energy that is their common source. In his drawings as well as in his writings, he tackled the problem of forces in action— water, steam, storms, and even floods (depicted in several sketches at Windsor). He understands creation as making use of these forces, by capturing or directing them. Aeronautics, ballistics, and hydraulics are the themes that his hand treats, whether it is holding a pen or the silver needle of the draftsman. Leonardo recognized that the era of theoretical speculation had come to an end. What he inaugurates is the era of emphasis on life itself, on the lessons to be learned from it, its unpredictability, its continuous discoveries, its ever-changing spectacle (Fig. 124).

THE APPEAL TO SENSIBILITY.    In all this, Leonardo was far ahead of his contemporaries. Although he neutralized the dead hand of the past, and by blurring form anticipated the diminishing importance it would have, he also brought sensibility into play, stimulating its powers by contemplating the indefinite penumbra of endless possibility, attracted by its mystery. His fascination with the indefinite as provocative of reverie is strikingly expressed in his advice to artists to study clouds and the cracks in old walls, letting their imaginations gradually endow them with life, as a springboard to creation (cf. *Dialogue avec le visible*, p. 108).

*It is noteworthy that Piero della Francesca, poet of pure form, was one of the first painters to attempt to render different lights, as here and in* The Dream of Constantine.

**54.** - *PIERO DELLA FRANCESCA* (perhaps with the assistance of a pupil).
ST. FRANCIS RECEIVING THE STIGMATA (fragment from the predella of an altarpiece).
Pinacoteca Vanucci, Perugia

Thus, in the history of art, Leonardo occupies a curious moment when the past is beginning to be wiped out and the future is as yet unrecognized. In part, this accounts for his mysteriousness: one system of realization is receding into the past; another is moving closer. Leonardo stands midway between the two, in a shadowy void where dreams are born, yet which seems to suffer from a certain sterility more intellectual than sensory. He already employs means that point to the victory of sensibility over rationalism. Still, he is not motivated by passion, by any deep emotion, not really moved by some new mode of feeling such as might have caught him up to the point of his giving expression to it. If he expresses any passion, it is that of curiosity. He is turned toward the secret of things rather than toward some secret in his own heart. Hence, we find in his art a kind of cold insensibility rather than lucidity, expressed in a language more suited to the expression of emotion than reflection. With him silence enters painting; in his pictures we are oppressed by an air of expectation, kept waiting for the opening measures of some triumphant song that is forever about to begin.

The first musician to break this silence is Giorgione. He takes the decisive step: the mist in which ambiguous creatures move about he populates with a presence—his own. Has

94

this been noticed? Leonardo's *sfumato* is almost mono-chromatic, faintly tinged with blue or green. His painting evolves within the scale of values, but it has not yet really opted for color. Giorgione does not only make his own the penumbra where everything blends and merges; he colors it. And, thereby, he defines it, endows it with urgency, enables it to attune itself to his own inner lyricism. Hitherto, art had represented things; henceforward, it will suggest them. We will discuss in the next chapter the great step forward that this was: we shall see how color supplies a language for sensibility, just as form had provided the intellect with the language of forms. And then, from intensity, which had added a new potentiality of art to quantity, we should advance toward a third potentiality—quality. Leaving behind the domain of the more and the less, art enters the domain where nothing is distinguishable save by the unique and irreplaceable value it presents to sensibility. But, since our purpose here is limited to a study of light and its vicissitudes in history such as bear upon the evolution of the human mind, we shall, for the time being, leave Giorgione as he embarks upon his liberating exploitation of color (Figs. 162 and 50).

The revolution effected by Leonardo had still another consequence. Light ceased to be the accepted yet mis-understood instrument of art, a mere means of making forms visible. Now it became aesthetic reality. Hitherto cast in an indispensable but minor role, now it was pro-moted to the leading role: it became rival to the form that it had hitherto served and been content to serve. Leonardo insured its triumph at the expense of drawing and made its presence felt to the extent that he minimized the impor-tance of line and volume.

All this came about as the result of a long and arduous process. In progressively developing his means over the course of centuries and even millennia, man first addressed himself to the most urgent and elementary matters: he concentrated on material reality, on solid, concrete things, things his hands could touch and control, his mind order and measure. Similarly, the earliest painters recognized no more than what might be called the negative existence of

*The more sensual Northern artists attempted to capture different lights at a very early date.*

**55. -** *FLEMISH SCHOOL.* THE ADORATION OF THE SHEPHERDS (detail). Sixteenth-century Antwerp Mannerist. Young Memorial Museum, San Francisco (cf. Figs. 296, 297, 298)

light—such light as is needed to make perceptible whatever is not light, i.e., an even, discreet, anonymous light. Light so conceived is an ideal, neutral medium, based on assumptions rather than on observation, a light at bottom indistinguishable from air. In such a light the forms could erect their architecture as impersonal as an architect's blueprint (Fig. 96).

THE DISCOVERY OF LIGHTS.   Does light exist—not just as something that serves to make things visible, but as something visible in itself? Just what does it consist of? Does it have a character, a sensibility, a soul? It was enough to ask the question to see that this soul has innumerable faces. Man became aware of the existence of different lights at different times and places, of the infinite plurality of light.

This discovery was parallel with those being made in the domain of form at about the same time. Ways were being found to render various materials and textures. The fifteenth-century Flemish Primitives, equipped with the flexible technique of oil, capable of imitating anything, filled up the abstract volumes conceived by Masaccio and Giotto with specific substances: they transformed them into metal, wood, drapery, and flesh. Similarly, light was acquiring materiality—a materiality more fluid, to be sure, than the most fluid materials, indeed, a well-nigh "immaterial" materiality, yet nonetheless visible and infinitely changing. For the substance of light belongs less to the realm of space—which we conceive of as the realm of forms—than to the realm of time. Light comes and goes and is indistinguishable from its successive metamorphoses in time. If the modeling created by light constitutes a modulation of form, light itself—pure light—constitutes a modulation of time.

The new era was opened by the last of the miniaturists. It was heralded in the Turin *Book of Hours*, most of which has unfortunately been destroyed. Van Eyck recorded all the subtle nuances that the atmosphere takes on, especially in the vicinity of water. But the great innovator, the first "luminarist," to use a term that was to be current until Impressionism—was the enigmatic master of the *Livre du cœur d'amour épris*. In this manuscript, now in Vienna, which was attributed to King René personally, we witness the procession of the hours in nature. There is a knight in a meadow at dawn, his shadow projected on the grass; there is a sunrise, with light dispelling the night—and it is a very specific light, "a certain smile" of light that appears with the dawn. Other painters were discovering that there may be such a thing as a specific absence of light. They are interested in night scenes and in the struggle of light with encroaching shadows. In the same manuscript of *Le cœur d'amour épris* we see a knight in his bed, illumined by a flickering light. However, it was in Italy, at Arezzo, that Piero della Francesca was bold enough to paint a fresco, *The Dream of Constantine*, in which gleams of light shoot through darkness. Whereas Giotto and the Primitives had not dared to portray *The Dream of Pope Innocent III* in any other light than habitual daylight, Piero della Francesca addressed himself head on to the problem of a light very nearly swallowed up by darkness (Figs. 54 and 55).

Then we come to some paintings of tragic beauty, such as Bellini's *Agony in the Garden* (London, National Gallery), which depicts dawn rather than night. Christ is shown kneeling, "His disciples... asleep at the foot of the hill," as the poet said, and we feel that this must have been a terrible moment of time, an icy, black hour when Christ must have shivered with cold as well as with anguish and loneliness. Bellini succeeds in rendering the transition from dark to light: in the hollow of the valley it is still night, but the top of the

Form ma

With Caravaggio and his disciples, the antagonism between form and light comes into the open. Light is no longer used to model and give greater accuracy to form; it violently breaks up form, sometimes with surprising effects.

**56.** - *MATTIA PRETI.*
THE CONCERT. 1630–40.
Municipio, Alba.

The extraordinary fifteenth century that inaugurated the modern era also made the discovery of this antagonism. It was at first treated timidly, episodically: bodies had for so long been bathed in a light both unreal and conventional that they had forgotten how to cast their shadows. Now these began to be discovered. Conrad Witz was one of the first painters to make a real study of them. He watched how a shadow fell across a floor, as cast by a column or a person walking, and how it struggled to make room for itself among the reflections of light all around it, from a window or an open door, for example. Chipped and dented by its antagonist, the shadow surrenders parts of itself until it is more than half eroded by the light. Meanwhile, it comes to terms with light in others of its parts, and, in the end, turns in upon itself in one central focal point as into an impregnable refuge. Its various withdrawals in different sectors constitute so many gradations of light, and the artist now has learned to render them legibly (Fig. 142).

This battle between light and dark, as it got under way, could not fail to become ever sharper, to take on an ever more dramatic character. By the end of the sixteenth century, the two adversaries were in open conflict. Canvases by Bassano and by Tintoretto served as the battleground. To Tintoretto, every color is derived from a corresponding darkness, from a black that assails it and bites into it. The contrast is brutal; it is like the noise of swords or pikes clashing. We seem to be witnessing a pictorial restatement of the rivalry between day and night—always at the same time a rivalry between life and death, as the ancient mythologies expressed it. (In Egypt, for instance, the rivalry centered around threats to the solar god.)

Some years later, the conflict becomes still sharper. In the beginning of his career, Caravaggio seemed to be wholly on the side of night. It was his ruling element, his perpetual point of departure. Suddenly, however, he introduced light into his characteristically compact darkness—much as one might use a knife to cut through a solid mass. The rays of light in his pictures are like the blows of an ax or a sword: their effect is to open wounds, to make breaches in a wall. Light is no longer the servant of form, as it had been in Classical painting—where no chance of a misunderstanding could be tolerated and contours had to be complete and continuous. Now light is an assailant; it wrests bits of brightness from the encroaching dark. They are mere stumps of forms, flashing salients emerging like islands hitherto covered by the sea. Out of the massive dark, bumps and bulges of light appear (Fig. 56).

From this time forward, light will never again be taken for granted. It is something to be conquered, and the victory will not always be easy. Light, henceforward, becomes precious to the painter, perhaps the most precious of all material aspects of his medium, for he has to work hard to obtain it.

Some individuals have been startled by the opinion that Vermeer, painter of the most luminous radiance, is at bottom an heir to the achievements of Caravaggio. At first glance he seems the latter's dramatic antithesis.[1] But it was thanks to Caravaggio, who influenced his early works, that Vermeer learned to appreciate the value of light. He made of

---

[1] How did Vermeer come into contact with Caravaggio's influence? It is generally supposed, not without reason, that the School of Utrecht served as intermediary. Vermeer never went to Italy; but we know that he was an art dealer and that a number of Italian works passed through his hands. For my part, I should like to point out some disturbing affinities between Saraceni and Vermeer: both disclose the same feeling for compact and full volumes caressed by light as against the aggressive divisions by Caravaggio; both exhibit the same quiet spirituality and sweetness. Even the "drops" of light so dear to Vermeer are anticipated by Saraceni. Now, it should not be

it the rarest and subtlest thing. It is locked into his paintings as some precious substance might be inclosed in a crystal. His love of light explains his fondness for pearls, each a translucid prison cell holding a drop of light. When we look at his paintings, we cannot decide whether the pearl is so highly prized because it is a rare jewel or because it is a symbol of light.

Light has very nearly come into its own. Soon it will have routed utterly its principal rival: form. To achieve this, what better means than to address oneself to the task of painting formlessness, the void?

A new illusionistic device—aerial perspective—now replaces linear perspective, which had been the blind tool of form. Instead of geometrically divisible space, we now have an opening onto a limitless expanse. The eye is no longer confined, no longer directed toward some given point, but drawn into the dizziness of infinity. The world of the earth, long undisputed in its sway, yields place now to the sky—a sky envisaged no more as the neutral, bright background that it had been since the beginning of the Renaissance. Originally conceived as an alternative to the gold grounds of Byzantine artists, the sky was now to an ever greater extent becoming the very medium of painting. In the course of transition from the Classical to the Baroque era, ceiling paintings more and more frequently led the eye into imaginary depths of light, populated with flying figures and clouds of ever-changing form. Tintoretto was the ancestor of this development; in him we find the first evidences of an effort to escape from the gravity and materiality of the heavens by recourse to speed of movement.

In Venice, Tintoretto's rival Veronese went on calmly with geometric discipline, constructing his sumptuous accretions of forms, but he left plenty of room for large luminous areas. Thereby, he paved the way for a scintillating poet of the void and formless: Giovanni Battista Tiepolo. With him, the heavens consisted of no more than a few infinitely light clouds, a few scattered figures floating in an ocean of light. Now light really comes into its own. Although masses and bodies subsist, they lose their darkness and density; they no longer play the leading role. Where formerly a compact army of forms held sway, only a few scattered survivors remain to remind us of the rout—like a last few clouds in a limpid sky swept clean by the wind (Fig. 174).

Light, the humble servant, now become mistress of the house, will prove a true tyrant. She will refuse to share her dominion with other elements of the work. The day will come when her lover, the painter, will make her the sole object of his concern, will have eyes for none but her: this is Impressionism. Drawing and contour, the first discoveries of the Paleolithic artists, will in time be banished. What light had helped to discover—masses, volumes, density—light now increasingly dissipates. Form primarily suffers, and since matter constitutes form, matter disappears, too. Increasingly, there is only light—light intoxicated with its own beauty, changing costumes with every passing moment of time, putting on and taking off, one after another, every sumptuous pattern of floral design, every fleeting appearance of a precious fabric. The painter gradually becomes the

forgotten that the latter worked with Leclerc, a native of Lorraine who lived in Italy. Through him Saraceni was brought in touch with Northern artists. There are also disturbing affinities between Saraceni and Georges de La Tour, a native of Nancy. They both painted *The Ecstasy of St. Francis,* and their versions are similar in the way they proceed from the simplification of smooth, rounded volumes to musical evocation of the inner life. This latter affinity is also accounted for more directly through the Lorraine filiation (Figs. 2 and 306).

mere slave who holds the mirror up to light, so that light can contemplate herself and study each and every one of her successive changing appearances (Fig. 59).

The very excessiveness of light's imperial dominion, her jealous tyranny, in time led to a reaction. Cubism's significance was to come at long last to the defense of form. Freeing itself at the same time from all concern for representing reality, Cubism conceived of the canvas as a flat area subject to the regulations and divisions of geometry. But that passionate cult of form and combinations of forms was unable to conceal how much it sacrificed— painting's grasp of the appearances of reality. Since remote prehistory, painting had set itself the organization of appearances as its primary task. Now that Impressionism had completed the divorce between form and reality, form found itself devoid of substance— a lonely survivor from other epochs, reduced to consuming its own substance. Its resurgence in the twentieth century has been a highly precarious venture: indeed, does not the most recent school, which calls itself "nonformal art" and aims only at the transcription of vital energy, confirm this view?

The conquest of form corresponded to a first conquest of the human mind—that of reason and logic in human thought, of organization and harmonious measure in artistic space. With light there came to the surface a restless awareness of another domain to be conquered—one that eludes the traditional means of apprehension. This is the domain of forces, energy, and intensity, now become a new measure of the world we live in. Space is, indeed, still the locale of these forces, this energy, this intensity—and is indeed agitated by them—but now it is they that impose their conditions upon it.

THE SIGN OF THE IMMATERIAL. Light has accomplished still more: to the sublimest artists it has opened the door to a world that had long seemed beyond the ken of art—the invisible, a world not only beyond space and matter, but also beyond measurement (and intensity was still governed by measurement). Although it is a truism to say that without light nothing would be visible, we are now faced with the paradox that light also makes it possible to express and show to the mind's eye things that elude the physical eye.

For although light is seen, it can also be thought. Man has always tried to exorcize his solitude in a universe unlike himself, by efforts to feel it as nonetheless related to him, possessed of a life, a soul, similar to his own. During the day he observes the existence of light and it seems to him an image of his own existence. Does not light go through similar stages? It is born in the morning, struggles to assert itself, and attains its full development at noon (high noon, summer's peak). Then it gradually declines and withdraws. Dusk is followed by night—which is a kind of death. When the light has gone, it is as though nothing were. Light is like the soul; without it the material world might as well not be. And yet—like the soul—light exists apart from matter.

Soon light comes to seem a kind of soul of things. It becomes the image of our own soul: immaterial, imponderable, and withal visible. It presents itself as a visible symbol of the invisible.

According to Plato, the highest peak of reality is the Good; its reflection in the sensory world is light, and in the world of the mind it begets truth and intelligence. The most poetic of all philosophers attributed to light a significance that is not physical: it becomes the equivalent of the highest spiritual principles. It is the sign of the absolute,

*With Impressionism, light becomes supreme and eliminates form altogether. Contours, modeling, and even continuity of the pictorial medium have gone.*

**59. -** *CROSS.* THE GOLDEN ISLES. Musée National d'Art Moderne, Paris

of God who descends to our souls in the form of the Good, the True, the Beautiful.

Several centuries after Plato, the real founder of Neoplatonism, Plotinus, constructed out of this doctrine a philosophy that frequently sounds strangely modern. The *Enneads* contain admirable passages on light. Plotinus discovers its beauty: "And why is gold beautiful, and what accounts for the beauty of the lightning one sees at night? Fire is beautiful in itself.... It is at the level of the Idea.... It lights up and glows.... The things inferior to it, eclipsed by its dazzling light, cease to be beautiful.... Matter is dark." Thus there are things that are not beautiful in themselves, by virtue of their form or substance, but solely because they reflect the beauty of the light that falls on them.

The opposition between light and matter now takes on symbolic force. Primitive man felt that blackness or darkness expressed matter, whatever is opaque or dense, and light the void, whatever is rarefied or immaterial. From the prehistoric wall paintings of the Iberian Levant and the Sahara to the black-figured Greek vases, the dark spot stands for mass.

Plotinus merely put the depth and ingenuity of his thought to the service of this old axiom: light enables us to escape from our physical fate. "Matter is darkness: the colors are kinds of light; they testify to the approach of the invisible soul." Light is the sign of the mind, of the *nous,* and Plotinus goes so far as to say, addressing himself to his reader: "You—yes, you—are entirely light, true light, nothing but light...."

This philosophy of light, which necessarily entails a specific aesthetics, was handed down to the Middle Ages, for Plotinus was the ancient philosopher who most profoundly influenced Christian thinking from the third century onward. In the fourth century, St. Augustine was a great reader of Plotinus and was much impressed by him. But, above all, Plotinus left a deep imprint on an anonymous thinker who, by a misunderstanding that greatly assisted his fame, was believed to be St. Denis, martyred at Lutetia after having been looked upon (according to the Roman breviary) as the Bishop of Athens, called St. Dionysius the Areopagite, one of the followers of St. Paul. Actually the work attributed to him dates from a much later period; it has been established that the pseudo-Dionysius wrote it early in the sixth century. But benefiting, because of this false attribution, from the prestige associated with St. Paul, it took on considerable importance, and because of it the mystical aesthetics of light influenced the Middle Ages. This aesthetics accounts for certain major aspects of medieval art otherwise incomprehensible to a realistic mentality. My eminent colleague André Grabar has shown this irrefutably: it is because Byzantine art was steeped in Plotinism that it sought to express things other than material forms; this was why it made such great use of mosaic and gold in order to produce scintillating images more suggestive of light than of matter. This is why Byzantine art is so glowing; this is why, for instance at Ravenna, in the Mausoleum of Galla Placidia, you find yourself, on emerging from a somber low-ceilinged corridor, under the sublimest of all mosaics, which represents nothing but expresses everything. You raise your eyes to the low cupola, and in this nocturnal vault, golden stars suddenly light up everywhere, gravitating around a sparkling cross. You have come into the night and what awaits you there is the revelation of light. You expected a stage setting, but you are caught up in dizzying vistas.... (Colorplate XI and Fig. 60).

Medieval Western thinkers were very familiar with this spiritual heritage derived from Plotinus and the pseudo-Dionysius, partly through the intermediary of Johannes Scotus Erigena. Robert Grosseteste, for instance, wrote: "What constitutes the perfection and beauty of corporeal things, is light." And was not St. Bonaventure the great poet of light? Among medieval theologians, light gradually took on a sacred significance that the thirteenth-century scholastics liked to justify by subtle arguments: light multiplies itself, and in this it is like God; it acts upon any movement whatever; it has properties that are also those of God, and, hence, in some ways, it participates in the nature of God.

As Grodecki has also observed, stained-glass windows gradually took on so prominent a role in churches because they are as though sanctified by light. Whereas it merely falls on paintings, it actually passes through stained-glass windows, becoming an integral part

*In the art derived from Byzantium, the use of brilliant gold expresses spirituality.*

**60. -** *NIKIFOR SAVIN.* CHRIST IN GLORY (middle panel of a triptych). Russian icon. Tretyakov Gallery, Moscow

of their coloration, with which it merges. Some theologians even see a likeness to the Holy Ghost's coming to the Virgin in the Annunciation.

The fifteenth-century Flemish Primitives are always referred to as realists. This is certainly true, but they are also men of medieval outlook and, hence, to some extent mystics. If they rendered light with so much love as well as with such subtle accuracy, it is because light to them was as much divine as it was visible. The infinitely pure and gentle light that bathes Van Eyck's Ghent Altarpiece is that of meadows in spring, but it is also the light of Paradise.

Fra Angelico, for his part, discovered his crystalline lights only in order to depict the dance of the elect in a Paradise where the song of the angels resounds with light.

As we come closer to the Renaissance, the work of Grünewald marks the final disintegration of the medieval spirit, which now falls apart like a worn or overstretched fabric. Like a fabric? Would not a better simile be like a piece of flesh torn off and spurting blood and screams? But in this agony, light, resembling the soul in process of breaking its ties with the dying body—*lama sabacthani!*—bursts forth as though at last liberated, explosively. The Isenheim Altarpiece radiates flames and colors with all the hues of the prism and others—supernatural colors, one would say—around *The Virgin Adoring the Child* and *The Resurrected Christ,* which, together, dispel the darkness of the tomb.

HOURS AND SEASONS OF THE SOUL.  With the end of the Middle Ages, light was bound to lose its sacred connotations; these did not, however, give way to some simple visual positivism. Light now acquires a human meaning. The artist no longer assimilates light to God, to the universal soul, but to his own soul. He seeks in it and projects onto it echoes of his individual being, and, thanks to this spontaneously perceived analogy, makes it the language of his innermost nature. Some artists, like Botticelli, are fond of the light of the morning, of the light of spring. The secret of this affinity may have been disclosed to us by a philosopher who was also a poet—Rabindranath Tagore. He tells us how he discovered the splendor of dawn as a ten-year-old boy: "One day, at the first glimmer of dawn, as I stood waiting for the sun to send its rays from behind the trees, it seemed to me suddenly... that the morning light was revealing a splendor of faith on the face of the world. The invisible veil of banality was removed from all things and all men, and their ultimate significance became more intense in my mind: this is the significance of beauty" (Colorplate XV).

Other painters who, like Rubens, more fully embody the virile force of maturity, and who, like it, are more material, more sensual, more sumptuous, feel a greater affinity with the afternoon light, the light of late summer, the light that has taken on the exact shape of things, has warmed them, fertilized them, and nourished them root and fiber. Just as a fruit, when fully ripe, grows heavy, bends the branch toward the ground, and then falls, so light, when extremely rich, is transmuted into color (Colorplate VI).

In Titian, this light achieves the greatest density where it suggests sunset. To other men, this moment of the day marks the advent of shadows, the transition to night, and from them the sumptuous richness of twilight evokes a lyric melancholy. In this form it was perceived by Giorgione, the friend of Titian's youth. But whereas Titian, who was to live to a majestic old age, is the painter of beautiful warm days and long evenings, Giorgione, who died young, had a kind of premonition that his life would be short. He was the first of the painters of evening and its secret sadness (Fig. 162).

Then there is Claude Lorrain. However constrained he may have been by the proud, rigid, Classical architecture of his century, he managed to open up broad vistas onto the sea, onto ships setting sail on unknown adventures. Like Poussin, he expressed security and rationality, and yet he slips in hints of evening nostalgia. In the extreme distance of the space that he opens up he lingers over the death throes of a dazzling sun (Fig. 45).

There is Van Dyck, too, whose preferred figures are beautiful, fragile young men, promised to death, looming up against a background of twilit woods, where, in the distance, hunters are sounding the mort.

And there is Watteau, who also died young, and who paints for us the same woods where Van Dyck's hunters roamed. Now, however, only lovers are wandering casually about them—moving away from us, plunging deeper in the shadowy thickets—lovers who have not had time to live out their lives.

*It is through light that painting attempts to rise above physical limitations.*

**61.** - *POUSSIN.* THE AGONY IN THE GARDEN. Upper part of a drawing. Royal Library, Windsor Castle
(By gracious permission of H. M. The Queen)

The time comes when light, after blazing up one last time, is dying, rapidly fading away; the flaming carrousel of sunset now gives way to shadows, and we are on the threshold of darkness, in the cold, ashen light that announces night. This is the light to which Leonardo referred when he wrote in a manuscript now in the Bibliothèque Nationale: "As for a portrait, paint it in gray light, at dusk.... At nightfall observe the faces of men and women in the streets—what grace and softness they reveal" (Fig. 242).

Thus, every painter picks a favorite time and season, which we can discern by his treatment of light.

FROM NIGHT TO DAY.   Night has fallen, and must be coped with as a fact of life. But is not night incompatible with painting, indeed, its very negation? Does it not exclude light? Not at all. There have been artists who look to night to provide them with light at its most sublime (Fig. 61).

Still, at first glimpse it does seem as though darkness is opposed to light, much as nothingness is the antithesis of God the Creator. Manichaeism was wholly based on a struggle between good and evil so conceived; it referred everything to this dualism which has impressed mankind in every age.

Delacroix's painting is in part an attempt to deal with it, nowhere more clearly than in the vast mural that decorates the ceiling of the Galerie d'Apollon in the Louvre. What else are we to make of Apollo's exploit, his striking down of the steaming snake coiling in the mud? This is the battle between light and night, between the God of the mind and the power of darkness. *Sol invictus,* the unconquered sun, was the shout that went up at the close of Classical times when the Roman legions brought back from the east *(ex Oriente lux!)* the cult of Mithra, another sun-god, another god of light, slaughterer of the Beast. Was not Delacroix restoring the deeper meaning of Apollo, when he said, describing his mural: "The god mounted on his chariot has already hurled part of his arrows.... The bleeding monster writhes, exhaling his last gasp of life and impotent rage in a fiery vapor. Meanwhile, Victory comes down from the celestial heights to crown the victorious Apollo, and Iris, messenger of the gods, waves her scarf in the air, symbolizing the triumph of light over darkness and the rebellious waters."

In this text worthy of a great writer and thinker, Delacroix restores the eternal struggle to its full significance. To Plotinus and, even earlier, to Plato, God was light. To the Middle Ages, too, God was light. But what light? Is not the light we see no more than a symbol of another light, infinitely more beautiful, which is inaccessible to human vision? Plotinus had long since, in order to describe that other light, invoked another kind of vision—the inner vision. Thus, there gradually emerged the idea of opposition between two kinds of light—the physical, i.e., material, and the spiritual, which illumines the inner life, just as the physical merely reflects or suggests the spiritual. This distinction may seem remote to us as drawn by the Neoplatonists and medieval theologians, but it has been expressed in more recent writings as well. In the nineteenth century, in the *Cahier vert,* for instance, Maurice de Guérin tells us how, intoxicated with nature, he would lie down in the grass, close his eyes, and become a new being. "I was like a man under hypnosis: his eyes are closed, it is night, his limbs are relaxed, all his senses are shut off." All ties with the outside world have been broken. He is alone with himself, within himself. And then, "under the veil that covers nearly all the phenomena of physical life, his soul is far more alert than it is in the waking state, in the state of natural activity. It pierces through the thickest darkness, beyond which it sees revealed certain mysteries laid bare, or enjoys the sweetest visions; it carries on conversations with apparitions; the doors to a marvelous world lie open to it."

Maurice de Guérin was a Romantic, close to the contemporaneously newest trends of German poetry. I could as well have quoted Novalis and other Romantics. What we have here is the discovery of a new world, which is perhaps dominated by night but within which a new light will shortly rise, a light situated on the uttermost boundaries of the world of painting.[1]

---

[1] This ultimate transcendence in which the soul attempts to find itself by sacrificing visible light and exploring the night will be dealt with at the end of the book (Part II, Ch. V, 3, *Lux et Nox*).

62. - *HOGARTH*. SELF-PORTRAIT (detail). 1758. National Portrait Gallery, London

CHAPTER IV

# COLOR AND THE SPIRIT OF MAN

ART could not discover the magic powers of light without becoming familiar with those of color, produced by the continuous decomposition of light around us. In this domain, which is related to that of light (though the source of very different experiences), art at first found analogous revelations. However, these gradually led to other discoveries and opened up revolutionary possibilities. It was by exploiting these possibilities that art succeeded in faithfully expressing the soul and transposing its innermost stirrings.

Before achieving this result, it had to travel a long way—the whole distance between the extremes of art conceived in terms of architecture and art conceived in terms of music —that is, from space-determined art to time-determined art.

Color was to travel the whole distance from one to the other of these two fundamentally different modes of expression, which, together, go to make up the richness and complexity of art.


COLOR BOUND UP WITH SPACE.   In the beginning, color was merely an ornament of form, and, so long as form ruled supreme, color kept a subordinate position. Obedient to the laws decreed by the contour, it was limited to filling up the areas assigned to it and to making them stand out clearly from one another. This is the same as the geographer's use of color when he assigns a different tint to every political or administrative division on a map. Color will continue to be used in this way by all adherents to a strictly Classical art, for whom color is inseparable from flat areas or volumes (Colorplate X).

This dogmatic conception of color was most emphatically asserted in the period of Neo-Classicism. Winckelmann, its theoretician, formulated the view, which held sway until Ingres, in the following terms: "Color contributes to beauty, but does not constitute it; color merely enhances it and sets off the forms."[1] David, too, stressed the subordinate role of color: "If you know how to draw, the application of color will not do the slightest harm to the drawing." Ingres, for his part, called color "a lady's maid." This is why Delacroix was right when he likened paintings by the Master of the Sabine Women to "painted statues," almost echoing Balzac who said, "All France feels the effects of his correct drawing and his love for ancient forms, which made of his painting a kind of colored sculpture" (Une double famille). Such was indeed the ideal of the last of the Classicists: everything—drawing, values, colors—had to serve the purpose of dividing up space between full volumes and luminous empty areas.

When Gauguin set out to react against Impressionism's sacrifice of filled-in areas, the better to concern itself with the void (which left room for the free deployment of light), he went back to the compartmentalization of space. To that end, he repudiated not only the Divisionist brush stroke—which made color vibrate like a scattered flock of birds flapping their wings as they escaped the cage of drawing—and reflections as well, thanks to which colors had long been enabled to leap across linear boundaries and echo in other areas; he also repudiated modeling, although the latter did no more than modulate colors in order to suggest relief. Going back to archaic sources, he divided the painting into colored sectors dovetailed like the pieces of a jigsaw puzzle. He allowed only flat areas, each provided with its local tone, like those found in the earliest Egyptian paintings. Color has continued to be subordinated to surface divisions right down to our own day, as we can see in works by the Fauves (Matisse), the Cubists (Léger), and certain abstract painters (Mondrian).


COLOR BOUND UP WITH LIGHT.   In the examples just mentioned, color is closely bound up with space and purely intellectual patterns traced in space. So conceived, color merely adds a kind of sensory nourishment to the painting, serves as a blood transfusion, as

---

[1] Geschichte der Kunst des Altertums, quoted in H. Guerlin, La Couleur, an anthology of quotations, which I have drawn upon in what follows.

*XI* - MADONNA AND CHILD

Mosaic, Cathedral of Torcello

it were, sufficient to animate the forms. Nonetheless, color has also been very much bound up with light. It is capable of performing a different, rather more glamorous service in painting. For it need not merely "ornament" light—as with surfaces—it can also merge with light to become indistinguishable from it. There is a give and take—color gives light a hue and light gives color its brilliance. This partnership delighted the barbarians as well as the Orient, but it was repugnant to a Greco-Roman civilization firmly attached to more intellectual plays of form, which saw in it mere crudity of effect, the sort of effect given off by ordinary substances—metals or precious stones, for example, independently of the human mind. On these grounds Classical art condemned this effect as inferior and impure. In a significant passage, Lucian denounces "spectacles such as barbarian eyes rejoice in." The mark of the barbarian is to care "less for what is beautiful than for what is rich," and his ignorance is defined by his failure to grasp the principle that beauty consists in "the rightness of proportions" and in "the elegance of forms."

Very revealing is the technical difference between Roman and Byzantine mosaics. In Roman mosaics, fragments of soberly colored marble are grouped to establish a pattern and to diversify separate areas. In Byzantine mosaics, use is made of translucid stones: color becomes inseparable from its surroundings and is endowed with depth; the rays of light take on tones of color or make the gold leaf sparkle and glow. In the Byzantine mosaics, light no longer falls upon a dull-colored surface that absorbs it. Rather, the golden ground serves as a stimulant to light and makes it more brilliant by reflecting it (Colorplate XI).

This marked a great advance over barbarian art. From the Scythians to the Merovingians, barbarian art had been content to set off the colored brilliance of gems with the sparkle of gold. With the coming of Christianity light was endowed with a moral and even divine significance. It no longer served merely to enhance drab things, to draw sparks from them; now it bore witness to splendors that are more than physical, that are of the soul. The wedding of light with color in the actual substance of the glass invested Gothic stained-glass windows with their well-nigh sacred significance, such that they could be likened to the Godhead's infusion of the Virgin by a ray of light. Color gained stature through such developments. Where Classical antiquity had intellectualized color by making it participate in form, Christianity spiritualized it, making it participate in light. Now the symbolism of light was extended to color, which became endowed with a number of new meanings: henceforward, color became a vehicle of *meaning*.

By the same token, however, color, which previously had been bound up with the surface only and, thus, subjected to the conditions of quality and measurement, now, as a result of its association with light, began to fall under the sway of another consideration: intensity. Degrees of luminosity now modified the brilliance of colors—whereas the flat, dull tones of Classical mural painting had been unchanging, uniform in intensity. Color was now no longer defined exclusively by its fundamental hue—red, blue, yellow. It could also be strong, vehement, brutal—or pale, soft, attenuated. Light provided it with infinite modulations (Colorplates I and III).

Color now acquired great variety. It had been used in so few tones in antiquity that many theories have been advanced to account for this poverty. Some scientists, for instance Hugo Magnus, went so far as to blame the capacity of the retina, which according to

Magnus had been insensitive to the bottom range of the spectrum. He maintained that violet did not make its appearance as a color until much later. This allegedly scientific statement is actually unfounded: we need only examine somewhat closely the surviving traces of color in ancient works to realize that shades of purple were combined with pinks and blues to enhance, for example, the subtlety of the Tanagra figurines. Moreover, although the earliest Egyptian frescoes exhibit no more than five colors (not counting black and white), ten additional colors appear in Middle Kingdom frescoes. It is noteworthy that some of these colors were obtained by varying the same basic hue: two blues, two greens, and three yellows. Arguments based on the vocabulary of color are unconvincing; quite apart from the fact that language is a dubious guide in this field, it is only natural to suppose that man perceived hues with his eyes that he did not distinguish intellectually or verbally until much later. Nor does the ability to name colors necessarily imply the ability to render them with the brush; technique does not necessarily keep abreast of vocabulary. It is always easier to feel than to provide a name for one's feelings, and it is also easier to provide a name than to reproduce feelings in an artistic medium. The latter accomplishment requires natural resources and technical knowledge, which only develops gradually. Are we to say that medieval man was unaware of certain colors around him simply because he did not use them in his stained-glass windows? The color range of these windows is as limited in one way as the range of archaic primitive frescoes was in another. Nevertheless, in the fourteenth century, Cennino Cennini listed no fewer than twenty basic colors, among which he mentioned five different yellows and seven different reds.

Actually, color did not really embark on any new adventures until a technical discovery was made that had other important consequences as well. This was the discovery of oil painting, as first practiced by Van Eyck and his successors. Oil admits of an endless range of transparencies and opacities and makes it possible to blend colors and spread them thin. The chromatic scale was suddenly revealed as seemingly limitless. A world of infinite nuance was opened up to the artist. The fresco painter had been compelled to apply simple colors in delimited areas, taking into account the drying time of the plaster; this is why painting, for so long, had to comply with a conception of form as defined by contour. Oil, however, permits continuous transitions, not only over the surface of the painting, but also in depth: this is the function of superimposed transparent glazes. They deploy the full gamut of tonalities passing from one to another by intangible transitions, which are even less consistent than degrees of shadow in modeling. When shadows are added to a color, they tend to neutralize it, modifying its value as well as its fundamental purity, dirtying it. Now color would have the same brightness everywhere.

As Baudelaire explains in his *Salon de 1845*, "instead of modeling with a single tone," which amounts to modeling with a stamp, it is possible to model with color. "This—if the shadow is green and the light is red—consists in finding at the first try a harmony of green and red, the former dark and the latter luminous, which produces the effect of a monochrome and revolving object" (Colorplate III).

The same is true of perspective. The Italian Renaissance rendered depth by the linear organization of space and of forms in space; henceforward, aerial perspective would also be used, and would employ hues modulated according to the varying thickness of the layer of air that interposes its light coloring in the manner of a glaze. As Félibien, the friend of

Poussin, observed, "Air is... a diaphanous body—though not absolutely diaphanous, for it is colored—through which we see objects."

This first—and already keen—perception led to others as the artist's eye became more highly trained in catching the nuances of tonality. Air, if colored, is colored diversely, according to changes in the light. This was another discovery, recorded by Vicente Carducho: "Color alters and changes in accordance with the *quality* of the light that illumines it—whether sunlight, moonlight, or reflected light. Shadows inevitably share in the same color." Thus, at the threshold of the seventeenth century, as oil-painting technique advanced, observation of the properties of color led to the discovery that shadows are not a mere darkening of the local tone, but have a tonality of their own. Light, far from being the bright, even, neutral medium that it had been in earlier painting, can also vary in color. And, finally, it was realized that local tones—an abstraction with reference to nature—are not merely affected in their integrity by all these modifying agents, but that they act upon one another in the sense of reflecting one another—as Leonardo da Vinci had long since noted. In his *Treatise on Landscape* he considered the case of a lady "in a field illuminated by the sun." In such an arrangement of light, "you will see that all the parts of drapery that can be influenced by the field are tinted by rays reflecting the color of the field, and this... changes the colors of adjacent objects, whether the latter are luminous or nonluminous."

THE REALM OF INTENSITY.   As a result of these developments, the permanence of form ascribed to solids—through which, one might say, man developed a sense of form in the first place—began to disappear. The spectacle of the world was thrown back into the current of time; henceforward it would never stop changing under the impact of multiple influences, all of which affect and modify color—the very color formerly believed to be a property of the surface. Nothing would appear stable any longer in this new way of looking at the world, in which the intellect no longer exercised a regulatory control. Now all was seen as change, transition, nuance; everything belied intellectual definition and measurement. The autonomy of things guaranteed by the artifice of contour (in obedience to the demands of the intellect) is now put in question by the eye. Vision became divorced from the intellect—and even opposed to it—or rather, it began to influence the intellect and made it more flexible.

At about the same time, Leonardo saw and made us see the world as bathed in a penumbra of reflections, by which all things are interrelated and made to seem interdependent. He conceived the universe as a field of forces; to grasp how these forces work is more important than to subject the bodies they act upon to abstract analysis. Clearly, art was undergoing profound transformations; a new era was coming about. Color, for which Leonardo's *sfumato* had paved the way, was now becoming the principal element in art. In the seventeenth century, color became the rival of form; in the eighteenth it became supreme. For a time, in the early nineteenth century, it was eclipsed under Neo-Classicism, but, thereafter, it established its supremacy once and for all. Impressionism, which made color the very incarnation of luminous energy, crowned its triumph, freeing color of all obligation save that of expressing chromatic vibrations. Form was sacrificed to color, and space given over wholly to its needs: it now served to render light. It is tempting to conclude that, with the victory of color, form disintegrated. The roles of master and slave were completely reversed (Fig. 107).

What have been the consequences of this revolution? To be sure, color has ceased to be an ornament, a mere extra, added treat supplementing the principal element of painting—form, at first, then light. But these profound changes in the elements of art, in the importance of different means of expression, are more far-reaching than a mere glance at the most recent painting would suggest. A new principle has come to serve as the foundation of art: neither quantity (measurement and proportion)—nor form—nor even intensity, the principle that light had imposed thanks to the possible variations in its brilliance. This new principle was bound to assert itself once light had surrendered to variations in color. One might almost say that this development took place somewhere in the period between Leonardo and Giorgione. Carducho, in the text quoted above, called the new principle *quality*. Of course, there is a sense in which this principle is as old as art, but, as though fearing to come face to face with the secret of its own nature, art long ignored it, preferring less exacting substitutes. Form and space, with all the problems of dimension and proportions they involve, occupied the mind with the resources of analysis; things were reduced to their constitutive elements, to units of measurement; and thus the intellect preserved supremacy over sensibility. And, yet, the work of art worthy of its name has at all times aimed, however unconsciously, at a certain quality of form and formal relationships. This had been called "harmony"; elevated to the rank of philosophical category, it became "beauty." But many theorists labored under the illusion that beauty could be analyzed and even achieved by applying rules and measurements, i.e., by a system of numbers. Such canons as the Golden Section and other proportions to which marvelous properties were ascribed strikingly illustrate the effort to reduce art and its aesthetic goal to problems of measurement, that is, to purely quantitative considerations. And yet Plato had already warned against such an illusion when he compelled beauty to take wing and soar beyond human grasp, into the inaccessible world of pure ideas.

By asserting its existence, light compelled man to follow his perception. More accurately, by making him aware of intensity and its variations, it favored the immediate appreciations of sensibility. Of course, men long believed that intensity, too, could be reduced to a problem of measurement, i.e., to quantitative considerations. But this belief served merely to give the intellect a kind of Platonic gratification; at all events, the intellect would have its say only *ex post facto*. Light, with its degrees of brilliance, its subtle nuances, and its modulations, could be directly apprehended only by the sensibility. The elusive penumbras of Leonardo's *sfumato* succeeded in baffling all attempts to grasp light, save by sensibility, to such an extent that his universe of lights and shadows, susceptible to no system of accurate measurement, summoned up the irreducible presence of mystery and gave it ambiguous poetic expression.

THE REALM OF QUALITY. We have pointed out that, because light admitted of the more and less, it was possible to imagine that the degrees of light, however nuanced they might be, could be analyzed. The moment light is colored, however, the moment that the scale of values began to be replaced with tonalities, the irreducible existence of quality had to be acknowledged. Quality now becomes the basis and instrument of art. The problem of the more or less gives way to the problem of the "other."

One color differs from another because I feel it to be different, because the reaction it provokes in my nervous system is unlike any other. The colors of the rainbow or those produced by a prism constitute a continuous sequence of chromatic variations, between which I cannot—as I can in the realm of form—trace boundary lines. Here, all is change—and not just in the matter of degree, as with light, but also in basic nature.

The intellect, as a matter of convenience, tries to determine which colors are fundamental by isolating certain centers of "density." Seven of them are customarily listed, in analogy with the seven tones of the musical scale. The distinction is crude and, at best, of purely practical significance. We are forced to recognize an infinite number of tones of color; and our vocabulary can never keep abreast of them. More recently, numerical scales of color have been suggested, such as the Ostwald table. Although it enables us to detect and enumerate an extremely large number of hues, and, thereby, comes close to recognizing the infinite variety of colors, this method is still caught up in the problem of assigning a finite number to infinity. The problem is something like the problem of the contrast between the continuous curvature of the circle and the multiple-angled polygon, which tends to the circle but never quite matches it. By such means we may reach the limits of perception, but, beyond that limit, tones of color continue to be differentiated: the polygon is never quite identical with the circle, however many times we multiply the number of the sides (Colorplate XIII).

The tones of color may be very like, but they can never be identical. Moreover, the name we assign to each of them suggests something definite only insofar as it recalls an actual experience. It presupposes that we know, thanks to our eyes, the actual color spoken of; in other words, it presupposes our ability to perceive its special quality. Our experience of it is unique and incommunicable, whereas any form can be determined by the mind on the basis of geometrical definition, and, with the aid of mathematical calculations, in accurate detail. Chemical analysis of the constituent parts of a pigment, however, can never take the place of empirical knowledge of the hue so produced. If it could, than a blind man would know as much about color as anyone else. Furthermore, no definition of a color can ever be more than an abstraction: this is because no color is ever entirely identical with itself to the same eye, since it varies with the light and with the colors next to which it may appear. Color cannot be grasped by the intellect; it can only be perceived by the sensibility. It can only be apprehended affectively, not comprehended.

Quality—in the literal sense of the term (for there is another sense, as we shall presently see)—is that thanks to which a thing is what it is and cannot be reduced to anything else without losing its very nature. Quality is that which makes a thing what it is. Quality cannot be defined or discerned by intellectual means. It can only be the object of a distinct sensation.

The term "quality" is ambiguous. In the sense in which we have just used it, it provides access to the elementary reality of art, which requires that we renounce the intellectual and (as it were) mechanical devices of thought, in order to develop the faculty of direct perception, the direct experience of a flavor or taste that defines the perceived object and makes it unique.

Quality in this sense merely provides us with the foundation on which art is built. Art comes into existence only to the extent that the term "quality" acquires still another sense. Space and matter come under the jurisdiction of quantity and measurement. Physical life, which unfolds in time, involves another experience—intensity in its varying degrees, which is apprehended by sensibility, though also quantitative in nature. Affective life, however, requires a further broadening of the field and endless modalities. These are provided by quality in the sense of the specific nature of an experienced sensation, inso-far as it is irreducible to any other sensation.

At this point, we encounter a phenomenon that is also designated by the term "quality." Although a sensation can increase or decrease according to the degree of its intensity, we can also apply to it another scale of values, a kind which only man seems capable of experiencing and which could almost serve as a moral definition of man. This definition is not based on any quantitative calculation of the more or less, but on a judgment of what is "better." Here, mankind seems to postulate a new dimension, belonging neither to space nor to time (though it can unfold only in time)—a dimension which mankind is striving to realize in the course of its progress by suc-cessive advances in value. We do not perceive these advances externally, but solely in terms of inner experience. A scale of approximate measurements based on psychophysical parallelism does not apply here as it does apply with intensity—for intensity has roots in the outside world. The particular quality we now deal with is confined to the moral domain, and is hard to find words for. Language is based on material reality, to which we cannot refer in this situation. Quality in my sense marks a given degree of man's ascension toward the horizon of his future evolution, which orients his progress and his aspirations. In the mathematical sense, it might be said that man tends toward this infinitude, which is, for him, an image of the absolute, the total actualization of his potentialities, the realm where Plato situated ideas.

Two parallel paths lead toward this goal; one, which defines our actions, is the moral sensibility, the domain of ethics; the other, which defines our creativity, is our sense of beauty, the domain of aesthetics. Only persons who can experience them may be said to know them. Nor does the fact that they cannot be explained to someone who does not know them (just as light cannot be explained to someone born blind) detract in the slightest from their reality. The same is, no doubt, true of any abstract notion, however current; no such notion would be intelligible if not based on actual experience. To take an elementary example—number—it may be asked whether we would employ the decimal system, had man not originally learned to count with his fingers. It is the permanence of the physical basis of an experience—its objectivity in a situation independent of the individual—that insures its universality and its self-evident character. The experience of quality is entirely internal, without reference to the material world, and its existence cannot be demon-strated, save possibly by its continually being lived by individuals upon whom mankind is irresistibly drawn to model itself—geniuses, heroes, and saints. Quality, thus, is the law of art, its goal. Art is an effort to manifest quality, to give it external, objective em-bodiment. The work of art resembles a moral act insofar as it enables us concretely to experience a spiritual order of existence that would otherwise remain hidden within us. It is, in a way, its own proof of its existence.

Quality as a unique perception of a unique sensory reality is the raw material of art. Quality as a degree of value that can only be felt intuitively and, to an extent, determined by the quality of the man who experiences it is the purely spiritual realm in which art grows and develops.

Color, which can be apprehended only in such terms, made it possible for us to arrive at a clearer idea of these two fundamental meanings of quality. Now, perhaps, we also realize more clearly than before that spatial form and vital intensity, although more concretely measurable, attain the level of art only insofar as they are governed by quality in both senses of the term. A given form is not beautiful because it expresses a numerical relation or because it is modeled on a geometric figure, but because the artist has felt it qualitatively, has experienced a particular emotion before it—and, also, because he has made what he has of it. Because he has conferred a particular meaning upon it, he endows it with a quality that it did not have before, that it did not possess simply by virtue of its abstract definition. The very term "harmony" implies that art goes beyond the realm of material things, that it is a spiritual reality.

COLOR DISCOVERS ITS EXPRESSIVE POWERS.   Thus, the problem of color brings us face to face with the very problem of art, whose nature is so elusive. No one will deny that we perceive art as a reality. However, it stubbornly eludes all definition, all rationalization, all mechanical explanation. The moment we pin it down, it dies. Sturdy, practical-minded men, confident in the universal applicability of the intellect, have always been disposed to locate art in the domain of tangible form. However, to those artists most conscious of the location of artistic activity somewhere beyond definitions, color has always seemed the essential element of art.

According to whether they are closer to the first or the second opinion about art, artists have used color in different ways. Those attached to the formal tradition, even when they used color more inventively than in the mere coloring of volumes, even when they used it as a major element, have always been dominated by the spatial conception of painting. They assemble distinct elements and link them by means of composition; they tend to define areas by use of distinct colors, the relationships between such areas being frequently based on contrasts. As a result, the use of complementary colors plays a major part. To some extent these features still characterize the art of Gauguin and, to an even greater extent, that of Matisse. This is why we are so conscious of the latter's affinity with decorative art, for instance, that of Islam. Decoration is, by definition, the ornamentation of a surface conceived as dependent upon it to give pleasure to the eye.

Another family of artists treats color very differently. These persons are less interested in its sensory quality or in the quality of its harmonies than in the echoes it awakens in the depths of the soul. They feel that, whereas distinctness is, by nature, an object of the intellect, indistinctness is a more suitable object for the sensibility. Therefore, they are less likely to juxtapose two colors, exploiting the particular tone produced by their contrast, than to blend them, giving free play to every sort of transition, nuance, and reflection, to the infinite variety of color mixture and fusion that becomes possible once form becomes immaterialized. The aim of these artists is to link colors so intimately that, in the end, they produce a complex, unified whole vibrant with modulations, an over-all effect to which each individual tone contributes. Leonardo obtained a similar effect by an almost monochrome play of lights and darks—that "atmosphere" to which we have already alluded (Colorplate IV).

At this point, the question of art as a language takes on its full significance. For, even though color is by no means its sole vehicle, the properties of this language are most clearly illustrated by color. Intellectual apprehension proceeds analytically: first it determines the constituent elements, and then the way they operate. It is admirably expressed in Cartesianism and the mechanistic theory of the cosmos. Opposed to it is apprehension by means of sensibility—a global apprehension incapable of distinguishing separate elements within the flux of impressions that it sets down in their totality. These impressions are only identifiable in terms of their special effect on the sensibility, the special flavor they imbue it with. A typical example of how the flux of impressions may be set down is the use of color to provide ambiance. Delacroix, who commented on this phenomenon more lucidly than anyone else, noted, "We see that the objects that come into our field of vision are in some sense linked with the *atmosphere* that envelops them; *reflections* of all kinds, as it were, make every object participate in a kind of over-all harmony" (*Diary*, Jan. 25, 1857: "Liaison"). It is by making use of this insight that the painting derives "unity of impression and totality of effect," as Baudelaire wished it (Colorplate II).

This fundamental distinction, though one of which the Western mind is prone to lose sight, had been noticed long before Delacroix and Baudelaire. As early as the third century A.D., Plotinus spoke of a direct affective perception "which is not *thought*, but a kind of ineffable, nonintellectual contact or touch." And he went on to say, "To touch is not to think." He sharply distinguished between what is expressed "by propositions" and what is expressed "by beautiful images." Likening such images to hieroglyphics, he said again and again that it is possible to represent a "reality grasped at a single glance, not by reasoning or deliberation" (*Enneads*, V, iii, and V, viii, 6).

It is interesting to note that Delacroix repeated Plotinus almost verbatim when he observed that comprehension by means of grasping spoken or written words is replaced, in painting, with apprehension "at a single glance." In a famous passage (*Oeuvres littéraires*, I, 63) Delacroix analyzed this simultaneous, indivisible action of a whole unified by a common spirit—a soul, one is tempted to say—seeking to express itself to others. Such a whole, according to Delacroix, procures "a pleasure very different from the pleasure we find in a work of literature." It is a "special kind of emotion... and impression," and it results "from a given arrangement of colors, lights, shadows, etc." His conclusion is already familiar, namely that "this emotion addresses itself to the innermost part of the soul.... It arouses feelings."

Among the active elements in this emotion, Delacroix gives first place to color, ranking light and shadows next—in short, he emphasizes the elements that further the emergence of an over-all atmosphere with a specific, individual tone that provokes a movement of the soul no less specific and individual.

The idea had long been coming: certain artists had recognized the emotional power of color, the directness of its effect upon sensibility, its independence of logic. They had noticed that every color exercises an action of a special quality.

Poussin's theory of the modes (cf. Part II, Ch. IV, 2) expounded in the letter to Chanteloup was an attempt to explain this emotional accord between the subject treated and the means of pictorial expression employed. However, he did not go into detail

about the "appropriate" manner. For all that, Poussin's paintings prove that he believed color very important. Under his influence and the inspiration of Classical sources, Paillot de Montalembert, long before Delacroix, distinguished "beautiful coloring" composed of "brilliant color... a felicitous combination of tones" from coloring that becomes beautiful by "conforming to the subject," even when the result is "a gloomy, somber, pathetic harmony." In the latter case, "beautiful coloring is the coloring appropriate to the mode of the painting, and just as it must almost always form an ensemble pleasing to the eye, so must it constitute a perfect moral accord between its own character and that of the subject, so that the soul of the viewer is drawn into the same harmony." This is the very idea that Delacroix expressed more concisely when he wrote, "Color is nothing if it is not appropriate to the subject and if it does not intensify the effect of the painting upon the imagination" (*Diary*, Jan. 2, 1853). Color must not only be consonant with the subject—like a musical accompaniment—it must also communicate a secret shock that touches off a kind of subconscious reverie.

## A LANGUAGE WITHOUT WORDS.

A LANGUAGE WITHOUT WORDS. To account for this power of an instinctual rather than an intellectual order residing in color, it should suffice to recall what takes place in oratory. The listener is persuaded by the meaning of the words, which his intellect grasps, but, in addition, he is carried away by their tonality and rhythm. These exercise upon him the direct physical action typical of eloquence. Diderot likened color to eloquence in his essay on painting, where he compared drawing with logic, and added that "there are more good logicians than there are eloquent speakers." This idea, which Diderot merely touched upon, is expressed more trenchantly by Custine, who was a keen, even brilliant thinker. In a passage that Delacroix copied out, Custine made a comparison between "intonation" and "coloring." "Every new affection lends its particular *harmony* to the words designed to express it: this is why the coloring of a style is the surest gauge of its newness, that is, of the sincerity of the feelings. However, the harmony of the speech will never deceive you. It is an involuntary revelation that comes directly from the heart and goes straight to the heart ['from soul to soul' was Delacroix's phrase]. It is born of emotion; in short, this music of words reaches further than ideas do; it is the most involuntary, the truest, the most fertile element in the expression of thought." The very essence of color is captured in this passage. But, as early as 1824, Delacroix observed that paintings, "just as music is, are above thought" (*Diary*, Jan. 26, 1824). This remark occurs in a passage about Madame de Staël.

Now we have tracked down the source of the new psychology that made it possible to recognize the previously ignored possibilities of color in particular and of art in general. This psychology originated in Germany, where, at the close of the eighteenth century, Germanism, irrational to the core, rose in revolt against Cartesian logic. Lessing recognized that a work of art enables the viewer to identify himself with the feelings it expresses, but—like Poussin—he associated feeling only with the subject treated. Herder (d. 1803), at first a disciple of Kant, later an opponent, laid the foundations for the characteristic nineteenth-century developments that culminated in the theories of Delacroix. Edgar Quinet translated Herder's *Philosophy of History* in 1827, and thus introduced Herder's theories into France on the eve of the Romantic revolution. Herder no longer stressed the

8

importance of the intellect or the communication of rational ideas. He believed that the source of art does not lie in conceptual thinking but in inner feeling, as experienced by the individual. In it resides the affective force that will impress its character *(Gemütscharakter)* upon the work. To be sure, Herder was dealing with poetry, but what he says about the poem applies even more naturally to the work of art, and to color especially. The poet or artist provokes a "magical" communication (Delacroix borrowed the term and applied it to painting). "Just as the electric shock penetrates everything, yet remains present every-where, and nothing can stop it, so [the poet's or artist's] lightning strikes the soul where he wants to strike it." In consequence, we feel "our soul powerfully flooded with the obscure or ineffable."

This brilliant intuition, which casts so much light on the resources and inner meaning of art, was confirmed by psychology a century later, in William James's theory of emotion. He demonstrated that "the perception of an exciting fact" produces physical changes directly, and that an emotion can be born of such changes even without the intervention of consciousness. The sensibility, in other words, can react directly to a fact. And the "exciting fact" may, of course, be a painting. Relevant here also is Wallon's observation (he studied the psychology of children and primitive peoples) to the effect that emotion "establishes direct communication between individuals, quite apart from intellectual relationships." In this connection, the phenomenologists use the term *contagiousness*. Art utilizes just such a possibility of communication: color is one of the most active emotional elements by means of which the viewer's soul can be affected, brought into direct contact with the artist's feelings, and made to share them.

Delacroix and his friends were very much aware of all this. Baudelaire, in one of his notes, said that he was trying to "penetrate the (vague and general) significance of colors."[1] Silvestre, the next most eminent critic of the nineteenth century, went further when he pointed out how many things painting can show by "I know not what color-magic, each color simultaneously bringing to mind some vigorous feature of external nature and stirring some passion within the human soul." Silvestre's remark is extremely keen. It may even take us to the heart of the problem of color's expressive powers. To be sure, the action of color is in part immediate and physical, since our nervous system reacts to colored rays of light within the range of a given wave length, and, in addition, color affects our sensibility in ways we are aware of: memory associates each color with certain deep impressions. This is what Silvestre expressed so laconically when he stressed the link that memory sets up between certain features of external nature and certain "passions of the human soul." What are the further implications of this ob-servation?

THE ASSOCIATIONS OF SENSIBILITY.   The states of sensibility are hard to define or even to grasp. We are subjected to them; we experience them; but how can we fix them, were it only in memory? It is easy to remember an objective fact, perceived by our senses, but it is difficult to apprehend the fluid, indistinct moment of inner life. This is why we tend spontaneously to link them with physical phenomena that can provide solid points

[1] This aspect of the question is treated in *Dialogue avec le visible*, pp. 269 ff.

of reference. When man sought to distinguish among the temperaments—though only in a most general way—he resorted to an analogy with the elements of nature. Earth, fire, water, and air served as signs or symbols to define the various human types, in accordance with vague similarities that were universally recognized nonetheless. Our discussion of light has shown how the same instinct drove man to compare the rhythm of his own life with that of the universe: the day and the season, as they unfold in time, *demonstrate* our own developmental stages—youth, maturity, decline, and death—as we *experience* them ourselves. Forms, in their fixity and permanence, resist such mutations. Light, in its freedom and infinite mobility, is governed by them and expresses them. But how does this come about? By variations of intensity, to begin with, but, even more obviously, by variations of coloring. Color is all the more expressive because variations in it seem to obey a kind of organic logic. Do we not find similar variations in the cycle of the hours, which gives internal articulation to the day, and in the cycle of the seasons, which gives internal articulation to the year? Fresh, bright tones serve to characterize the morning as well as the season of spring. Dense, brilliant tones serve for noon as well as for summer. Sumptuous but less bold tones render dusk as well as autumn. Lastly, nightfall and winter occasion the freezing and extinction of color. Thus, what might be called "the chromatic system" becomes a universal system of signs for rendering the ebb and flow of vital states. And, by the same token, it serves to express human types in their various degrees of intensity, now fitted to apprehend and embody a particular state, now attuned to another climate of organic possibilities and sensibility. Every great artist belongs inevitably to one of these human types, and his prophetic sensibility induces him to choose a palette that will best serve to express his particular range. This is not to say, of course, that every artist does not in addition impress upon his palette the particular seal of his personality—but his basic tonality will remain constant and essential.

Sometimes, the mood of a whole generation of artists is given expression in this way. The Italian Renaissance, at its dawning in the fifteenth century, was joyfully aware of its vitality, and, at that time, realized some of its freshest, most youthful harmonies. Botticelli, who celebrated the birth of Venus and Spring, gave expression to its paganism, Fra Angelico to its religious spirit. But the one and the other make use of the same color equivalences: the pure, delicate youth of figures, the crystalline quality of morning light, and the gentle breath with which they infuse the season of spring. All are condensed in a flowery bouquet of airy blues and pinks bathing in silvery brightness. We shall find the same tones again in the works of Boucher and Fragonard, Tiepolo and Guardi, in the course of an eighteenth century that recaptured the joy of untroubled youth, having freed itself from the austere discipline of the great French seventeenth century and from Italian pictorial *tenebrosismo* (Colorplate XV).

In the preceding chapter, we noted that certain artists devote themselves to specific aspects or moments of light because they feel inner affinities with them. The full scope of these affinities is now revealed. In Rubens' painting, the light flesh tones are brilliant and scintillating, and even the fruits are sensuously rendered. We find almost the identical quality in Renoir: he gives us healthy undraped bodies that have cast off all adolescent fragility and are generously endowed with warmth, joy, and the juices of life. All this is reflected in glorious colors, above all, by a range of reds whose lavishness is echoed by complementary greens, just as the rising sap of the plants is echoed by the pulsing blood in human beings (Colorplate VI).

In some old popular engravings the ages of life are represented in an ascending order from birth to maturity, thereafter declining to death. It would be possible to allocate each of the great colorists a place on some similar graph of artistic vitality. Once the point of climax has been reached, the stored-up heat seems to become more oppressive than before —the oppressive heat of afternoon or early autumn. High tide is a superb peak of self-possession, just before the waters begin to recede; such a moment might be assigned to Titian, whose work coincides with the majestic exhaustion of the Renaissance. Its period of most rapid growth was the fifteenth century, and Titian already exhibits signs of decline.

Similarly, Largillière's sumptuous palette reflects the first signs of exhaustion in seventeenth-century French painting. The colors are more brilliant, and yet they are less intense, less glowing: they are beginning to get sleepy, even as they blaze up in glorious sunset. Similarly, Titian as a human type is less vivacious, heavier; he brings to mind the bearded gravity of Venetian doges and senators, apparently all old men. His yellows are more golden, his reds more coppery, his blues deeper; an almost rusty-red atmosphere enhances but also envelops and subdues the glow of his somehow solemn colors. This is the supreme moment that precedes twilight, or heralds autumn, or marks the beginning of old age.

With Giorgione, Van Dyck, and Watteau, as we observed earlier in discussing light, night—like autumn—is approaching and threatens on the horizon. The tones are still Titian's, but they are beginning to change; they are less warm. Clouds take on orange hues, but shadow saturates them more and more. Cold tones gain ground—violets and blues; the coloring reveals a secret decay, as of dead leaves. As a result, color is more turbid; its ambiguous nuances and silky iridescence are not far from a certain morbidity. A feeling of prematurely exhausted vital force, a dreamy, refined langourousness reflects the moment when the first fresh wind of evening begins to blow. It is getting late in the day—the year is drawing to a close. Such are some of the wider extensions of color harmonies.

The wheel comes full circle: as the shadows rise, colors are strangled and supplanted by values. That old Faust, Leonardo, lies in wait at just such a time. Despising uncontrolled or even expressive impulses, he scrutinizes the objects of his curiosity with the cold clear-sightedness of experience. Not even vegetation is allowed to disturb an austere mono-chromaticism: rocks, glaciers, high altitudes where the air is thin combine to create the climate of some bloodless, dead planet—the dark side of the moon. Does he not more than a little resemble our satellite, which gives off neither heat nor light but mysteriously returns, reflects (and how the double meaning of this term fits him!) the heat and light it receives, at the same time freezing them with its bluish breath?

Now darkness has fallen. Man fights it, kindling fires and lighting lamps, making ready for the heroic moment when he will be wholly on his own, alone in the black silence of the external world.

And now comes Rembrandt. Color has vanished with the advent of night and winter, but man revives it: he brings light into the family circle to dispel the blackness. As he treasures the lamp, he treasures jewels and precious metals—they, too, were extracted from depths of darkness by unaided human hands, carved and fashioned by other human hands to create new colors. Gold and blazing reds play a predominant part, and their mysteriousness is enhanced by the fact that they are set off against velvety backgrounds—whether darkness or dark draperies—or glow amid the thickness of fur. Occasionally a blue or a green appears—an ephemeral spark. Rembrandt's color is forever flashing, unstable; it breaks through its own negation—dark shadows where mingled browns subdue and neutralize the chromatic scale (Color-plate XVI).

El Greco, too, wrenches his colors from the night, but more harshly, more radically; they no longer emanate out of darkness, they are in strident contrast with it. The opaque veil that concealed them is slashed as though by a knife; so suddenly awakened, they look haggard, and the electric lightning that strikes distorts them, endowing them with a fleeting sharpness, a vibrant hypertension such as the modern eye meets again only in the eeriness of fluorescent light. A previously unknown chromatic scale makes its appearance—outside time, outside the habitual cycle of the hours and seasons. It conjures up a new reality, a reality such as Lazarus found when he had risen from the grave. Here, color no longer feeds on memories of nature; it opens the gates to the supernatural, to the unknown (Colorplate IX).

Another great colorist escaped being imprisoned within the vital cycle, though he did so by entirely different means: Vermeer. Unlike Rembrandt, he felt no compulsion to paint old men on the very threshold of the grave, nor to create a light without resemblance to daylight. He does not extract colors out of time, from absolute blackness. Instead, he discovers absolute whiteness. Self-imprisoned in a cell of limpid walls built by himself, he ends up by ignoring the cycle of times and seasons altogether—despite the luminous window that brings him faint echoes of them. Clear and calm, his colors—soft yellows and sky-blues—are those of the pure, serene light of contemplation, without fire or brilliance.

Thus, the rainbow of colors is also a kind of clock face upon which successive artists have learned to mark the times and seasons of the soul and to disclose—by their choice of colors—their own innermost dispositions, the human types to which they belong. To this end, they merely offer the viewer equivalents perceived in nature—accessible to all—of their own natures, of what they alone feel.

With this development of color, new horizons were opened up to the painter. Form required of him primarily that he apply his intellect to the task of analyzing the constituent elements of things, first in isolation and then linked together in accordance with the canons of proportion, combined according to their capacities to act upon one another. The harmony so pursued was a little like assembling a marvelous piece of machinery, bit by bit. To be sure, sensibility played a large part in this work, but primarily by exercising a certain control: that of taste. Color, however, appeals exclusively to the sensibility, to the artist's deepest nature. It lets us identify ourselves with what is not ourselves, to recognize ourselves in the other by virtue of attraction, of love. Thanks to color, man learns to merge with what is distinct from himself but which, in the merger, ceases to be other. The artist has learned to recognize what are *his* colors in a spectacle hitherto merely external to him. Now they have become his innermost possession, and he compels those who contemplate them with him to recognize themselves in them—and in him as well. Unlike form, color is no more thought of as a segment of space; it is a vibration. Hence, it is not felt to be a fixed thing. It is not, like a concept, something extracted from the mobility of life by a will to permanence. Rather, it is a wave length, and it affects us in the manner of a musical harmony—which has the same source—because its rhythm is that of our own life. For this reason, it reflects directly, with no need for intellectual assistance, the psychology of the painter himself, who instinctively chooses colors attuned to his inner nature.

A SLOW VICTORY.   Discovery of the full range of the powers of color was a slow, gradual development. Thanks to its ability to convey the most intimate nuances of personality, the importance and resources of color increased as man became gradually more aware of his individual nature and needs.

During the first millennia of artistic history, many potentialities of color remained undiscovered; it followed in the wake of form, as the latter's helper. Ruskin proved his acuity when, discussing the role of color in antiquity, he said that, for the ancients, color did not as it did for medieval artists possess a pleasant, joyful, or melancholy meaning; it was merely a more or less pleasing qualification of space and was pursued only for the sensory pleasure of the eye. This was what for a long time was called "beauty"; and this notion, preserved over the centuries, has, down to this day, opposed the strongest resistance to an art based upon expression of the soul.

The Middle Ages, which associated color with light far more than with form, endowed color with meaning, but failed to recognize its spontaneous expressiveness, linking it arbitrarily and indirectly to mental notions, to abstract ideas that it was supposed to suggest by virtue of one or another intellectual convention. Color, in a word, became allegorical. In the course of the last few years, we have learned to recognize and interpret the Christian color symbolism of the Middle Ages—all awareness of which had disappeared during the period of Rationalism. Its validity is easily confirmed even in secular art —for example, in coats of arms, where every color is assigned a traditional meaning. In heraldry, according to an ancient tradition, gold is bound up with the sun and stands for faith and constancy, and red is related to Mars and stands for charity and valor. Vulson de la Colombière, author of a *Traité des couleurs des armoiries*, pointed out in an earlier work, *Science héroïque* (1644), to what extent these traditions, after vanishing from religious art, survived in heraldry. For instance, he records: "The gules or red of armorial bearings denote ardent love of God and one's fellow men, and valor, but also fury, cruelty, anger, murder, rapine...."

With the Renaissance, however, color abandoned this allegorical phase, and artists became aware of its deeper powers, which are less easily codified. Today we must break with a long-standing historical cliché and look at the Renaissance as something very different from any mere revival of the ancient ideal. Actually, many medieval traditions survived and flourished in Renaissance art, though clothed in the new garb of the epoch. The conventional meanings given to colors in the Middle Ages helped the Renaissance to sense in them an expressive power, eventually to be transmuted into a directly poetic meaning, as something experienced rather than deliberately intended. Venice, following in the footsteps of Giorgione—for whom Leonardo had paved the way—contributed powerfully to this transmutation. Is it not significant that Venetian artists closely associated painting with music, from Giovanni Bellini's angels playing musical instruments to Titian's organ and lute players lulling Venus to sleep? Was this not tantamount to recognizing that painting, which creates atmosphere by means of color, is capable of the same emotional magic as musical harmony—a truth that, as we shall see, Delacroix stated explicitly? Beauty changed camp: hitherto linked to subtle measurements, it now became the confidant of the human heart. Rodin's saying, as recorded by Paul Gsell, might have been uttered even at this early date: "There is actually no such thing as beautiful style, beautiful line, or beautiful color; there is only one beauty—that of Truth revealing itself." And human truth, above all! This had been a conviction of Venetian aesthetics, as opposed to Florentine and Roman formalism. It propagated a new freedom in European painting—to render "what the soul discovers stirring it inwardly, in objects that affect our senses only," as Delacroix said when he was still a young man. And it is above all by color that objects affect our senses and, through them, stir the soul.

★
★  ★

By replacing rational insight with private musings that carry each man along the path of his own talents and aspirations, inclosing him in his own inner labyrinth, art recognized the irresistible progress of individualism. Rembrandt and Vermeer effected a real withdrawal from the outside world, a descent into the individual's inner depths. As man explores himself and gains greater self-knowledge, he becomes more individualized. The traditional division into general types is now differentiated. The extreme variety of personalities is revealed as the self comes to be cultivated more. The chromatic scale, with its endless possible combinations of chords and dissonances, will provide art with ever richer means for rendering the subtlest nuances of psychic life. Chardin's famous saying, quoted as early as Haillet de Couronne's *Eloge*, "We make use of colors, but we paint with our feelings," now takes on full significance. In a development anticipated by Giorgione, the first of the twilight painters, art from Van Dyck to Watteau and from Gainsborough to Prud'hon will now increasingly become a monologue of personal reflections whispered in the gathering dusk.

There was still the problem of explaining the full extent of color's powers and its capacity to express the soul. There was still the task of founding an artistic credo upon it. A painter who was also a thinker was needed, and the nineteenth century found such a painter in Eugène Delacroix.

Throughout the period dominated by Impressionist aesthetics, when color was subordinated to the rendering of light, Delacroix was looked upon merely as a forerunner of the great optical discoveries that had made the new technique possible. Signac spoke of him in these terms in his book, *De Delacroix au néo-impressionnisme*. But such a view is unfair to Delacroix's larger contribution. He did not merely transform the role of color by assigning it the most important functions—by his discovery of reflections and of the part played by complementaries, which he inferred from Chevreul's discoveries. Nor did he just, besides, invent new harmonies that influenced the vision of his successors. Delacroix did nothing less than formulate a new conception of the powers of color.

DELACROIX AND COLOR SYMBOLISM. If, by his technique, Delacroix was indeed the initiator of Impressionism, he was also, through Baudelaire, the indirect initiator of Symbolism and of the art of Gauguin. These two currents flow from the same source. When, in 1824, at the age of twenty-six, he said of great artists that "they painted their soul when they painted things, and now it is your soul's turn," he was showing the way to Gauguin. The latter was to declare that there could be no question of seeking the source of art in "the eye," but only in "the mysterious center of thought." Similarly, when Delacroix said, "It is within yourself that you must look, not around yourself," he anticipated Gauguin's remark, "I am content to explore myself, rather than nature." To the traditional realist, color, like drawing, is no more than a means for describing the visible world, for reproducing it; to the Impressionist, color is the *only* means. Delacroix assigned drawing and color alike a very different task: that of "production," i.e., of manifesting and making visible what the artist has experienced inwardly. For, as he said, "man possesses in his soul innate feelings that the painter's or the poet's imagination can endow with life and form." If art remains a sign, it is no longer a sign of the known, i.e., of the visible, but of the unknown, of what is invisible. Art transposes and communicates. It becomes a means of psychic action, the means for provoking a specific emotion—something very nearly equivalent to the emotion experienced by the artist, which has demanded expression in just this particular way and no other. "This emotion addresses itself to the innermost part of the soul." What Delacroix is saying is that, unlike ordinary language which alludes to the most general, most universal elements of our inner life—namely, ideas—art appeals directly to the sensibility, to its most personal, individual part, the part as yet unaffected by systematization of our intellectual resources. The emotion it arouses "stirs feelings that words can only express in a vague manner." For, just as our feelings are imprecise in comparison with our ideas, the content of which is delimited and the form of which is determined, so, conversely, what we think is vague, precisely because of its neutral generality, especially in contrast with the incisive particularity characteristic of our feelings.

Thus, the art of form, based upon drawing, clearly fixes its elements and combines them by a method of articulation, producing a type of painting that, again and again, suggests analogies with sculpture and architecture. But there is another art, which brings into play the over-all *ambiance* of light and its colored modulations—an art that is comparable to music, because it creates an atmosphere instead of elaborating a construction. "The impression resulting from a given arrangement of colors" is "what might be called pictorial music."

Pictorial music! As they became aware of the powers of color, more and more nineteenth-century painters began explicitly to refer to music and ceased to conceive of their art in sculptural terms (with respect to form) and in architectural terms (with respect to composition). They repudiated David's conception of "colored statues." From now on, forms and lines, following the example of color and combining under its aegis their evocative potentialities—analogous to those of sounds—would aim at arousing emotion. The reaction against positivism and naturalism seized upon music as a palladium, as a weapon. This is not surprising, for, more than any other art, music embodies purely spiritual realities. In the light of this comparison and in the image and likeness of color, poetry worked out a new orientation. Baudelaire was to discover it: "Poetry comes close to music by a mysterious and profound prosody." And Verlaine will demand, "Music,

above all else." Gauguin, for his part, referred to "the musical sense of color," and to "the musical part color will henceforward play in modern painting." In his letter to Fontainas in March 1899, he observed: "Color, which is vibration to the same extent as music, can capture the most general and yet the vaguest element of nature—its inner force." Van Gogh, at Arles, summed up the change that had taken place. Painting, which previously had referred exclusively to space and forms in space, now entered the realm of time, with all its variations of intensity and quality. "Painting, as it is today, promises to become subtler—more like music and less like sculpture—in short, it promises color."

Here, too, Delacroix was the first to have stated explicitly that color was, par excellence, the element of painting invested with magic capacities henceforth inseparable from it. Whereas subject, form, and line appeal primarily to the intellect and are recognized by it, color has no intellectual *meaning*, but it can affect the sensibility in every possible way. Color precludes all attempts to compensate for the absence of emotion by the subterfuge of comprehension: color can only be felt. For this reason, it is color that must be given priority as the messenger of the soul, as the bright-feathered arrow that flies straight to the heart of the viewer and implants itself there (Colorplate VIII).

Thanks to color, in addition to the rational and positive language of the known, man can avail himself of the language of the unknown or the unknowable, for color acts upon our unconscious. As Delacroix put it, it acts upon us "without our knowledge, as it were." Thus it can communicate or suggest things that lucid thought is incapable of expressing. It is color that provides the essential foundation for poetry, which, according to Delacroix and Baudelaire, is the ultimate goal of art.

Art is no longer the expression of clear ideas; it is rooted in the most secret depths of our being and expresses *them*, revealing the artist's soul to a greater extent than he himself can realize.

This is a very different outlook from the one that concentrates on the amusing but anarchic diversity of visible appearances, whose shimmer was cultivated and amplified by Impressionism, bringing to its highest point of development a realism that had long been the conscious goal of art. Delacroix had an inkling of the truth that the work derives its unity from the inner life that it interprets. Therein lies "the dark and profound unity" referred to by Baudelaire. Color is but one of the roads leading to it—the broadest and most direct road, the main road, the royal road. Henceforward, the unity of the work will be found in the domain of the soul: the soul alone perceives the play of the correspondences and sees unity emerge from the tracery of sensations—not only visual sensations but all sensations. "*Les parfums, les couleurs et les sons se répondent*" ("Perfumes, colors, and sound all correspond to one another"), Baudelaire said in a famous line. But Delacroix also wrote in his diary in 1854 that on hearing "the diamond-studded song of the nightingale," he felt the desire "to paint this song for the mind by means of the eyes."

After Baudelaire, Symbolism, under the impulse given by Delacroix, was to become more and more clearly aware of the chain of secret reactions touched off by the impact of color on the optical nerve. Look at Redon!

Thanks to color, painting gradually gained awareness of its nature and inherent potentialities, and has become the spearhead of art. This development embodies a radical change. Formerly, art imitated the outside world, its sole purpose apparently to record visible appearances; now art is restored to its true vocation, which is to turn to the inner world, to listen to the soul, to break the law of silence and communicate what the soul is saying to others, borrowing from the visible world only the necessary vocabulary. And all this may only have become possible when painters discovered, as Baudelaire said, that "color [I hope I will be forgiven these linguistic subterfuges to express very subtle ideas] thinks by itself, independently of the objects it clothes."

**63.** - *MONSU DESIDERIO*. IMAGINARY ARCHITECTURE. Seventeenth century. V. Horda Collection, London

CHAPTER V

# DREAMS AND THE IMAGE

## 1. ART

ONCE art had emancipated itself from the severe rules of form and, giving itself over to the sway of color, had begun to create a more poetic image, it went on to explore ever deeper ranges of the inner life. The alternative to the pursuit of intellectual lucidity was the pursuit of sensibility, of feeling—even of the unconscious feelings. This was a broader approach to art, for images are created by the combination of form and color. True, the form-loving mind can represent specific facts and embody ideas. But images can be more than that: they can be a direct emanation of sensibility. According to whether it is more nearly confined to intellectualized fact or is spontaneously emotional, the image (in this respect, like color itself) is more or less closely related to the deeper ranges of the inner life, and especially to dreams, in which the image serves as the very language of the mind, organically conceived.

ANALOGY BETWEEN ART AND THE DREAM: ITS LIMITS.   Sometimes it is very hard to draw a clear distinction between dreams and daydreams, or between both of these and poetry or art. "He is a dreamer," we say of a man when we mean to convey that he is or might be a poet, an artist. Ordinary speech thus recognizes the overlapping of the domains in question. In point of historical fact, painting was ahead of poetry in grasping the affinity between art and the dream and sensing what they have in common. Dürer in Germany, Goya in Spain, and Dosso Dossi, Marcantonio Raimondi, Gianfrancesco Penni, and Salvator Rosa in Italy all made efforts to set down dreams in paint. That so many Italians made this particular kind of effort is significant, for Italy is nothing if not a rationalistic nation. Many other artists, with etching needles as well as brushes, early betrayed their fascination with a dream world, felt as obscure and yet somehow an animal basis for their more conscious inspirations (Figs. 64 and 270).[1]

The similarity between art and the dream, however, cannot be carried too far; to make them appear identical is a mistake. Even the Surrealists, who went farthest in this direction, have acknowledged this—André Breton has done so. The Surrealists did not so much produce art as use it, make of it an instrument for the exploration of the unconscious. Instead of treating art as an end in itself, they made of it a means to something else.[2]

Actually, in his work the artist pursues infinitely more varied possibilities, within the enormous range of which only a few are really close to what goes on in dreaming. It is matter for debate, of course, which of the possibilities open to him is most important. At the most elementary level, reproduction of natural phenomena is his sole aim. A little beyond this, the artist aspires to create, to invent, to add to the world something that was not already in it. At this moment, he is aware of that something as latent within himself. And does it really matter whether he thinks in terms of forms or images? Ah, but it does matter—very much. If he concentrates on the achievement of form, his aspiration is essentially plastic achievement. If he concentrates on the creation of an image, his aspiration is essentially expressive. At the same time, in the actual course of artistic creation, these theoretical distinctions meet and merge.

At this point of our argument, the most orthodox members of the latest schools of art will rise to object: "But is not the creation of images the most banal and ordinary concern of realistic artists?" Actually, nonfigurative painters have a good deal in common with realistic painters, for all that they profess antithetical intentions. To set down combinations of pure line and color on the canvas, or—like Courbet—to set down "just what one sees" is in either case to invent an image. Even though the realist repudiates fiction, he still makes choices and—if he is anything more than a mere artisan—follows personal preferences in making those choices, thereby exposing elements of his inner nature. The abstract artist either shifts and combines familiar geometric forms according to his own— sometimes obsessive—bent, or else gives way utterly to personal impulses, all the more unmistakably rendering an image of the gesture or other inner preoccupation that haunts him. Both realists and abstract artists, in other words, are caught up in a certain mechanism of producing images—though to what extent either is thereby doing something analogous to dreaming remains a question. However, the artists who most self-consciously set out to

[1] Cf. *Dialogue avec le visible*, p. 301.
[2] *Ibid.*, p. 372.

externalize their dreams are caught up in the same mechanism—perhaps most especially—and are also making visible unknown layers of their inner lives.

Take the last-mentioned, the most dream-conscious artists. Where do their images come from—from what depths of being and through what germinating process have those images arisen? Somehow, on the canvas, phantasms out of an obscure, deep-flowing layer

*The idea that the artist may paint his own dreams occasionally asserts itself even in rationalistic Italy.*

**64.** - *GIORGIO GHISI.* THE DREAM OF RAPHAEL or THE MELANCHOLY OF MICHELANGELO.
Engraving after Gianfrancesco Penni. Bibliothèque Nationale, Paris

of being have been given form, language, and order. This is very like what we all have the impression of doing when we dream. Painter and dreamer, we seem very much akin, drawing upon the same unconscious source of images and governed by the same laws.

But to just what extent are artistic images and dream images of the same nature? To be sure, both derive from the same source, but they do not follow the same development—indeed, they follow separate, divergent paths. The dreamer is passive; images unreel before him aimlessly and indiscriminately. The artist, on the other hand, is all activity, preoccupied with making something new, and the images of his unconscious are subjected to especially sharp, alert faculties that recombine and reorder those images according to such principles of understanding and conduct as he possesses or has acquired.

Still, dreams have this in common with artistic inspiration that the initial flow of images (insofar as they are spontaneous) is determined by faculties nothing if not obscure. The unconscious or the subconscious is the inner force they have in common. Certain images tend to recur—some more insistently, more obsessively, than others. In individual artists, as in individual dreamers (who are not artists), it is possible to chart a graph of unconscious forces, though just how we are to interpret it is not always clear. Psychoanalysis was the pioneer scientific effort in this domain, concentrating upon dreams and the less controlled states of the imagination; and, unquestionably, a similar method can be devised for coping with the spontaneous flow of images we call "inspiration."

There is a reservation to be made in this connection, however. Based essentially on clinical observation, psychoanalysis still reflects its origins, and even exaggerates this tendency in certain disciples of Freud, though, fortunately, Jung and Adler reacted against it.

The art historian must guard against the psychoanalyst's professional deformation, which is to stress mental disturbances and morbid aspects of the psychic life. Nevertheless, we owe to analysis the information that there are far more residues of conscious preoccupation in the dreams of healthy, well-balanced persons than in the dreams of more disturbed persons. The sort of obsessive, symbolic image that psychoanalysis stresses reflects its clinical origins; the dreams of normal persons are more episodic, more reflective of preoccupations waking life had left uncompleted, unrealized. The point is important, for there is a romantic prejudice against recognizing the fact that great artists were (and are) most often normal—normal in a superior way. The greatest geniuses have striven for and achieved mental balance above all else—a mental balance reflected to the world in the images they created.

FROM THE OBJECTIVE TO THE HUMAN ORDER.  From the individual essence of his being, from that part of it which he feels to be his very own and to constitute *his* value, the artist seeks to extract a reality that can survive him, that will serve as his own monument, so to speak. Moreover, he extends and amplifies this reality in order that it may stir the emotions of the greatest possible number of his fellow men. The creation of works of art is a prodigious attempt to go beyond the confining limits of space and time, to find a way out of them, beyond the individual, ephemeral aspects of the human condition. The beauty man conceives of as an absolute and sets out to pursue is perhaps the most brilliant and most enduring of all the weapons he has ever devised to protect the fragile flesh of heart and thought from all that would limit his capacities and reduce him to humble particularity, alone and transient in the world. In creating beauty, he extracts from his strictly personal self a universal object, which serves as nourishment for the other, and for the greatest possible number of others.

This may cast light on the complex nature of the work of art. To begin with, the work is rooted in the individual's innermost depths, at some remove from the mental mechanisms

The nineteenth century recognized the imagination as the artist's principal faculty, and the artist himself as the creative source of the dreams embodied in his works.

**65. - BRESDIN.**
MY DREAM. 1883.
Engraving.
Bibliothèque
Nationale, Paris

changing. Nothing in this other world is explained by causes; everything in it asserts itself as such, enters into associations with other things or generates them according to affinities that seem to us more mysterious, imperative, and absurd the deeper we plunge into an individual soul, leaving behind the narrowly organized zone of consciousness. These inner depths are our particular reality, for which the duties and demands of modern civilization leave less and less room, so that they have scope or freedom save in dreams. Must we then ignore our inner depths? Must we, like a ship's figurehead, look only in front of us, our eyes fixed on the next obstacle to be penetrated, no longer aware of our own substance, of which our thought is only the busy outrunner? Or should we try to penetrate more and more deeply into ourselves, utilizing the mysterious means of art? At a first, superficial glance, art seems to give us no more than reflections of the outside landscape, such as we might catch glimpses of through any window, but those who know how to scrutinize it are enabled thereby to plunge more and more deeply into the penumbra within. There, imagination is king.

Imagination (used here in the strict sense of the act or power of creating mental images) is thus the foundation of dreams and artistic creation alike. Spontaneous, well-nigh animal in dreams, elaborated and intellectualized in art, in both it is the act or power by which the mind secretes, in the form of images, certain inner contents that press upon the subconscious and eventually overflow into the conscious mind. These active and still formless contents seem to emerge from the incandescent core of the psyche—the unconscious—and, pressing outward, meet and merge with consciousness. There they are condensed, so to speak, and take on mental form, to be embodied in images or ideas. Pressing ever outward, they take on externalized existence in the form of concrete works and acts. Imagination is what first gives them body, however obscure; with the act of creation alone they take on solid material body, such as others can see—as works painted on canvas or carved out of wood and stone. The imagination merely prepares the inner contents to become visible, borrowing from the appearances of the outer world. Such is the function of realism in art. However, what gives real substance to the inner contents—at once concealing them and making them graspable as such—what gives shape to the inner contents, is the artist. Thus, the inner and the outer worlds converge and are indissolubly united in the work of art. The visions of the mind, struggling to attain visible existence, are defined and embodied in matter by the creative human being through one or another exercise of technique (Figs. 63 and 65).

THE PASSIVE IMAGINATION.   The imagination thus plays the major, essential part in the creative process. However, analysis discloses that it has many aspects, and, before going further, we must identify them. At the most elementary level, the imagination comes close to memory and is almost indistinguishable from it, but, as it develops, it gradually throws off the imprint of memory. There is a kind of passive, noncreative imagination, which, both in dreams and in artistic activity, merely reconstructs and releases the images that have left their deepest mark in memory. But, whereas memory reconstructs them accurately or, at least, boasts of being accurate, imagination preserves no more than what might be called their "character." The recorded sensation is dissolved, as it were, like a solid in a liquid, so that its components are set free and, although now present everywhere in the liquid, are visible only in the coloring they give it. Similarly, the components of an original impression are dissolved and color the new images to which the impression has given rise. This phenomenon is common in everyday life. For instance, after reading a book many times, we either in the end have memorized certain passages, or else we unconsciously plagiarize the style in our own writing—putting down sentences that seem our own but that are actually imitations of those we have read. Similarly, on leaving the theater, we sometimes imitate the intonations or mannerisms of an actor whose performance has struck us.

In art, what are called "influences" operate in a similar way. Satellite imaginations group in formation around the creators; there is a swarm of Rembrandtesque painters around Rembrandt, just as around Ribera there is a swarm of painters whom Dr. Perez pleasantly dubbed "Riberoids."

Banal though this observation may seem, it is pregnant with consequences. For it is noteworthy that this specifically passive imagination formerly predominated in art. It did not give way to the actively creative imagination until our civilization became aware of the importance and primacy of the individual. In the Middle Ages, the individual was lost in the collective, and as a result his imaginative autonomy was extremely restricted. Every artist treated a given episode according to the same rigorous rules, in terms of the same appearances; and his personal genius was expressed only in the degree of intensity with which he invested his subject and in the degree of talent with which he portrayed it. The Classical epoch is still largely confined to collective images, which every artist repeats with a submissiveness that would today be branded plagiarism. Not until the modern era, especially with Romanticism, did every artist begin to feel in himself the possibility of, and begin to cultivate, a more original, inventive sort of imagination, determined by inner necessity far more than by external compulsion. This is not to say that influences no longer play a large part. The example of Picasso alone has powerfully affected the formal invention of our contemporaries. But, today, such influences are unconscious, and every artist prides himself on his creative autonomy. Rarely, today, do you find a preface to an exhibition catalogue that does not tell you that the artist belongs to no group or school and owes everything to himself and his personal inspiration, without outside influences. In former times, artists never laid claim to any such degree of utter independence, neither desiring it nor so much as conceiving it. This is why iconography is so important in the study of the art of the past: all these repertories of collective images with rigidly uniform rules of treatment. Emile Mâle was a historian of art who conceived art in almost exclusively iconographic terms, and made important contributions precisely for this reason: of course, his field was medieval art. However, he registered surprise at the extent to which iconography remained effective, even dominant, in the post-medieval epoch. It was only under the impact of such great personalities as Tintoretto and Caravaggio, whose creations went contrary to tradition, that the passive imagination was gradually supplanted by the active imagination. Only as our civilization gradually evolved to the point where the individual began to occupy the forefront of our preoccupations, in all his uniqueness, was originality elevated to the rank of a new value of the highest importance. Only then did poets and artists begin to draw upon their personal, private imaginations and begin to give expression to the innermost secrets of their souls.

THE ACTIVE IMAGINATION. With possession of the active imagination, the individual is opposed to the world outside himself, which he now reconstructs, as well as to the worlds of other individuals, from whom he differs. How does it operate? How does it enable man to make manifest his innermost essence, even in its most ineffable aspects? It is the language of desire or, in psychoanalytic terms, the language of the *libido*. Life moves forward in a series of successive aspirations which, as they are realized, constitute progress in time. Life does not lag in this respect: no sooner has an advance been made than mankind darts off in pursuit of another. Desires can either be gratified effectively, in terms of action, or mentally, in terms of the imagination. What dreams achieve organically and unthinkingly, the artistic imagination achieves by supplementing desire with all the resources of will and intellect and by sublimating it as beauty. Whether in the animal language of our dreams or in the human language of our art, our desires supply the fabric of our existence, expressed in images, in mental visions (Fig. 66).

But how can we distinguish expressive from merely repetitive images, these mere vestiges of old sensations to which we have just alluded? False judgments about the value of a work are almost always the result of a viewer's inability to distinguish between the two types of image. What separates the genius who creates from the disciple who reproduces him faithfully, what separates the original from the copy, is that in the first case the image is equivalent to a sign and in the second to a residue. Though seemingly analogous, the two kinds of image are radically opposed by nature. How, then, can we distinguish the one from the other? The images that are signs, that possess creative import, are recognizable by their obsessive character. They are not the transient results of accident, but constantly repeat, in different embodiments, one and the same stubbornly asserted need. Their recurrence, like those patches of green that point to the presence of an underground river, provides a graph of the lines of desire operative at the solid substructure of mental life. Who has failed to detect, underneath the apparent diversity of images invented by a particular artist, a kind of steady consistency—the sort of thing that led Proust to say that the greatest works are always characterized by a certain "monotony"? Similarly, among the crowds filling the streets of a large city, those persons born in it always display a certain resemblance to one another—for all that we may not see it at first. It is up to us to discover the key images in an artist's work, the recurrences and resemblances. It is up to us to question them and listen to them, since it is through them that artists speak to us.

The language of images is a singular language that has nothing in common with the language of reason. It is a purely associative language that takes some time to learn to decipher. Sometimes it is direct and immediate, designating the object of desire most explicitly and in a manner easy to grasp. Sometimes it is indirect, operating by allusions—that is, by symbols. Dream analysis has confirmed the existence of these two states.

A man consumed by fever, tossing on his damp bed, or an explorer tormented by thirst in the desert, evokes in his dreams images of springs, of iced water—the object of desire is directly designated. Some artists speak exclusively in such silent language. The sensual daintings of Rubens and Renoir are crudely eloquent of desire for the female body. Did not Renoir say quite openly, not beating around the bush, that he was "making love with his brush" (Colorplates VI and VII)?

SYMBOL FORMATION.   Even in ordinary dreams, however, psychoanalysis has long since discovered the presence of another language of the imagination, a language of symbols. Symbols are particularly deceptive and hard to analyse, for they often take diametrically opposed forms. They, too, can be either direct or indirect. They can *reveal*—make visible—what by nature is invisible, or, on the contrary, they can *conceal* something which is striving to become explicit but which the conscious mind disapproves of and refuses to accept. It is easy to see what traps the duplicity and contradictoriness of symbol formation create for the investigator. Many psychoanalysts have been taken in themselves, supposing symbols to be always—what is far from the case—devices of mental camouflage. Primarily symbols are a language, man's oldest, most spontaneous language.

When primitive man wanted to designate concrete material objects, all he had to do was to point to them. But the day that he sensed other, immaterial, invisible realities behind them, he was at a loss. He could easily point to a flame, but how was he to express the power that he sensed in the flame—something over and above appearance, yet cause of its light and heat? The reality could not be more unmistakable, and yet no finger could touch it, no word convey it. The abstract language that was eventually developed to meet this need had not as yet been coined. Primitive man could only designate the invisible by means of the visible—that is, he had to grasp analogies between the known and the unknown, and by indirect reference to material reality express what eluded the capacities of positive language. It was then that symbols—and myths—made their appearance. Practical experience suggested that every act is the effect of some living person's will; consequently, the primitive assumed the existence of a manlike being, a genius or god, who embodied the immaterial power of fire. He assumed the presence of similar beings behind every natural phenomenon.

The dreamer's imagination works the same way: it bears witness to the unknown whose effects it perceives by recourse to some familiar analogy. I hear in my sleep the crash of a falling frame; I perceive the noise, but I do not know its cause; the unidentified sensation suggests to my imagination a possible cause—and I dream that a bomb has exploded.

This is not to imply that the artist who makes use of a similarly symbolic language can be reduced to the level of the primitive man or the dreamer. The primitive man and the dreamer make use of this language because they are below the stage of abstract language—at the so-called prelogical stage. The poet and artist have gone beyond the stage of abstract language, and it is precisely because they *have* left it behind that they find themselves in a similar situation requiring similar solutions. For their purpose is to express spiritual realities so unique and so new that the social language has as yet no words to designate them. Thus, they too are confronted with the inexpressible, and once again the symbol—which suggests the unknown through analogy with the known—is the only means available. Since the effectiveness of the speech of the tribe stops short at that precise point beyond which the tribe has never passed, all they can do is give the old words a new meaning, as Mallarmé put it ("*donner un sense nouveau aux mots de la tribu*"). In painting, this implies giving new meaning to the customary images of the visible world. It is up to us to identify these images and to make out what they are telling us.

Alongside neutral and accidental elements, works by great artists seem to contain

*The artist sees himself in the world around him, choosing the element best attuned to his own nature. The earthly element, vegetation...*

**67.** - *COURBET*. LANDSCAPE IN THE FOREST OF FONTAINEBLEAU. Ny Carlsberg Gallery, Copenhagen

*...the immaterial element—air, light, reflections...*

**68.** - *COROT*. VILLE D'AVRAY. National Gallery of Art, Washington, D.C. (Johnson Collection)

*...the fluid element—water, mist...*

**69.** - *TURNER.* ENGLISH WARSHIP BEACHED OFF FORT-VIMEUX. Thomas Agnew Collection, London

*...the element of energy, fire....*

**70.** - *VAN GOGH.* STARRY NIGHT. 1889. The Museum of Modern Art, New York

representations endowed with mysterious expressive character. Human figures or objects, themes of inspiration, or modes of composition, lines, forms, and colors, however diverse they may be, seem to have entered into some secret understanding, some complicity of their own. Silently, they all point in the direction of a certain attitude of the sensibility, and, as they converge upon it, suggest it the more imperiously. It becomes clear that lines, colors, and objects have a meaning different from their customary meanings, even as they duplicate them—an analogical meaning that gets through to us without our quite knowing how.

This symbolism is not artificial, nor is it a convention in any sense. It appeals to deep, confused notions that vibrate in us in unison with, almost as an echo of, the artist's own sensibility, superimposing it on ours—almost, indeed, supplanting ours. The language these symbols speak is part of no intellectual system; it is addressed to the oldest experiences that life has stored up in us from earliest childhood. Because of these experiences, every element, every part of the body, every hour of the day, every direction in space, and every material object duplicates its habitual meaning with another, more obscure meaning, which is, however, endowed with the certainty of animal instinct. The fact has often been observed that true and spontaneous symbols, far from being the product of fantasy, recur, identical and unchanging, everywhere in the world, in every epoch and among all peoples. They obey secret laws, grasped by interpreters of dreams in ancient times as well as by medieval compilers of treatises on heraldry.

AN EXPRESSIVE UNIVERSE.   The artist possesses this symbolizing instinct in his sensibility. By imperious, expressive choice he creates a world composed of the same elements as the real world, but selected or omitted according to whether they confirm or deny the meanings he wants to give to things. In the familiar forms of composition and drawing, there appear obsessive patterns like those graphologists seize upon when they study a sample of handwriting. To take only one example, the division of nature into four elements is immemorial; every one of them has been directly experienced by every man and has aroused in him certain sensations historically associated with a particular state of sensibility which these elements still suggest irresistibly.[1]

Earth is compact and stifling but generous and rich with nourishing saps; its brown color evokes the mixture it consists of; it is matter and, being passive, seems to breathe only through its vegetation and verdure. Earth was the element that Courbet saw and handled, and he instinctively finds in it the gigantic counterpart to his own robust, voracious nature so evident in his own physical features, though in his painting translated into a lyrical symbol (Fig. 67).

Air is the opposite of earth: transparent and luminous, it all but eludes our senses. It is the subtlest condition of life, yet to be without it is to suffer the horrors of strangulation. Weightless, animated by invisible exhalations, shimmering with lights and associated with the sky—thus foreshadowing the infinity of space—it is ethereal, immaterial. It is open to flights of fancy and to the freedom of the mind. Gentle, delicate, divine Corot was for-

[1] Cf. Bachelard's masterly psychoanalysis of the four elements—water, fire, air, and earth; he has devoted a volume to each.

ever dazzled by it, like the skylark to which he once compared himself. He sees everything through its caressing shimmer. What other element could have been as appropriate to his winged, angelic nature (Fig. 68)?

Water is ambiguous and mysterious; less material than earth, it is less fluid and translucent than air. Submerged in it, man loses part of his weight, only to find his breath stopped in its opaque depths. Its form is illusory, being determined by gravity and by the receptacle that contains it. Docile and ungraspable, it reflects when it is motionless the appearance of what is not itself. It merges with light. It gives body when it is violent to the energies it borrows from winds and storms and joins forces with the furies of the air. It can also be as light as air when scattered through it as mist, dissolving forms into mirages. Still more subtly suspended in the air, it provokes every possible play of color, from the faintest atmospheric haze to the motley design of the rainbow. Turner, the strange Englishman who led an enigmatic, paradoxical double life, saw everything through water, spellbound by its rages and perfidiousness as well as by its mirages (Fig. 69).

And what about fire? Splendor, heat, light, furious and consuming dance, it seizes upon everything—earthy matter, air, and water—to destroy them all if it can in extreme convulsions. For the ardent, liberating thrust so early evident in Van Gogh's graphism as an ascending, flamboyant arabesque (cf. p. 59 and Figs. 28 and 29), for his attempt to escape from the materiality and mediocrity of the human condition, the painter of Saint-Rémy could find an appropriate symbol only in fire—the destroyer of physical fetters—which as a specifically heavenly fire had illumined and consumed the night scenes of the mystic El Greco. Throughout his too short life, Van Gogh sought out the destruction of fire the better to magnify himself. As a young man he thirsted after the saintliness of the Gospel preacher, and the dramatic moment when he cut off his ear at Arles was another kind of sacrifice—amputation of a part of his body—that alone satisfied his notions of punishment and redemption. What more fitting symbol than fire for the need to transcend the self, to transcend the drabness of reality? The Impressionist light he had discovered in Paris was but a poor approximation of it. Its full revelation for him was the blazing sun of southern France.

There fire dictated his every line, every stroke of his brush, every form. All emulated flames. Fire suggested to him the background of wavy flames for his self-portrait; fire dictated to him his favorite color, yellow, which he celebrated with pen as well as with brush. "How beautiful is yellow!" (Letter 522). "Everything now contains old gold, copper, bronze, and all this with the green azure of the white-hot sky results in a delightful color" (Letter 497). "To achieve the supreme yellow I have achieved this summer... that is something more important that the matter of being well or sick." Occasionally he rose to orange tones, "oranges as effulgent as red-hot iron" (Letter 520). Finally, fire provided him with his major object, the focus of a vision engendered by waves of light—around which the sky, nature, and the whole painting swirl. His paean of praises to the sun never flagged. "Ah! to paint over all this a yellow sky with a yellow sun...! a sun, a light, which, lacking a better word, I can only call yellow, pale-sulphur-yellow, pale-lemon-gold" (Letter 522), "a sulphur sun on a pure cobalt sky" (Letter 543). Even of the figure of the reaper whom he wanted to make a symbol of death, he said: "This takes place in full light with a sun that floods everything with golden light" (Letter 604). "Ah! those who do not believe in the sun of this place are very impious" (Letter 520). Even at night, he seeks fire out and finds it:

143

in the lamps and candles of his interiors, surrounded with luminous haloes, in the landscapes where distant suns and stars make the sky dizzy with their gyrations. The sun had such a hold over him that his favorite flower was the sunflower, and he wanted to paint half a dozen pictures of it to decorate the walls of his studio (Fig. 70).

Such is the hallmark of the great artist: whether he finds what he needs in previous works, in the fashionable currents of his time, in nature, or in his own imagination where his dreams germinate, he *finds* it and unconsciously puts it to the service of what he has to say. Everything that the mediocre artist learns and repeats, the great artist chooses, absorbs, and *endows with meaning*, the very meaning of his soul, which he would be unable to define in words.

But it happens—and here the situation is more complex—that a man is tempted, obsessed by certain impulses that his upbringing and morality had taught him to condemn. The domain of sexuality is particularly fertile in such cases. Lucid consciousness strongly represses what it forbids, exercises its censorship, forces desire back into the unconscious. There it continues to press forward and is externalized in the form of symbols, in which form they appear permissible, their true identity concealed. Thus, they gain access to the conscious mind that rejected them. Psychoanalysis has familiarized us with such processes; it has focused—perhaps too exclusively, to the detriment of residual images—on images directly designating forbidden sexuality. However that may be, dream analysis has provided us with methods for investigating this sibylline zone, methods that can easily be applied to the symbolic images used in art.

Freud himself was the first to attempt such an investigation, in his essay *A Childhood Memory of Leonardo da Vinci*. His conclusions, however, are highly debatable.

# 2. ARTISTS:
## JAMES ENSOR, MARC CHAGALL

Such is the complexity of the human psyche, to which art has always borne witness to some extent. Western civilization, however, with its inveterate rationalism, long covered that complexity with a (frequently impenetrable) layer of positivism or logic. Now and then the layer has been pierced by a sudden flash of genius. There came eventually a day of general dissatisfaction, followed by revolt. Whereas the eighteenth century, toward its close, turned toward sensibility, though still clumsily and aridly, the nineteenth century championed sensibility passionately and tumultuously. Yet even the nineteenth century did not separate it from a certain logical lucidity, for all the mounting enthusiasm of the non-Latinized races.

At the end of the nineteenth century, the crisis made itself unmistakable. Rationalism and the chains that it had laid upon free exercise of the expressive function of art met with increasing distrust, often with resentment close to hatred, of which Surrealism is the end result. With it, art plunged into the obscurest depths of the inner life.

ENSOR AND THE CRISIS OF 1880.   Half a century earlier, Symbolism had broken away from the misunderstood realism, then prevalent, of which Impressionism was merely a more refined version. Symbolism, as the term itself implies, marked the recognition of the essential function of art: that of expressing the human soul in a language of images whose meaning could be only indirect and vaguely allusive. At the same time, more explicitly Nordic tendencies began to shake off the long Latin tutelage. They provide us with a complete, fully revealing example of the mysterious detours which the human soul may take, with all its obscurities and complexities, in order to disclose its secrets through the selection and elaboration of images.

One such example is provided by the Belgian painter, James Ensor. This belated Symbolist succeeded in avoiding literary pitfalls and inaugurated the development of modern art. With the Frenchman Odilon Redon and the Norwegian Edvard Munch, he was among the very first artists to dislodge the traditional values of rationalism and humanism. Romanticism, also a Nordic current, had enriched and broadened, rather than undermined them. Ensor perceived keenly, in his own inner depths, the antagonism that was asserting itself; toward the end of his life he forcefully voiced the demands of the new spirit, which was still being strangled by Cartesian discipline: "Above all, let us condemn the infamous doctrines of Descartes, that dull valet to the odious Christina of Sweden, and the foolish Malebranche; the doctrines of this wretch tend to sterilize the heart in the name of reason." He considered himself one of those painters who are "the slaves of vision" (i.e., visionaries) and who "rebel against the positive rays and positive reason as well." Like them he turned toward the "beauties closed to positive minds steeped in reason and in futile, cruel, crude, and ridiculous science." "Deeply moved by the charms of red moons," he sacrificed at the altar of "the goddess of dreams and the marvelous."

"Beloved king to sirens, emperor to pink seashells, pope of the dunes, doge of the docks and piers, god of grotesque masks, angel to sick cats"—as he defined himself with his characteristic blend of malice and bombast—James Ensor made his debut in the history of art at the turn of the 1880s.

In 1880, Impressionism was at last recognized, but the moment of its triumph also marked the beginning of a reaction against it on the part of forces that it had failed to gratify. Symbolism demanded an art that would be an art not merely of the eye, but also of the soul.

Art historians have, for too long, given greater importance to the combination of external circumstances and influences that account for an artist's work in historical terms than they have given to the secret of his personality. To situate an artist historically is merely to perform preliminaries to the real task, which is to understand the artist himself. We shall not, however, omit the preliminaries—in that way we shall be able the better to circumscribe the central problem and to point out what remains impenetrable.

Ensor may indeed be located at the point where the two co-ordinates of Impressionism

*For Ensor reality disappears behind empty masks, the most terrible of which is the skull.*

**71. -** *ENSOR.* PIERROT AND SKELETONS. 1907. C. Jussiant Collection, Antwerp
(communicated by the Marlborough Gallery, London)

and Symbolism intersected. The Cercle des XX, founded in 1884, where Ensor exhibited
his early works, merely revealed to the Belgian public the masters of the former school at
its apogee, and those of the second at its birth.

By his frenzied treatment of light, Ensor was still an Impressionist. "Painting speaks to
me the pure language of the sun, the sky, the daylight. It says, 'Light, more light, always
light.'" But his is a light that exalts color, just as his color exalts light: "My Lady Color,
my dearest one, is beckoning to me.... Color, adornment of the sea, of sirens and women,
joy to our eyes, enchantment of painting, color, life of Beings and Things.... Let us
brighten our colors, let them be enchanting, let them laugh, let them shriek with joy!"
Ethereal, brilliant, subtle, pure colors, which exalt light—but which exalt also that fluid
and changing element par excellence, the sea—for their sake Ensor joyfully gave up heavy
matter, the earth with its clays and muds, leaving all that to sculptors (for whom, inciden-

tally, he had nothing but contempt). Watching the sea from his window high above Ostend, he called it "the fairy who presides over multicolored skies and waters," bathing in a sun "with rays of purple brightness." Colors are also eloquent of life and flesh— and he was very fond of flesh pinks born of the union between brightness and blood. In all these respects, he was an Impressionist, harking back to Watteau and Fragonard by way of Renoir, as well as by his obsession with light, color, and water. He found and worshiped these qualities in mother-of-pearl, a prism within which light becomes chromatic scale, in the nacreous light of Flanders' sea and sky, and in seashells, all reflected in the sensuous nacreous colors of *Siren, Gardens of Love,* and the last *Gestures of Nymphs.*

But Ensor was also a Symbolist. He was not fascinated by the mirages of light just because of their color complexity and variety, as the Impressionists were, but because every spectacle conceals its hidden truth, which does not lie in the appearance but in the soul that it expresses. A whole primer of Symbolism could be made up from statements scattered throughout his writings. "In former times, before I appeared, painting gratified primarily the senses of touch and taste," but now it has finally got rid of its materialism. "Triumphant sensibility is indignant; painting is becoming spiritualized; a more refined feeling is predominant.... Today rhythms swing, musical nuances sustain painting.... I prefer a picture when it speaks to me musically." What he likes even more is the fact that "between the appearance and the substance of things the discord remains profound."

Before giving full rein to light in outdoor paintings, Ensor—an intimist before Bonnard and Vuillard—had captured an infinite range of transitions of light in interiors crammed with fabrics, as in his *Salon bourgeois,* which served as his first pictorial theater. Even then he was abandoning the pursuit of light the better to sneak up on its other half—shadow— where invisible presences lurk. *Russian Music* shows a room full of draperies, thick-figured rugs, and Oriental vases; amid shadows steeped in reverie, a lady whose face is hidden plays the piano. Shadows are full of mystery in *Dark Woman*; the figure is shown seated with her back to the light, her face impenetrable, her arms crossed; also in *Waiting*, where we see a woman (is she the same woman as before, only now dressed in white?) next to a door opening on the void of the outside world. Shadows are steeped in anguish in *Lady in Distress*, where the figure sinks like a dead body into the insidiously soft couch, behind curtains. And yet, the date is only 1882. The following year, masks come in through the open door in *Scandalized Masks*; they will, from now on, take irrevocable possession of this world shut off from the rest of the world, yet wide open to inner depths. Henceforward, they will fill it with their cluckings and their sneers. Old rags thrown on the floor, they rear up suddenly like snakes, become animated, wag their heads, and hover in mid-air, false bodies surmounted by false faces. Or perhaps they are as hollow of life as the skulls alongside them, no less frozen in grimace, no less sardonic (Colorplate II and Fig. 71).

ENSOR IN THE KINGDOM OF MASKS AND INSECTS.   Is this some sort of show or carnival, these mocking works perpetrated by a pink-faced, white-haired jack-o'-lantern who actually survived into the middle of this century, never having stopped exploring the lands of "Tetasia, Cracozia, Phoosia, Caramelia, Mirandolia, Parabolia, Boudinia,

*Monsters and devils jeer at reality and God alike.*

**72. -** *ENSOR.* THE DEVILS DZITS AND HIHANOX LEADING CHRIST TO HELL. 1895. Engraving.
Bibliothèque Royale, Brussels

Grommelia.... The country made of dreams and multiform, multicolored enchantments"?
"Serious and pleasant trips," he called his expeditions. Pleasant? Yes, certainly. "I have
joyfully confined myself to the lonely country of banter, where the mask is king, all
violence, light, and brilliance." But they are serious, too. For if he laughed, ironized, and
mocked, if, in his strange country, he defied the yokels and ridiculed the pedants, he knew
very well that the nods and becks had to be engaging if they were to tame real monsters
closer to home, from whose actual presence he suffered greatly.

The painter of suffering masks, he exposed himself to long encounters with these tor-
menting inhuman companions of his solitude, and he engaged in long and lonely dialogues
with them. They were his familiars, his "guardian devils" (the term is revealing!). They
kindled his verve and they became his obsession. The rattling skeletons, sly masks, devils,
and demons that he portrayed in an engraving of 1895 as "harassing him" sometimes
surged up inside him to a hallucinating degree. He made up dreams and sometimes

148

succumbed to their obsessive presence, whereas, on other occasions, he escaped them by a sneering somersault, his laughter breaking through the threatening compulsions (Fig. 75).

Does this give us a complete definition of Ensor? Into the twin crucibles of Impressionism and Symbolism he threw a nature in which macabre Anglo-Saxon humor (inherited from his father) mingled with damn-all Flemish truculence (inherited from his mother). He gave this mixture shape in his own native surroundings—in Ostend, where sea and sky unfold and blend their bright, iridescent lights. Is this all there was to Ensor? Yes—all that Ensor has left to history, the better to escape from it—the cloak of contingencies he allowed the clutching hands of history to seize, the better to leave himself naked, reduced to his own resources, a latter-day Joseph.

For if Symbolism tried so hard to convince us of the presence of the unknown and the invisible, this was because they really do exist, and in every individual soul. It remains now to try to penetrate them.

Every great artist, as we have said, discloses to the observer who picks his way through

*Ensor's broken, vermicular line suggests the slow corrosive action of a worm.*

**73.** - *ENSOR.* CATACLYSMS. 1888. Engraving on zinc. Bibliothèque Royale, Brussels

the diverse elements of a life's work certain constants—or *leitmotivs*—that appear in many embodiments, that recur in matters of inspiration as well as in those of execution, in the choice of subjects as well as in the choice of color harmonies. They are elusive, capable of pronounced changes as well as of subtle modulations; however, in the course of their avatars they disclose a mysterious invariant that persists despite all transformations and is reborn in every aspect of the artist's creation, material or spiritual. This constant which provides us with indefinable and yet manifest—sometimes even obsessive—meanings (both of the works and of the artist's inner being) is what we are left at the close of every analysis. Whether we study a cross section of all the manifestations of a given artist's personality or a longitudinal section of his career, this constant is always there, an irritating key to his genius, the supreme reason for his being.

Drawing or graphism provides one important clue. Apart from what the lines represent, they form a strange labyrinth whose character discloses analogies with the spirit that thus inspired the artist and his themes. Over the course of his career, Ensor's line became more and more legible and dominant in his paintings. At first he painted in *impasto*, and, later, in thinly applied color, almost a kind of wash. However, his line asserts its special character most clearly in his graphic work, which is quite as important as his work in oils. Whether we are dealing with fantasies or with landscapes, where a sharp needle analyzes the stones, leaves, masts, and skies of Flanders, his line always evokes the scratching of a tiny clawlike paw. There are hatchings, dotted lines, and vermicular curves suggesting the wavy, over-elaborate track of a worm gnawing its way through old wood or the meticulous labor of some gnawing insect's mandibles. "Singular insects" is a phrase he often used when describing a picture "dear to insectophyles" *(sic)* or one that evokes "the hard shells that harbor soft beasts." In one of his drypoints we find again this phrase, now applied to a singular insect that could be one of Kafka's characters. Another engraving shows his "animalized friends" in the guise of scarabs or locusts. In one corner of *Terrible Archer*, he shows a man with pincers, crawling like a crab. His line, which sometimes suggests the threading of a screw, attacks the classical conception of line as defining form; he either erodes it, reducing it to a vibrating, dusty haze, or makes it wavy, tormented, and twisted. In this way, he captures the spirit of the Impressionist revolution more fully than the Impressionists ever did. What they accomplished by their breaking up of the brush stroke into vibrations of colored light—the dissolution of form—he completed by reintroducing line, but distorting it, robbing it of its sharpness and plastic power, overelaborating it, twisting it, warping it. His line wriggles and fidgets like the waters of some narrow mountain stream (Figs. 73 and 74).

ATTACK ON THE TRADITION OF THE WEST.   We find the same qualities in Ensor's ideas. At the close of the humanistic period that had, for so long, shaped Western culture, he was as unable to keep from disintegrating man and the moral personality as he was unable to keep from disintegrating form. He subjects man to the same crumbling, sarcastic treatment. Sometimes, he reduces him to caricatural types—ridiculous, grimacing—replacing the human figure with dehumanized monstrous masks. At other times, he annihilates individual man, portraying him as swallowed up in crowds. The obsession with crawling, wriggling life that his graphism discloses appears also in those astonishing

II - *ENSOR*
LADY IN DISTRESS
Musée d'Art Moderne de la Ville de Paris

visions where the figures are not only frozen stiff in the distortions of their vices, but are, at the same time, lost in a collective torrent that sweeps them in a confused mass. This is what we see in *The Cathedral*; there is the same torrential catching up or dispersion of the human individual in *Capture of a Strange City*, *The Roman Triumph*, *The Battle of the Golden Spur*, and, above all, in the brilliant, bombastic *Entry of Christ into Brussels*. Outdoing Bruegel, Ensor pulverizes crowds of people so that they become anonymous legions, animated particles of dust, insect swarms.

His imagination invades the inner life and disintegrates those solid, clearcut forms on which all rational order is based, ripping them open to reveal their eroded worm-eaten substance. His irony, like his line, undermines and hollows out the human form, dislocates it, caricatures it, assailing "the constituted bodies: justice, the medical profession...." He jeers at it with his masks, frozen and sardonic travesties with empty eyes and no insides. Like Rouault—though long before him—he portrays human failings, but his human figures are terrifying only in their inanity; eyes wide open, they stare at you stupidly, and an insidiously gentle breeze, redolent of madness and nothingness, whips around the empty eye sockets.

Norms and rules, physical and spiritual conceptions of beauty alike, are all assailed to the accompaniment of the same choked laughter. Spiritual depravities vie with one another in the faces of Ensor's puppets, who are so much less real than the vices that they act out. Only thanks to the latter do they have some semblance of life. Ensor made two engravings entitled *The Deadly Sins*, and he never missed an opportunity to conjure up devils, imps, and horned demons, as in his *Sabbath*. He is fascinated with impurity and profanation even as he acts the buffoon, makes private jokes, and indulges in schoolboy satire. He really succumbs to temptation, giving in to the attractions of the lower depths. Ensor rediscovered themes treated centuries earlier by Bosch and Callot, two artists with whom he had strange, secret affinities.

To begin, there is his scatological vein. As though the *Stools of Darius* were not enough, we also have the male figure relieving himself against a wall on which has been scrawled, "Ensor is a madman." Ten years later, we get *The Scavenger* (Nordic humor can sometimes be obscene without being malicious). But more recurrent, more obsessive, slipping in wherever the occasion permits—as in teeming crowd scenes—is what the psychoanalysts pedantically call "the anal complex."

In Ensor there is also something rather more disturbing, more serious than his indulgence in dirty jokes. As in Bosch, there is an unconscious tendency to invoke Christ only in order to surround him with the threat of grotesque or dramatic profanations. For one *Adoration of the Shepherds*, he produced countless versions of Christ in Hell, Christ exposed to insults, Christ flogged, in pain, tempted by the Devil, struggling against a storm, etc. As late as 1920, in *The Holy Ghost Descending upon the Apostles*, the religious subject is transformed by his pencil into the broadest possible parody. Bosch and Bruegel had portrayed struggles between angels and demons, and Bosch had rather tended to ignore Paradise in order to devote himself to its counterpart, Hell; he excluded it altogether from his *Last Judgment of the Damned*. Ensor went further, and, obviously, took pleasure in portraying the messengers of evil triumphant, for instance in *Devils Thrashing Angels and Archangels* (Fig. 72).

But Ensor was not content with blasphemy; this obsessed prankster went on to the pleasures of destruction. He frankly celebrated the true, the ultimate wrecker, the only one who

151

need not tear off his mask (for Death's sneering skull needs no mask). And yet it was in a jeering, bantering spirit that Ensor confronted death. He painted himself as a skeleton "in the year 1960," and also anticipated death in a macabre self-portrait where his remains are seen turning to dust. In *Game of Human Pins* he is using a skull instead of a bowling ball. Also the artist has Death take part in a dance of masks, attired in bizarre rags or wearing a motley hat. He portrayed skeletons trying to warm themselves grouped around a stove. In the hideous *Revenge of Hop Frog*, the charred and shriveled corpse on the ground portrays man as returned to the insect stage of evolution. Everywhere, Death is more and more often, more and more openly, evoked. Its wings enfold the final chorus of *The Deadly Sins*. In *Cataclysms* it sweeps away the human insects (again!). In the *Exterminating Angel*, in *Death Pursuing the Human Herd*, in *King Plague* (a theme borrowed from Edgar Allan Poe), he multiplies the masks of the omnipresent Azrael. *Peste dessous, peste dessus, peste partout*, proclaims one of his engravings with sarcastic self-confidence.

On the margin of one drawing he made of a sleeping woman, Ensor wrote, "Make a face." And yet his fantastic art is never arbitrary; it is a deliberate, constant, unleashed

*Human beings, including Ensor himself, are metamorphosed into insects.*

**74.** - *ENSOR.* THE SINGULAR INSECTS (ENSOR AND MADAME ROUSSEAU). 1888. Engraving.
Bibliothèque Royale, Brussels

*Two great wreckers—death and laughter.*

**75. -** *ENSOR.* PIERROT AND SKELETON IN YELLOW GOWN or DEATH AND MASKS. 1893.
Collection Madame de Lange, Antwerp

fantasy that takes on seriousness only when confronted with the beauty of *things*. It becomes burlesque the moment *man* is involved. This is one of the keys to Ensor's art, to his unconscious aims and instinctive methods. This artist who, for so long, has enjoyed only a minor reputation, actually played a major part in the vast intellectual and spiritual movement that, at the end of the nineteenth century, began to drive out the Classical and Latin spirit from its comfortable, traditional, academic home. It remained for the twentieth century to complete this process—to move in for the kill.

Grafted onto an Impressionism that, for all its realism, went beyond the traditional "rational" vision, and stimulated by a Symbolism that condemned positivistic science and glimpsed vast territories extending beyond sensorially, rationally grasped reality—the still virgin lands that Odilon Redon was exploring in France, though still imbued with Classical *noblesse*—the art of Ensor recklessly smashed the Pandora's box of objective reality. He let loose the heady fumes of an imagination inspired by unconscious forces. Pandora? He would no doubt have preferred the less ancient image of Asmodeus—the devil who was locked up in a bottle.

He advanced the dissolution of line in his complex, effervescent handwriting, and, also, the dissolution of the human figure, which he submerged in crowds, froze, and jeered at with his masks. He advanced the dissolution of rational thought by continuous clownish jibes. And upon a universe so dismantled, devalued, fragmented, and waiting for a new order, he let loose Death and the Devil, presenting them, in contempt of the entire literature on these subjects, as a circus turn, brought on to the accompaniment of a brass band and the roars of good-natured, hearty Flemish laughter.

The laughter is reassuring. And yet, under cover of it, Ensor is no less a member of the generation which witnessed the birth of the twentieth century and which—from Huysmans through Jean Lorrain, Barrès, and Proust—flirted with preciosity and ambiguity, sometimes with evil and perversion, always with death. Freer than others from the stranglehold of Classical culture and Latin blood, he signals, with greater deliberation and intensity than his contemporaries, the revolution already occurring underground—that revolution which, with Picasso on the one hand and the Surrealists on the other, was shortly to find ever more emphatic and subversive expression. The fantastic pirouettes of Ensor's imagination and the dazzling *entrechats* of his palette mark the beginning of a human transmutation that is taking place in our time, that is reshaping us and the civilization whose end products we are.

In Ensor, this transmutation still has the features of a reaction against the existing state of affairs; his laughter has a grating, sardonic quality. His generation paved the way for artists who would more spontaneously give birth to strange and colorful images, bringing up into the light of day rich trophies of explorations underground in hitherto unknown strata of the inner life.

CHAGALL, THE PLAYBOY OF THE EASTERN WORLD. Chagall indubitably provides us with the most striking single example of how the image unfolds once its resources have regained their scope and freedom. Unlike Ensor, he does not belong to the West; he was born at the gates of the East, in that baffling Russia which has scarcely been touched by Latin culture and which harbors so many mysteries. Born into the ancient Jewish people, this playboy of the Eastern world has been marvelously successful in keeping the gifts of childhood intact.

From the images of the outside world, he keeps those that can serve as vocabulary for him, those that were so firmly welded to his being in his youth that he can no longer distinguish himself from them. They became part of him in his childhood, at an age when the soul, still without a protective shell, lends itself to the delightful wounds of the unforgettable. At a very early date, he sensed that his childhood images would provide the answer to his prayers—though, at the time, he did not know that his were the artist's prayers par excellence. In his autobiography he tells us that he wandered in the streets of Vitebsk,

*Chagall conceives of painting as a piece of music.*

**76.** - *CHAGALL.* THE MUSICIAN. 1912. Stedelijk Museum, Amsterdam

praying: "O Lord who art hidden in the clouds and behind the cobbler's house, grant me that my soul reveal itself, the aching soul of a stammering boy, reveal my path to me. I do not want to be like all the others, I want to see a new world." In answer to his prayer the city begins to appear strange and wonderful to him. Its inhabitants walk in the air and are otherwise displaced. Familiar characters settle down on the roofs of the town and make themselves comfortable... (Fig. 76).

These everyday images, these signs of vision and feeling were singled out by the avid eyes of childhood, taken away from their original surroundings, and transferred to other surroundings, the surroundings of the artist's inner life. This displacement is betrayed by a recurrent feature: the force of gravity is no longer operative. Moved to another planet, the images are no longer aware of their own mass or of the earth's attraction—which, in actual fact, had subjected them to its law. At last liberated from physical circumstances that had been looked upon as constituting their essential nature, the appearances are now restored to their secret subjective meanings, obeying only the magnetic force of sensibility. They whirl about, come together, move apart, hover in the air, merge with one another, even turn upside down. The fish flies, the cow floats in the air, the people in the street do not distinguish between up and down. Meanwhile color rises like a tidal wave—flamboyant, like the filament of a bulb released from the vacuum in which it has been kept, now suddenly consumed in one supreme flash of iridescence.

Some of these images evoke actual personal memories. The child has pressed to his heart "the big-bellied cow," the clock that swings along with its pendulum, the lamp and the violin, the isba and the golden bulb, the moon and the night sky. From adolescence survives the way his fiancée looked in her white gown, hair as black as her gloves, eyes lost in a reverie of love—the embracing couples gliding through space, even outside space, as pleasantly and dizzily as comets. And of the traveler who is subsequently to discover France and the Impressionists there survives the fragrance of flowers and light (Fig. 78).

But all this is joined and jostled by images that have emerged from within to open like water lilies on the surface of consciousness. These are not so much striking as haunting, obsessive images nurtured on the inner juices of the soul. In fact, they are almost the same as the others, for the choice made by memory was dictated by inner needs no less than the gambits of the imagination. Chagall's dreams are hand and glove with his recollections.

Light when it passes through a prism takes on colors derived from it, and yet it comes from far away. Similarly, Chagall's inner needs come from far away; they arise out of time immemorial. To these images—of which Chagall believes himself to be the master or at least the inventor—they dictate the message of eternal and universal humanity. Psychoanalysis has learned to decipher them: it would demonstrate that the cow and the obsession with the foetus or egg gloriously visible through the belly, as well as the moon, are associated with the haunting memory of his mother, for whom Chagall has an indelible love. It would explain to us why the horse and the rooster, from time immemorial associated with the Beyond, here recur so frequently around the figure of Bella since she died.

Like those of his figures obsessed with reversibility, the visible world teeters and turns upside down in Chagall, sliding into his own inner depths. "Time is a river without banks," he has written. And yet the river of life flows between the banks of reality; from

*The whole of Chagall's childhood with its dreams slumbers in his imagination, like the dead awaiting resurrection.*

**77.** - *CHAGALL.* THE JEWISH CEMETERY. 1917. Private collection

them we borrow such images as we ever reflect, but at the same time we make them convey the very movements of our inner nature.

"Art seems to me primarily a state of mind," as Chagall himself put it *(My Life)*.

★

★ ★

The foregoing discussion suggests the possibility of a method of investigating works of art perhaps capable of yielding richer results than the analysis of dreams, since it would be applied to exceptional personalities. We have no more than indicated the possible avenues it opens to research.

Such research would have to proceed very cautiously. It is only too easy, when approaching secret and uncontrollable phenomena, to indulge in the most adventurous—and hence peremptory—hypotheses. Some of the excesses of psychoanalysis have made us only too familiar with the errors to which pigheadedness and credulity can lead. The exploration of souls requires prudence and respect, particularly when the souls in question are among the sublimest mankind has produced—those of artists and poets. Too great reliance upon keys or special lexicons, as well as a taste for shocking revelations, may lead to offenses against the spirit. A number of great writers have been subjected to such treatment because those who discussed them were less interested in understanding their essential contributions than in finding the quickest possible route to the lower depths of their sexuality.

Under the pretense of scientific ruthlessness, such investigators merely gratify their own lower instincts. Analysis of a work of art must serve the work of art, not just analysis as such.

If the work of art—or, in the broad sense, every poetic work—embodies the attempt of a soul to reveal its innermost essence and to let other men benefit from its perishable riches, the deeper and subtler psychological knowledge acquired by our epoch should be used to gain a better understanding of the language that the great creators of images and words have employed. And we must always keep in mind that this language is not just only the vehicle of a secret to be divined, but that it is dedicated to beauty—whose presence in nature and in man it seeks above all to reveal to us.

*As life goes on, memories, both past and present, crowd in upon the painter and dance to the music of art.*

**78. -** *CHAGALL.* THE CONCERT. 1957. Maeght Gallery, Paris

# PART II

# THE HUMAN MEANING
# OF ART

*The true artist has something to say in*
*addition to what is visible in drawing or*
*painting. True appreciation of art begins*
*with discovery of that "something."*
Samarandrenath Gupta

*Art has long been aware of its magic power to evoke the soul: Dosso Dossi's* Apollo *paves the way for Chagall's* Musician *(Fig. 76).*

**79. -**
*DOSSO DOSSI.*
APOLLO
AND DAPHNE.
Borghese Gallery,
Rome

*Nothing can seduce us, nothing can attract us—*
*nothing makes our ears prick up, nothing arrests our*
*glance—nothing is chosen for us among the multitude*
*of things, and nothing disturbs our soul that does not*
*in some way pre-exist in our being or is not secretly*
*expected by our nature.*

Paul Valéry (Eupalinos)

In Part I of this book we reviewed the principal means available to art for conveying the essence of human nature, for acting as its transmitting station, as it were. Everything shaped by the artist's hand becomes by the same token one of the faces of his soul. This is true of drawing, which lends itself to graphological interpretation, and of form, which is its result. It is true of light, in which form is immersed and which is the counterpart of form, sometimes even supplanting it. It is true of those children of light, the colors, which can be combined to give rise to a musical symphony. And, finally, it is true of the whole in which all these elements are united and merge, and which gives rise to the image. The latter's recurrence in every artist's guiding themes increases the suggestive, obsessive powers of art.

What are the elements of human nature that art can express? To just what extent is human nature reflected in art? A language, but a language devoid of rational structure, art comes directly into contact with human nature in an uncomplicated enough way. Our sensibility registers the contact, but our intellect remains baffled. Does art really have much more to give us than rather vague impressions? If we suspect this to be true, possibly we have not tried very hard to get more than this out of art. In Part II of this book we want to show how much more in the work of art there is to be perceived.

Theoretical demonstration is inadequate in this connection; we need specific, living examples. And, in order to verify our conclusions, we must compare what history has taught us about a given artist and his age with what works of art themselves have to tell us. For this reason, our approach is historical and our observations about a given order of psychological insight based on art will be controlled by studies of specific instances. We speak of "orders" of insight rather than of individual insights, because the work of art opens access to its creator's *total* nature. It is a mistake to destroy the given unity of art and artist—through analysis, for example—for the insights that we can obtain are richer and more varied when this unity is respected. The artist's entire inner life is expressed in his work, and it is possible to scrutinize it at every level: it reflects all his thoughts, his conceptions of art as well as of life, his philosophy as well as his unconscious instincts. Moreover, what the artist discloses is not only his individual personality, but, also, the collective soul of which he is a part, the soul of his nation as well as of his generation.

Proceeding from conscious thought to the unconscious, from collective to individual aspects, we shall try, by probing several specific cases, to reveal the full range of expression possible to this secret language whose grammar alone occupied our attention until now.

The secret of a people, its character and intellectual development, can be read in its art. The West, thanks to its Greek origins, is humanistic and rationalistic. It defines its forms for greater intellectual security. The East is caught up in the boundlessness of nature; reality is swallowed up in it along with dreams.

**80.** - Attributed to *MI FEI* (1051–1107). LANDSCAPE IN MIST. China. Wash on silk. Freer Gallery of Art, Washington, D.C. (Courtesy of the Smithsonian Institution)

**81. - *PHIDIAS*. THE ASSEMBLY OF THE GODS: POSEIDON, APOLLO, AND ARTEMIS.**
Portion of the east frieze of the Parthenon. 440–437 B.C. British Museum, London

CHAPTER I

# ART AND IDEAS

Art emanates from life—which attains its highest level of awareness in thought. We are, nonetheless, tempted to oppose thought to life: whereas thought feeds on ideas, art feeds on sensibility. And we know, only too well, how often the intrusion of thought into the domain of art—in the form of theories—has hindered its natural development.

Both come from the same source—the spirit of a man and the spirit of an age. Art translates them into images, resorting to unconscious processes; philosophy translates them into ideas, resorting to conscious thought. Inevitably, these two resulting products bear the imprint of a single origin, however they may diverge at the end, being identical with respect to initial impulses and goals. Today we are well aware of the fact that man varies and changes according to time and place, that he is constantly developing different conceptions of himself, of life, and of the world—i.e., specific new ways of thinking and feeling, reacting, and behaving. Both at the collective and at the individual level, he tries to express his specific way of thinking and feeling, not in action, merely, but in works—whether in terms of abstract theory or in terms of imaginative invention, whether in the form of a dogma, a book, or a picture. He will embody himself and his age in as many diverse forms as there are modes of expression, but each new embodiment will reveal an identical essence. Even when no reciprocal influence, no interaction among the various

163

*To the measured rhythms of the West, India opposes limitless profusion, without beginning or end.*
**82.** - LITTLE TEMPLE AT KUMBAKHOMAN, INDIA (detail of the roof)

embodiments can be detected, we are obliged to recognize that they all have a common spiritual root. I have often in the past pointed out that the theory of influences, which flatters our confidence in a mechanism of cause and effect, should be discarded in favor of a theory of deep inner affinities. It is the common task of the intellectual and of the artist to make manifest the fundamental soul that determines the face of an age, but whereas the intellectual transforms it into a *concept*, the artist supplies us with a *vision* of it. Both have the same essential meaning, and history is full of cases in point, to show how each confirms and illumines the other.

This parallelism becomes unmistakable only when we follow it up on a sufficient scale and with sufficient thoroughness to exclude the hypothesis of coincidence. Thus, we shall begin with a summary view of Western culture over the centuries, so as to bring out the constancy of the inner relationships linking art and thought, directing their development along essentially identical paths.

To be sure, to simplify is often to distort. It is not without some hesitation that we undertake to boil down to a few pages the various attitudes that human thought has adopted toward the problems presented by life and the world. But to simplify is also, perhaps, to come closer to essentials; searching out the main branches hidden among a shimmering mass of foliage, we sometimes manage to make out the trunk—the central body where realities that seem at first glance scattered and independent are in fact gathered together and directed toward a common goal.

164

EAST AND WEST.   We shall begin by asking just what our notion of a specifically Western culture stands for. Does it denote some underlying spiritual reality? Is our opposition of West to East merely a verbal convention? Specialists caught up in the ramifications of individual subjects are sometimes tempted to think so. And, yet, we are here obliged to surrender to the converging evidences of art and thought: in the East, as in the West, we discover certain fundamental tendencies that force us to acknowledge that each of these entities has a "spirit" of its own, however that spirit may have varied or even contradicted itself over the centuries. To be sure, these two spheres have been infinitely varied in time and space, yet each embodies a distinct conception of life and of the world. Each, despite innumerable vicissitudes, remains faithful to its essential nature. The two have been opposed ever since Greece imposed on the West the basic attitude it has never abandoned.

East and West have ever been in contact and have influenced each other strongly— beginning with Alexander's invasion of India, when elements of Greek anthropomorphism penetrated Buddhism. In the nineteenth century, the prestige of the East began to grow in the West, and, with Schopenhauer (among others), Germany appeared to be in the forefront of a new cultural interchange. However, such crosscurrents and confrontations must not obscure the fact that we are dealing with two radically divergent conceptions echoed by two distinct types of art, regardless of the frequency of instances of mutual influence.

This antithesis is strikingly illustrated with respect to the crucial distinction between the inner world and the outer world, and the nature of the relations between them. The West sees each of these worlds as autonomous and immutable: autonomous in the sense that they are separate and opposed; immutable in the sense that each is defined by what makes it permanent. In the life of the mind and the sensibility, the West regards the I as the center of gravity; in the outer world, it gives primacy to matter in space, to concrete reality. Furthermore, Western thought is primarily concerned with laws of structure, i.e., with the principles of constancy governing each of the two worlds—the inner world being governed by reason, the outer world by form. On the basis of these rigorous definitions, the West stresses the incompatibility between the two worlds. The I, armed with intellect, is opposed to the physical universe; the I is at the same time enjoined to observe it with its senses, to explore it with its ideas, to bend it to its logic, the better to act lucidly upon it.

However, in thus setting up two different powers face to face, in making them partners and, occasionally, adversaries, the West links them in its thinking. It assumes a unity between the two, were it only the unity of opposing sides in the same battle. Thus, it shows them as somehow attuned to each other, postulating between them a similarity of scale, an analogue, since it assumes that the world can be understood and mastered by rules inherent in the human mind. Moreover, a kind of affinity is postulated between the stability of matter, defined by its forms, and the permanence of rational laws. This entails a most important consequence: it dispels our two major fears—that of being lost in an incommensurable infinity, and that of being cast out into the instability and eternal transiency of time. Thus the West asserts and reassures the human condition.

The East, on the other hand, does not base the relations between the world and man on any so sharp a distinction, however attenuated in the end by mediating links of intelligent action. Because it aims at objectivity, Western knowledge requires things to be viewed from a certain distance; the East often prefers to think of all things as in essential union or fusion; to intellectual method it prefers the impulse of love. In the fifteenth cen-

165

tury, Kabir, the Indian disciple of Ramanand, said, "The outer and the inner world are mad eto be an indivisible unit." And G. Gaillart has concluded, "Asia tended to know the world by identifying itself with it." In the East, as it seems to us, everything is turned upside down—the artist's vision as well as the thinker's conception.

India shows this most clearly. It divests the inner and the outer world of just those basic features to which the West reduces them—the autonomy of the I and the reality of concrete appearances. This is enough to bring them together and amalgamate them. But the East carries this principle of their essential identity still further, making it explicit in a conception of universal life. This life is to be discovered in the innermost depths of individual human beings, lying underneath the personal self. Indeed, it is to be discovered everywhere in the depths of nature, once we have got beyond the deceptive curtain of illusion (Maya) with which material appearances disguise this essential nature. Thus the goal of Eastern thought is a return to primordial unity rather than the forging of links between two disparate worlds. In effect it is a flat negation or rejection of the Western view of the human condition.

In the sixth century B.C., Buddha proclaimed the abolition of the categories of the inner and outer. "For him alone who has disappeared, who has become extinct, ungraspable, there is no form any longer." The I has given way to the universal self, the *atman*; the mirage of the physical world has been dissipated, and all that is left is the unfolding ocean of life, the *samsara*. "The perfect experience in which subject and object become identical," as Coomaraswamy has written in our own day, is thus effected. Brahmanism, Buddhism, and Jainism all reflect this conviction. Logically, we should have expected the arts in India to have been limited to music—and music did, in fact, attain a high degree of development there. Moreover, the plastic arts were for some time suspected of being impure. In the Middle Ages, Vishnuism modified the terms of the problem by acknowledging that the universe is not a mere phantasm, but a manifestation of the divine. Earlier it had been recognized that the artist's effort to make visible the motif of his inner concentration was a valid technical method for achieving his spiritual goal, a true *yoga*. However, as Cakracarya observed in the Gupta period, the artist must "constitute images of the divinities he venerates according to his inner vision... not from direct observation." Thus the eye, which in the West lingers complacently at the threshold of external appearances, is no more than an instrument in an effort to communicate with the profound truth they hide; its function is to achieve a kind of symbiosis between the artist and what is essentially divine in the universe (Fig. 80).

It is not enough that this result should be achieved by the artist; the viewer too must achieve it, by an analogous process. And when he does, says Panshadasi, "the object seen by our eyes is felt by our mind." In other words, art has no descriptive value, but only a suggestive one; figuration of visible appearances is not permissible, save as a mode of perceiving and communicating the invisible. This requires "the power of suggestion" invoked by Mammata Bhata. Is not the Indian *sadharana*, an anticipation of the *Einfühlung* that was not discovered until the nineteenth century by German theoreticians, a variety of revelation imparted uniquely by the methods of art? Incidentally, it is also the basis of the Hindu theater.

It is not very different from the aesthetics developed by the Chinese, of whom Henri Berr said that "it does not occur to them to oppose subject and object; the two are inseparable to them." Like the Indians in the same sixth century B.C., the Chinese who had followed Lao-tse in going beyond the I and physical appearances went on to make an explicit search for "the unnamed, for being," for "the breath that mingles with that of the universe," for that vital spirit which is the foundation of the Chinese Tao as of the Indian *atman*. Hsieh Ho, critic and portraitist, who, at the end of the fifth century, formulated "the six principles of painting" (before the thirteenth century, the Hindu Jashodara also recognized six principles of painting, which are not without analogy to the Chinese), gave first place to "rhythmic vitality." The artist must discover it in nature and identify it with his own feelings. This teaching has been respected over the centuries, down to our own day. Similarly, Chinese artists resort to suggestion in order to reach the viewer, in keeping with the spirit of their calligraphy which, as Marcel Granet has observed, does not so much aim at recording ideas as at expressing emotional attitudes. For this reason, China, like India, feels that representation is independent of literal appearance: Chinese painting has taken the greatest liberties with the categories of time and space and has neglected the I, in order to pursue and attain being. This tendency, which the introduction of Buddhism to China in the first century assisted, was given particular emphasis during the T'ang and Sung dynasties when the genre of the scholarly landscape was developed. It marked the triumph of Hsieh Ho's principle that forms should be simplified to become primarily evocative. It is well known that Chinese painting of this type had an enormous influence upon the Japanese painting of later times.

Thus, the art of the East ignores well-defined forms no less than it ignores the I. The artist does not aim at originality, but, rather, applies principles and rules of long-standing authority. (In India these take the form of recipe books, covering both iconographic and plastic formulas.) He feels that he is an instrument of communication between mankind and the irrational life of the universe. For this reason, he is also driven to renounce the formal definitions so dear to the plastic arts of the West. He never reduced his work to a self-evident unity: fluid life and its endless rhythm always win out. The scenes depicted on the walls at Ajanta follow one another in unbroken development, much as the speech of India consists of continuous sentences rather than words. There are analogies, as well, with the doctrine of the transmigration of souls. It has been observed, very justly, that the Indian proportions, the *shastras*, are not based on arithmetical (i.e., static) symmetries, as in the West, but on geometric (i.e., dynamic) symmetries. The flux of life sweeps individual man along and tolerates neither a sense of his completeness in himself nor artificial divisions in his portrayals of it. Much the same may be said of the scenes that unfold interminably in superimposed relief bands executed in China as early as the third century, during the Han dynasty. And then there are the Chinese scrolls where the brush runs on for yards. These influenced the Japanese *kakemonos*. Just as Chinese artists dislike being confined by special limitations—and have nothing like our all-pervading sense of the picture "frame"—so they also dislike delimitation in time. Serge Elisséev has shown that, in Chinese portraits, "the expression of the right eye preceded... that of the left eye, and the line of the mouth showed expression at still a third moment." Moreover, this is done without loss of harmony (Fig. 82).

This principle of unity shared by the peoples of the Orient must not obscure undeniable differences. India, in quest of extrahuman perfection, turned its back on the human condition (as we understand it) and let itself be swept away in an immense, nameless ocean of infinity. In consequence, China and Japan are closer to us—Japan to the greater extent—because they are closer to everyday life. They seem never to have desired to abolish themselves, to emulate smoke, which spreads and dissolves in the air. They remain aware—Confucian China, especially—of the existence of organized society and are attached to its traditions and principles of order. China is more interested in morals than in mysticism or even metaphysics; her sensibility never becomes wholly detached from pleasure in concrete experiences, however subtly she may refine them in her art. In this respect, she is doubly positivist and shows affinities with the West—just as in Europe the German spirit often suggests affinities with the dreams of Asia.

ANTIQUITY: THE CONCEPT OF BEAUTY.   Unlike the East, which aspires to a universal life conceived as beyond man's natural limits, the West distrusts it. Western man sees it as a current that threatens to carry him off or swallow him up, as a perturbing force the effects of which he must neutralize. To escape from this infinite mobility, this boundless complexity, to tower above it, he seeks refuge in himself—the sole principle of beauty that he experiences directly. From Greek civilization onward, he has regarded himself as the basis and standard of truth, looking upon his sensations as accurate perceptions of reality, upon the fundamental rules of thought as conforming to the laws of nature and the structure of the universe. Similarly, he regards the forms and proportions of his body as units of the same universe scaled down to his own dimensions. "Man is the measure of all things," proclaims Protagoras of Abdera, a contemporary of Socrates. And Plato's Philebus asserts that, "in all things, measure and proportion constitute beauty as well as virtue." Never before had man felt, as he did in Greece, that nature was built to his scale and measure. Never before had he perceived, between himself and nature, the existence of a reciprocal accord or—still more explicitly—a harmony. In Greece, the image of man became the essential content of all representations, just as it was the unit of measurement of all edifices. The East sought to go behind appearances in order to rediscover the mystery of being; in Greece appearances were subjected to the laws of human reason, sole source of truth, and became the foundations of reality. The supreme rule of the West—objectivity and abstraction—was now formulated. The etymology of these words (ob-jacere, ab-trahere) clearly implies man's effort to make a distinction between himself and things, with a view to preserving his own unity. In the East, by contrast, man sought to become immersed in the all. Twenty-five centuries later, modern science was still respecting this founding principle of Western thought, although in the interval it had been modified in many ways.

The Greeks applied the same basic principles in their religion, their philosophy, and their art. In imagining their gods, they started from man, from his known constitution. In attempting to understand reality, they proceeded from facts to ideas. In creating beauty, they proceeded from nature to the ideal. In every case, the effort of the mind was to clarify a concrete datum perceived by the senses. This is the very opposite of what we observe in the East, which takes its point of departure in a divinity conceived as inaccessible to mankind as such and which strives to catch some faint glimpse of the divine through the veil of perceivable reality. Hegel saw very clearly to what extent Christianity—in which God is made man—differed from the anthropomorphic religions, thereby revealing its Oriental provenance. The iconoclastic controversies that shook early Christianity were Eastern in their origins.

Greek thought is so rich, so complex, that every conceivable contradiction may be

*In Classical Greece, forms are as sharp and clear as ideas; they are firmly outlined.*

**83.** - ATHENA (detail of a metope from the Temple of Zeus at Olympia:
ATHENA RECEIVING THE BIRDS OF THE STYMPHALOS LAKE FROM HERACLES).
470–455 B.C. The Louvre, Paris

found in it, but its dominant features are unmistakable. They are found everywhere in
Greek art—in the proportions of the Parthenon no less than in a marble statue by Phidias.
A balanced mixture of realism and idealism—of that objectivity and abstraction we
stressed above—it formulates the fundamental aesthetic principle of the West: to extract
beauty from nature—nature being the raw material in which beauty is latent—to release
beauty by processing this raw material with the help of the intellect (Fig. 81).

In the greatest period of Greek art, the fifth century, Plato's philosophy admirably systematized this view. He distinguished the material world perceived by our senses, where everything is continuous transformation—i.e., the world of illusion[1] or nonbeing—from the world of ideas, the home of the absolute, divine and immutable. Animated by Eros, the power of love, and by inspiration, the artist will take his cues from the nature that alone is visible, but he will imprint upon her the idea of the beautiful, which is unknowable in essence and which can be perceived only insofar as it is reflected in beings and things.

A seed of degeneration is contained in this doctrine: a desire to enclose the secret of the idea in theories, formulas, or even recipes, to codify it by the intellect. This facile oversimplification, which freezes creativity, is given a name derived from the very name of Plato's school—academism. But Plato, as though trying to forestall this eventual deviation, insisted that the beautiful is never ready-made, neither in nature nor in its rational principle. It "has no sensory forms," we read in the *Symposium*. In the *Phaedrus*, Socrates says, "He who without the divine madness comes to the door of the Muses, confident that he will be a good poet by art, meets with no success, and the poetry of the sane man vanishes into nothingness before that of inspired madness." [Trans. by Harold N. Fowler, The Loeb Classical Library.] That the gift of inspiration is indispensable was also stressed in the *Ion*: "The poet cannot begin to create before the god has entered him."

And yet it was very tempting to demand of reason a formula for the beautiful. Plato was really suggesting such a formula when he recognized the beautiful in certain geometric figures, such as the cube, the octahedron, etc. Because of their genius for abstraction the Greeks were seduced by the prestige of mathematical formulations, and, as early as the sixth century B.C., Pythagoras proclaimed, "Number is the essence of things." It is true that early in the sixth century, Heraclitus—who, significantly, was born in Asia Minor—had emphasized how the world, like the tides, is borne by a dizzy and incessant transformation. But the Greeks felt at home only in the defined and the definitive; they were tempted to enclose harmony in numerical relations, and originated the famous Golden Section which, based on ideal proportions of the human body, determined its measurements. The notion of the Golden Section leaped across the Middle Ages and Gothic architecture to haunt the Renaissance. Early in the sixteenth century, Fra Luca Pacioli devoted to it his treatise *De divina proportione*, which Leonardo da Vinci and Dürer both studied. Still later, it was revived by aestheticians of Cubism.

Directly opposed to this approach to art, which leads from the ideal to the formula, is the approach that leads to literal realism, to naturalism (academism's opposite number). Since ancient Greece, the West has always been torn between these two temptations. As Greek art declined, the sense of quality grew weaker, and closer and closer imitation of reality dulled art. Only superior minds such as Plato's were aware of the importance of a sense of the poetic and of the crucial role of creative inspiration. A Western tendency to action, to the mastering of immediate obstacles, furthered the confusion between art and technical skill. This confusion is illustrated in the famous anecdote about Zeuxis—a painter active at the end of the fifth century—who painted grapes so realistically that birds tried to nibble at them. A similar anecdote about Apelles tells us that Alexander's horse neighed in recognition when he was led up to Alexander's portrait—it was so lifelike! The

---

[1] It should be noted that Plato calls it "the world of illusion" for reasons diametrically opposed to those of Indian philosophy: it is illusion not because it conceals a life that eludes all form, but because it is tainted by the confusion and mobility of life.

As Greek art grew older it sacrificed the primordial notion of the idea to sensorial realism; with concern for details, it became naturalistic.

**84.** - YOUNG SATYR BACK FROM THE HUNT. Hellenistic relief. The Louvre, Paris

same confusion afflicted sculpture. There is a short poem that says, "Shepherd, let your herd graze farther away, lest, imagining that Myron's cow is breathing, you take it for one of yours."

The philosophy of Aristotle is symptomatic of this development. Aristotle discards the divine principle asserted by Plato. He excludes the universality of the idea and takes us back to the particularity of the sensation and its findings. Sensation it is that brings the artist into contact with nature, and not even the imagination itself is opposed to empirical reality, since it feeds on the residues of sensation. As a result, *mimesis* or imitation takes on greater importance. The idea of experience becomes dominant.

As the idea lost its absolute value and an empirical realism gained ground, the role of sensibility and the emotions took on increasingly greater importance. Aristotle stressed the function of catharsis, a ridding oneself of one's feelings by expressing them. Thus the way was opened to pathos, which is at odds with the perfectionism of abstract serenity (Fig. 85).

These developments were confirmed by the last product of Classic Greek art, in the fourth-century works of Scopas. Incidentally, after Alexander the principal centers of Greek art moved to the Hellenistic cities of Pergamum in Asia Minor, to Rhodes and Tralles. The Gigantomachy, the Laocoön, and the Torso from Belvedere proclaim an increasingly affected and brutal realism tending to colossal and dramatic effects.

Rome, the heir to Greek culture, did not fail to accentuate this regression from idealism toward naturalism and academism. In Roman art, abstract purity faded away. Whereas Greek architecture had been based on rigorous straight lines, Rome took pleasure in the curve, derived from "irrational" numbers. Similarly, in the figurative arts, a color that appeals to the senses took the place previously occupied by the purely intelligible perfection of line. Lionello Venturi justly stressed the significance of the following clear-sighted text by Dionysius of Halicarnassus, dating from the first century A.D.: "The old paintings had a very simple coloring and presented no variety of tones, but line was always perfect in its correctness.... Later on, purity of line decreased, and this was compensated for by more elaborate execution and a more lively mixture of lights and shadows, together with every resource of a rich coloring, to which the new paintings owed their vigor and splendor."

The eclipse of ancient thought had begun. Rome paved the way for the barbarians, whose art aimed at elementary physical effects and impact upon the sensibility.

THE CHRISTIAN EPOCH: IMMATERIAL BEAUTY. This development was inevitable: the Greek genius, robbed of its national basis after Rome conquered it, was scattered all over the shores of the Mediterranean and was often brought into close contact with the East. The specifically Roman genius was diluted in the immense *orbis terrarum* and everywhere became saturated with Oriental and barbarian elements. Classical antiquity, which had concentrated upon lucidity and had limited "feeling" to the domain of the senses associated with reason, was discovering a domain of existence that eludes both the eye and the mind. It is situated beyond the reach of man's normal means, and there the ineffable is king. Only mysticism can give access to this domain, and it can only be expressed in the language of images, whose symbolic power goes beyond the clarity of words and ideas. Now the ancient world began to be invaded by religions coming from the East. From Egypt, Roman mystagogues received the cult of Isis and Osiris; from distant Persia, that of Mithra; from the eastern shores of the Mediterranean, the most revolutionary revelation of them all—Christianity (Fig. 86).

What a transformation! From the perceivable, empirical, human world, the soul was launched upon a pursuit of the ineffable, the divine, the immaterial. It was now to seek "the invisible, ungraspable being" mentioned by Dion Chrysostomus as early as the first century, which, "since we have no model," cannot be expressed by means of a visible and sensory material," but only "by means of a symbol." The earliest Christian art, for reasons both external and internal, consists of no more than a schematic language in which allusion takes the place of imitation.

However, Plato's thought was not dead; nascent Christianity interpreted it in its own way, concentrating on the antithesis between the nonbeing of appearance and the absolute world of ideas where dwells pure beauty, inexpressible as such. There Christianity found the mold into which it could pour its preoccupations. This was accomplished by Neoplatonism, which, under the aegis of Plotinus in the third century, effected the transition from ancient to medieval thought. This took place in Alexandria, the ancient crucible where the West fused with the East. Even though the work of art may still give us "the representation and image of a thing," we must replace "the eyes of the body" with "the inner eye." As Plato had seen, the material world is nonbeing, absence of being—and being alone is real. To attain to being, "intellectual vision" must transcend not only sensory vision but also rational thought—"discursive thought." Through "contemplation," it will merge with its object and become identical with it. This was the movement that Plotinus demanded of the mind, which he would have guided by means of "enthusiasm, self-abandonment, rapture" toward pursuit of "the ineffable and indescribable vision," of an "ecstasy" where it would be united with the One, with God. Clearly, Neoplatonism colored Plato's legacy with Eastern thought.

The Neoplatonic current soon flowed into the Christian current, providing the Church with a mystical doctrine. Toward the fifth century, the Pseudo-Areopagite celebrated "the darkness" that "floods the souls, who have no eyes, with marvelous splendors." This anticipates "the night of the senses" and "the dark night of the soul," which Christian mysticism, with St. John of the Cross, was to proclaim as prerequisite to the perfect experience of union with God. Reality and reason can now alike be dispensed with, for, according to the Pseudo-Areopagite, we must "completely transcend the senses and the intellect."

Thus, the problem of art was reversed. It had become indifferent to appearances, to veracity, and to logical elaboration; its aim now was to give the soul access to the divine. This sums up Byzantine art in a nutshell. Realism gave way to abstraction, rationality to suggestion. André Grabar has shown how Byzantine art, in keeping with the new conception of the world, ignores the logical laws governing the rendering of nature—relief, perspective, imitation—replacing all these with elements capable of striking the soul, stirring it, and exalting it via the senses. Color in all its splendor, sumptuous materials like gold, and—above all—light dazzle the eye as a mystical reflection of Godhead. Meanwhile, forms are schematized, in keeping with a set of accepted conventions and stereotyped iconographic principles (Colorplate XI).

In the West, this new vision was grafted onto the legacy of barbarian art. The latter provided a perfect vehicle. It was based, on the one hand, on an exploitation of rich glowing materials such as gold, and translucid materials such as jewels. Their violent impact on the senses, even in an unworked state, was much appreciated. On the other hand, barbarian art was based on the exploitation of forms schematized to the point of abstraction, and these were appreciated for their memory-assisting value. As soon as Christianity breathed its sense of the spiritual into this art, we find successively Merovingian jewelry, the jewelry of the early Middle Ages, and the flowering of Irish miniature painting, with its Celtic traceries. Even Romanesque sculpture was to show the mark of daring stylizations.

THE DUALITY OF THE MIDDLE AGES.  The history of the Middle Ages is that of the formation of a homogeneous thought and art out of discordant elements that had begun to clash with one another. It is the history of the transition from Mediterranean to

*The Romans, practical-minded and direct, were fond of anecdotal portraits. In this one, the eyes are disproportionately large. This is a symptom of the Eastern influence and the spiritual crisis in the background of the rise of Christianity.*

**86.** - FIGURE OF A GIRL, called SAPPHO. Fresco from Pompeii. National Museum, Naples

European civilization. The Greco-Roman foundation seemed to have disappeared with the Roman Empire, yet it subsisted like travertine under the overlaying deposits of time. The miraculous balance that the Greek mind had achieved between man and the universe by closely linking the realism derived from the latter with the rationalism imposed by the former, broke up under the force of two opposing pressures. The barbarians glorified matter as such, in all its scintillating richness, scarcely troubling to process or refine it. In ornamentation they preferred the intricate, sinuous, all but physical line to the logical, intellectual elements of symmetry and proportion. At the same time, victorious Christianity sought to carry souls to the other extreme. Bearing the imprint of its Eastern provenance, it urged upon mankind the obligation to transcend its origins and, in following the revelations of religion, to soar to spiritual heights beyond all reason and logic.

The course of medieval art was thus charted in advance, but several centuries were needed to unify the seemingly incompatible tendencies at work within it. Though essentially spiritual, it made use of the richness of materials—gold, enamel, and later, stained glass—to give a foretaste of the divine splendors, light being regarded as the nearest equivalent in this world here below. It retained the ancients' fondness for proportions, for number, for geometry—elements that assist us in perceiving more sacred harmonies. It was not much concerned with the representation of reality (St. Augustine preferred architecture and music to the figurative arts). It studied reality only to the extent that appearances might lead to the ideas that this art symbolized. And, since these ideas were religious, the artist was not master of them: he was bound to respect a rigorous iconography drawn up and codified by representatives of the Church. The artist's sole task was to place his fervor, his talent, and his technical skill at the service of particular images, of which he was merely the copyist, so to speak. It is not surprising that, most often, he remained humbly anonymous.

The new synthesis that was to give birth to European art came about gradually and progressively. Merovingian art, under the aegis of a firmly established religion, held to the barbarian repertory in matters of decoration, but was compelled to draw upon Roman models in architecture. Similarly, recourse was had to such vestiges of older administrative structures as survived in the restoration of social organization. Carolingian art, under the powerful guidance of Charlemagne, and then Ottonian art (which attempted no more than to continue the former) applied themselves more consciously to renewing ties with the Roman past. This was the age when Europe revived the idea of the Roman Empire. While Romanesque art was developing, the secular monarchs, who were of Northern origin, co-operated closely with the religious and spiritual leaders in Rome to bring the souls of their peoples under authoritarian control—a process marked by several violent upsets.

Whereas Roman rationalism gained ground and was progressively re-assimilated, and whereas religious thought borrowed its logic from this rationalism to strengthen the intellectual foundations of the faith, Roman realism—which was contrary to both the barbarian heritage and the Christian spirit (with its Eastern provenance)—met with great resistance. That the Middle Ages saw two successive styles as different and, in many respects, as antithetical as Romanesque and Gothic would be inexplicable if we did not keep in mind that this epoch also saw a change in its attitude toward physical reality. Whereas early Christianity had looked upon it as contrary to spirituality, the Middle Ages was rediscovering the material world. For it is not enough to say that Romanesque art, conceived and developed primarily in the south, bears a strong Latin imprint, and Gothic art, predominantly under Northern influence, is rather removed from Classical art. Some theoreticians such as Strzygowski, for instance, have gone so far as to see in the Gothic style an extension of Scandinavian architecture, both in design and technique. However, the situation is not so simply accounted for: there is the paradox that Romanesque art, for all its Latin features, resists most strongly the Mediterranean tradition of realism, whereas Gothic art, for all its Nordic spirit, reintroduced the empirical vision that was to remain the basis of Western art down to our own day. More than a difference in artistic attitudes, it is a far-reaching difference in points of view that separates these two phases of medieval culture (Figs. 87 and 89).

The contradiction between Romanesque and Gothic seems to us readily reducible to a single, constant antinomy. The Romanesque style took its point of departure in ideas, in concepts that it introduced into real life and self-consciously elaborated. The Gothic style, on the other hand, lent itself to the dictation of real life, being molded by it and reflecting its influence—although all such influences were in turn transformed by the intellect and sensibility and invested with universality. The two approaches are consistently antithetical.

Everywhere it developed and in every aspect of its development, Gothic art preferred the vision of things—a new basis of knowledge—to thought made visible. This was a profound revolution: for can there be a more far-reaching change in human affairs than a shift of the very concept of reality? This was what the historical appearance of the Gothic style meant. Our present conception of reality was born then—the conception upon which our life is still based today, although the twentieth century seems to have undertaken its revision. Some readers may be surprised by this statement. How can the very meaning of reality undergo change? Is not reality the material, objective, concrete datum, which everywhere impinges upon our senses? Such is merely *our* definition of reality, however, and the revolution just referred to consists precisely in the historical adoption of this definition. The great conflict which marked the turning point was continued in the twelfth century in the quarrel between Realists and Nominalists. The revolution consisted precisely in the fact that the Nominalists triumphed over the Realists. What does—or rather, what did—the term "realist" stand for? Today, according to our dictionaries, it denotes those who believe in the reality of sensory appearances. In the Middle Ages, however, it denoted the exact opposite: Realists were those who believed in the reality of general ideas, "universals." It was in the eleventh century, at the apogee of Romanesque art, that this doctrine was most brilliantly represented by St. Anselm. In fact, it was associated with the latent conviction that sensory appearances have no reality in themselves. The thirteenth century reversed the situation and implanted the opposite thesis in the Western mind, so firmly anchored that we have mostly taken it for granted ever since.

Roughly speaking, it may be said that until about 1200 the Middle Ages had been nourished on the thought of St. Augustine, while from the thirteenth century onward that of St. Thomas became dominant. The former had been deeply influenced by Plato, whereas Aristotle was the primary influence on the latter. What we have here is two antithetical visions of the world. For Plato, the world of individual appearances, the physical universe, is nonbeing; it is merely a distorted reflection of the ideas, the pure models of reality, which have "neither form nor color," as Plotinus said in the third century—and the influence of Plotinus was as great as that of the bishop of Hippo. True being is in the ideas. However imperfect our thoughts may be, they are closer to the ideas than they are to things, which are counterfeit reality: a snare and a delusion to the mind. It was thus not surprising that a tendency to abstraction characterized the art of the early Christian centuries and that of Byzantium, which was also influenced by Neoplatonism. We may

*The forms current in antiquity (cf. Fig. 34)—rectangles, triangles, and (since Roman times) circles—and their symmetrical arrangement remained the basis of Romanesque and Renaissance art.*

**87.** - NOTRE-DAME-LA-GRANDE, POITIERS. Middle of the twelfth century. West façade

**88.** - CHATEAU OF ANET. Sixteenth century. Entrance

recall that St. Augustine had been perturbed at the sight of too concrete beauty and suspected it of being sinful.[1] Medieval philosophy begins with Johannes Scotus Erigena, who taught in Paris c. 847 at the moment when Romanesque art was just about to make its appearance. Scotus was steeped in Neoplatonism; his Latin translation of the works of Dionysius the Areopagite was referred to as the "Vulgate." According to him, the highest reality is in being, i.e., in God. The visible world partakes in being only to the extent that it is a sign or symbol of God; it is like an obstacle that one must encounter the better to be thrown back to one's point of origin. Toward the close of the Romanesque era, in the middle of the twelfth century, when the earliest Gothic work was under construction at Saint-Denis, the Abbé Suger, who had so much to do with the new development, was still professing the traditional formula: *mens hebes ad verum per materialia surgit*—"because the mind is weak, it rises to truth by means of material things"—which is tantamount to recognizing them as inferior makeshifts, mere supports or handmaidens to the mind, ultimately to be transcended.

As Emile Mâle has pointed out, a significant feature of Romanesque art is its "contempt for reality." The intellectual method current at that time derives from such a contempt, no less than does the art. Truth was not to be pursued by exploring the secrets of nature; indeed, the term "nature" had no meaning, almost no existence. Where, today, we see her as both very full and opaque, she was conceived as a kind of transparent veil interposed between the individual and God, through which, however, the individual could glimpse Him. Truth was to be deduced by employing a skillful logical apparatus, by the exercise of a dialectic initially founded upon a divinely revealed *logos*. Thus everything was seen to

[1] "The mind must be diverted from corporeal images," he said, and, "Woe to those who love Thy signs instead of loving Thee."

*Gothic art breaks with the Classical tradition. It has a more living sense of form, greater indifference to abstract patterns, and its soaring structures scorn regularity.*

**89. -** CATHEDRAL OF SAINT-ETIENNE, BOURGES. Fourteenth century

179

*Gothic architects do not combine basic geometrical forms, but, rather, organize forces, thrusts, loads. To channel these they rely more on a structural system of elastic ribs than on the elevation of the walls, which are replaced with stained–glass windows.*

**90. -** VAULT OF THE CHOIR IN THE CATHEDRAL OF BEAUVAIS. Collapsed 1284; restored 1337 arise from a pre-established, preconceived idea, whether the divine *logos* creating the universe or human thought busy with its own creations. Matter, the objects of our perception, bore the imprint of the *logos*, and was valued only in so far as it could be seen to bear that imprint. This system of thought, which owed so much to Platonism and Neoplatonism, conceived every thing in terms of its essential or original principle, as a particular application of it. This approach pervaded the philosophy of the period, but it is also recognizable in its art, where the material realization is always the consequence of some pre-established notion, which is copied more or less felicitously. Identifiable images are used only to suggest to the mind the symbolic significance, associated with them, that has inspired them. Similarly, both decorative and architectural forms are derived from the simplest, most fundamental, most regular geometric figures—square, rectangle, triangle, circular arc, etc., and the builder's art consists solely in compelling stone—regardless of the force of gravity—to respect and adopt those forms. Romanesque art is born of a concept that antecedes its embodiment, and serves solely to give it a concrete, visible garment or appearance (Fig. 87).

The thirteenth century saw the victory of contrary propositions. At the end of the eleventh century, Roscellinus' Nominalism tended to deny the reality of general ideas, which he regarded as *flatus vocis* (mere vocal utterances). Now, reality began to be located in individual things empirically observed. In the twelfth century, Abélard, a pupil of Roscellinus, consolidated the decline of Platonism; Aristotelian doctrines were steadily gaining ground. During the twelfth century, Platonism offered firm resistance, however, thanks to the considerable authority of St. Anselm, who threw the whole of his weight in support of it. In the thirteenth century, Aristotle won the upper hand: translated into Latin at Toledo early in the preceding century, and propagated by Arab philosophers, Aristotelianism imposed its theory of knowledge to an ever greater extent in the University of Paris. The latter institution, which was organized in 1215, took the place previously held by the schools of Chartres, which subscribed to Platonism.

THE NEW GOTHIC SPIRIT.    The reign of Augustinianism was approaching its end. Under its authority, the Platonic tradition had led to repeated efforts to go beyond the images of the sensory world, as St. Augustine had called them, and beyond the limits of the human reason as well, to attain to God. Now came the turn of Aristotelian belief in the world of concrete realities. The Franciscans had helped to pave the way, even though they remained faithful to St. Augustine in the thirteenth century. Their discovery of the importance of nature was of great indirect influence.

St. Francis taught that God is to be loved through love of the physical world. He loved the creation because in it he saw the hand of the Creator, and yet he brought to his study of it a previously unknown closeness and fervor of attention. The rise of realism in Italian art, at the expense of Byzantine abstraction, was encouraged by this doctrine: we can follow its progress in Cimabue and Giotto. St. Bonaventure, a general of the Franciscan order, combined the doctrines of St. Augustine and St. Francis, but he remained faithful to the view that man accedes to God through love, and he looked upon created things and beings as signs of God's presence in the sensory world. Moreover, he admitted that the science of things does not derive from the ideas, but from things themselves: this marks an important step in the eventual revival of the Aristotelian view of physics, according to which created things are real in and of themselves. Roger Bacon, a Franciscan genius and an Oxford celebrity, went further. Whereas his teacher Robert Grosseteste had still believed that science could do without the experience of the senses, he introduced the term "experimental science." He did not, for all that, become a true Aristotelian; indeed, he referred to Aristotle as an adversary. But he acknowledged that sensory data must supply the starting point for science, if there is to be any certainty, and that a science wholly of "arguments" is inadequate. Reasoning, he said, can never take the place of visual observation, nor even of tactile manipulation by the hands, and the reason mathematics eliminates doubt is that it makes "everything manifest to the senses... because it traces figures and makes computations." Even though he argued against the Aristotelian system, he saw in it the most advanced philosophy of his epoch, and called Aristotle a great precursor. "There are two modes of knowledge," he says, "reasoning and experience. Theory draws conclusions and makes us accept them, but not until the conclusion has been ascertained by way of experiment does it give us that complete certainty in which the mind can rest." He arrived at this formula: "No reasoning can give us certainty; the latter depends entirely upon experiment." Similarly, Leonardo da Vinci, who knew the works of the Oxonians, advanced this principle: "The sciences which have not been born of experience, mother of all certainty, are vain and full of errors." Indeed, Leonardo was the heir and continuator of Roger Bacon, inventor of the term "experimental science," *scientia experimentalis*, which would become the catchword of the nineteenth century. The term "experiment" was often used in the twelfth century. In France, Pierre de Maricourt earned the name *dominus experimentorum* for his treatise on the magnet. In the thirteenth century, William of Occam, who had much to do with the victory of the new theses, spoke explicitly of "experimental knowledge," *notitia experimentalis*.

Thus, Franciscans, Nominalists, and men like William of Occam, each man in his way and for his own reasons, gave increasing weight to the importance of sensory data and helped to bring about the triumph of an experimentalist conception of knowledge. Without always realizing it—indeed, sometimes under the impression that they were its adversaries—they contributed to the victory of essentially Aristotelian doctrines.

Moreover, Aristotelianism penetrated the medieval world by some unusual routes. Early in the thirteenth century it reached Paris, tainted by the Neoplatonism of Aristotle's Arab translators and commentators, Averroës and Avicenna. In addition, Aristotle had long been known for his logic (in the twelfth century, John of Salisbury had already venerated him as "The Philosopher"). He had been the master of the Scholastics, whose reasonings and ratiocinations were to prove the principal obstacle in the evolution toward empiricism. Albertus Magnus had observed this confusion: according to him, the commentators saw in Aristotle "the supreme perfection of the human intellect. But they expound him in different ways, according to the views of each." And yet, it was Aristotle who, by destroying faith in the Platonic ideas, inaugurated the method of dealing with sensory reality which has endured down to our own day.

The opening stages of the battle present a somewhat confused picture. The statutes of the University of Paris, drawn up in 1215, still ban Aristotle's *Metaphysics*, and his *Physics* was several times condemned by the Holy See, down to the second third of the thirteenth century. But these were the last gasps of a steadily weakening resistance. The

*XIII - CONRAD WITZ*
ST. CHRISTOPHER
Museum of Fine Arts, Basel

Sorbonne, as it gained ascendancy over the Platonist schools of Chartres, took the lead in the Thomist revolution. For St. Thomas, matter or objective reality is endowed with concrete existence (*esse in re*, in the Thomist formula), a concept that makes it appear more important than the being of essences. Etienne Gilson's characterization of Albertus Magnus, who had been St. Thomas' teacher, may perhaps also serve as a definition of the new developments in art. Albertus, he says, "resumed contact with nature," and he adds: "He knew that in arriving at the *particular* the syllogism loses its value, and that *experience alone* then becomes cogent." The new philosophy imposed recognition of a reason that operates inductively on the basis of sensory experience, in contradiction to a reason operating deductively on the basis of established truths. Does not the passage from Romanesque to Gothic art confront us with exactly the same *volte-face*? The new method of thinking established the primacy of nature, making it the major reality to be explored by the senses, the means through which the intellect discovers general laws. The approach of the Gothic architects, sculptors, and painters was no different. They discovered nature and were filled with wonder at it; they made it the source of all knowledge, whose principal means now became the sense of sight (Fig. 93).

What brought about this radical change? Perhaps the fact that the West, which had long been overrun by foreign civilizations, was, with its second adolescence, attaining

*In sculpture, too, Gothic art asserts life in contrast to the abstract, preconceived form of the Romanesque.*

**91.** - QUEEN OF SHEBA. Twelfth century. From the portal of Notre-Dame de Corbeil. The Louvre, Paris

**92.** - THE VISITATION (detail). Thirteenth century. Central portal, Reims Cathedral

maturity at last—a stage at which, more aware of its own nature and potentialities, it tended to go back to its own foundations, to that combination of realism and rationalism that is its inborn characteristic. The change is perhaps also to be accounted for as a repercussion of the social evolution that was bringing about the formation and gradual rise of a new class, the middle class. The commercial activities of this class also furthered a taste for concrete reality. However that may be, the change that was revolutionizing the West found its intellectual expression in a parallel revolution in philosophical thinking. Albertus Magnus and St. Thomas reversed the current of Western thought. The latter, especially, restored the primacy of sensation: from it he derived both ideas and imagination, and it is on sensation and on experience that he founded knowledge. Even though faith, according to Thomism, retains a certain character of mystery irreducible to human logic, St. Thomas restored considerable importance to reason with respect to concrete truths. Even in the sphere of the contemplative life he assigned it a certain role. Thus, the twin foundation of ancient science—sensory experience and the laws of reason—was fully restored. The progress of idealism, with its arbitrariness and abstraction, to which the early Middle Ages had added suprasensory and mystical ambitions of its own, was now checked by the growth of a rational realism, which frequently compelled it to give way. The evolution in art marked by the rise of the Gothic style discloses strikingly similar features.

As Gothic art succeeded Romanesque art, the artist's attitude was profoundly modified. To be sure, Gothic art continued to exalt the soul by means of sensory impressions; being more Northern in origin than logical-minded Romanesque art, which had been born in the Latin provinces, it perhaps exploited sensory impression more fully. Never before had jewels been more scintillating, glowing mysteriously in the penumbra; never before had the union between light and color been more intimate than in stained-glass windows; never before had greater use been made of the intoxication of incense, chimes, and organ music to enrapture the faithful. The mystical strain of the Middle Ages was as evident as ever. What was new, however, was the artist's attitude toward reality. Not only was the lowliest nature—the most ordinary of the field plants—admitted in the decoration of churches, supplanting purely geometric designs; not only did sculpture mark steady advances in the close imitation of reality, so that before long one could speak of its "naturalism"; but architectural theory was completely revolutionized. Instead of being forcibly imposed on matter, the forms were now made to express and adjust themselves to its laws —including that most important of them all, gravitation. By studying gravitation, by seeking to eliminate its action whenever it imperiled stability, and by exploiting the lines of force it necessitates, the Gothic architect invented a whole repertory of forms, as new as they were unprecedented—the forms that have been called *ogival*. Instead of imposing, as the Romanesque architect had done, the most abstract Euclidean figures—square and circle —upon a hostile power of gravity, the Gothic architect let himself be guided by practical considerations of balance in determining the appearance and the structural elements of his edifices. The forms that emerged were startling in their originality, but they were logically deduced from experience. The pointed arch derives from the diagonal rib—a pure problem in the balancing of forces; the flying buttress and the pinnacle were born of the need to shore up the walls and to strengthen the bridging piers. These functional concerns soon resulted in a style that was less bent on combining compartmentalized geometric figures—as had been done earlier—than on giving free play to sinuous, gyrating, undulatory movements that occasionally bring to mind the dynamic line of ancient Celtic art (Fig. 90).

As Gothic art developed, it progressed ever more resolutely in the direction of realism; less and less use was made of symbolism, and, by the fifteenth century, religious iconography did not any longer so much address itself to the mind as try to strike and move the viewer by eloquent narrative representations (even of sacred episodes) of an almost theatrical verism—they were in fact influenced by the theater (Fig. 94). The large Entombments, with their life-size figures and their dramatically emphasized facial expressions, strikingly disclose the radical change that had taken place. Painting became infatuated with a new—and revealing—problem: the rendering of materials with an accuracy bordering on illusion. Van Eyck perfected the oil technique that makes literal imitation possible. By the middle of the century, the *Pietà* of Avignon in France, the Schools of Venice, Ferrara, and Padua in Italy, with Giovanni Bellini and Mantegna, and even Portugal with Nuno Gonçalvès were all so obsessed with the concrete that they created a quasi-international style of works in which the figures take on the appearance of sculptured reliefs, together with the density of stone or carved wood. Sensory, and hence material truthfulness reached its apogee in the art of the Netherlands, the product of a more middle-class and positivist-minded people, without however abandoning the intense religious fervor of the Middle Ages (cf. Part II, Ch. II, 1 and 2).

Henceforth, the Western schools would be characterized by a growing tendency to realism and by an erroneous belief that art consists in faithful reproduction of the appearance of nature. In one form or another, this was to remain the fundamental credo of European aesthetics right down to the end of the nineteenth century, when the competition of photography led to profound self-examination on the part of artists and to the revolution that gave birth to modern art.

This realism, which was steadily to strengthen its hold on art, enjoyed its greatest successes in the Northern countries, where the monarch and the aristocracy played a limited role and where the middle classes developed most rapidly. The absolute monarchies and principalities developed mostly in the South. The religious conflicts touched off by the Reformation accentuated such differences, which were political as well as social and cultural; they even isolated entire regions, such as the northern portion of the Low Countries, which became Protestant Holland. It is hardly surprising that in Holland the realistic aesthetics attained its most considerable and most exclusive development. Furthered by

fifteenth-century Flemish art, it appeared in its most radical form in this Protestant, middle-class country in the seventeenth century. An exclusively realistic art leaves no room for an explicit aesthetics: ideas and theories are incompatible with so passive an

*The Gothic capital uses realistic representation of foliage.*

**93.** - CAPITAL WITH FOLIAGE, Reims Cathedral

*Whereas the late Middle Ages displayed a passionate interest in empirical reality, the Italian Renaissance revived the Greco-Roman spirit, subjecting concrete reality to the laws of logic.*

**94.** - THE ENTOMBMENT (detail of THE VIRGIN AND ST. JOHN). 1515. Chapel of the Sepulcher, Church of St. John the Baptist, Chaource (Aube)

**95.** - *Opposite page: DONATELLO. THE CURE OF THE YOUNG MAN.*
Middle of the fifteenth century. Relief. Basilica of S. Antonio, Padua

attitude toward nature. Such artistic ideas as are encountered in these regions were imported directly from Italy and gave rise to Romanism, an indigestible compromise between native *verismo* and borrowed idealism. The naturalistic tendency was transcended only by a few isolated, individual geniuses such as Rembrandt, Vermeer, and Ruisdael, all of whom, by their preoccupation with the individual inner life, anticipated the nineteenth century.

THE RENAISSANCE AS OPPOSED TO THE MEDIEVAL HERITAGE.   If in the Northern countries, the Middle Ages drifted steadily toward realism, a new aesthetics in reaction against it made its appearance quite early in countries of an older culture, where vestiges of antiquity had never been completely erased. This new aesthetics justifies the term Renaissance. Its center, needless to say, was Italy, and it was there that all artists eager to go beyond realism went to study for several centuries.

At first, the Italians, too, thought that the revolution that they were carrying out would be confined to reinstating a cult of reality and reviving the means of rendering its exact

appearances. The pressure of realistic currents at the close of the Middle Ages was very strong. However, perhaps atavistically, the Italians unconsciously added other elements to the realistic spirit of the late Middle Ages, though they remained unaware of this until the end of the fifteenth century. Then experimental curiosity, which goes hand in hand with artistic realism, underwent a profound change, influenced by a revival of ancient art and thought. Although a profoundly Mediterranean and Latin country, Italy had never really assimilated the medieval spirit, least of all that of the Gothic epoch. It had always cherished its own memories of Greco-Roman Classicism and longed to go back to its sources. No one, perhaps, felt this longing more keenly than Petrarch, whose fate it was to spend most of his life in exile. In the first half of the fourteenth century, he launched a passionate search for ancient manuscripts and urged their widespread copying and circulation among men of letters. At about the same time, Greek scholars in flight from Byzantium in its extreme decadence were flocking to Italy. The trek to Italy had begun as early as 1308 with Pachymeres; the number of such refugees increased stedily throughout the century. In 1396 Manuel Chrysoloras was teaching Greek in Florence and, later on, held classes in Milan, Pavia, and Venice. The capture of Constantinople by the Turks in 1453 was the signal for the final dispersal of the Greek scholars and their mass migration to Italy.

At about the same time, the invention of printing was bringing about a revolution in the propagation of ideas. At first, only Bibles were printed, but, before long, the rediscovered ancient treasures had their turn at publication: in 1470 Virgil, in 1498 Aristotle, and in 1512 Plato. The sixteenth century was the century of great publishers all over Europe. Although Aristotle had, in actual fact, been responsible for the revival of the notion of experience or experiment, he was nonetheless discredited because, in the eyes of the new thinkers, he was inseparable from the scholasticism which had owed so much to his *Logic*. This misunderstanding favored the revival of Aristotle's great rival Plato, whose works the Byzantine scholars had brought to Italy with them. The reading and discussion of Plato now became a topic of widespread interest. Manuel Chrysoloras played an important part in this revival; his courses in Florence were devoted to the philosopher. But the prodigious vogue of Neoplatonism was due primarily to Gemistus Pletho, whom John VIII Palaeologus had sent in 1438 to the Council of Florence as the delegate of the Greek Church. The Medici, from Cosimo the Elder to Leo X, did much to encourage Platonic studies. The vogue was also furthered by Marsilio Ficino's founding of the Platonic Academy in 1460. Now Aristotle's reign came to an end in Italy; at the close of the next century Giordano Bruno could brand him "the enemy" and attack him as such.

Guarino da Verona, a disciple of Gemistus, used the expression "a ray of sunshine in the darkness." Thus was born the image of a "dark age," which was to become so popular and mislead so many. And yet the revival of Platonism did not really affect a powerful intellectual tradition that was opposed to it: the experimental spirit, which was to be the foundation of modern science and which, actually, was launched in the Middel Ages toward its eventual triumph. Contrary to what is generally believed, it was not in the Renaissance that the great discoveries of modern thought originated. Nicole Oresme, bishop of Lisieux in the fourteenth century, was certainly a "Gothic" man—and yet his genius anticipated the diurnal rotation of the earth long before Copernicus, the law of bodies subject to gravity long before Galileo, and analytic geometry long before Descartes. He certainly belongs to the medieval tradition and was steeped in Aristotle, like his contemporary Albert of Saxony, who was also on the trail of a theory of gravity. The latter wrote a commentary on Aristotle's *De coelo et mundo*. The powerful mind whose brilliant insights make him an especially outstanding pioneer of modern civilization—Leonardo da Vinci—belonged to this same intellectual tradition, as we shall show in detail later. It is important to keep clearly distinct the idealistic, aesthetic spirit of the Renaissance, based on freedom of thought, from the development of empirical research which was to give birth to modern science. If the faith we inherited from the Gothic and Romanesque Middle Ages were one day to crumble away, all that would be left would be our experimental civilization, whose champions, incidentally, have been well aware of their own filiation. Condorcet admired Aristotle, and Auguste Comte, the pope of nineteenth-century positivism, spoke of "the incomparable Aristotle." The new spirit of the thirteenth century and the proud scientific spirit of the nineteenth century really had a great deal in common, were more profoundly akin than has sometimes been recognized. When the nineteenth century rejected all statements not experimentally confirmable in the physical world, it was merely bringing to its conclusion a great undertaking first launched and formulated in the thirteenth century. The infatuation of the Romantics with Gothic art is rather better known, but as compared with this inner affinity it is a mere epiphenomenon. The practical-minded functional architecture of the nineteenth century, in which the engineering spirit gradually conquers the aesthetic spirit (the latter a reactionary tendency inherited from the Renaissance), led to creation of simplified, unfamiliar, dynamic forms analogous to those of Gothic architecture. Once again, traditional forms gave way to lines of force. The anti-quarian spirit imposed by the Renaissance, which had, at the time, undermined the Gothic spirit, was now in turn discarded, and the link with Gothic art restored. Leonardo da Vinci, Francis Bacon, Hume, and Condillac are only a few of the landmarks along a road that leads uninterruptedly from the thirteenth to the nineteenth century. We recognize this continuity in the simultaneous flowering of positivist, sensualist philosophy, experimental science, naturalistic painting, and architecture dominated by engineers.

All this points up close affinities between the thirteenth and nineteenth centuries. During the Augustinian Middle Ages, the predominance of abstract thinking had given grammar and logic a leading position in culture; then observation and computation supplanted them, and all that could be perceived, seen, and measured came to the fore. The thirteenth century, like the nineteenth, was a century of the primacy of the visual and the quantitative. *Figuratio et numeratio*—these, for Roger Bacon, were the pillars of the new temple. Although to him the domain of faith remained the object of another, inner, experience, in every other connection he praises mathematics for having for all things "a sensory example and sensory experience, because it traces figures and makes computations, so that *everything becomes manifest to the senses*; whence the impossibility of doubt." But in the nineteenth century, when the special powers of faith had crumbled away, Courbet said that the reason he did not paint angels was that he had never seen any, and surgeons in the same period questioned the existence of the soul on the ground that they could not touch it with their scalpels. If the analogy seems strained, recall that early in the fourteenth century Nicolas d'Autremont ventured to declare that "nothing authorizes us to assert that there exist things outside what we perceive with our five senses and through our experiments." Was this any less positivism? A contemporary of d'Autremont, the Aristotelian Jean de Jaudun, for all his cautious reservations, also seems to have agreed with the materialists and to have given credence only to factual data.

It was inevitable in such an age that, just as in the nineteenth century, visual realism became a major concern. Roger Bacon worked on a theory of vision, and the Franciscans of Oxford looked upon the treatise on optics by Alhazen as an essential book; another treatise, by the thirteenth-century Polish mathematician Erasmus Vitello, inspired Kepler and Leonardo da Vinci. The latter, who was both a painter and a scientist, carries this visual avidity of the thinker to its logical conclusion. Nineteenth-century pictorial realism, too, was led to an ever more thorough analysis of the conditions of vision, with which thinkers had been so much preoccupied at the close of the Middle Ages, and the end product of this analytic tradition was Impressionism. We can perhaps now better grasp a major peculiarity of modern Western culture: it is and professes to be dualistic, clearly distinguishing between its literary and its scientific side. Our school system has sanctioned this division by providing separate formations for the mind, according to whether it selects the one or the other discipline. In this way, the two essential impulses received by Europe—Platonism, which gives primacy to the idea, and Aristotelianism, which gives it to experimental knowledge—have survived to this day and continue to be opposed. For many centuries Western art bore their imprint; the two traditions alternated or clashed—on the one hand, there was ideal beauty, conceived and imposed by the mind, and on the other, realistic truth, which accepted dictation by the eye. It would not be absurd to maintain that the present-day conflict between figurative and abstract art is but the latest manifestation of this irreducible dualism.

The waning Middle Ages founded positivism, even though the power of the Christian faith still provided a counterweight. The religious struggles contemporary with the Renaissance split Europe into two warring factions and, later, gave rise to free-thinking agnosticism. The earlier religious quarrels set this tendency in motion, although it is a gross oversimplification to regard the Renaissance as a victory of paganism. Actually it was a resurgence of spiritualism, closely linked with Christianity, and it reacted strongly against the contemporary rise of positivism and materialism. It was delighted to discover an ally in Platonism, which was revived in this period with the publication of ancient manuscripts.

Thus, the Renaissance traveled back along a trail that the thought and art of the Gothic age had blazed. To some extent it reoccupied the positions that had been taken, with other means, by Romanesque art. It is noteworthy how easily Italy made the transition from Romanesque to Renaissance art, scarcely passing through a Gothic stage at all. It is almost as if we were witnessing a straight-line development, and that the art of the Renaissance were a late flowering of the Romanesque style. Conversely, who would venture to say today that the Renaissance ever really existed in countries where Gothic art had been intensely alive? In such countries it was merely a fashion, a modernism, usually confined to the borrowing of decorative patterns. On the other hand, the Gothic inspiration, which originated in direct contact with life, facilitated transition to the Baroque in these same countries, and superficial implantations of the Renaissance failed to break the continuity. This obviously happened in Germany, Holland, Spain, and Portugal. The unfortunate tendency of textbooks to divide history into successive chapters is responsible for the impression that the Romanesque, Gothic, and Renaissance periods are three indispensable acts in the same play, as distinct from one another as though a curtain were lowered between them. Closer examination of European thought, art, and social development restores awareness of the existence of continuous currents in the great river of history, now distinct from each other and now inextricably merged.

*The rational a priori structures regain dominance: intellectual order prevails.*

**96.** - Attributed to *FRA CARNEVALE.* THE BIRTH OF THE VIRGIN. 1484. The Metropolitan Museum of Art, New York (Purchase, Rogers and Gwynne M. Andrews Funds, 1935)

THE DUALISM OF EUROPEAN CULTURE. The vistas thus opened from century to century down to our own day—the successive epochs usually designated as the modern era—suggest that all have in common a dualism that can be traced back to the opposition of Platonism and Aristotelianism. It can be summed up even more simply in two antithetical formulas: truth lies in the mind; truth lies in the senses.

Does not the medieval experimentalism and sensualism, which the nineteenth-century positivists felt so close to, seem as remote from us today, in our own century, as does the artistic realism of our grandfathers? The burning faith of the Middle Ages was strong enough to restrict the domain of physical knowledge; however, if that faith was eventually undermined and the way paved for the religious reactions and emancipations of the Renaissance, it served for a long time as a natural counterweight to materialism, which only in the nineteenth century became systematic and exclusive. So exclusive, indeed, that a reaction was bound to take place, and did take place even before the century had ended. Then the excess of scientism resulted in the discredit of realism in art and of positivism in philosophy.

Symbolism was the first sign of the coming reaction. Clearly, it did no more than reoccupy the position of the Platonists, with a view to destroying the prevalent Aristotelianism. In literature and in art, the sectarian cult of realities perceived by the senses gave way to the rehabilitation of spiritual realities. We must go back to "the powers that elude our senses." Who said it? Olympiodorus—in the sixth century! Next to the "realistic representation of objects" there is "the meaning disclosed to the mind by images," and this meaning "arouses and enraptures you." Who said it? Delacroix—in the nineteenth century, and his words were directed against naturalism.... Thus art should serve as a means "to collect oneself," it should lead to "a contemplation which is not that of spectacles but *another* form of vision—ecstasy." Delacroix again? Not at all. Plotinus said that, in the third century. "The impressions produced on the sensibility by the arts... present a curious mystery.... A mysterious and profound sensation." Plotinus? No, Delacroix! What, then, is the value of the visible appearances evoked by the artist? "They are like Egyptian hieroglyphs: to the physical eye they show a sparrow hawk or a scarab, but for the mind they contain a meaning to be discovered." This time the comparison is by Plotinus; but we find it again, almost identical, in the writings of Delacroix, and later in Baudelaire who was a forerunner of the Symbolists. *Mens hebes ad verum per materialia surgit*—*per*, i.e., through, by means of.... As we saw above, this was said by Suger at the midpoint of the twelfth century.

Thus, modern art, unwittingly embracing the Neoplatonic and Augustinian convictions at the basis of Romanesque art, reduces reality to a mere allusion that conceals and reveals a spiritual meaning. This was the belief proclaimed by Gauguin, by Odilon Redon, and by many others. "Nature is not what it seems to be... it is the sign and symbol of a deeper reality." We owe that statement (which would not have been disavowed by Albert Aurier around 1890) to Etienne Gilson, commenting upon St. Augustine, reconstructing the latter's thought along with that of the entire Middle Ages with awareness of contemporary trends. Are not so many coincidences revealing?[1]

---

[1] Gilson's recent book, *Peinture et réalité* (1958), proves, incidentally, how easily a specialist in medieval thought can switch to problems of modern aesthetics and adopt its point of view.

Before long, a discredited reality, reduced to the role of intermediary, mere symbol of all that is not in the domain of reality, would be eliminated altogether. The modern painter no longer feels obliged even to use it as the stuff of his language; he no longer follows visible appearances and instead elaborates free constructions obeying the demands of his thought and sensibility alone. Once more abstraction triumphs. Art is more and more exclusively inspired by the form "pre-existing in the artist's mind"—to use an expression which contemporary art criticism is perfectly capable of uttering but which happens to have been uttered by Plotinus.

Is not the recent vogue for styles which profess scorn for conformity with visual appearance and which see in it no more than the manifestation of abstract principles an admission of this secret affinity? Byzantine and Romanesque art were the first to benefit from this revival; the Romanesque paintings, especially, have become familiar today, thanks to the copies in the Musée de la Fresque and numerous volumes of reproductions. At the same time Gothic art is gradually relegated to the background of present-day taste. Forms current in the nineteenth century are no longer found inspiring and have been supplanted by Romanesque forms, even in religious art.

"These reflections apply to literature and artistic tendencies," some readers will say, "but how about science? More than ever it dominates our world, more than ever its voice summons and we obey. It remains experimental, and if the mutations of the spirit of an age were really effective, would we not discover their effects in this primordial domain, too?" Very true! The dominant scientific conceptions never stop evolving, according to the same unknown laws as those which govern human transformations. We can do no better than to refer the reader to Bachelard. He has pointed out to what a great extent modern science tends to go beyond the exploration of concrete reality in search of general properties, and to what a notable extent it is more interested in the relationships among elements than in the elements themselves. "Relation bears upon being," he writes. "More than that, it is identical with being." In the scientist's mind, ensembles play the leading role. He no longer confines himself, in the positivist spirit, to cautious generalizations and, step by step, the results of localized, individual experiments. He ventures to conceive relations that, so to speak, compel experimentation to confirm them. The most striking example is, perhaps, Mendeleev's table, which, far from organizing experimental results, anticipated reality and, as it were, assigned it its task. Of course, the classification was based on the concept of atomic weight; in 1930 Moseley translated it into the far more abstract concept of atomic number, retaining only the most elementary properties, those determined by the electric charge of the nucleus. According to this table, nature was bound to contain 92 elements; but the elements as yet empirically isolated were far fewer, and the table had many gaps. Bidden by the intellect, nature was set the task of filling in the blanks gradually. There are many other instances of how reason, on the basis of rigorous calculations, has anticipated reality. The pressure of light waves, the diffraction of electrons, and Dirac's positron are all the offspring of pure concepts deduced by mathematical logic. According to Bachelard, "the determinism of ideas has taken precedence over the determinism of facts." Facts have been obliged to obey the injunctions of the human mind, and, in the end, have confirmed them.

But are we wrong to recognize here the same formula by which we summed up the antithesis between the Romanesque and the Gothic age? The former subordinated everything to a determinism of ideas, the latter to a determinism of facts. It would seem that

193

the course of human history has once again carried us away from the domain of facts and back to ideas.

We, too, are turning our backs on factual data, on the evidences of our senses; every day we move farther away from them. The moment has come when science, in order to conceive the universe, is compelled to give up trying to represent it materially; it must leave the domain of sensory perception. "The more deeply we penetrate into the intimate structures of matter," Louis de Broglie observes, "the more we realize that the concepts forged by our minds in the course of everyday experience, and most particularly those of space and time, have become inadequate when it comes to describing the new worlds we are exploring." Neoplatonism, and, above all, Plotinus, had already taught that the ultimate reality, being, is beyond the reach of our senses and cannot be imagined by their poverty-stricken resources, which can only take in material appearances. He went further: he maintained that being eludes even the domain of the intelligible, with its imperfect grasp of possibility. Does science in its latter-day language say anything so very different? Not only are the structure of the atom, $n$-dimensional space, and the curvature of space-time impossible to visualize, but our thought is confronted with an inconceivable that, like a blind man groping with fingers for something he cannot see, it can designate solely through the intermediary of mathematical symbols. How could our minds "think" a function without a differential coefficient or a number greater than infinity? The physicist concludes that "reality is mathematical in its essence." But had not St. Augustine long before stated that "the numbers are God's thoughts"?

It must be emphasized that we are not playing up superficial similarities in order to arrive at factitious coincidences based on this or that detail. On the contrary, the analogies we have noted between the Gothic Middle Ages and the nineteenth century, on the one hand, and between the Romanesque Middle Ages and the twentieth century, on the other, are to be discerned at the deep level of fundamental patterns in the mind. Those whose eyes would linger over external circumstances, over the various detailed embodiments that history has imposed on basic currents of thought, will fail to grasp our meaning. Such analogies are valuable insofar as they bear upon the whole of a mental attitude, such as entails the same parallel consequences in different times and places.

If I had more space I could verify the relationship by attacking another aspect of the question; I shall instead confine myself to formulating it. Ideas—abstractions—are of the order of the universal; sensory data refer to the particular. The Platonic[1] mentality ignores and despises what is not universal, and looks upon it as mere accident. The Aristotelian mentality knows only and wants only to know the individual: individual perception, and hence individual expression. Now observe this new antinomy: the Platonic epochs aspire to the discovery of rules and drive out individual exceptions; thus, they are associated with authoritarian social forms that standardize the individual in the name of an all-powerful collectiveness. They are also associated with Classical intellectual forms, according to which everyone subordinates himself to traditionally fixed principles. From Plato's *Laws* to the Renaissance tendencies flowering under Louis XIV—what can be found to contradict this? In the Aristotelian epochs we witness the inevitable growth of private tendencies, particularisms, and subjective expression. Thus, Greek art of the fourth century is suc-

---

[1] The terms "Platonic" and "Aristotelian" are used here only as convenient designations, almost as symbols, as points of reference, without laying claim to any such rigorousness as the philosopher demands.

ceeded by the more emotional art of the following centuries. Thus, beginning with the thirteenth century we witness the rise of an individualism that had been altogether missing in Romanesque art. Thus, French Classicism was routed by eighteenth-century sensualism and carried away entirely by nineteenth-century Romanticism. The latter age carried the pursuit of originality so far as to give rise to the conception of *artistes maudits* irreducible to any common measure.

Have we not now been witnessing, for the past several years, a revival of collective imperatives and an increasing hostility toward that very individualism which, not so long ago, seemed to be triumphant all along the line? The pressure of this revival is exercised everywhere in the social and political domain, quite apart from the more extreme forms of collectivism that would require artists and writers to make public commitments. Clearly, individualism is on the way out.

Thus, it may very well be that mankind's intellectual history is governed by a strange ebb and flow that keeps a certain regularity beneath the surface of continuously changing circumstances. Such an alternation accounts for the spiritual affinities between the age of the Romanesque and of the Renaissance. Now that we traced the recurrence of similar attitudes down to the twentieth century, it will be easier to admit that both the epoch before the Gothic and the epoch after it correspond, *mutatis mutandis*, to analogous swings of the eternal pendulum. With the Romanesque age the Renaissance shares not only its Platonism and a strong admixture of Neoplatonism—under the influence of St. Augustine and his disciples in the one case, of Marsilio Ficino in the other—but also analogous conceptions of art. To be sure, the outward appearances are very different, because the Romanesque style is exclusively associated with the Christian Augustinian world, whereas the Renaissance frees itself from that world and attempts to go back directly to the pagan world. Its grammar of decoration, since it derives from other sources, does not much resemble that of the Romanesque, and the superficial dissimilarity strikes the eye first. But it is nonetheless a fact that, in architecture, the Renaissance abolished the practical, functional forms of Gothic art and restored the abstract forms that Romanesque art had borrowed from the fundamental elements of geometry. Once again we find combinations —subtler and more elaborate than before—of triangles, rectangles, and globes. Similarly, in painting, designs of intellectual origin turn their backs on the scrupulous realism of the Flemish Primitives, last of the Gothic artists. Everywhere the preconceived idea regains its prerogative. It is noteworthy, moreover, that the Renaissance spirit achieved full self-awareness only in the fifteenth century, at the very moment that Platonism was being revived and gaining widespread intellectual currency.

The Romanesque age found its aesthetic guide in Augustinian Platonism. The Italian Renaissance went back to Classical sources, and its thinking about art flows from them. Just as in Greece—indeed, in the West as a whole—the basis of art still lay in observation, in knowledge of reality. But the passive kind of knowledge supplied by the senses gave way to a more active concept of knowledge according to which the task of the mind is to remove the veil of appearances so as to discover the ideas that constitute its rational principles. The intellect formulates laws that determine visual appearance itself, such as the rules of perspective; laws that go beyond visual appearance and disclose its structure and organization by means of forms; and, last, laws that track down a truth which is different from any perceivable by the senses and which can only be formulated as beauty, subjecting things and their accidental combinations alike to absolute concepts of thought (Fig. 95).

From the ancient world, too, the Renaissance inherited the Pythagorean temptation to seek out a key to harmony in numbers from which proportion derives. This tendency is exemplified by Piero della Francesca, in painting, and by Alberti, in architecture. Even the German Dürer succumbed to the same temptation when he went to Italy. As the theory of the beautiful gradually hardened into a formula, Italian art set itself up as the Classicism of all classicisms, the academism par excellence.

THE REFORMATION AND THE BAROQUE.   During the Middle Ages all things were thought to have derived from God, in Whom alone they found their ultimate meaning; now this pre-eminent role was taken over by man, who in Northern art relied on the experience of his own senses and in Italian art on his own proud intellect. To man, writes Ficino, "the sky does not seem too high.... In all things he seeks to impose his decrees, to be praised, to be eternal like God." Humanism was reborn; man's critical mind stood up against divine authority. Religion did not die out, but it began to reflect the new spirit, as the Reformation attests. Luther and Calvin demanded that the faithful be allowed to read the Bible for themselves, in their own languages. This insistence on the direct acquaintance by the individual with the sources of faith, which laid the foundation for criticism of the Bible, betrays the influence of the experimental spirit. More than that— beyond all collectively conceived humanism, the Reformation foreshadowed the advent of an individualism that would succeed humanism and inspire the modern era. Albert Dufourcq has shown that even before the appearance of Protestantism, Catholicism was tending to an individualistic disorganization. One of its manifestations was the idolatrous realism which from the fourteenth century on characterized representations of Christ, the Virgin, the saints, and so on, in such a way that the individual worshiper could relate them to the requirements of his personal piety. Protestantism encouraged recourse to the individual conscience; direct study of the sources permitted the individual to weight for himself matters formerly envisaged as universal objects of unanimous belief. Now any and every man could claim to be in direct contact with the Lord through his private prayer and meditation on the Bible. The critical mind was not slow to assert its rights. Montaigne subjected all authority to what he called "doubt"; he set out to examine and discuss any and every topic on its own merits. "What I am putting down here is my own moods and opinions.... My sole purpose here is to disclose myself." We should not be surprised, then, to learn that the iconography of the same period bears witness to the beginnings of a pursuit of originality and personal vision, both in the Catholic countries with such artists as Tintoretto and Velázquez, and in the Protestant countries with such an artist as Altdorfer, for instance.

Protestantism spread primarily in Northern or Germanic lands, where the revolution that was taking place favored realism without gaining much headway for Platonic idealism. Northern artists, especially when they were really cut off from the Catholic world (as were the Dutch from the seventeenth century on), found themselves alone with nature, on their own without a guiding principle in the form either of ecclesiastical or aesthetic authority. The more mediocre of them confined themselves to faithful copying of what they saw; those endowed with exceptional sensibility developed individual reactions and went beyond passive contemplation to personal visions that transformed all

*With the advent of the Baroque, the Renaissance spirit collapses. Forms swell and lines swirl, illusion gaining ascendancy over regularity.*

**97. -** *BERNINI.* THE CORNARO CHAPEL, SANTA MARIA DELLA VITTORIA, ROME. 1644–51.
After an eighteenth-century painting. Staatliches Museum, Schwerin

197

*The Germanic Rococo, continuing the Baroque, stirred aspirations long repressed by the Latin spirit. Here all is vibrant energy.*

**98.** - DOMINIKUS ZIMMERMANN. PILGRIMAGE CHURCH "DIE WIES." 1749–50. Bavaria

things into harmony with their innermost feelings. Rembrandt, who was the greatest of such artists, portrayed his own emotional reactions to the Bible and to objective reality alike. Ruisdael's landscapes, although faithful depictions of real places, also convey the melancholy of the individual thrown upon his own resources. Vermeer's interiors, though rendered with meticulous accuracy of detail, are pervaded with the presence of a soul. Personal expression now gradually took on a place in art which it had hitherto possessed only unconsciously and exceptionally—in a few very great artists, such as Michelangelo, Giorgione, Titian, Tintoretto, and El Greco.

The Protestant countries thus paved the way for modern Romanticism from an early date. Catholic Europe, meanwhile, recognizing the enormous danger at its door, recovered its balance and proceeded to organize its own defense. This task was performed by the Council of Trent, which went on, with interruptions, from 1545 to 1563, inaugurating the movement eventually known as the Counter Reformation. Luther died just as the Council began; Calvin was in the heyday of his power. To counteract the movement they had touched off, the Church called upon a spiritual army, the Society of Jesus (founded in 1537), to mobilize and propagate throughout the Catholic world the conceptions of art decreed by the ecclesiastical authorities who assembled at Trent and later at Bologna. Jesuit art merged with the rising tide of the Baroque. Consciously opposed to the individualistic tendencies of Protestant realism, it exalted the collective powers of art, with respect both to its sources and its effects. To this end, it began by limiting the artist's freedom, decreeing iconographic rules and obliging him to observe them strictly. At the same

*French Classicism opposed to the Baroque a stiffening of rational norms.*

**99. -** STAIRCASE OF THE AMBASSADORS, VERSAILLES. 1671. Engraving by Surugue.
Bibliothèque Nationale, Paris

time, this art was encouraged to appeal to the emotions of the Christian public, the *ecclesia*. In banishing the spirit of individual free inquiry, it furthered everything that could arouse instinctual reactions, collective impulses. A primary requirement was sumptuousness of effect, for, as Molinus wrote, "the Church is an image of Heaven on earth. How can we fail to adorn it with the most precious things?" Another requirement was vivacity, vibrancy of sensation, the exaltation of feeling. In this spirit, Baroque drawing aimed at tumultuous contours and effects of proliferation; color and materials tended to be warm and brilliant; forms were vehement and exaggerated. "The Church wants to inflame the souls of her children," Cardinal Palleoti said in 1594. The appeal was not just to sensation, but also to emotion, and hence the Church favored polished, insistent, dramatic treatments representing saints in ecstasy and martyrs in the extremity of their sufferings. The austere ideal of the Renaissance, along with the tested knowledge of Guido Reni and the Carracci, was swept away by a torrent—the sumptuous and sensual Baroque that produced Bernini's sculpture in the seventeenth century, and the frenzied canvases of Tiepolo and his central European imitators in the eighteenth; and, too, the crude realism cultivated by Caravaggio to the point of shock and brutality, as a reaction to the artificialities of his day. The most brilliant single representative of the true Baroque, which sacrificed subtle individual nuances to effects of vast, tumultuous movement, was Rubens, the artist of Catholic Flanders (Fig. 131).

199

SEVENTEENTH-CENTURY CLASSICISM.   The bitter religious conflict, which generated such antithetical approaches to art, produced a reaction of renewed fervor in Spain and France. Spain, the one bastion of Catholicism which the Protestant movement never penetrated, was touched by a mystical current which, originating in Persia with El Hallaj (tenth century), passed to Western Islam and was brought to Seville by Abu Medin and to Murcia by Ibn Arabi. A Christian tradition of mysticism, Alexandrine in origin and continued by the Pseudo-Areopagite, converged in Spain with the Moslem tradition illustrated by Ibn Ata Allah of Alexandria. At the confluence of these two mystic traditions, Christian and Moslem, then appeared, in the sixteenth century, the energetic mysticism of St. Theresa and of St. John of the Cross. Into the direct, brutal Iberian realism, this mysticism introduced a spiritual fire that lights up the canvases of Zurbáran as it had, earlier, consumed those of El Greco. In sculpture, it combined the most intense expression of inner life with an insistent materialism in treatment. (This treatment is also exemplified by the violent Ribera and the subtle Velázquez.)

In France, two distinct currents appeared in the seventeenth century. One was oriented toward Northern art; its chief representative was Philippe de Champaigne, the painter of Port Royal, who displays a severity of temper analogous to Protestantism. The other current, softened by the proximity to the South, inspired St. Francis of Sales with an amiable and subtle devotion, whose echo we perceive in Le Sueur.

The horrors of the spiritual schism of sixteenth-century Europe, and the anarchic tendencies furthered by a nascent individualism challenging the universality of the medieval Church, promoted aspirations for a new, more firmly established order. Religion could no longer provide such an order; the only possible foundation for a new universal faith was human reason.

This is why, just as Italy had dominated the sixteenth century, France held sway over the seventeenth. Sufficiently Nordic to appreciate realism and the experimental approach, and sufficiently Mediterranean to conceive them only in the broader terms of universal laws of reason, France assumed the role of mediator. More than that, she provided the West in general with just that synthesis of conflicting tendencies—that principle of order—for which Europeans had long been waiting. This synthesis was masterfully formulated by Descartes.

Man, reduced to his own resources, had to find such certainty as he could within himself, as the ancient Greeks had done, much earlier. Though still cognizant of divine revelation, he now gave up the attempt to found reality upon it. Setting out from self-evident truths that he discovered in his own mind, he displayed a new awareness of himself ("I think, therefore I am") and of his own powers (laws of the intellect confirmed by the experience of the senses). Unlike the English thinkers, who remained faithful to a native positivism—and who, a few years earlier, had with Francis Bacon placed concrete experience above intellectual classifications, seeking to arrive at general laws by "amplifying" particular findings—Descartes was first and foremost a mathematician, and, hence, a rationalist. Reason comes first: "I thought that I could not do better than devote my whole life to the cultivation of my reason." For reason dominates and precedes experience. Through the senses, we can only apprehend signs and symbols; their findings can serve only to complete and give substance to the absolute definitions posited a priori by inner necessities of the understanding as clear and distinct ideas. The sovereign order that reason discerns in things gratified Descartes' taste for universality, for the subordination of the

*Cartesianism starts from direct observation, but subjects it to the rule of the intellect. In Poussin we find the same sense of balance.*

**100. -** *POUSSIN.* THE CHILDHOOD OF JUPITER (detail). 1637. Dulwich Gallery, London

interests of the individual to those of the whole of which he is a part. Universality and permanence thus come to seem indispensable attributes of truth, as Bossuet was shortly to demonstrate in fresh arguments for Christian belief (Fig. 99).

French Classical art, of which Versailles is the most accomplished expression in both architecture and decoration, and which was learnedly formulated by the Royal Academy under Le Brun, has no other foundation but this. Nicolas Poussin, a contemporary of Descartes, made this clear in both his works and his writings (for all that his successors lapsed into academicism). His was an effort to put art on "a rational basis." "My disposition is such that I look for and love well-ordered things and fly from confusion." He refused to let himself be dominated by visual experience and distinguished carefully between l'*aspect* and le *prospect* (the latter depending on the intellect).

And yet Poussin's art is not dry, as it sometimes seems to hasty or superficial viewers. He cultivated observation of nature, just as Descartes admitted experimentation, but assigned it "its proper place." His realism is vigorous and compact in his wash drawings, but, the moment he turns to oil, he subordinates realism to the guidance of the intellect. "It is by *observing* things that the painter acquires skill, rather than by taking the trouble to copy them." And when he observes the passions, he renders them by means of a skillful mechanism of features and gestures, a mechanism which was systematized by Le Brun and which is utterly Cartesian in spirit.

Poussin transcends the narrow limits of the system that his disciples erected upon the basis of his ideas; he opens the door to the future. What Descartes did for philosophy, Poussin did for painting. He contributed to its liberation from exclusive domination by the Church. It was in part thanks to him that painting became aware of its autonomy, and this autonomy was in time recognized as one of its essential characteristics. Painting is made for man. "Its purpose is delight." Spinoza, a more radical thinker than Descartes, was in the same century to proclaim the independence of secular thought as such, under obligation to none but its own laws. Similarly, Poussin launched the modern conception of art, the notion that the artist's explorations are determined solely by artistic reasons, and that the aim of art is to procure a specific, aesthetic pleasure (Fig. 100).

One aspect of Poussin which is often overlooked reveals him as a precursor. He feels the need to correct a too rationalistic universality by recourse to a certain diversity, a certain "relativity" such as psychological intuition or feeling insists upon when assailed by too-rigid logical convictions. He said of himself that he "does not always sing in the same key; he knows how to vary his manner according to the different subjects" (cf. Part II, Chap. IV, 2). This new feeling for nuances is also to be found in his contemporary, Pascal, who, without contradicting Descartes, believed with Francis Bacon that nature's subtlety surpasses that of reason. Pascal recognized that a universal logic must be supplemented by the mind's adjustment to the problems it sets for itself. Thus Pascal distinguished between l'*esprit de justesse* and l'*esprit géométrique*—one required in physics, the other in mathematics.

One of these forms of the mind, l'*esprit de finesse*, has nothing to do with pure reasoning: according to Pascal, the *esprit de finesse* sees "things at a glance, not by any process of reasoning." In a flash, by a kind of intuition, it perceives what the meshes of logic alone are not fine enough to catch and hold. Poussin, too, and about the same time, glimpsed the importance of the artistic sensibility. It is not enough to describe things correctly and logically; there must be a certain current passing from artist to viewer, making it possible for the latter to experience the emotions of the former. In other words, art is not confined to representation, it also employs suggestion, the importance of which was glimpsed for the first time by Poussin. "Try not only to represent the passions... in the faces... but also to arouse and to give birth to the same passions in the souls of those who view your pictures." To achieve this end, Poussin, like Pascal, had to go beyond Cartesian immutability and conceive a certain relativity with respect to the means for arousing emotion. In order to suggest emotion, the artist must vary his expressive resources and adopt a different style or "mode" (Poussin's term) according to what he intends to convey. We shall take up this subject again in the chapter dealing with Poussin.

It is noteworthy that the germs of all subsequent modern aesthetics are to be found in the most Cartesian of all painters, who foreshadowed both of the two goals that art will pursue more and more explicitly—*plastic form*, which procures a specific pleasure (Poussin calls it "delectation") by pictorial means alone, by combinations of line and color, and *expression*, which transmits the artist's inner experiences to the soul of the viewer.

EIGHTEENTH-CENTURY SENSUALISM.   Whereas France tended to rely entirely on rational thought, English thinkers had long displayed a certain repugnance on this score. Bacon was inclined to take sensory experience for his guide rather than a priori logic, and regarded the former as indispensable in knowledge. Thomas Hobbes, although he was a friend of Descartes, brought philosophy back to the world of material bodies, eliminating absolute concepts. His ideas led to Locke's, according to whom the human mind has only sensations and reflection at its disposal; and reflection can only be exercised on the data provided by the senses: *Nihil est in intellectu quod non prius fuerit in sensu* (there is nothing in the intellect that was not first in the senses). Leibniz's thoughtful addition, *nisi ipse intellectus*, was held of little account in the eighteenth century. These theoretical views gained ground with Newton's discovery of the universal laws of gravitation (he presented his findings to the Royal Society in 1686). Reversing the order imposed by Descartes, he showed that facts must come before logic. By merely stating a physical fact, he destroyed the Cartesian concept of mechanism, his theory involving an essential though seemingly absurd idea: namely, that one body can move another body without coming into material contact with it.

French thought now came round to the English view: Condillac, d'Holbach, and La Mettrie acknowledged that the universal and absolute principles of thought derive from insights and habits acquired by sensory experience. According to Helvétius, the mind is a "blank page" on which only residues of sensations are inscribed. D'Alembert and Diderot recognized that a priori reasoning can lead to conclusions that are contrary to experience, and hence inadmissible.

It is therefore not surprising that art, and more especially painting, now began to pay less and less attention to rational principles, and relied more and more on sensory perception. Although the eighteenth century as a whole tended to lose faith in all moral rules, let alone abstract principles, the figurative art of the age aims primarily at visual delight and the pleasure of the imagination, and architectural decorative art at convenience and attractiveness. Like the age in general, its art rapidly passed from sensualism to sensuality, from charm to frivolity, and finally to pleasure seeking. The passage of three generations takes

*In France, as elsewhere, the rise of the bourgeoisie initiated an art of homely observation. Chardin is a particularly fine example of this new sensibility.*

**101.** - *CHARDIN.* LADY WITH A MUSIC BOX. The Frick Collection, New York (Copyright)

us from the profound inner reveries of Watteau to the sensuality of Boucher and then to the voluptuousness of Fragonard.

With the decline of logical reason, not only rules and constraints went overboard, but, also, the desire for an immutable, perfect absolute. The senses can only recognize the warmth and fleetingness of life in time. Increasing preoccupation with dynamic energy gradually supplants the cult of fixed form. Cartesian mechanism had conceived of matter as distinct from the reason that imposes its laws on matter. Leibniz, who died early in the eighteenth century, had already advanced an entirely different conception, in which the essence of bodies is movement. According to him, substance is not defined spatially but in terms of forces; the monads are the "atoms" of life, and the principle of the conservation of motion is supplanted by that of the conservation of kinetic energy. France, too, was evolving: like d'Holbach, Diderot rebelled against the conception of an inert matter; he emphasized movement and believed that the universe was produced by a "fermentation."

Art reflects an equally dynamic orientation. Everything in it begins to stir and becomes more animated. More and more, curves swell, roll, and undulate, dislocating rigid geometric patterns. Even the rudimentary regularity provided by symmetry is rejected; marble, and particularly clay, which sculptors prefer because of its malleability, throb under the fingers of Houdon and Pajou; Fragonard's brush bubbles and seethes with excitement.

Everywhere the Baroque was victorious, giving rise to the Rococo. It gave a new lease on life to German artists, who found in it an opportunity to gratify their old instinct for the vital thrust destructive of the established order (Fig. 98). Aesthetic theory took cognizance of the new developments: in his *Essai sur le Beau*, which he presented to the Academy of Caen in 1741, Father André contrasted essential beauty, which he saw primarily in geometric forms, with natural beauty, which marks the triumph of light and color. He stressed the importance of the inner life, and detected a rudimentary form of it in flowers, which he enjoyed because they had "a certain appearance of life... an appearance of sentience."

Now that all permanent a priori models were discarded, the very conception of human history was revolutionized. Religion looked back to a paradise lost prior to "man's first disobedience and the Fall." Humanists looked back to the perfection of antiquity. Since Plato's theory of recollection, the movement of thought had been conceived in terms of a steady regression. Suddenly this movement was reversed, and men began to look forward, to the future. In time, the new faith would become faith in "progress." The notion of evolution appeared in Diderot; it gained ground with Laplace, who applied it to inanimate matter. Lamarck extended it to living nature, and it triumphed with the doctrines of biological transformism and historical relativism in the nineteenth century, completing the rout of all absolute dogmas.

However, this impatient forward march was checked at the end of the eighteenth century by a reaction on the part of the Western—and very French—love of order. The bourgeoisie—a class traditionally attached to the principle of order—whose political importance was growing, was disturbed by the new trends. Moreover, it was trying to discredit the aristocracy by exposing its irresponsible and dissolute ways of life, to this end exalting principles of morality. The middle classes had reacted similarly toward the Church in the sixteenth century, when they rallied to the cause of Reformation. Now, virtue and moral conscience became immensely popular; by means of an appeal to conscience, which he internalized as instinct, Jean-Jacques Rousseau was able to restore the moral law without appeal to rational principles. For his part, Diderot, one of the earliest art critics, reacted against the idea of *delectation*, which the ruling class had carried to extremes, and he subordinated art to social usefulness, assigning it the task of setting an example, of teaching good conduct, of *endoctrinement des mœurs (moral indoctrination)*. Besides appreciating the authentic bourgeois probity of Chardin, Diderot praised the pictorial sermonizing of Greuze. He laid the aesthetic foundations for middle-class culture, which would, increasingly, be infatuated with realism. Referring to a painting by Chardin, he writes, "This is nature itself. The objects come out of the canvas with a truthfulness that deceives the eye...." He was a lay preacher: "Every work of sculpture or painting should be the expression of a great maxim, a lesson to the viewer.... To make virtue attractive, vice odious, ridiculousness emphatic—such is the purpose of every decent man when he takes up his pen, brush, or chisel" (Fig. 101).

The excavations of Pompeii (begun in 1748) revived interest in Classical antiquity, and more particularly in the virtues of the Roman Republic. David embraced the doctrine formulated by Winckelmann, which would restore moral austerity to the subjects treated and aesthetic austerity by cultivation of rigid sculptural forms (Fig. 102). His disciple Ingres was subscribing to this doctrine when he called drawing "the probity of art." This surprising revival of Classicism benefited from a series of social events that provoked fears of disorder and anarchy. Born of bourgeois indignation against aristocratic "corruption," Classicism served as the foundation for the art of the French Revolution. It remained the foundation for art under the Empire, reflecting bourgeois reactions to the violent excesses of the Terror. Under the Restoration, the aristocracy in turn became the champion of Classicism, as a cult of the past, out of attachment to traditional values which it felt obliged to exalt. At the same time, philosophy, in keeping with the political program that the Holy Alliance imposed on Europe, was also advancing a number of reactionary doctrines. Joseph de Maistre, Bonald, and even Lamennais launched attacks on the spirit of eighteenth-century political liberalism and freethinking. Diderot and the Encyclopedists were increasingly held responsible for the Revolution. Contradictory in origin and bolstered by successive appeals to order, Neo-Classicism received more and more admixtures of realistic platitude as the bourgeoisie continued its rise. Eventually it became the official art of the nineteenth century. With support from conservative, impeccably orthodox elements, it gradually declined, from Ingres to Bouguereau.

The existence of an official art in the nineteenth century led to a divorce between the artist and society without parallel in earlier Western history. This divorce lasted down to 1914. The most creative and valuable artists were no longer supported by society or even by the public. On the contrary, they were targets for open hostility on the part of the public. Those who did gain recognition had to struggle a long time to obtain it, and it was they who developed the new tendencies which Poussin had foreshadowed and which had been given further encouragement during the eighteenth century.

THE NINETEENTH CENTURY: HEYDAY OF GERMANIC THOUGHT. The humanism that succeeded the theocratic Middle Ages could maintain itself only as long as thought and society remained subordinated to the universality of reason. The moment

*But the bourgeoisie, in search of order, revives Cartesian Classicism. David introduces into it a tension that heralds Romantic dynamism.*

**102. -** *DAVID.* LICTORS BRINGING THE BODY OF HIS SON TO BRUTUS. Sketch.
National Museum, Stockholm

reason collapsed and eighteenth-century sensualism replaced absolute principles with the relativity of the senses, the way to individualism was opened. Its advent was accelerated by a social evolution that the middle classes furthered, eventually demanding freedom for all. Barrès observed justly that the Declaration of the Rights of Man was "the charter of individualism." It was also spurred on by intellectual developments, giving more and more substantial credit to individual experience in all its immediacy—whether in terms of sensations or of a moral sense. France encouraged this development, with its bent for psychologizing, which, after a long line of moralists following Montaigne, produced another great precursor in Maine de Biran. Describing himself as a man "disposed to observe internal phenomena," he emphasized introspection, "immediate apperception" of

*Baroque influence in the eighteenth century produced a greater liveliness.*

**103. -** *GUILLAUME COUSTOU.* One of the HORSES OF MARLY. 1740–45. Place de la Concorde, Paris

the data of consciousness. Thus, he rejected dogmatic principles in favor of inner experience. He taught the need to break away from "habit," i.e., from social and personal codifications of thought, and to discover within ourselves the "voluntary effort," which is a living "immaterial force" and which gives us the sense of freedom of choice. He thus foreshadowed an eventual reaction against the determinism so unrelentingly demonstrated by Spinoza: in art this assertion of freedom was reflected in the assertion of the individual's freedom to give expression to his inner experience, even at the expense of long-cherished traditions.

However, France, because of her Cartesian tradition, favored Classical tendencies rather than any such individualism of expression as the German Romantics exalted, and denounced individualism as anarchistic. Ever since the seventeenth century, the main current of German thought had been opposed to Cartesianism; now, in the course of the nineteenth century, it came to occupy the leading position that French thought had held in the eighteenth. The German victory was of limited scope, however, for even though Germany now determined the direction of the new ideas, France was almost alone in giving them creative expression. Already in the eighteenth century, France had disclosed a change in its tastes. Symptomatic in this respect was the fact that it turned away from the Italians in favor of the Northern schools, particularly the Dutch. The English, for their part, had at the same time supplemented the moralizing middle-class realism of Hogarth

*A comparison between Géricault and Coustou shows that the passionate violence of Romanticism derives from an eighteenth-century strain. The Baroque implied a return to living experience, and hence a progressively greater awareness of vital energies, such as David displayed, for all his Neo-Classicism.*

**104.** - *GÉRICAULT.* SIGN FOR A BLACKSMITH'S SHOP. Private collection, Paris and the aristocratic facility of portraitists such as Reynolds and Romney with a Nordic sense of nature. It first appeared, perhaps, in the dreamy art of Gainsborough. The direct emotion of Constable and the visionary poetry of Turner both helped to alienate nine-teenth-century art from preoccupation with the human condition in all its limitations and to orient it toward what lies beyond. Long before this, Shakespeare had observed that "there are more things in heaven and earth, Horatio, than are dreamt of in your philos-ophy." However, it was the Germanic genius more than any other, with its preference for intuition rather than logic, that took the plunge into the mysteries of the unknown—the mysteries of the cosmos and of the darker zones of the inner life alike, situated outside the sway of reason. The time had come for a new assault on the Latin world. According to Schmidhauser, the Reformation "broke upon the Platonic and Aristotelian theology of the Middle Ages, just as the German barbarians had overrun Greco-Roman civilization." In the nineteenth century, this observation acquired new topicality: the antagonism referred to is indeed recurrent!

Thus, a France, which we have just seen ready to renounce abstract generalities and to plunge more deeply into individual particularity, was encouraged by Germany to take the path of subjectivity and to repudiate a static logic in favor of a dynamic vitalism. These two impulses favored the emergence of an art expressive of the dark drives and forces of the sensibility, an art bent upon originality rather than any observance of rules (Fig. 105).

Germany had long been pressing in this direction. The *Aufklärung*, the "Age of Reason," which had reached Germany in its French form during the eighteenth century, never gained much national or popular adherence there. Already, at the end of the preceding century, the philosopher Leibniz, though he was steeped in Cartesianism, had opened philosophy to currents that were to swamp Cartesianism. His theory of the differential calculus pointed to the exploration of the continuous and the infinitesimally small; the "confused" perceptions that he opposed to clear perceptions had introduced the notion of an unconscious mind; his monads, because they were never identical, suggested the limitless diversity and originality of individual forms and, unlike the inert matter in space of Cartesian mechanism, they imposed the conception of a universal dynamism. Inciden-tally, Maine de Biran in France claimed kinship with Leibniz, who had admitted "no reality save that of simple beings whose essence is *active force*." And Leibniz originated the idea that "to be and to be active is one and the same thing." He also conceived the idea of evolution: "Every present state of a simple substance is a natural consequence of its preceding state, so that its present is pregnant with the future."—What a contrast with Descartes, who saw the universe as essentially motionless, "a machine of which there is nothing to study save the forms and movements of its parts." It could almost have served as a definition of a painting by Le Brun! Leibniz extended his revolutionary dynamism even to psychology. Anticipating the Romantics, he declared: "Restlessness is essential to the felicity of creatures, which never consists in a perfect possession [this had been the ideal of Classicism] such as would make them insensitive and stupid (as it were), but in contin-uous, uninterrupted progress toward greater happiness." Once this seed had had time to germinate, we were ready for a modern art conceived as creative force— ormented, never repeating itself, in perpetual innovation.

Kant dealt an even severer blow at the foundation of Classical thought. He robbed not only reason but material reality as well of all absolute value. The sensibility by means of

*Germany inaugurated Romanticism. Its art began to express the deep and obscure aspirations of the soul.*

**105.** - *KASPAR DAVID FRIEDRICH.* CROSS AND CATHEDRAL IN THE MOUNTAINS.
Museum, Düsseldorf

*Landscape becomes the place where the artist's avid search enters into communion with nature's grandeur and mystery.*

**106. - THÉODORE ROUSSEAU.** THE WOODS

which we experience things, the understanding which transforms experience into concepts, and the reason which unifies concepts—with their respective forms (space and time), categories, and regulative principles—secure for us no more than a knowledge of appearances, never a knowledge of things in themselves. This meant the end of objectivity. The impulse given by Kant drove art ever more resolutely toward finding new bearings. Kant asserted that the judgment of taste "is not a cognitive judgment; hence it is not logical but aesthetic, that is, the principle that determines it is purely subjective." Thus the art of the future was now authorized to ignore visible reality and logical principles alike, and to prefer the personal vision. Nor has art since Kant's day been slow to take advantage of this new permissiveness....

The *Sturm und Drang* group glorified creative genius, freed from the discipline of the real world and from well-defined rules of thought. The genius is an exceptional individual. These early Romantics invoked the philosopher Fichte for having gone further than Kant in exalting the spiritual energy of the absolute I. According to Fichte, the conscious finite I projects what it does not contain into the non-I; it is this non-I that we call the outside world and that is actually a creation of the I. There is no reason now for art to reproduce external models or even to observe rules; what matters is solely the genius's original personal vision.

This radical subjectivism was only gradually arrived at. Novalis and Schelling—though the latter emphasized the importance of unconscious energies as stimulants of conscious activity—still ascribed positive reality to nature. They saw it as the symmetrical counterpart of the soul, but inseparable from it, and it is reality that provokes the creative spark. Madame de Staël, in her book *De l'Allemagne*, found a beautiful image to express this duality: "The poet succeeds in restoring unity between the physical and the moral world: his imagination forms a link between the two." The evolution of science was meanwhile helping to discredit mechanistic materialism and building to a conception of life as "fluidic" energy. The discoveries made by Galvani and Volta in the domain of electricity and magnetism struck every imagination at the close of the eighteenth century, making the world seem suddenly endowed with new and different features. According to Schelling, the artist uses outward forms as symbols to translate his own creative power, and acts in the manner of nature within the human soul (Fig. 104).

This profound change in ideas had multiple repercussions. It resulted in a new and fervent effusiveness by which mankind was linked with the rest of life. It encouraged a confused mystical religiosity. Artists felt it intensely: they persuaded themselves that the emotional purity of the early Italian Renaissance from the Primitives to Raphael (painters who enjoyed a new vogue with Romanticism) reflected a similar religiosity. The movement started in Germany with the Nazarenes was continued in France by the analogous group founded in the wake of Ingres, and in England it led to the Pre-Raphaelites.

This religiosity takes on the form of pantheism in the landscape painters: individualism favors solitude, and in solitude man communes with the universe; in portraying it he finds the pleasures of confession combined with those of deeply moving contemplation. The leader of the Barbizon School, Théodore Rousseau, seems to be echoing Schelling when he exclaims: "When we look at nature with all the religion we have in our hearts, we feel and express a real world all of whose fatalities enfold us.... The artist's soul attains plenitude in the infinite of nature..." (Fig. 106).

NINETEENTH-CENTURY INDIVIDUALISM AND POSITIVISM. The conception of beauty had undergone a radical change: it no longer had any objective foundation outside the individual sensibility. How could it have when Kierkegaard denied to the universal and the impersonal the power to stand for truth? There was no longer any model for beauty, either external or ideal; every artist must create it for himself all over again. But to relativism arising out of awareness of limitless individual variety was added a growing awareness of historical relativism. The development of historical research, particularly in France, occurred over the same period that produced the doctrine of evolution, from Geoffroy Saint-Hilaire to Darwin and the systems of the philosophers. As early as the beginning of the eighteenth century, Vico had outlined a dynamic theory of social development as a succession of states, which, however, he still saw as moving cyclically. The eighteenth century went further: it outlined the idea of steady progress. German thinkers, obsessed with a desire to substitute Germanic "becoming" for Latin and

Cartesian "being," systematized this tendency. Hegel adopted the view that the artist's most important attribute is an intense personality, but he subordinated evolution to historical necessity. The earliest symbolic form of art was relegated to the past; the second form, Classicism, suffered the same fate. Mankind had arrived at the latest, contemporary form of art—the Romantic. Moreover, Hegel formulated his famous triadic concept of dialectical progression—thesis, antithesis, synthesis. Previously, it had been thought that art was at best capable of perfecting or surpassing earlier achievements; now it seemed necessary to struggle against all that had been hitherto recognized as art and to negate it. It was now even possible to conceive of negation as a means of creating future truth and reality. The "moderns" who had been victorious over the "ancients" in the eighteenth century were now left behind in their turn. They had merely believed that tradition was perfectible; now the notion of a revision of values was asserted. Art no longer possessed the conservative function that the Classicists had ascribed to it; its function was now recognized as revolutionary.

Outside philosophy, the profound writings of the greatest nineteenth-century painter, Delacroix, give striking and lucid expression to all these themes, confirming the fact that the artist creates in accordance with theories current in his time. In 1857, Delacroix published a long essay, *The Variations of the Beautiful*, in which he stressed the diversity of notions of beauty in different civilizations: "The beautiful, like customs, like ideas, undergoes every sort of metamorphosis." Occasionally, Delacroix suggested geographic and economic causes for this diversity, such as, in sculpture, the availability of specific materials in a given country. But he also pointed out "the influence of the way of life... more effective than that of climate." It is interesting to note, incidentally, that Karl Marx was born twenty years after Delacroix, and that it was not until 1865 that Taine published his *Philosophy of Art*, in which he declared: "The work of art is determined by an ensemble consisting of the general state of mind and the manners and customs of the artist's environment." In the same work he applied his famous theory that the determining factors are period, race, and environment.

Delacroix also stressed the relativism that arises out of the individual nature of every artist who, by definition, is "a unique man. Is it not possible to say, without paradox, that it is his singularity, his personality... the new face of things he reveals" that constitute his greatness?

Later on, we shall have to come back to this theory of individualism as developed by Delacroix and, after him, by Baudelaire. Let us keep in mind for the time being that, in the eyes of Delacroix, the artist is a creator of life: the beautiful "emerges from within amid travail and torment, like everything that is destined to live." It is not the fruit of imitation, nor of the application of rules. It springs from the imagination, "the queen of faculties." Reality merely gives "a kind of consecration to the imagined part"; nature serves only to provide the words of a "dictionary" with the help of which the artist translates the "idea" he conceives into a new and personal language. In the last analysis, that idea is a manifestation of his own innermost soul, which he makes visible to others.

Now, it must be observed that as early as 1810, in the book *De l'Allemagne* which introduced Germanism to France, Madame de Staël had defined poetry as "an ability to reveal... what one feels in one's own heart," an ability "to release the feeling imprisoned in the depths of the soul." She said that the new German poetry "made use of our personal impressions in order to move us." More important is the fact that Hegel's *Aesthetics*,

214

*Impressionism, perceiving light instead of forms, sees reality as a flow of energy, thus anticipating modern science.*
**107.** - *MONET*. IMPRESSION, SUNRISE. 1874. Musée Marmottan, Paris

which was published in French translation in 1852, contains similar ideas. Hegel speaks of the manifestation of inner life, and says that color is its principal means. He celebrates music, which expresses the sensibility unfolding in time, without recourse to space. He celebrates poetry as describing external objects only in order to communicate to the reader a vibration of the soul—"the ideal" in a subjective sense very different from its objective, Platonic sense. As early as 1841, the Collège de France founded a chair of Germanic languages and literatures, the first occupant of which was Philarète Chasles.

Baudelaire, who was no doubt the greatest of all art critics, never concealed his debt to Delacroix in this field. His own contribution was to define the suggestive powers of art more exactly, as in his theory of correspondences, which had been foreshadowed by Hoffmann. Appealing to different senses according to the techniques of each art, "odors, colors, and sounds correspond to one another," for they have a single source in the indefinable affective reality that they communicate. In Baudelaire a triumphant Romanticism is heralding Symbolism.

Greco-Roman rationalism was well-nigh swamped under this largely Germanic on-slaught. But traditional Western thought staged a comeback by modernizing itself. Abandoning the positions maintained by a rationalist Classicism now obsolete, passion for objectivity and clarity was given new foundations consistent with faith in concrete reality and in logic. Science led the way in this development. In his masterly *Introduction à la médecine expérimentale*, Claude Bernard demonstrated that sensory perception controlled by reason can lead to certain knowledge. The same idea underlies Auguste Comte's elab-oration of positivism. The latter went back to the eighteenth-century tradition of objective sensualism and rationalism, revising it in the light of historical relativism. At the same time, he sought to eliminate Romantic individualism, and "to bring the revolutionary period to a close," so as to restore to thought the objective universality that it had lost. According to him, the theological epoch and the metaphysical epoch that followed it were dead and gone, and a third epoch was beginning—the positivist epoch—which would no longer concern itself with the "why" of things but seek to determine, in accordance with rigorous universal laws, the "how" of the phenomena we perceive and the constant laws that govern them.

After a period of intoxication with Romanticism, which enriched it by shattering its traditionalism, French art also went back to the exact observation of phenomena, banish-ing all interpretation according to aesthetic or idealist principles. Courbet proclaimed, "Painting is the representation of visible objects.... The essence of realism is its negation of the ideal." Thus, artistic naturalism was born. However, like Daumier and Millet, and to a greater extent than they, Courbet was haunted by social problems, which were also leaving their mark on the positivist philosophy of the day. These problems were taking on alarming urgency as the peasants and the workers rose against the dictatorship of the bourgeoisie. Courbet knew and admired Proudhon and other Socialist theoreticians. The year 1848 marked a high point in the rise of the new spirit. Auguste Comte crowned his doctrine with a sociology—in 1847 he had declared that art had "an eminent social des-tination." All over Europe, in sculpture as well as in painting, naturalism was being tinged with humanitarian social preoccupations. As early as 1833, the journal *Charivari* had observed: "Today painting must inevitably become popularist and democratic." And in 1857 Paul de Saint-Victor called Millet's famous *Gleaners* "the Parcae of pauperism"—and the artist was far from pleased by the tendentious epithet.

THE TWENTIETH CENTURY AND MODERN ART.   The two adverse currents—realistic objectivism and expressive subjectivism—gained strength about equally, and the conflict between them had its ups and downs. The positivist vision seemed victorious in Impressionism, which stripped art of social implications and reduced it to an accurate rendering of optical sensations divorced from intellectual notions, even those of space and energy. Cézanne said of Monet, "He is nothing but an eye." Neo-Impressionism, dom-inated by Seurat, was more submissive to science and systematized the application of its laws, particularly the law of "simultaneous contrast of colors" formulated by Chevreul as far back as 1827. Insofar as it aimed at harmony, it sought its formula in mathematics, under the influence of the scientist Charles Henry (Fig. 107).

However, in the same period—at the close of the nineteenth century—the objective current, which was more and more associated with science (then dominated by the materialism of Marcelin Berthelot and tinged with social concerns under the influence of Herbert Spencer's evolutionism), encountered renewed resistance from the ranks of the neo-spiritualists. Oriented to inner experience, thinkers like Ravaisson and Boutroux consistently criticized "scientism," which had two still more powerful adversaries in Renouvier and Bergson. At the same time, the Symbolist movement in literature and in art was denying the priority—or even the existence—of the outside world. Gauguin, who had begun as an Impressionist, now saw in things no more than "the visible signification of a thought." He reduced art to the expression of inner realities, different in each being; "I am confining myself to the exploration of myself, not of nature." This implied a shift in the means used. "In short, we must look for suggestion in painting rather than for description." Once again, subjectivism was taking precedence over objective reality.

As the twentieth century approached, it seemed that we must do without the attempt to restore a stable, permanent truth such as realism had affirmed. In opposing it, twentieth-century thought once again based itself on the individual, opposing his originality to the concrete certainties of believers in science, and his capacity for revolt to the values accepted and imposed by society.

In France, Augustin Cournot had prophesied that the progress of a materialist civilization would result in the degradation of life and abolition of the individual. Renouvier refused to surrender the human person to sociological necessity; he sought to protect it against the strangle hold of scientific determinism. In Germany, Nietzsche thought that culture was threatened with a "weariness with life." As it seemed to him, weariness was vitiating all established values, from Christianity to Socialism, and including rationalism. Our only hope of salvation, according to him, was negation of these values by the individual, however respectable they might seen. The individual must assert his "will to power."

The contemporary mind was being formed. It, too, would mistrust all curtailments of the individual's creative energies. It would look suspiciously at every established value, whether the objectivity of realism or the validity of traditions and rules. André Gide formulated the new catechism in L'Immoraliste: "What mattered was what separated, distinguished me from the others; what I had to say, what no one but I was saying or could say." Art was to be the instrument for making manifest an irreducible pursuit of novelty, deliberately aggressive with respect to all accepted ideas. This intransigent drive was checked by two major obstacles—material reality, and the laws of reason, both of which enter into the problems of identity and community. Surprisingly, the very science which was based on them and in turn supported them with the prestige of its achievements, which founded truth and order on them, now began to undermine them in a strange way. On the one hand, the inexorable consequences of experimentation continually carried forward led to a far-reaching revision of the most familiar concepts. The discovery of radioactivity revolutionized the conception of matter, Einstein's theory of relativity the conceptions of space and time. On the other hand, it became necessary to revise and broaden the logic that had been recognized since Aristotle, if not to replace it with an altogether new logic. Philosophy, meanwhile, showed with Bergson that the principles long regarded as the rational foundations of science were no more than a practical but schematic systematization of life, of "the vital current," which scientists distort in their efforts to make it intelligible.

*Freed from rational constraints, modern art projects the instinctual anxieties that rise from the uttermost depths of being.*

**108.** - *MUNCH.* IN HELL: SELF-PORTRAIT. 1895. Museum of Fine Arts, Oslo

Suddenly liberated from what had long been obstacles to its progress, left to its own devices and obliged to determine its goal and its function without outside help, art saw only two courses open: either it would be an instrument of enjoyment or an instrument of expression. Each school and individual temperament would have to choose between them according to inner disposition, but the extremest consequences were drawn in either case. For art was no longer restrained by any external consideration, whether derived from nature or logic; its course was now entirely determined by its own explorations.

As an instrument of enjoyment, art makes free use of the means at its disposal, its vocabulary of lines, forms, and colors. By "assembling them in a certain order" it discovers new and more autonomous resources; this is the road traveled by nonfigurative art from Gauguin to Cubism (via Cézanne's constructivism) and on to abstraction.

As an instrument of expression, art will oppose to normal vision the vision revealed by the artist's inner life. Carried forward by the most violent and most disturbing impulses, it progressed from Van Gogh to Fauvism in France, and from Munch to Nordic and

Germanic Expressionism. With Surrealism it set out to explore the unconscious mind that Freudian psychoanalysis had discovered in the depths of the human psyche. Much recent abstract art, proclaiming that it is "nonformal," has confined itself to projecting the most organic drives on canvas (Figs. 108 and 109).

Has the West renounced its old dream of setting up objective, universal foundations of art? Discarding all a priori rules, has it handed art over to the chance results of experiment? Still, in the face of a hypersubjectivism that, today, goes so far as to scorn communication, we find that there has been an unexpected comeback, furthered by political considerations, of the nineteenth-century current of evolutionary positivism. Invoking Marx and dialectical materialism, it has culminated in the official art of the USSR, though not all of the Socialist republics subscribe to it. The most modern movements find ardent followers, for instance, in Poland. In its new form, the dogma still negates the individual, denouncing him as a symptom of the decline of a civilization. It seeks the truth in what might be called the law of the greatest number: since the foundation of all objectivity has become precarious, an equivalent is sought in the consciousness of the majority, the masses. The goal is an art that should reflect both the beliefs of the masses—that is, a banal realism—and their aspirations, i.e., an art confined to subjects expressing their needs and struggles.

*Freed from realistic constraints, modern art records uncontrolled bursts of primordial energy.*

**109. -**
*GEA PANTER.*
DUALITY. 1959.
Owned by the artist

Must, then, art again be reduced to the role of docile spokesman for collectiveness? The antagonism that has been gradually more apparent since the nineteenth century has today become irreconcilable. More tragically than ever before, the inner affinities between art and thought, between thought and history, assert themselves. A social and political conflict—a world conflict—looms behind the narrower conflict that opposes a traditional culture to a new ideology.

And now, suddenly, the East has joined in this game of giants, and the West is no longer the sole master of its fate. Two aesthetics and two social systems confront each other. On the one hand, China joins Russia in the will to a popular objectivism; on the other, the West leans ever more willingly toward abstract art, in which national particularities become no less blurred.

The United States, in its impatience to be the spearhead of civilization, has failed to recognize that culture does not necessarily keep step with material progress and has neglected its own cultural development. The very advances of its technology have called attention more dramatically to the gap between a dizzying material progress and a spiritual life that is in complete confusion. Alternatively, it exhibits a cultural narrowness closed to all historical development, or else improvises too hasty and too spectacular remedies. The American avant-garde, impatient to throw off the yoke of European tradition, is plunging headlong into an art that sweeps aside every achievement of the past and relies on the raw energy of instinctual impulses. American Abstract Expressionism, as it is called, is finding growing favor in Europe as well.

Thus, in the second half of the twentieth century, we have our choice between two extremes. On the one hand, an art which calls itself popular but which actually is a prolongation of the bourgeois realism of the past century, and whose exclusive materialism is a dogmatic reflection of the latter. On the other hand, an art that aspires to utter novelty but puts aggressive improvisation above maturity. Caught midway between the two, old Europe, pregnant with the past—and, it would seem, with the future—is divided between concern for preserving its heritage and desire to throw itself into the creative adventure. Under these chaotic conditions, art reflects the truly geological fault that divides mankind in two today. Culture seems to have liberated itself from obsolete traditions only to be faced with a choice between blind collective certainties and the anxieties of the submerged individual, which frequently drive him to negation and destructiveness. Once again, the solution cannot lie in a choice between two such antithetical attitudes, both as pregnant with danger as they are with promise. It can only lie in striving toward a synthesis of the two, such as has scarcely as yet been attempted.

# AN ARTIST AND THE THOUGHT OF HIS TIME:

# LEONARDO DA VINCI

Our bird's-eye survey discloses a certain parallelism between the evolution of art and of thought over the centuries of Western history. The one and the other seem to be transpositions in different keys of a single structure that defines a given epoch, its position in relation to its own past and in relation to the future it is preparing. This parallelism is obvious with respect to general trends, but is it also valid with respect to particular instances? Is not the great artist—who is by definition original and exceptional—exempt from the effects of this parallelism? Actually, although his value is measured by the personal quality that he confers upon the data serving as his point of departure, he finds these data in his own epoch and shares them with his contemporaries. He does not appear suddenly, like a meteor fallen from some unknown star; he is more like a plant that grows in a specific soil, distinguished from other plants only by the fact that it produces flowers of incomparable brilliance and grows taller than the others. It is primarily the artist's sensibility that distinguishes him from his fellow men; his thought obeys the same laws and is confronted with the same problems as that of his contemporaries. Moreover, thought's role in art is as important as sensibility's. Thought orients sensibility's explorations, assigns its goals, and is responsible for its initiatives as well as for its constraints. In short, the contents of art are poured into molds prepared by thought.

It is not enough to assert that there are over-all, collective relations between thought and art. Every artist expresses them in his own way, and there are as many ways as there are individual artists of genius. For this reason, it seems that to study some one case with thoroughness could best convey the rich complexity of the problem—and what case could serve our purpose better than Leonardo da Vinci's? He is almost unique in having secured for himself a prominent place both in the history of art and of thought. He appears at a moment of transition—between the waning Middle Ages and the emergent Renaissance. It is on this great divide that Leonardo is situated, historically speaking. We think of him as a man of the Renaissance—if there ever was one—but let us look more closely at this possibly oversimplified view of the matter.

LEONARDO ON THE MARGIN OF THE RENAISSANCE. The historian can never be sure that his Penelope-like task has come to an end. In order to gain understanding of the infinitely complex facts confronting him, he subsumes them under a few key notions, which serve for his orientation. These are soon seized upon by the public at large and, reduced to routine formulas, perpetuated in textbooks. By the time this has happened, however, the historian is beginning to revise his thinking in an effort to recapture the original richness of life.

The men of the Renaissance were very emphatic about their own originality. Their earliest historians, led by Vasari, turned out a series of medal-like effigies of them in this spirit. In order to present their masters in the best possible light, the Neo-Classicists heaped abuse on the Renaissance's immediate past. Thus the medieval epoch fell into discredit; for a long time thereafter—apart from a rehabilitation of medieval art in the nineteenth century—its character and achievements were simply ignored. The prevalent view was that the Renaissance had emerged out of total darkness, like some new sun, the sole and original source of light.

Eventually a reaction against this view got under way. Philosophers, one of the most important among them being Etienne Gilson, recognized the richness and value of medieval thought, which had for long been contemptuously dismissed as "Scholasticism." Before Gilson, a great student of the history of science, Pierre Duhem, had demonstrated the falseness of the myth according to which all modern discoveries originated in the Renaissance. To the contrary, he established, they were the fruits of a slow gestation begun in the Middle Ages.

Debate between champions of the Renaissance and of the Middle Ages continues. Rather than simply choose between them, we shall begin with the premise that the Renaissance represents a complex stage of Western development, and that it introduced elements in sharp reaction to what had come before it. We see it as incorporating these new elements in a revived comprehension of antiquity, but in other respects we see it as continuing and bringing to maturation elements it inherited directly from the centuries immediately preceding. Among the most important of these elements, was the experimental spirit that was to create modern science. It had been a-borning since the thirteenth century, and the Renaissance happened to be the moment when, after having been formulated, the experimental method began to be applied.

Leonardo da Vinci played a crucial part in the history of experimental science. Berthelot contested his value as a scientist, no doubt because, living himself in a epoch when men of science and men of letters thought it necessary to despise each other, he disliked the idea that a famous painter should be among the founding fathers of modern experimentalism. Pierre Duhem (whom Berthelot, by the way, treated with marked animosity) showed on the basis of a careful study of the texts that Leonardo had not been a creator *ex nihilo*, and that writings dating from an earlier epoch had provided him with a good deal of material. (Duhem stressed the fact that this was also true of Copernicus and Galileo.) This is not to diminish Leonardo's achievement in any sense. He was a man of genius, the first to translate into practice an aspiration to experimental knowledge for which men had been groping for two centuries. He cannot be truly understood or put in his rightful place unless his ideas are seen as the end result of medieval aspirations. They remain among the constituent elements of the fifteenth and sixteenth centuries, which were the legitimate heirs of the thirteenth and the fourteenth.

*In the larger of these pages, Leonardo portrayed himself meditating on the secrets of "that which is," and particularly the most elusive secret of all, the nature of fluids. On the other page, unable to resist the curiosity for "that which could be," he distorted his own features in a caricature.*

**110. -** *LEONARDO DA VINCI.* LEONARDO MEDITATING ON THE MOVEMENT OF WATER.
Drawing. Royal Library, Windsor Castle. (By gracious permission of H. M. The Queen)
**111. -** *LEONARDO DA VINCI.* SELF-PORTRAIT. Drawing. Royal Library, Windsor Castle.
(By gracious permission of H. M. The Queen)

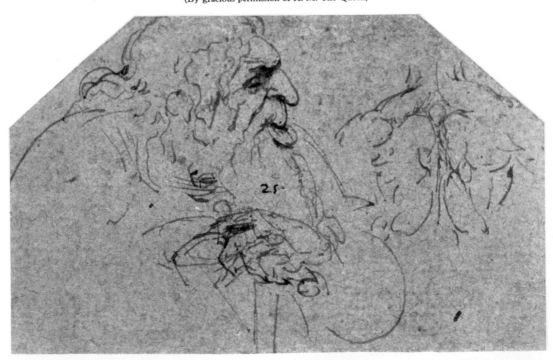

*Leonardo was a Renaissance artist only when he pursued ideal beauty—the beauty incarnated in this pure-faced Madonna, composed according to the principle of the pyramid. His pupils lack his depth and richness; his ideas are echoed most closely by the German artist Dürer (compare the treatment of the hair).*

**112.** - *LEONARDO DA VINCI.* THE VIRGIN OF THE ROCKS (detail). 1483–90. The Louvre, Paris

**113.** - *GIAMPETRINO.* SALVADOR MUNDI. Institute of Arts, Detroit

Vasari placed at the summit of the Renaissance pantheon the three exemplary figures of Leonardo, Raphael, and Michelangelo. But, actually, only Raphael embodies the contribution of his epoch. Leonardo marks the culminating point of a previously existing spirit, and Michelangelo foreshadows future developments. Leonardo is a man of the Renaissance only insofar as he carries to completion a constructive synthesis that the Middle Ages had begun—something very far from a turning of his back upon the past. And this accounts for his ambiguous position among his contemporaries.

For, after all is said and done, was Leonardo really recognized, appreciated, and duly honored by the Renaissance? It reserved for him a fate very different from that it bestowed upon Raphael, in whom it saw its own admired image. Leonardo had to struggle to carve out a place for himself. His contemporaries respected him, rather than liked him; their admiration was for a strange kind of miracle worker, and they mostly gave him a rather wide berth. In Florence, his native city, his welcome from Lorenzo de'Medici was not unequivocal. Lorenzo appreciated him mainly as a musician, a manufacturer of strange new instruments—Leonardo was the violinmaker he recommended to Ludovico Sforza! The potentate of Milan, too, was reticent in his enthusiasm: he saw in Leonardo primarily an engineer, an organizer of public festivities; and we know how long it took him

**114. -** *DÜRER. SELF-PORTRAIT.* 1500.
Alte Pinakothek, Munich

to commission the famous equestrian statue. In Rome, Leo X, another Medici, scarcely favored his fellow countryman. In fact, he kept him almost entirely out of public projects in papal Rome, and called upon his services mainly for the reclamation of the Pontine Marshes. In Rome, too, his artistic gifts seem to have been regarded as secondary, and he was looked upon primarily as an inventor. As for his pictorial masterpieces, it would seem that Leonardo's father, the notary Ser Piero, played a large part in the complicated scheme that resulted in the contract for the first of these masterpieces, *The Adoration of the Magi.* The enthusiastic admiration displayed by Louis XII contributed much to the success of *The Last Supper*; but, except for Isabella d'Este, no Italian prince made a serious effort to hold the artist in Italy. His wandering life ended in exile at the court of Francis I. The relations between Leonardo and his most prominent contemporaries—there can be no doubt about it—were always marred by a certain awkwardness.

This latent disagreement between Leonardo da Vinci and the spirit of the Renaissance will seem less surprising when we recognize to what extent he was profoundly alien to its essential program—humanism. This statement calls for an explanation. Taking humanism in its latter-day sense of universality, such a statement would certainly be absurd. However, it is not absurd when we take the term in the sense Leonardo's contemporaries gave to it. The humanism of the Renaissance was essentially a revival of the Platonic ideal, and it rapidly became the age's chief rallying point. Now, we are compelled to recognize that Leonardo remained alien to this ideal, that he was in fact much more closely related to a current of thought that had asserted itself at the close of the Middle Ages. Within the complexity of the Renaissance, he seems far less bound up with the new Platonic current than with another, the one that, in continuation of impulses initiated in the preceding centuries, in the end gave birth to experimental research (Figs. 110 and 111).

In this connection, let us make sure there is no misunderstanding. The art of Leonardo da Vinci, as embodied in his paintings, easily takes its place in the aesthetic development of his epoch. These paintings were conceived, for the most part, to accord with contemporary tastes and preferences, and they largely fulfilled contemporary expectations. And yet, do not his works stand out from among those of his contemporaries by a certain strangeness and mystery? Who can fail to perceive in them, along with the pursuit of ideal beauty, the outcroppings of enigmatic inner preoccupations unmatched by anything around him? As for the famous, unique smile and his exhaustive, painstaking study of draperies, would we find them incongruous set next to the sculptures at Reims (Figs. 112 to 114)?

When we leave the domain of his public realizations and enter that of his private explorations—when we leaf through the countless pages of drawings and, most especially, the precious manuscripts in which he set down his reflections, we discover materials on which to base a definition of his personal approach and the historical currents to which it is most closely related.

BETWEEN HUMANISM AND SCIENCE.   Leonardo da Vinci's writings prove that he disagrees with the majority of his contemporaries. He belongs far less to the present—his present—than to the past, a part of the waning Middle Ages whose development he extends and completes. But he also belongs to the future: he outlines a system of thought and a conception of the world that did not fully assert themselves until after the Platonic principles of the Renaissance had once again gone into eclipse. This is why we see him as a precursor, and this is why his modernity was so abundantly stressed during recent commemorations of his birth five hundred years ago.

Not only the spirit of Leonardo's conceptions, but also his conduct of life sets him apart from his contemporaries.

The very circumstances of his birth and upbringing set him off from the others. The son of Ser Piero, a lawyer, and born out of wedlock to Caterina, a peasant of Vinci, he did not receive the education normally given to boys of good family. Although the validity of an old tradition to this effect has been doubted, it seems true that up to the age of five he was brought up by his mother as a little countryboy—this may account for his feeling for nature, which was exceptional for his time. Once he had gone to live with his father, he was given a rather summary schooling which included Latin and mathematics but which fell far short of that given to well-born boys. Thus, Leonardo's mind was formed outside the customary norms of the epoch, and he always cut the figure of a prodigious autodidact, curious about everything, but, all the same, a self-taught man. In his remarkable studies of the Leonardo source materials, Solmi contests the thesis of Leonardo's lack of schooling, but he is compelled to admit that he had only rudimentary notions of Greek and that his Latin was mediocre. There can be no doubt that the contemporary mandarins made him painfully aware of his shortcomings in this regard, which, in their eyes, were most reprehensible. Early in his career, he felt keenly the contempt—more or less thinly disguised—of the respectable people he was seeing at that time. He sets it down with bitterness: "Because I am *omo sanza lettere* (a man without letters), some are presumptuous enough to hold this against me, alleging that I am not a humanist—the stupid tribe!" (Cod. Atl. 119). Elsewhere he uses the familiar argument: "Good letters are the result of a good disposition, and since the cause has greater dignity than the effect, a good disposition is more valuable than learning without disposition" (Cod. Atl. 76). He was to some extent regarded as a person of "common" background, and he suffered from this. Leon Battista Alberti, whose strong personality dominated Florence when Leonardo went there at the age of sixteen (in 1468), said: "A man who knows nothing, a man without letters, will be looked upon as a yokel even if he be a gentleman by birth."

Leonardo's legitimate pride took on a note of defiance. Far from trying to minimize the gulf separating him from others, he boasted of it and called attention to it. There is only one master, he declared—nature. And those who flaunt their familiarity with ancient works are nothing but bookworms, unaware of the fact that the works they admire originally took nature for model. Excluded from the proud group of the humanists, he passes judgment on them in the name of an opposed conception of knowledge: "My adversaries will say that because I am deficient in the humanities, I cannot say well what I want to express. They do not know that my works are dictated by experience rather than by the words of others, and experience has always been the teacher of those who wrote well. I, too, take her for my teacher.... If, unlike them, I do not cite authors, my source is higher and nobler—experience, the teacher of their teachers...." (Cod. Atl. 117). This is what he says about men of bookish learning: "They walk proud and pompous, clothed and adorned not with their works but with those of others, and they challenge my works and despise me"—"they" here being further qualified as "reciters and declaimers of the works of others." And this is what he has to say about the men who let direct experience guide them: they are "the inventors who interpret nature to mankind." He went further. "I, an inventor, and greatly superior to them, the trumpeters and declaimers, the reciters of other people's works, contemptible on other grounds as well."

In the same spirit, he draws a line between the scientific-minded and the "sophists": "You, with the crowd of sophists, you deceive yourselves and you deceive the others, by despising the mathematical sciences which contain the truth" (Richter, 1210). The conflict here alluded to is still very much alive in our own day, for we inherited it from the Renaissance. It sometimes seems as though we do not often enough realize to what extent the basis of European culture is divided against itself. Has any other civilization split its educational system into two distinct branches that sometimes belittle each other—the humanities and the sciences? The conflict referred to by Leonardo is still very much around, but we have become used to it to remark it very often. The humanities, based on Classical culture, primarily promote the free play of ideas. The sciences, based originally on direct sensory experience, stress primarily the application of mathematics. Thus, we are still living within a dual tradition: one, from the Renaissance on, has been nourished by knowledge of the ancient languages and other similarly "impractical" matters, study of which develops, as well as ornaments, the mental faculties as such; and another, the scientific tradition, is synonymous with the spirit of exactness, objectivity, and disciplined knowledge, seeking verification of its activity in the outside world where—as Paul Valéry observed so subtly—"perceiving" counts far more than "conceiving." We must, however, note that perceiving and conceiving tend to come closer to each other and to merge in twentieth-century science, which is much more abstract than nineteenth-century science. So far as that goes, the whole of post-Renaissance culture seems increasingly to be put in question and to be in process of being revised.

However that may be, it is important to note that the current of scientific thought did not originate in the Renaissance, as the current of literary thought did. To be sure, the Renaissance contributed to its irresistible development, but added nothing of its own substance to it. For it had existed earlier, at least in rudimentary form—its principles, however badly applied, had been formulated during the Middle Ages, an epoch long deprecated and little known, and perhaps especially that period of the Middle Ages beginning in the late twelfth century, when the new tendency to experimental research first raised its head in opposition to the older Scholasticism. Roger Bacon, *doctor mirabilis*, formulated its main outlines; in the fifteenth century Leonardo took his place in the family of thinkers founded by this precursor, a full century before Francis Bacon. Thus, Leonardo was not the founding father of this tradition—as has sometimes been assumed—but he nevertheless occupies an important place in it. For he not only contributed to the growth of the experimental spirit, but may very well have been the first clearly to discern the new aspirations and to have asserted their validity and autonomy, without getting sidetracked by the problem of reconciling them with religious revelation.

The above evaluation of Leonardo is more than a theoretical inference from the premise that the experimental spirit has developed continuously; it is confirmed by reliable documents. For we know what authors Leonardo read; he often made notes, listing the books he owned or borrowed. I refer those interested in this matter to the remarkable essays by Pierre Duhem, *Sur Léonard de Vinci, ceux qu'il a lus et ceux qui l'ont lu* (three series, Paris, 1906–9). However, Pierre Duhem seems mainly to have listed the texts that Leonardo studied with special attention, above all those by Albert of Saxony and Nicholas of Cusa. A more complete list will be found in *Leonardo da Vinci e la sua libreria* by Girolamo d'Adda (Milan, 1873) and *Le fonti dei manoscritti di Leonardo da Vinci* by E. Solmi (Turin, 1908), a work completed in 1911.


REPUDIATION OF THE PLATONIC CURRENT. Examination of Leonardo's reading enables us to ascertain the most familiar tendencies of his thought. What was his attitude toward Classical humanism? As might be expected, on this score the results of scrutiny are disappointing. He did know Latin. The *H* manuscripts (dated 1497) and *I* manuscripts disclose daily exercises in declension and conjugation. It is also clear that he read certain Greek authors in Latin translation when no Italian translations were as yet available. He did this, for instance, with Euclid and Archimedes. There is no doubt that he would have had much trouble with them in Greek, for, even though Benvenuto Cellini tells us that Leonardo had some knowledge of Latin and Greek, and even though he occasionally wrote down sentences in Greek, his knowledge of Greek seems to have been rather superficial. He consulted elementary works: the short Latin syntax by Donatus and the Latin grammarians (3rd Forster ms. and ms. *F* of the *Institut*); he mentions "the author of an Italian-Latin dictionary." All this suggests study at a fairly elementary level.

What kind of interest does he display in Classical literature? The fact is, his interest is more practical than literary. He reads Ovid for the latter's moral reflections; it is primarily instructive facts that he looks for in the great authors. He notes that Horace "wrote on the swiftness of the heavens" (ms. *F*); he borrowed from the same poet the name of a weapon. It was the same with his reading of Lucretius, from whom he got information on primitive armaments. Virgil interested him in connection with a shield, Lucan because he described a sword, Greek fire, and a military pontoon boat! The historians attracted him more than the poets—Livy and Justin, for example—but the scientists still more than the historians, especially Pliny the Younger with his *Historia naturalis*. This concern for practice rather than theory is very significant. When he read Euclid, it was in search of names of engineers! Is this not the very opposite of the Greek spirit, which always neglected engineers and assigned them a decidedly inferior place? We may recall Plutarch (*Quaestiones convivales*, VIII, i, ii) who tells us that mechanics "has long been despised by philosophy"—and by Plato, especially. For, he goes on to say, "everything that is valuable in geometry is destroyed or perverted when applied to sensory things instead of being

Leonardo's art is inspired by an eagerness to scrutinize nature and to discover her secrets. This interest in nature is not a Renaissance characteristic. It was inherited from the Middle Ages, from a current of realism that had emerged with Gothic art.

**115.** - *LEONARDO DA VINCI.* FLOWERING LILY. Drawing. Royal Library, Windsor Castle. (By gracious permission of H. M. The Queen)

The duality of Leonardo's genius is illustrated by these drawings on two sides of a single sheet of paper. One shows his obsession with human form, a throwback to Classical concerns; the other exemplifies his meticulous observation of reality and his predilection for its surprising, strange, or even monstrous aspects.

**116. -
LEONARDO
DA VINCI.
STUDIES FOR
THE
ADORATION
OF THE
MAGI.**
Wallraf-Richartz
Museum,
Cologne

**117. -**
STUDIES OF
CRABS
(reverse of
the sheet shown
in Fig. 116)

231

elevated to... the eternal and incorporeal ideas." Here we get to the core of Leonardo's quarrel with the ancient tradition. It had maintained—and the Greeks above all—that science is essentially theory, not practice, and that its dignity rests upon ideas. But Leonardo instinctively rushes to the defense of Archimedes, who created the engineering spirit proper. He also went often to such writers as Vitruvius, Galen, and Frontinus, always looking for exact information, for precise formulas. He even drew up a list (ms. *B*) of names of engineers—a rather thankless task as far as the Greek legacy goes.

His interest in Italian literature is of the same kind. He alludes to Dante and a poem of the latter's imitated by Frezzi da Foligno, to Petrarch, to Burchiello, and to Luigi Pulci. But in his notes it is works on morals, algebra, arithmetic, surgery, medicine, agriculture, music, and travel that are most often mentioned—and even works on chiromancy and the symbolism of precious stones.

What was his attitude toward Alberti, the great man who at the time ruled Florentine thought, and who was so deeply imbued with Platonism? Certain writers, carried away by the traditional views, have very nearly made Leonardo appear a disciple. But how much did he know of Alberti's ideas? He quotes the *Ludi rerum mathematicarum* (ms. British Museum), a highly untypical work. At one point he mentions a calculation on the speed of ships from Alberti—only to criticize it! There is not a trace in Leonardo of Alberti the influential aesthetician, not even a mention of his contribution to a burning question of the day—perspective. On this point Leonardo follows Vitello, a contemporary of St. Thomas Aquinas. It is true that among the authors he mentions we find a certain Albertuccio, "the little Albert." Ravaisson-Mollien as well as some more recent writers have supposed that this name stood for Alberti. But it is clear today that Leonardo was thereby designating Albert of Saxony, who was called Albertutius or Parvus Albertus to distinguish him from Albertus Magnus. Once again we find that we are back in the Middle Ages.

His intellectual bent is even more clearly revealed in his philosophical tendencies. Two great names at that time shone in the metaphysical sky: Aristotle, dear to the Middle Ages, and Plato, god of the Renaissance. Which of the two most appealed to him? Leonardo's notebooks supply the answer: Plato is mentioned once in them, while Aristotle's name figures about a dozen times. This may be the heart of the matter, and it is worthwhile to dwell upon the point.

On Plato, Leonardo read *Theologia platonica, sive de immortalitate animae* by Marsilio Ficino, the pope of Platonic humanism, published in 1482. This book does not seem to have inspired him with great love for the philosopher. "Regarding the rest of the definition of the soul, I shall leave it to the monks, the fathers of people who know all secrets through inspiration" (Windsor ms., An. IV, 184). Through inspiration—this was where Plato shocked Leonardo, who described himself as *discepolo della sperienza* (Cod. Atl.). Even in the domain of geometry, he criticized Plato for being too exclusively theoretical and attacked his doctrine of the five regular bodies—which so profoundly influenced the Renaissance conception of aesthetic form, and which directly inspired Piero della Francesca's famous treatise *De quinque corporibus*, published at the end of the fifteenth century. The influence that this treatise exerted on Leonardo's friend Fra Luca Pacioli is well known; this disciple of Piero, who more or less plagiarized him, composed the famous book *De divina proportione*; the illustrations it contains are attributed to Leonardo. Now, in ms. FI 27 v., the master of the *Gioconda* criticizes those "five regular bodies," which Plato

Leonardo the scientist is inseparable from Leonardo the artist: his vision reflects the interests of both. But while the artist focuses on appearances, although he goes beyond surface effects and anticipates problems (for instance, the structure of clouds), the scientist aims at discovering the causes and constitution of things. A landscape, a map....

**118. -** *LEONARDO DA VINCI.* LANDSCAPE. Drawing. Royal Library, Windsor Castle. (By gracious permission of H. M. The Queen)

**119. -** *LEONARDO DA VINCI.* STUDY OF TERRAIN. Drawing. Royal Library, Windsor Castle. (By gracious permission of H. M. The Queen)

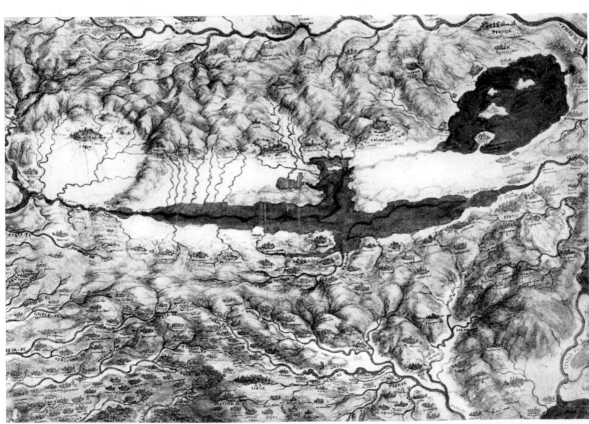

placed at the basis of the world of forms, seeing in them the fundamental structure of the elements themselves. Leonardo rejects the idea advanced by Plato that the surfaces of the elements are those of these bodies, i.e., the five regular polyhedrons. According to the *Timaeus*, the elements of fire, air, earth, and water have respectively the forms of the tetrahedron, the octahedron, the cube, and the icosahedron. As for the dodecahedron, "God used it to compose the final arrangement of the Whole." The regular polyhedrons were predestined to be used in this way because of their intellectual perfection, for "all the genera thus constituted were given by the Arranger their shapes through the action of the Ideas and Numbers." To such arbitrary views Leonardo opposes the data of experience, which teaches him that "every fluid element necessarily has a spherical surface." This conception, diametrically opposed to Plato's, is that of Albert of Saxony, that of the Middle Ages. As early as the beginning of the thirteenth century, Robert Grosseteste, the great founder of Oxonian thought, had looked upon the sphere as the dominant form in nature because it corresponds to the mode of diffusion of light.

Leonardo went further: he indicts Plato's very method. "It has nothing to do with true geometry," he says, "because geometry proceeds by means of instruments, the rule and the compass, and Plato is not confirmed by experience." Plato's theory is solely based on "entirely mental proofs," which are purely abstract, and hence invalid in the eyes of Leonardo. By way of the Middle Ages, he rediscovers Aristotle and takes the Aristotelian position in basing knowledge on sensory experience rather than on "the eternal and incorporeal ideas," which the Platonists placed above all else and thereby created the Renaissance theory of ideal beauty.

At the very time that Leonardo was confiding such opinions to paper, the Greek scholars from Byzantium were spearheading the irresistible wave of Platonism in Florence, which led to the founding of the Platonic Academy. However, the followers of Aristotle had not acknowledged defeat.

BACK TO ARISTOTLE. One center of Aristotelianism remained active. It was presided over by another Greek, George of Trebizond, who was invited to Venice in 1428 and later taught in Rome. In Florence itself, Johannes Argyropoulos, who had taken refuge there after the capture of Constantinople in 1453, taught until 1471, when he left for Rome, where he died in 1473. In Florence he lectured on Aristotle's philosophy of nature at the Studium Generale; he translated his works into Latin; and since Leonardo mentions him in his notebooks, it has been surmised that the painter attended his courses.

At all events, Leonardo was attracted to Aristotle's empirical approach, his interest in the physical world. He frequently quotes from or refers to Aristotle's *Ethics*, *Physics*, his treatise *De coelo et mundo*, his *Meteorology*, and even to "*The Floods of the Nile*, a little work by Aristotle." On the cover of *Notebook F* he cites the *Philosophy of Aristotle* and his great eleventh-century commentator, Avicenna. He mentions the latter's treatise on liquids, and in *Quaderni d'Anatomia* (now in Windsor) he notes: "Have Avicenna's *On Utilities* translated. The book on the science of machines precedes the book of the utilities."

Duhem has shown in his scholarly studies that Leonardo owed a great deal to Aristotle's physical theories, which he studied in their medieval commentaries. Aristotelianism, which was introduced to Europe by the middle of the twelfth century, mostly through the intermediary of the Arab commentators Averroës and Avicenna, had been integrated with Western religious thought, primarily by Albertus Magnus and, later, by his pupil St. Thomas Aquinas. There are numerous references to these two authors in Leonardo's notebooks. Albertus is mentioned in the Codex Atlanticus and in ms. *M*; Leonardo even records that he found among Fra Bernadiglio's books the *Alberto, De coelo et mundo*, which he thus distinguished from the treatise attributed to Aristotle that he mentions elsewhere ("*vedi Aristotile de cielo e mondo,*" Cod. Atl. 5). Ms. *I* shows that Leonardo associated Aristotle with the two powerful thinkers who with his help had revolutionized medieval thought in the twelfth century. For we find there a reference to Aristotle in a note dealing with "movement" and "recoil," to which he adds, "and Albertus (Magnus) and Thomas." Thomas' book is mentioned in ms. *L* I, v., x (cf. Cod. Atl., 120 r.d.).

In the fourteenth century, one of the principal commentators had been Albert of Saxony, a pupil of Buridan and an Occamist, who incidentally revised his teacher's scientific conceptions. Leonardo, in keeping with the critical attitude of the fourteenth-century Occamists, discusses the Aristotelian doctrines just as freely, but—let us not forget it—from the experimental point of view stimulated by Aristotle's revival.

It becomes clear that Leonardo refused to take part in the wave of Platonism that Leo X, a Medici pope, placed at the center of the age that bears his name. On the contrary, Leonardo belongs to a tradition that had been born in the Middle Ages, at the close of the twelfth century, when works by Aristotle were brought to light. In the thirteenth and fourteenth centuries this tradition broke away from Aristotle and anticipated—nay, founded—the positivist, materialist experimental method that was to give birth to modern science. In this development Leonardo played a crucial part.

I pointed out above that the close of the twelfth century witnessed the beginning of a revolution in art as well as in intellectual life. This revolution was completed in the thirteenth century, and divided the Middle Ages into two parts—the earlier dominated by St. Augustine and embodied in the Romanesque style, the latter dominated by St. Thomas and embodied in Gothic art. What the twelfth century inaugurated was the idea of nature —a concrete nature, with laws of its own, observable by the senses—a nature no longer (as in the early Christian centuries) dominated in many respects by St. Augustine's Platonism, a mere symbolic language, a perpetual reminder of God. "What had been lacking," Etienne Gilson writes, "for a concrete reality to be superimposed on this world of symbols, was the conception of a nature with reality and value in itself, however low its place in the scheme of things.... It was to Aristotelian physics that the thirteenth century owed such a conception."

Brought to Europe by the Arabs in the twelfth century, Aristotle gained definitive dominance in the thirteenth when Albertus Magnus and then his great pupil St. Thomas Aquinas integrated his philosophy with Christian doctrine. He gave rise to two major intellectual currents; they might be called a narrow and a broader Aristotelianism, respectively. The former blindly followed the teachings of the Stagirite in a spirit of *magister dixit* and kept closely to the letter of the Arab commentators. It led to a desiccated and narrow conservatism, provoking opposition even from those who most profited from Aristotle's sense orientation and put it into practice. The broader current of Aristotelianism threw off any authoritarianism so rigid and carried this doctrine, which rehabilitated sensory knowledge. Its followers founded the dogma of experience as the sole valid source of knowledge, at least where the physical world is concerned. One example should suffice. One of the most remarkable Averroist philosophers was Jean de Jaudun, whose companion in arms in the struggle against the papacy, when he lived in exile at the court of Ludwig of Bavaria, was Marsilio of Padua (d. c. 1340). Jean de Jaudun went so far as to declare that the creation of the world and the immortality of the soul were not susceptible of proof, on the ground that—for creation—"we cannot know it on the basis of sensory things, nor demonstrate on the basis of ideas in accord with sensory things." We have seen that Leonardo used almost the same words to stress the primacy of "sensory things." Jean de Jaudun goes on to say that we must follow only those ancients "who inferred all knowledge from reasons based on sensory things." Now, what more does Leonardo have to say in the Codex Trivulce? "All our knowledge derives its principle from sensation." And starting from the same premises he is led to infer the same inability to decide the question of the immortality of the soul, "which cannot be demonstrated." Did he not also observe sarcastically that "the definition of the soul" was something he "left to the monks"? Vasari, too, tells us that "Leonardo's conception of the soul is so heretical that it belongs to a philosopher rather than to a Christian." And this conception was characteristic of only one type of philosopher—the follower of Aristotle.

NATURE AND EXPERIENCE. However, Leonardo was not so close to Averroism as to the experimental current that came into being at the same time and was steadily to broaden its perspectives. It had been merely implicit in earlier Aristotelianism. Albertus Magnus declared that whereas St. Augustine must be followed in "matters concerning the faith and mores," Aristotle "knew nature best... *experimentum solum certificat in talibus.*" Where Aristotle taught that general ideas derive only from experience, St. Thomas for his part declared that such ideas "are abstracted from sensory things," and hence that the soul "must derive from the senses all its knowledge, including knowledge of intelligible realities." Neither of them admits, as did St. Bonaventure, for example, that God can be known directly. Leonardo shares this view: "*Le cose mentali, che non sono passate per il senso, so vane e nulla verita partoriscono*" (Coll. Rouveyre, B. F. 7 v.).

Whereas Thomas was victorious in Paris, with the Dominicans, the Franciscans, in their Oxford stronghold, proceeded to develop the experimental method, going beyond Aristotle and often opposing him. Recognizing with St. Bonaventure that God could be known directly, independently of the senses, through love, they upheld religious revelation; but at the same time, they made the physical world the exclusive domain of the senses, that is, of positive experience. In this way they foreshadowed the development of the scientific spirit as something unrelated to religion, capable of developing alongside it. Although they criticized Aristotle, and particularly the Scholastic version of his philosophy, they did not ignore him. Roger Bacon said that he had been the most accomplished philosopher of his epoch. Grosseteste translated the *Nicomachean Ethics*. Knowledge, according to them, has two foundations—first, mathematics (primarily geometry, according to Robert Grosseteste), and second, concrete experience, as known in direct observation, which Roger Bacon stressed. Grosseteste lived from 1175 to 1253; Bacon from 1214 to 1294. Grosseteste proclaimed "*veritas geometriae....* It is extremely useful to consider lines, angles, and figures, for without these things it is impossible to know

*This profile, which seems to be that of the artist (cf. Fig. 111), although beardless, shows to what extent Leonardo's art is inseparable from the laws of vision, and the latter from the exercise of the intellect. This is confirmed by the copious notes in Leonardo's cramped mirror-reversed handwriting, which is characteristic of his secretiveness.*

**120.** - *LEONARDO DA VINCI.*
PERSPECTIVE VISION. Drawing.
Royal Library, Windsor Castle.
(By gracious permission of
H. M. The Queen)

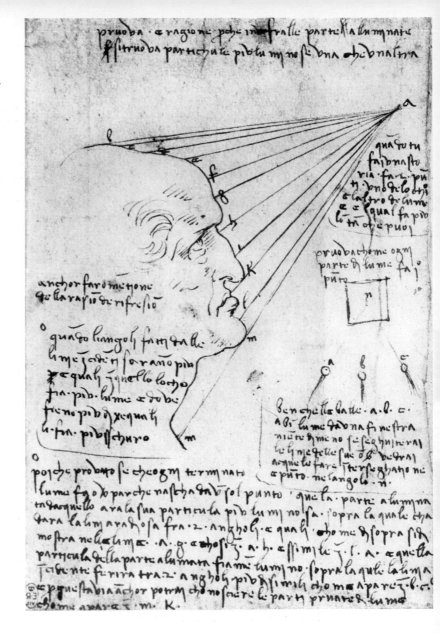

natural philosophy." Roger Bacon wrote: "If we deprive ourselves of the benefits of mathematics, all that is left is doubt, opinion, error." This is also Leonardo's fundamental tenet: "Here one no longer asks whether two plus three is more or less than six, or whether the sum of angles in a triangle is less than two right angles; on the contrary, the quarrels dissolve in an eternal silence, and among the disciples of this science there prevails a peace never achieved by lying intellectual speculations." This barb was directed against the adversaries of experimentation, i.e., the Platonists. For although they, too, praised mathematics and geometry, they did so for purely speculative or aesthetic reasons, while Leonardo's attitude toward them was essentially practical. Incidentally, it is odd to note that few men interested in mathematics have had less concern for abstraction and beauty than Leonardo. He loved mathematics because it provided him with precise units of measurement, and geometry because its truths could be expressed visually.

That was exactly what Roger Bacon had asked for—*numeratio* and *figuratio*, computation and figuration. As he observed, they give us "a sensory example and a sensory experience for all things." Similarly, Leonardo looked upon his countless drawings as visual records of experience. Like Bacon, he said that all things must "be verified by experimental constructions of figures and computations."

Such experiments must be completed by direct sensory observation of the physical world. Bacon had noted that in order to extract "the evidence of truth" from *res hujus mundi*, "the things of this world... reasoning is not enough, but experience is." It provides us with "certainty exempt from doubt." And Bacon had uttered the phrase that was destined to ring down the ages: *scientia experimentalis*. It is too often forgotten that this term "experimental science" was coined in the thirteenth century—that this century saw the beginnings of the profound intellectual revolution that created the modern world. On this score Leonardo repeats Bacon almost word for word. Rational investigations, he says, "are vain and full of errors when they are not based on experience" (*Trattato*, § 93). The Codex Atlanticus celebrates "sound experience, common mother of the arts and sciences," and the *Trattato* (§ 93) "experience, mother of all certainty" (Fig. 115).

The same internal logic led Bacon and Leonardo to the same conclusions. Bacon repudiated the principle of authority, and Leonardo repudiated "those who study authors rather than the works of nature."

Such a conviction, which discounted pure speculation, gave a new importance to physical knowledge and to the manipulation of objects in particular: *industria manuelis* in Bacon's phrase. We know to what extent Leonardo enjoyed doing things with his hands, how, for example, he liked to surprise people with conjuring tricks. But sensory experience is primarily visual. The eye is the chief beneficiary of the devaluation of abstraction and revalorization of the senses. To the Oxonians, the model of science was Alhazen's optics. What a revolution! The intellect is no longer formed primarily by the study of grammar and logic, but by visual perception of the world. Hence the importance of Vitello, the Polish mathematician who was still studied in Kepler's day. Few names are mentioned so frequently as his by Leonardo. Before leaving for Rome with Ligny, he noted, "Take along the book by Vitolone" (Cod. Atl. 247 r.).

Leonardo borrowed from the Middle Ages not only his cult of vision, but also his theory of it. Whereas the Platonists believed that the beam of light starts from the eye and moves toward things, Leonardo embraced the opposite theory, that of Aristotle. He marvels at the fact that "figures, colors, and parts of the world of all kinds are reduced to a single point" where they converge (Cod. Atl. 337). This is why he conceives vision as a pyramid: "The air is filled with pyramids, with radiating straight lines, which start from every point of luminous bodies." What we have here is the very theory advanced by Grosseteste: vision suggested to him a pyramid formed by the concentration of every point of an object on another single object—the eye (Fig. 120).

*"Knowledge is power...." The investigation of the familiar world is only a prelude to the creation of imaginary worlds. Leonardo reshapes reality into new patterns.*

**121.** - *LEONARDO DA VINCI. DRAGON.* Drawing. Royal Library, Windsor Castle.
(By gracious permission of H. M. The Queen)

**FROM ROGER BACON TO LEONARDO.** Bacon went further: he foresaw the consequences of this new mode of knowledge—and here, too, he anticipated Leonardo. Experimental science makes it possible to discover the unforeseen—i.e., not only what is implied in principles and can be revealed by deductive reasoning, but entirely new things: it is the mother of creation. More than that, "the third dignity of the art of experimentation" consists in this, that it makes possible the shift from knowledge to power. For unlike the other kinds of science, it possesses not only the past—what has already been—but also the future, what can be. And this was why Bacon regarded it as so important to the Church.

According to Paul Valéry, Leonardo was the first to conceive the idea that knowledge is power, a notion put forward by the other Bacon—Francis—early in the seventeenth century. In a letter addressed to this writer in September 1943 (the essential part of it was published in *Quadrige*, No. 3, October 1945, pp. 6 and 7), Valéry said, "Actually, science can increase only that knowledge which is and provides us with power." Leonardo, for his part, had noted, "Science, knowledge of things that are possible, that can happen."

A coincidence? Not at all. The mention in the ms. of the British Museum (71 v.) *Rugieri Bacon fatta in stampa* (Roger Bacon printed) proves sufficiently his interest in his great predecessor. However, the exact sense of the mention remains enigmatic. For, as Anna Maria Brizio observed in her remarkable edition of Leonardo's *Scritti scelti (Selected Writings)*, the earliest known printed publication of a work by Bacon with engravings did not appear until 1529. This work is *De la pierre philosophale (On the Philosopher's Stone)*, translated into French by St. Girard de Tournus, Paris, 1529. Solmi, too, has noted that nothing by Bacon had been printed at the end of the fifteenth century and the beginning of the sixteenth. The 1529 edition was followed by works published in 1542 and 1590. It seems probable that Leonardo was referring to Bacon's optics.

Leonardo was not unfamiliar with medieval English science, for in ms. *M* he mentions "Suisset, that is to say, the calculator." This refers to Richard Suiseth, who, in the fourteenth century, advocated the extension of mathematics to research. All the same, Leonardo was interested in all medieval works. When he met the French painter Jean Perréal (in the home of the Maréchal de Chaumont), he borrowed from him the *Speculum mundi* by Vincent of Beauvais, the famous twelfth-century Dominican. The work is a kind of encyclopedia.

It is possible to find other links between the school of Oxford and Leonardo. Thus, the Franciscan current leads back to William of Occam, student and later teacher at Oxford, who died in 1350. It was he who elaborated the idea of *notitia experimentalis* (experimental knowledge) in his commentaries on Aristotle's logic and physics. Although he criticizes Aristotle's theories, they remain the basis of the theories he opposed to them. In Occam, we find Leonardo's fundamental formula, "Experience, mother both of the arts and the sciences," for Occam says, "Experimental knowledge, cause of the universal proposition, which is the principle of art and science... *principium artis et scientiae*" (Figs. 116 and 117).

The path that leads to Leonardo can be followed after Occam's death. Occamism, though condemned in 1339, triumphed in Paris. Its advocates were called *moderni*, the moderns. Tracing this development, we come progressively closer to Leonardo's ideas. For example: one of the most famous of these "moderns," Nicolas d'Autremont (d. after 1350), was fond of the following formula: "Nothing authorizes us to assert anything except what we know by our five senses and by formal experiments." We have already seen that in his *Trattato* Leonardo says similarly that investigations are "vain and full of errors when they are not based on experience... that is to say, when their origin, means, and ends do not pass through any of the five senses."

Finally, we have already pointed out the important place occupied by Albert of Saxony in Leonardo's thought; through him alone Leonardo could have become familiar with Occamism.

AFFINITIES WITH THE MIDDLE AGES. Does not Leonardo's position become entirely intelligible? Nothing arises out of nothing. Leonardo's thought represents the flowering of ideas that had been brewing since the thirteenth century. But this contemporary of the Renaissance differs from his medieval predecessors in that, unlike them, he makes no effort to reconcile the truths of religion with those of experience; he leaves the former entirely alone and is concerned only for the latter. Moreover, although this method had been clearly conceived before him, it was he who translated it into action; it was he who proved its effectiveness. And yet, even on this score, there is more to be said for the Middle Ages than might be generally realized. We must not forget that, as early as the fourteenth century, the great Nicole Oresme, who was also an Aristotelian and who wrote several commentaries on Aristotle's works, made discoveries foreshadowing those of Copernicus, Galileo, and even Descartes, on matters that are sometimes credited to Leonardo. Among other things, he outlined the earliest laws governing falling bodies, by observing their behavior on an inclined plane. Leonardo did not merely contribute to the constitution of modern scientific method, he also provided modern science with its permanent elements, assigned it its goal, and foresaw its achievements. Thereby, this continuer of the Middle Ages appears a precursor of genius. To be sure, he escapes the limitations of the Middle Ages, but only in order to herald the future, for the *scientia experimentalis* outlined in the thirteenth century was to be the true foundation of the modern world.

This is why Leonardo's full significance could not be grasped until recently. So long as the Renaissance and its tenets—upheld by seventeenth-century Classicism—ruled supreme, he could be only partially understood. He was looked upon as merely one of a number of leading Renaissance figures, and his painting alone received attention, especially the elements of ideal beauty and purity of form that herald Raphael. Because of the extremely graceful quality of his work, he was classified as a Platonic idealist. His strangeness, his mysteriousness, were looked upon merely as added charms. Discovery of his manuscripts was required to alter this view, and also the development of a new approach—one more capable of gauging their importance. However, the non-Renaissance aspects of his personality are to be found not only in his writings, but in his art, also.

Thus, his predilection for the abnormal and the fantastic continues one of the familiar veins of the Middle Ages. He pushes this predilection to a point of concern for ugliness, which he studied thoroughly in his caricatures, for monsters (he manufactured lifelike monsters by applying make-up to lizards), and finally for death and destruction. This is attested by the series of floods which he was so fond of drawing and describing. This aspect of his art is scarcely discernible in his paintings, which catered to current taste, but it comes to the fore in his sketches, in everything he did for his own eyes only, when he was alone with a sheet of paper. The throbbing restlessness of his drawings is worlds away from the static calm and perfect purity of his paintings, where there is no disorder or degradation, in keeping with the essential spirit of Classicism (Figs. 121 to 123).

Many other aspects of his thought, so familiar to the modern sensibility, are completely alien to the Renaissance. For instance, there is his obsession with a shifting, gliding light in which forms are dissolved, and which, through Giorgione, may have made possible the flowering of Venetian art—the latter, with its Nordic soul, also very far from the rational clarity of the Renaissance art of Florence and Rome. And is not Leonardo's obsession with movement, with every aspect of action—especially notable in his *Battle of Anghiari*—at the opposite pole from Raphael's untroubled depiction of beautiful movement? What other Renaissance artist ever showed as much interest in—indeed, paid the slightest attention to—the phenomena of water, wind, light, and fluidity, similar in that all of them are resistant to formal definition? He was as obsessed by them as by the inexorable flight of time, which destroys and sweeps everything away, or by death and nothingness, which he treated in a number of drawings (Fig. 124).

*Leonardo's monsters are scientific in the sense that they are not gratuitous, but based on plausible deformation of actual structures.*

**122. -** *LEONARDO DA VINCI.* HEADS OF FANTASTIC ANIMALS. Drawing. Royal Library, Windsor Castle.
(By gracious permission of H. M. The Queen)

TIME, THE NEW DIMENSION.    *Panta rei,* "all things are in flux," Heraclitus said—but long before the time of Plato! After Plato, the Greco-Roman tradition ignored or negated the existence of a frantic, destructive flux in the universe, opposing to its recognition barriers borrowed from the domain of the absolute and perfect.

Leonardo, on the contrary, meditated endlessly on the unending instability of things, on a domain of perpetual becoming in which death alternates with life. This had been a

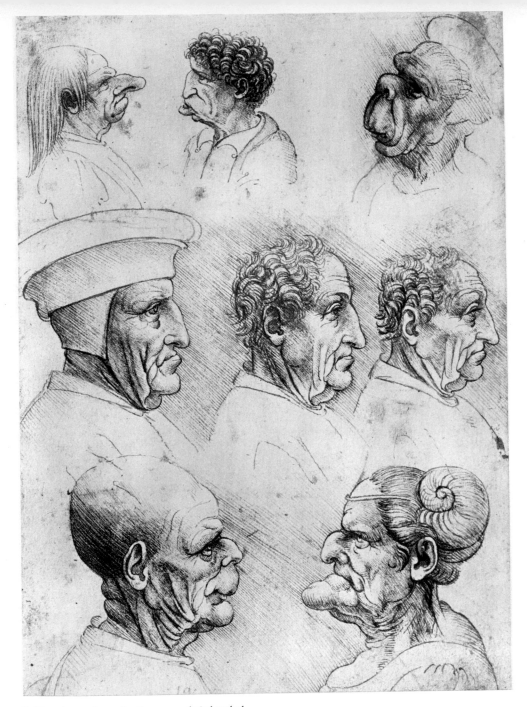

*In his caricatures he applies the same analytical method.*

**123. -** *LEONARDO DA VINCI.* CARICATURES. Drawing. Royal Library, Windsor Castle.
(By gracious permission of H. M. The Queen)

central medieval preoccupation from which the Renaissance conspicuously kept aloof. Only with the Baroque did this theme reappear in European art.

In Leonardo, Aristotelian dynamism achieved a first fusion with the characteristic anxieties of the modern soul. In his notebooks we frequently find remarks that fall under the heading of the medieval *memento mori*, and that yet sound strangely modern. "O Time, consumer of all things," Leonardo noted after Ovid, but this is not for him a philosophical cliché, as can be seen from the following lines, which bring to mind the Proustian time lost: "The water you touch in the river is the last of the wave that has passed out of sight, the first of the wave coming in. And so it is with present time..." (Codex Trivulce, 68). In the unceasing abolition of the present, Leonardo perceived the secret of nothingness: "Of the great things that dwell among us, the existence of nothingness is the greatest. It dwells in time and spreads its limbs into past and future..." (Cod. Atl. 398 v.). And again: "In the domain of time, nothingness is found essentially between the past and the future, without possessing any of the present" (British Museum ms., 131 r.).

No, this is not the language of the Renaissance. It is that of Pascal, of the world we are living in. In a flash of anticipation, Leonardo, who was obsessed with these problems, realized clearly, long before Bergson, that "lived" time is very different from the abstract time measured by clocks. Again in the British Museum ms. he notes, "Write on the nature of time, so different from its geometry."

Little of this was grasped about Leonardo until our own day. Before he could be fully appreciated, the development of an experimental culture had to take place—one the seeds of which had been planted in the thirteenth century, one which was revived and extended in the eighteenth, to be triumphantly asserted in the nineteenth. The tide of Platonism that the Renaissance had renewed had to recede again. It is amusing to see the scientific nineteenth century once again paying tribute to Aristotle. Condorcet had earlier expressed his admiration, and Auguste Comte called him "the incomparable Aristotle."

It was in 1797—note how revealing the date is!—that one J. B. Venturi, professor in Modena and the namesake of an illustrious latter-day historian of art, presented to the Institute his *Essai sur les ouvrages physico-chimiques de Léonard de Vinci*. Nineteenth-century scientists, such as Humboldt, felt the importance of this side of Leonardo's genius, which would only attain full recognition in our own epoch. Péladan wrote, "We would have to wait till the nineteenth century—until the very end of the nineteenth century—to find a just appreciation of this unlimited intelligence."

But have we not, in all this, lost sight of the artist? This analysis of his thought, some will say, is of no matter for it casts little light on his art. Such a view would be mistaken.

To begin with, to Leonardo, science and art were linked far more closely than they are to us today. According to Valéry, Leonardo regarded his art as the equivalent of philosophy and science. Until him, all of man's faculties and talents had been regarded as belonging to God, to whose service mankind was dedicated. Henceforward, man would devote his faculties and talents to knowledge, and this would mark the end of the medieval epoch when it succumbed to forces that it had itself released. To Leonardo, thinking and drawing are merely different methods of exploring reality. Through them he analyzes and understands it; through them, and starting from insights gained with their help, he arrives at new syntheses; and in these syntheses he discovers the sources of creation, both artistic and scientific. The method and the process are identical in thinking and drawing.

*Leonardo went so far as to imagine catastrophes caused by unleashed natural forces. His swirling floods illustrate the laws of hydraulics, in which he was particularly interested (cf. Fig. 110).*

**124.** - *LEONARDO DA VINCI.* SWIRLING WATERS. Drawing. Royal Library, Windsor Castle.
(By gracious permission of H. M. The Queen)

Perhaps never before had the parallelism between art and thought been more effectively demonstrated. For, although Leonardo's works of art also pursue beauty, in conformity with the Renaissance ideal, it is obvious that he regards beauty as an object of intellectual curiosity rather than spiritual gratification. It presents him with a new riddle to investigate. How can the impression of beauty be produced, he asks himself, in the spirit with which he seeks out a technique of mystery and an art of suggesting mystery. The problem of beauty, no less than anatomical problems or the problem of flying, stimulated his lucid intelligence. He wants to discover the secret of beauty in order to become capable of producing it at will (Figs. 118 and 119).

But if art and thought share their methods and goals, can we say the same of their respective natures? It will be enough to refer to what we wrote above on the transition from a static, spatial conception of the world to a dynamic, temporal one, to see how close is the parallelism between the nature of art and the nature of thought in Leonardo. He effects the transition in both domains, in turning his back on abstract, absolute categories—the revelations of religion and theoretical principles on the one hand, the architecture of forms on the other. He plunges into the maelstrom of experience; and its great lesson for him is awareness of time—of the fact that everything is in motion, in action, in process of being transformed. He looks upon science with the eyes of an engineer—as a study of forces; upon art as the rendering of imperceptible transitions of light—he created *sfumato*. Possibly, he was not himself fully aware of the underlying unity of his multifarious efforts. But at this distance it emerges clearly, confirming that both in the innermost recesses of a solitary mind and in the general currents that encompass several generations, art and thought have a common denominator—which is the secret and key to each successive age.

*Realistic rendering of materials and textures.*

**125.** - *QUENTIN MATSYS.* THE MONEYLENDER AND HIS WIFE (detail).
The Louvre, Paris

CHAPTER II

# ART AND SOCIETY

A RT faithfully reflects the evolution of fundamental ideas at the basis of knowledge; the preceding chapter has shown that this is true not only for collective entities, but also for exceptional individuals such as Leonardo da Vinci. However, art also records and expresses—and no less directly—phenomena of which we are far less conscious than those of our intellectual life, for all that they are at least as important. I refer to transformations in societies and in ways of life, which powerfully affect our ways of thinking and feeling. As our conception of reality changes, our interpretation of its appearances, too, is modified.

247

# 1. THE FLEMISH MIDDLE CLASS AND THE
# DISCOVERY OF MATTER

IN the fifteenth century, as the Middle Ages drew to a close and modern times began, Western culture underwent major changes. Men found their lives and the life about them taking on different aspects and new meanings.

Although it is correct to see, in the realism that asserted itself at the time, the end result of a philosophical effort begun in the thirteenth century and still felt as a conscious influence by Leonardo da Vinci, it is also possible to detect in it the effects of a deep social change.

THE RISE OF THIS-WORLDLINESS. The Middle Ages with its aristocratic structure, whose major expression was the feudal system, gradually saw the rise of a new class—the burghers. This class championed a new realism in keeping with its tastes, needs, scale of values, and way of life. In Northern Europe, where the new class was victorious, a strong tendency to realism and positivism asserted itself, taking on a character very different from Italy's. In Italy, this tendency reflected an intellectual need, whereas in the North it was more spontaneous and instinctive. To study this new mutation of Western culture is to acquire a better understanding of how the most varied factors, from the most intellectual to the most material, meet and merge to produce a single end result, a new stage in the march of civilization.

Fifteenth-century Flemish art cannot be reduced to a simple formula, as Léo van Puyvelde was right to insist. It is realistic, indeed, but it is also glowing with faith. The medieval soul bursts forth in one last concentrated expression—somewhat stiff, withal—through the sumptuous matrix of materiality, like an overelaborately mounted precious stone. So dazzling is the superficial aspect of realism—as heavy and richly substantial as the brocaded stuffs lovingly portrayed—that historians may surely be excused for long having seen no more than this in Flemish art. Yet this is not the essential part of its beauty, for all that it is the most strikingly original part of its contribution. Certainly it is this about it that most immediately catches the eye (Fig. 126).

Who has not been entranced to follow those winding paths with his eye, as they vanish and reappear again between rounded clumps of green trees, while far away a tiny white horse ambles slowly off toward the horizon? Sometimes the horse has gone, it is getting late, and the setting sun lengthens the shadows of the bushes on the empty road. Who has not enjoyed watching from the railing reflections of the arches under some microscopic bridge in a painting by Van Eyck the ripples in the water around a silently gliding barge —or waiting for the night to fall while resting his eyes on Memling's swan, which seems to grow whiter and whiter as the pond darkens in the gathering dusk? Similarly, we like to direct our eye, this time using it as a magnifying glass rather than a telescope, at a human

*The meticulous detail of the Flemish Primitives evokes a peaceful walk in a miniature world where the shadows of trees and people carefully record the time of day.*

**126.** - *MASTER OF FLÉMALLE.* LANDSCAPE (detail of THE NATIVITY). Museum, Dijon

face, to explore the detail map of its innumerable wrinkles and the tiny bristles of a budding beard. And we like to catch a glimpse, through the myriad details so meticulously supplied, of an almost materially rendered inner life, to measure the exact grief mirrored in the tears filling a pair of eyes, arrested at the moment just before they fall. We study the Virgin's red-rimmed eyes and try to divine the words that she is silently reciting, hands folded motionless in front of her, caught forever in some attitude of prayer. Really to explore the world of the Flemish Primitives in detail would be to attempt to reduce the infinity of things to an exhaustive list.

The enchanted eye lingers on and is diverted by reality—but does not go beyond it, for it is through this reality and no other that it must divine the rest. In this sense, Flemish art may well be the most clear-cut, most emphatic expression of our culture—I mean that culture which was born with the Renaissance and is today in process of being transformed and supplanted by another. That culture might best be summed up in the word: this-worldly. It is a civilization firmly anchored in reality.

But has not man always believed in reality? In a sense, yes—but how many different conceptions has he formed of it! Actually, the conception of reality as the totality of material things perceived by the senses has been current for only a relatively short time and over a relatively restricted area of the planet: for approximately five centuries, and only in Europe. The arts of other civilizations have treated concrete reality as mere appearance, often as no better than a mirage—sometimes even as vanity, illusion (Maya). What was called reality was not, as in modern Europe, the substantial sensory aspect of things, but on the contrary, what lies beyond matter, what matter covers and conceals. For primitive man, reality is magical, a curtain that mysterious powers cause to billow and subside, and only occasionally lift. Similarly, to Classical Mediterranean art, what we call reality was no more than a mask. True being was conceived of as lying behind it, invisible but capable of being divined, as a more hidden and purer essence. For Plato, true reality was the idea, for Pythagoras it was number, a certain principle of harmony that cannot be explained but only formulated mathematically. Thus, Classical art sought the eternal type or the perfect proportion behind the accidents of appearance (Fig. 125).

In the Middle Ages, our own conception of reality seems gradually to have asserted itself with the approach of the modern era, although always as an image of the omnipresence of God. True reality to the Middle Ages still lay beyond the visible world that envelops and reflects it; it is the soul of things, i.e., God. What we call realism in Gothic art—and was its main impulse—was still conceived as a means for bringing us into closer contact with God, through a better grasp of His nature. As we have seen this realism did not appear before the close of the Middle Ages, after ten centuries during which Augustinianism had taught that "the contemplative eye" rather than the corporeal eye must be resorted to, if we are to discover the essence, the *logos* that lies beyond the visible world. When, most notably with Thomism, experience began to be granted admission to the life of the intellect, art began to reflect closer observation of nature. Theoretically, it was the beginning of modern realism. Once it gained a foothold in philosophy, it conquered a parallel importance in art.

We are now very close to the fifteenth century and the Renaissance, when the new attitude asserted itself. Reality was transposed from the world of abstract ideas to the world of the senses; speculation gave way to experimentation. There began a vast movement of

*Early in the fifteenth century, Van Eyck succeeded in defining not only the various textures of things (porphyry or limestone?) but also the infinite diversity of lighting—direct sunlight, glancing rays, light reflected from the ground, cast shadows....*

**127. -** *VAN EYCK.* Detail, THE ANNUN-CIATION (from the outside of the GHENT ALTARPIECE). Cathedral of Saint Bavon, Ghent the claims of the physical and the claims of the spiritual. Only one school of painting surrendered exclusively and totally to reality in all its concreteness and substantiality—Northern painting.

At this point we must turn from intellectual developments to social conditions. Realism made its appearance with the rise of the middle class. Untouched by philosophical culture, and hence unhampered by Scholastic or Classical traditions, this class of traders and craftsmen had always been closely associated with material things, fashioning them, evaluating them, and selling them. It had a highly developed sense of concrete realities. This is why realism in art flowered only where and when this class gained ascendancy. It was only after feudalism had been undermined and the middle class asserted and extended its power that the medieval speculative and mystical spirit began to be gradually supplanted by an empirical approach to reality.

In France, the sixteenth, seventeenth, and eighteenth centuries are marked by the complex struggle between an aristocratic spirit clinging to Mediterranean conceptions and a bourgeois, realistic spirit. It is enough to mention the bitter rivalry that bourgeois painters like Le Nain and the *peintres de la réalité* in the seventeenth and Chardin in the eighteenth century encountered from monarchic and aristocratic art circles that sought to stifle their art in the name of Italian Classicism. Classicism became, to such a degree, a state doctrine that a revolutionary painter like David—who, left to his own devices, was a realist—felt obliged to practice a stiff academism whenever he worked for the government. Centuries of the French monarchy had identified Classicism with "official" art. And even as late as the close of the nineteenth century, the French bourgeoisie (which really preferred the photographic platitudes of Meissonier) felt obliged to embrace a stilted academism whenever it acted in an official capacity, i.e., as the ruling class.

The situation was very different in Flanders, which has no aristocratic national past. It is true that in the sixteenth and the seventeenth century, when Flanders was ruled by princely, Catholic Spain, it too felt morally obliged to pay tribute to Classical Italianism. But in Flanders in the fifteenth century, when the towns were free, and in Holland where the burghers retained their hegemony, realism flourished unhampered.

Realism is closely associated with the middle classes throughout history. In the nineteenth century, when positivism reached its culmination—socially with industrialism and technology, intellectually with experimental science, artistically with naturalism—the middle classes were triumphant all over Europe. The Second Empire in France marked the apotheosis of the bourgeoisie. It was at that time that a radical materialism, which recognized only the findings of the senses, gained dominance. It was the official doctrine and unacknowledged religion of the century. Its Bible was Claude Bernard's essays on methodology and Auguste Comte's philosophy of positivism. Whatever is not substantial or cannot be verified by the senses was looked upon as nonexistent. Need we add that many people today are still so imbued with the nineteenth-century spirit that such an assertion seems perfectly natural to them and the expression of intellectual maturity?

And yet this conception, still in many quarters taken to be the norm, has lost ground everywhere, not only in an art torn by conflict between figurative and nonfigurative tendencies, but also in the domain where this conception was born and developed, in science itself. Solid matter, the positive substance which was regarded as synonymous with reality—we are told today that it has no real existence. Modern physics reduces it to a mirage: its constituent particles, we are told, are scattered about in an immense void, like the stars in infinite space. These ultimate specks are not even solid, they are merely points of concentration of energy—the very energy that was once regarded as the antithesis of matter and described as immaterial. More than that—and this is the final blow—the specks that are not material in the traditional sense do not even occur at some place, for they cannot be situated simultaneously in time and space. Thus, the conception under-lying the positivist, middle-class civilization that flourished for four centuries and reached its culminating point in the nineteenth century is today disintegrating under the advances of the very science from which it sprang.

This is not to say that it is influenced by science—such a view is false. But science, art, and philosophy are merely different faces, simultaneous incarnations of a single reality, the soul of the epoch. This is why they are linked by an obscure, deep affinity, which is fasci-nating to decipher. Take the disintegration of the concept of matter. Impressionism recognized it as volatile at the very moment physics was breaking up the atom; abstract art supplanted it with mental constructions at the very moment when an Eddington, for instance, was proclaiming that, in the last analysis, the structure of the universe is math-ematical, and that numbers and numerical relationships are the only reality. Whatever became of that "reality of the senses," so laboriously evolved in the modern era, once the Middle Ages had been left behind, and now being dissipated by new concepts in process of evolution?

THE RENDERING OF MATERIALS AND STRUCTURES.   Primitive Flemish art was the first and perhaps the most accomplished expression of this reality of the senses. Born with the fifteenth century's mounting respect for physical truth and furthered by a positivistic-minded middle-class society, Flemish art was profoundly, essentially, realistic. I say essentially, but not exclusively, for it is never possible to break with history com-pletely. The Flemish Primitives always kept a faith in inner life, in spiritual presences, in a religious rationale that illumined physical nature and transfigured the materials they were beginning to worship, bathing them in an invisible light. None of these spiritual qualities survives in the minor Dutch masters of the seventeenth century—only Rembrandt, Vermeer, and Ruisdael preserved them by the sheer power of genius. For these elements were the last residues of the medieval soul and were only gradually driven out by the cult of the concrete rendering of appearances.

But what prodigious achievements this new art has to its credit! When fourteenth-century Italian art represented the external world, prior to any exposure to Flemish influences, it made use of colored forms—forms that were still close to the abstraction that had generated them, forms that had a contour and a surface but were singularly stripped of all substance, or at least of all individual substance. No magic wand had as yet released them from the limbo of abstract thought and invested them with flesh. What are Giotto's objects? Volumes and colors defined with authority. They possess weight and mass—like the bodies of physics—but unless we identify them, we can scarcely say whether they are made of wood or flesh, of stone or fabric.

The moment Van Eyck appears and Flemish art emerges, there springs full blown a ceases to be what it had been in Italy—a luminous void, a steady clarity in which forms arise. Turning its back on this immaterial vacuum, Flemish art defines air, too, as material, perceiving it as a substance and elevating it to the rank of atmosphere—an infinite variety of particular lights endowed with transparency, brightness, nuances, and reflections. The crystal column lets itself be penetrated by the luminosity of the space around it and freezes it. In exchange, it casts a shadow just there, a shadow that grows longer and fades away altogether on the flagstones (Fig. 127).

Italy will not delay in going to this school, but her mind will remain too rigid to capture what can only be recognized by touch. Prodded to emulation, she also was obsessed with matter in the fifteenth century, but with her, this resembled an act of will more than an impulse of the sensibility. Under the precise hands of the Florentine jewelers, painting will transform nature into a metal etched with line. Mantegna and the Ferrara artists will prefer stone—compact, jagged rocks, sharp as flint, out of which they carved faces as well as mountains, and drapery as well as flesh. In Italy, pursuit of the concrete misses the point, goes too far, does violence to it. The artificiality of the approach is revealed in lack of balance (Fig. 139).

Later, in the sixteenth century, Flemish art attempted to extend its dominion over reality, to add to its conquests. In its eagerness to analyze the matter it was trying to seize, it froze the world into immobility the better to observe it, and rendered detail ever more meticulously. "Don't move now," it seems to be saying to the world it contemplates, much as the earliest photographers were to do in the nineteenth century. Neutralizing time—life in terms of time—it conquered space, truth in terms of space.

But there is something else besides the substantiality of things—an essentially spatial feature. Things are alive, they move, they change from one moment to the next, they are not only fixed appearances but also forces at work, active energies. Flemish art in the seventeenth century made this second conquest, and it almost seems that Bruegel, who pioneered this development, had felt the need to free himself from the grip of space. He towers over it, dominating it, and at the same time renders the swarming existence of beings and things. Then the great bugle call of Rubens settles the matter once and for all, injecting nature with life—a kind of massive blood transfusion—thanks to which nature is transmuted and begins to evolve in time (Figs. 130 and 131).

Thus, over the course of three centuries, Flemish art gave painting the concrete world. As such, it marks a major stage in the development of the West: it determined the vision of a culture that was to play an immense part in human history.

# 2. A HISTORICAL MILIEU:
# FLEMISH REALISM IN PORTUGAL.
# NUNO GONÇALVÈS

FLEMISH realism appears to be closely bound up with a specific people and even with a specific stage of its social development. In order to prove this more convincingly, we might try to imagine this art transported to another country, where it could be studied in a new environment. How would its development be affected by the changed circumstances? There could be no better demonstration of the unbreakable ties that link a given art with the society that produces it. Fortunately we need not just imagine such a situation. Historical instances are not lacking, for just this experiment has been carried out.

Portugal learned the Flemish lesson. But thrown into a new crucible, it produced very different results. What we find is a new phase of realism, as well as a gradual shift toward an entirely different chapter in the history of the West. From concern for matter, the painter's explorations shift to the soul, and we see the first signs of the rise of the individual, whose emergence and eventual ascendancy revolutionized European art.

THE AGE OF PORTUGAL.    Every great nation has its day in the sun, its great century, during which it steps into the forefront of history. No longer a mere extra in the wings, it takes over the star part. There is more to this than mere chance: actually, every nation, by virtue of its peculiar aptitude and genius, seems to be created in order to rise to the fulfillment of certain expectations related to specific events. If these events take place, it moves to the forefront, ready to embody the aspirations of the moment or even to solve the problem that happens to be confronting civilization as a whole at that time. Thanks to it human history as a whole moves on to a new stage.

Thus, the thirteenth century belonged to France, just as the sixteenth was dominated by Italy; the fifteenth was shared by Flanders and Portugal. That Portugal came second must not be interpreted in the sense that its role was that of some mere imitator or follower. Portuguese painting of the second half of the fifteenth century, when we compare it with the Flemish art of the first half of that century, is just as original and creative as Flemish art in relation to the French illuminations before it.

The day Flanders attained a fully middle-class society—that day realism found its full expression in art. All Europe had been waiting for such a development, and Flemish art spread with lightning speed, even to Italy, though there it was resisted because a parallel but different development was under way. We may recall here that Jan van Eyck traveled several times to the Iberian peninsula. It seems fairly certain that in 1427 he accompanied the Burgundian embassy sent by Philip the Good to negotiate his marriage with the daughter of Don Jaime d'Urgel; at all events, the following year he landed at Lisbon with the embassy that was to obtain the hand of Isabella of Portugal. The arrival of the creator of a new form of art must have been a momentous occasion for Portuguese artists. But even had this trip never taken place, the commercial relations between Flanders and Portugal in this period furthered the establishment of artistic relations. Even earlier, at the close of the fourteenth century, there was a Portuguese consulate at Bruges, and historians tell us that many Flemish works and artists were sent or invited to Portugal and that several Portuguese painters worked at Bruges and Antwerp.

Until then, Portugal seems to have been under the complete domination of Italian painting, particularly of the School of Siena. It showed itself receptive, however, to the new Flemish art that so brilliantly embodied the aspirations of the time. But did it confine itself, as some historians tend to think, to creating a variant of Flemish art, a kind of local branch of it? There is much more than that in the art of Nuno Gonçalvès and his school, more even than the individual contribution of his genius: this art marks a stage in the Western soul's conquest of itself. Chronologically the work of Nuno Gonçalvès is situated —since he was appointed painter-in-ordinary to the king in 1450—just between Van Eyck's and Roger van der Weyden's on the one hand, and Van der Goes's and Memling's on the other. Now, it is easy to see that Nuno Gonçalvès, far from being merely a link in the chain, moves far ahead in a direction that he was alone to take, just a little later. The fact is, although Flanders introduced realism into Western art, Portugal went a step further in revealing the essence of the modern spirit by introducing the theme of the individual and his problems. Fifteenth-century realism was no more than a stage on the road to individualism, an eventual development very much in keeping with the West's peculiar gifts. Ideas are by definition the domain of the general, the universal; the real fact is the domain of the particular. Albertus Magnus had stressed, following Aristotle, the primacy of the particular in the domain of experience. Moreover, realism, by making man pass from the domain of abstraction to that of sensory experience, compels him to become aware of his own personality, to know and test himself in terms of his own resources—in short, to become increasingly conscious of himself as an individual. It was thus inevitable that modern civilization should be as individualistic as the Middle Ages had been collectivistic; the development parallels the shift from medieval intellectualism to realism. Now, although Flanders had, from the first, carried realism to the very pitch of perfection, Flemish artists continued to share a common religious fervor. The inner life concealed behind their apparent objectivity is still at one with the religious sensibility, as it had been in the Middle Ages. There are, to be sure, individual nuances, but there is no apology for the individual as such. Individualism, the growing need for which manifested itself in the West as the inevitable sequel to realism, found its earliest expression in Portugal in the middle of the fifteenth century. Moreover, it was formulated with a power of characterization and a restlessness of sensibility that were not surpassed for several centuries. What has been called "the Flemish miracle" was almost immediately succeeded by a "Portuguese miracle," no less fateful for Western art and culture as a whole. The achievement was the work of Nuno Gonçalvès.

NUNO GONÇALVÈS, EXPRESSION OF THE PORTUGUESE SOUL. While it is wrong to think of genius as the mere effect of social causes, its roots draw nourishment from the social soil. It was in his own country and in his own epoch that Nuno Gonçalvès

*Flemish realism tended to concentrate on the material surface of things. Nuno Gonçalvès used this approach as a means of psychological exploration. Here the individual makes his first appearance in art, with all his problems. His inner life and secret are hidden behind a public mask, but are hinted at by the expression of the eyes and by telltale wrinkles.*

**132. - 133. -**
*NUNO GONÇALVÈS.*
MONKS AND
CHURCHMEN
(from the side panels of the
ST. VINCENT
POLYPTYCH). 1458–64.
National Museum of
Ancient Art, Lisbon

261

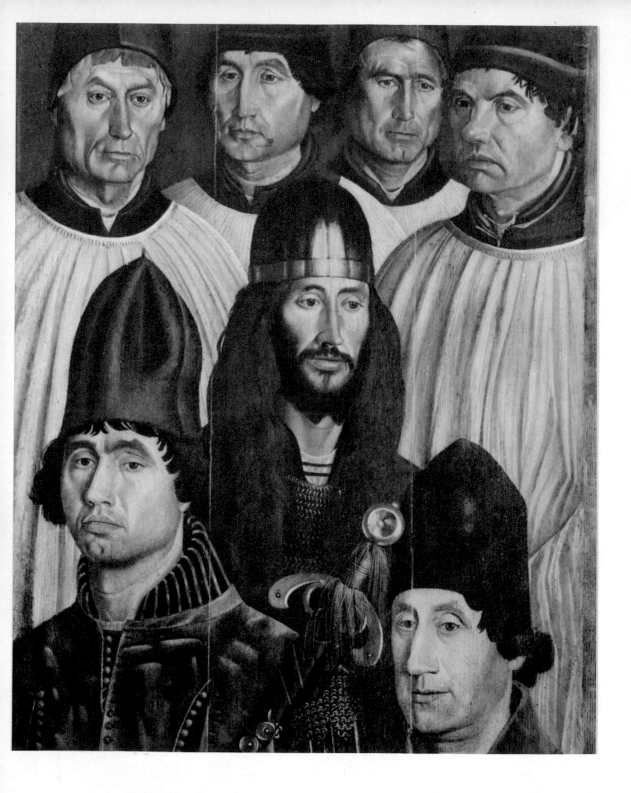

found the essential psychological forces which he embodied in plastic form. The period between the Battle of Aljubarota in 1385 and the battle of Alcácer-Kibir in 1578 was Portugal's golden age, under the dynasty of Aviz. It is marked by illustrious names— Henry the Navigator, Alfonso V, whose court painter Gonçalvès was (and whom the latter celebrated in the polyptych of St. Vincent), and Manuel I, who gave his name to an architectural style unique in history. In no other period, perhaps, had man more effectively displayed his will to power and appetite for conquest than in the fifteenth century; and nowhere, perhaps, had he expressed it more passionately than in Portugal during the age of the great explorations. From the thirteenth century on, Europe had been increasingly aware of the world outside its borders; from the fifteenth century on, it was possessed by an ambition to dominate that world. The epoch was marked by conquests in every domain of human activity. There were the conquests of the mind, which gave birth to science, and which in art found their expression above all in Leonardo's Italy. There were conquests of the eye, which were made by the Flemish artists, so adept at capturing the appearances of things. And there was the conquest of the seas, made by ships boldly setting out to circumnavigate the globe. In this latter task, Portugal played the leading part. Situated at the tip of the continent, facing the ocean, whose mists on certain days dampen the flagstones of the church where Camoëns lies buried, it had, at first, been alone in setting out to scour the seas and explore lands where no European had ever trod. By their maritime conquests, the Portuguese discovered the universe and reopened the faraway Orient, which Islam, for several centuries now, had sealed off from the West with a sort of iron curtain. And, in the course of their long sea voyages, the Portuguese navigators discovered another kind of *terra incognita*, that of the inner life, of the individual consciousness. To measure the importance of this other discovery, it is enough to examine the faces on the panels by Nuno Gonçalvès, faces that for the first time since the Middle Ages are endowed with a secret. Sailing the seas molded this new humanity, obscurely stirring in the fifteenth century. The seafarer was, on the one hand, a man bound up with the collective body into which the Middle Ages had absorbed him; on the other hand, he was thrown face to face with himself in the infinite solitude of sea and sky. Long hours of inactivity often compelled him to undertake that withdrawal into oneself which solitude generates (Fig. 134).

Who can be surprised that a hard school fashioned those highly characterized faces, which the brush of Nuno Gonçalvès brings to life for us with lines as hard and seamed as scars? It could not have been in the Mediterranean, that sun-drenched inland sea, where European man finds harmony and order above all. The individual and his anxieties could only have been discovered where he could feel himself more alone, either before the endless expanses of the great oceans or before the immensity of the Lowlands skies. The great outcroppings of the individual soul appear in art with the flowering of Portugal in the fifteenth century, in the work of Nuno Gonçalvès, and in Holland in the seventeenth century with Rembrandt and Ruisdael (Figs. 132, 133, and 145).

*Every man here seems to be thinking his own thought, to be preoccupied with his own fate, his eyes set on infinity.*

**134.** - *NUNO GONÇALVÈS.* KNIGHTS (detail from a side panel of the ST. VINCENT POLYPTYCH). 1458–64. National Museum of Ancient Art, Lisbon

MID-FIFTEENTH-CENTURY SCULPTURAL REALISM. In judging the importance of the fifteenth-century Portuguese School we must guard against two errors. One consists in underestimating it, in failing to single it out from the later work when Portuguese art fell under alien influences and lost its initial autonomy. The second error consists in overestimating it, in succumbing too completely to the mysterious attraction of this boldly individual art. Actually, the Portuguese Primitives present no riddle; what we have is merely the happy combination of a vigorous people and a pictorial genius equal to it. In the last analysis, the only real mystery is the fact of genius—in this case, the genius of Nuno Gonçalvès. But, just as on the human plane Nuno Gonçalvès was in perfect accord with the soul of his country in his century, on the pictorial plane the sole anomaly is his high degree of accomplishment. He fits in very naturally with the development of European painting in his time. His most striking gifts illustrate his continuity with tradition both in its most conspicuous features, the look of his paintings, and in its psychological features, those expressive of the artist's inner life, the inner meaning of his work.

To even the most superficial eye, the works of Nuno Gonçalvès and his disciples can hardly be confused with Van Eyck's, though their realism clearly derives from the latter. Not only is the technique different, the more or less plastery undercoating being absent, the oil applied directly to the wood panel, but also the realism, though just as striking, is of a different kind. Flemish realism seems to be an exact mirroring of nature (and incidentally, the symbol of the mirror occurs frequently in the works of the Northern Primitives). Portuguese realism, on the other hand, goes beyond nature; it seems to me to fall in the category of the something more-than-nature. It is as though the artist, intoxicated at having perfected an illusionistic technique, were no longer content to represent things faithfully, giving the illusion of their exact form, relief, and material textures. Rather, it seems that, having overcome the obstacle of his panel's two-dimensionality, he is trying to give greater density to form, greater salience to relief, greater hardness to matter. Illusion goes beyond itself and endows the living presence of things with such concentrated violence that the copy appears more emphatic than the original. Such attempts to be more realistic than reality always bring painting closer to sculpture. The volume, density, and hardness that naturally characterize sculpture are here suggested by the omission of modeling, and by what we might call a speeding-up of transitions. Instead of continuous modeling "in the round" we find the abrupt juxtaposition of light areas with dark areas, half-tones being eliminated. The result gives the impression of volumes freshly carved out of stone or wood. This feature is so basic to the technique of the Portuguese School that the pupils try to outdo the master, as is particularly evident in the *St. Theotonius* and the *St. Francis* in the Lisbon museum; these works come from the St. Vincent Palace, no less than the altarpiece to which they may formerly have been attached. It follows naturally that, as the contour loses its gentle curves, the line stands out in harsh angularity (Fig. 138).

It must, however, be acknowledged that Nuno Gonçalvès' enhanced realism, for all its

*After 1450, the passionate concern for the rendering of materials and textures led to a hard, sculptural treatment. The figure might be made of stone.*

**135.** - *ANDREA DEL CASTAGNO.* FARINATE DEGLI UBERTI. Fresco. S. Apollonia, Florence

DOMINVS FARINATA DEVBRTIS SVE PATRIE LIBERATOR

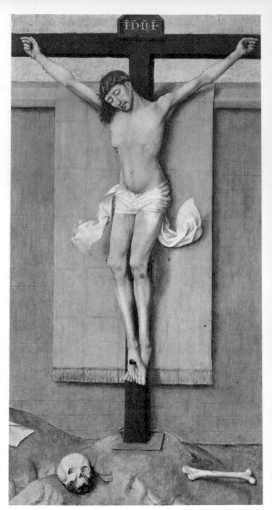

**136.** - *At left: BARTOLOMEO BERMEJO.*
ST. DAMIAN.
National Museum of Ancient Art, Lisbon

**137.** - *Above: ROGIER VAN DER WEYDEN.*
THE CRUCIFIXION. J. G. Johnson
Collection, Philadelphia

*The current of sculptural painting spread all over
Europe. Everywhere it imposed metallic flutings and
rigid folds, sharp modeling, incised boundaries. We see
here this treatment in works by a Spaniard and by a
Portuguese. The latter's Crucifixion is in all these
respects close to the works of the Flemish masters.*

**138.** - *Opposite page: SCHOOL OF NUNO
GONÇALVES.* ST. FRANCIS.
National Museum of Ancien Art, Lisbon

266

highly personal quality, is in keeping with the development of painting in the fifteenth century. Its equivalent, or echoes of it, turn up elsewhere. In Spain, we find it in paintings by Cordovan artists like Bartolomeo Bermejo and in the Catalan painter Jaume Huguet, whose figures are placed on grounds that are as though brocaded with gold—exactly like the *St. Theotonius* and the *St. Francis*. These examples might not, of themselves, suffice, for we may possibly be dealing with some mere influence of Nuno Gonçalvès. Such an influence is evident in the case of Bermejo, while another Cordovan artist, Master Alfonso, reflects Gonçalvès' psychological acuity and has adopted his direct and fluid technique. The latter may have been a pupil, as the Marquis de Lozoya has suggested, stressing his probable ties with Portugal. Master Alfonso and, even more, Bermejo would explain how these developments reached Catalonia, for the name of the same Bermejo appears in a contract along with Huguet's for the execution of the organ doors of the Church of Santa Maria del Mar (Fig. 136).

However, these sculptural features turn up in other schools in the same period, reflecting a widespread, inevitable phase in the evolution of fifteenth-century realism, a common effort to intensify it. Van der Weyden in Flanders shared this obsession with the sculptural, and even executed *trompe-l'œil* sculptures. M. Rolland emphasizes his close relationship with the Tournai School of sculpture. The example of Van der Goes, moreover, confirms that we are dealing here with a feature characteristic of a whole generation (Fig. 137).

In Italy, too, there is a new stress on volume in Masaccio, Uccello, and Andrea del Castagno, in marked contrast with the gently nuanced modeling of Fra Angelico. The same obsession with three-dimensionality appears only a little later in such Florentines as Verrocchio and Antonio del Pollaiuolo, and in such North Italians as Mantegna in Padua, and Bartolommeo Vivarini, Crivelli, and (somewhat later) Bellini in Venice. The School of Ferrara, especially, endowed forms with hard, angular, compact materiality, to such a degree that flesh and drapery alike are rendered as though composed of bronze or marble. The forms seem engraved or carved more than painted (Figs. 135 and 139).

The most interesting instance is that of the School of Avignon. Nowhere else do we find effects more similar to those of Nuno Gonçalvès. These derive from bold, violent treatment of lights and shadows, juxtaposed without transitions, almost syncopated. The *Avignon Pietà* is the most striking example.[1]

We are thus dealing with a specific stage in the development of European realism that seems to coincide with the second half of the fifteenth century. This stage follows naturally in the evolution of technique, which had begun with the miniaturists and illuminators of manuscripts—in other words, with a graphic or even calligraphic stage—then went through a stage of painting on wood panels, whose illusionism and nuanced modeling were largely the contribution of Flemish artists. The development then continued to the stage of emulating sculpture. Claus Sluter and the plastic School of Burgundy played a prominent part in furthering the obsession with sculptural volumes. In the first half of the century, Conrad Witz more than anyone else favored the passage from the one

---

[1] The obvious relationship between the author of the *Pietà* and Nuno Gonçalvès (Bermejo as well) was confirmed almost naïvely when Sampere y Miquel in 1906 thought he could attribute this masterpiece to the Spanish painter, and when J. B. Ford and G. S. Vickers, thirty-three years later, attributed it to the Portuguese painter.

*When an Italian's sense of form was combined with the exaggerated treatment of materials and textures current at the end of the fifteenth century, all nature seemed to consist of layers of rock.*

**139.** - *MANTEGNA.* THE AGONY IN THE GARDEN. National Gallery, London

technique to the other—the same Conrad Witz whose father, Hans of Constance, had worked at the court of Burgundy, and who has been assumed to have influenced the School of Avignon. Admitted to the corporation of painters in 1434 (the same year Van Eyck executed the double Arnolfini portrait), Witz introduced into European painting this exaggeration of volumes and densities, most masterfully expressed in the works of Nuno Gonçalvès and in the *Avignon Pietà*. But is it not curious to find in some of Witz's paintings—for instance, that of the knight Sabobay—the gold background as elaborately worked as brocade, much as we find it in the School of Nuno Gonçalvès and among certain Spanish painters influenced by it? The same background type turns up in the portrait of Cardinal Pierre de Luxembourg (School of Avignon, c. 1430). Is the background of the *Pietà* itself and its abstract golden sky, or the similar background in Enguerrand Quarton's *Mother of Mercy* of 1450 so very different? The accentuated, accelerated perspectives of the *St. Vincent Polyptych* find a curious antecedent, moreover, in some of Witz's last works, for instance, his *Annunciation* in Nuremberg. And also

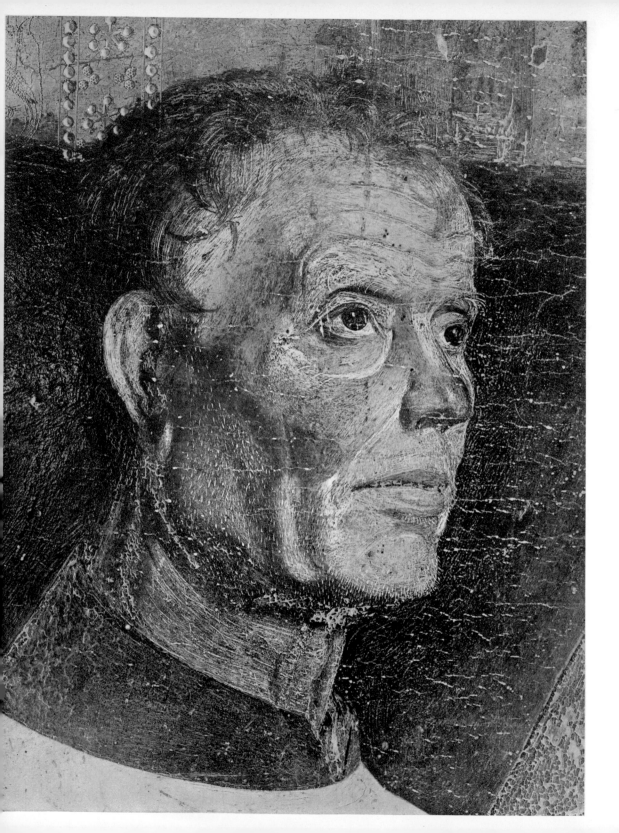

*A similar combination of strongly characterized spiritual intensity and inexorable modeling defined by planes reveals a disturbing affinity between this Portuguese master and the unknown artist of Avignon.*

**140.** - *Opposite page:* HEAD OF A DONOR (detail of the AVIGNON PIETÀ). About 1460. The Louvre, Paris

**141.** a and b. - *Above:* NUNO GONÇALVÈS. ARCHBISHOP'S PANEL (detail from the ST. VINCENT POLYPTYCH). 1458-64. National Museum of Ancient Art, Lisbon

in works by Witz there first appear those cast shadows, so subtly rendered as to seem to glide over the ground—the same shadows whose subtlety is so striking in Gonçalvès' masterpiece. These parallels and similarities are not advanced to suggest some hard and fast chain of direct influences, but to point out that the great Portuguese painter's sculptural approach was part of a movement that spread from Burgundian sculpture to Conrad Witz and from him to the whole of Europe, in an age when art was remarkably international (Fig. 142).

THE BIRTH OF THE INDIVIDUAL. More important than his technical achievements in the domain of art are Nuno Gonçalvès' achievements in the exploration of humanity. His figures are portrayed as so utterly caught up in themselves that only the accident of appearing in the same picture provides any link among them. Every one of them is closed off from the others; their eyes are not so much looking at the world around them as turned inward. We have come a long way from the undifferentiated conception of man, which was that of the Middle Ages! Now the human community has been dislocated, broken up. Each single face has become a distinct and separate pole of attraction, which further splits up our already divided, disoriented attention. These eyes stare fixedly, indifferent to everything save their own inner preoccupations. These men are individuals, at the ground intensifies to an almost painful degree the perpetual paradox of gravity (Figs. 132 and 133).

Bold though the technique is, we must once again note that it has not sprung meteorlike out of the blue. It reflects a general contemporary tendency. Italy was as yet too rational-minded, too Classical-minded to go in for this sort of thing, but Northern art had inaugurated the tendency. Even more than Van der Weyden, Dieric Bouts made frequent use of zigzagging diagonals and made the ground seesaw with vertical perspectives. And—again—at Avignon, in the *Pietà* especially, we find a type of composition eschewing regularity of arrangement and emphatically distributing heavy sculptural masses in a space that scarcely permits them to rest. Rather, they seem almost to hover in it, with as little support from gravity as from symmetry. Meanwhile, the abstract void of the backgrounds, which open up no vistas on nature, prevents them from being related to anything.

Psychologically, the impression is similar: individual man is lost in solitude, just as his form is lost in space. Nuno Gonçalvès' faces are unforgettable. Each man is centered around an innermost self, gravitating in a surrounding void. Almost wincing with the pain of his predicament, his eyes find nothing in front of them to relate to or cling to. The individual being is a sort of walking dream, endlessly prolonged. Emptiness, endlessness... perhaps we have here a specific "void of the infinite" such as man confronts at sea far from land. Even more terrifying is the *Ecce Homo* of the Gonçalvès School: the eyes of the figure are covered by a white veil as by a shroud, pierced only by the thorns of suffering. These men of action, energy, power—they seem somehow becalmed, caught by the painter at some moment of life analogous to the aimless drifting of a ship when the wind subsides. The hard-bitten faces are tense with unhappiness, an unhappiness that has a name —*saudade*—a word that every Portuguese historian uses again and again. By his *saudade* Nuno Gonçalvès perhaps transcends his own age and joins hands across the centuries with men who have felt no less bitterly their abandonment in time and space. The melancholy that these works distill is known to races that occupy vast deserts of sand no less than to those familiar with the vastnesses of the oceans—to the Arabs, with whom the Portuguese have always been in contact, as also to the Brazilians, a people of Portuguese stock, and to the Argentines. There is something of the same meditative resignation in Ruisdael's confrontations of the expanses of air and sky under which the flatlands of Holland lie. There is a kinship as well with Romantics of the type of Alfred de Vigny, with all whose souls have been invaded by the great empty waste spaces of the mind and heart. Portuguese painting was the first in the Western world to incarnate the theme of human solitude.

The modern soul is beginning to take shape. Therein lies the greatest originality, the unique contribution of Nuno Gonçalvès' genius. This is not to say, however, that some echo of it cannot be found elsewhere in his age. After 1450, much the same expressions of anguish or torment can be read on faces portrayed by other artists. In Flanders, Van der Goes gives us his dislocated, unstable compositions and his agitated, almost haggard

*The School of Nuno Gonçalvès produced several outstanding masterpieces.*

**143.** - *SCHOOL OF NUNO GONÇALVÈS.* ECCE HOMO. Fifteenth century.
National Museum of Ancient Art, Lisbon

a development that also helped to check the original drive so marked in the preceding century.

However, historians of Portuguese art have justly pointed out that parallel to the increasingly influential Flemish tradition, the Portuguese tradition of painting continued. To be sure, in style it owed much to Gerard David, Van Orley, and Quentin Matsys, but, among the supernumerary figures in many a religious scene, there still appear faces with haunted eyes and commanding individuality. Artists like Cristovao de Figueiredo and the Master of São Bento remind us that Portugal had been the first nation to become fully aware of the individuality of the human soul and its expression. Later, when the Portuguese School was more closely linked with the Spanish School, its characteristic contribution will be the same incomparable gifts. Sánchez Coello, who was a pupil of Maro, the founder of the School of Madrid, was a Portuguese. As a Cavalier of Christ he left the court of Jao III and his son for the court of Spain. The great Velázquez was of Portuguese parentage.

First to become aware of the infinite particularity of humanity and the enigmatic nature of the soul, Portugal passed on its discovery to the rest of European art. In its earlier expression by Nuno Gonçalvès, it remains unsurpassable. And yet Portugal perhaps achieved even more: over the centuries the seeds it had planted flowered in Velázquez, and, through him, reached Goya. This was a notable contribution to the shaping of modern man.

**145.** - *NUNO GONÇALVÈS*. HEAD OF ST. VINCENT (detail from the Archbishop's Panel, ST. VINCENT POLYPTYCH). 1458–64. National Museum of Ancient Art, Lisbon

# 3. POLITICAL ASPECTS:
# THE COURT VS. THE PROVINCES
# IN SEVENTEENTH-CENTURY FRENCH ART

IF the Flemish School invented realism in the depiction of materials and textures, this was because it largely expressed the tastes and preoccupations of a middle-class society intoxicated with recently secured power. If Portugal's adoption of Flemish realism transformed it and gave it new meaning, this was because the genius of Nuno Gonçalvès was nourished and guided by a society inspired with an ideal derived from other sources and directed toward other goals.

The psychology of societies, to which works of art so often seem to contribute, enables us to go further. In some cases, it supplies the solution of problems that art history cannot handle alone. One such problem has only recently been noticed: seventeenth-century France displays almost contradictory tendencies localized in different environments—Classicism on the one hand, Caravaggism and the Baroque on the other. It seems that the answer to this riddle lies in the psychology of French society in the period, and even in its political structure.


THE FALSE UNITY OF SEVENTEENTH-CENTURY FRANCE. It must be granted that historical truth is no more definitive or stable than scientific truth. It is a process always open to revision. Facts are facts, you may say, and it is enough to know them. This may be true of facts, but what about their interpretation? Facts are merely the past. Their interpretation is history.

As historical truths evolve, they undergo modifications, just like the shapes of continents. Sometimes they change very slowly, almost imperceptibly, sometimes by sudden breaks. The most untroubled, traditional area of opinion suddenly undergoes a seismic shift and, against all expectations, suddenly presents a new configuration. In the history of French painting, the seventeenth century has recently undergone one of those seismic shifts.

We have long known—for we were taught—that in the seventeenth century France was eager to put behind it the confusion (and profusion) of the preceding century. To this end, France accepted a deliberate discipline and disavowed the unconstrained facility of the School of Fontainebleau, in very much the same spirit that led Malherbe to disavow the poets of the Pleiade. From Vouet, who, upon his return to Paris, gave up the truculent Caravaggism of his youth, to Poussin, and on to Le Brun, French painting pursued an increasingly austere Classicism, increasingly subject to rationalistic controls and, eventually, to rules. It was nourished on Italian examples and ended up in authoritarian academism. In this view, it would have raised no argument to the inevitability of the new order, being content to supply a few shafts of brilliance around the Sun King, Louis XIV. Indeed, it has long been for this unity of purpose and achievement that we have admired seventeenth-century France.

Actually, this unity was officially imposed rather than spontaneously generated, a matter of policy more than of performance. To speak plainly, it was no more than a façade imperiously raised by the government, especially by Louis XIV himself—a façade behind which plenty of things went on that were hushed up as promptly as any family ever hushed up wayward or unconventional behavior on the part of its members. History, too, has its "family skeletons," long consigned to oblivion, long supposed dead and buried, that are suddenly discovered to have been very much alive all the time. The most sensational of these figures in French art history is Georges de La Tour. There can be no doubt that he was a well-known artist in his day, since he was painter-in-ordinary to the king. And yet he lay in limbo for three centuries. Now, of course, restored to daylight once again, he is not the only such example. Quite a lot of long-forgotten skeletons have, along with him, been released from the closet of history: Tournier, Baugin, Chalette, Linard, Vignon, Rivalz, Michelin. What in the world happened? In what secret dungeons had the seventeenth century buried these artists—and not only them but a whole busy seventeenth-century artistic production that contradicts (sometimes very flatly) the officially sanctioned art of the epoch? Until quite recently, only the brothers Le Nain had succeeded in slipping past the sentries and prison wardens of Classicism. It seems incredible that so many men and works could have been so thoroughly erased from the historical record for being at variance with a "history lesson" that generations of official writers had been interested in cramming down the throats of posterity. It is as though, in its own way, and in the domain of art, the *grand siècle* practiced the policy of the Iron Mask, dear to the Romantic imagination of a later age (Figs. 148 and 153).

Thus the long-traditional view of the seventeenth century is today under fire. The general problem raised is that of Classicism *vs.* the Baroque. For several years, the Baroque has been given a good deal of attention by art historians, perhaps in reaction to a somewhat narrow concern for form, for purely plastic qualities, also characteristic of art history in recent years. Writers drawing up genealogical tables of artists on the basis of form and formal systems have been led to emphasize the conflict between Classical and Baroque art for which seventeenth-century France was the major battlefield. Unfortunately, too clear-cut definitions have somewhat confused the picture that they are intended to clarify. Whereas the French seventeenth century had long been regarded as the expression of Classicism par excellence—the definition of the age, practically—a different view was taken by German scholars to whom the phenomenon of Classicism has always been something alien, an essentially Latin rather than a Germanic attitude. Under the influence of this new biased view, some American critics have even reached the conclusion that the seventeenth century marked the irresistible triumph of Baroque art, and hence, that French art of the century was an expression of that triumph. Some writers describe the palace of Versailles and the chapel of the Sorbonne as examples of Baroque architecture. Clearly such a view confuses ideas and values.

It is rare that a currently accepted thesis does not reflect some degree of truth. As the two theses confronting us are contradictory, ought we not to suspect that they are partial truths inflated out of all proportion? Seventeenth-century France was indeed part of a largely Baroque Europe, but, just as unmistakably, France tried to counterbalance the general tendency. It should surprise no one that she could hardly have been left untouched by features of the style she opposed—that she had to know a great deal about it in order to oppose it.

More than that. Closer examination shows that both these antinomial tendencies are to be found in the France of the period—though not always at the same place or under the same circumstances. No formal study of itself could disentangle the problem. In art history, it is not enough to study forms and single out sweeping categories, like Baroque, Mannerist, Classical, etc. The historian who asks himself why a Baroque or a Classical art

*French provincial art occasionally treats scenes from the life of the people in a spirit of realism similar to that of Flemish art, but is distinguished from the latter by the austerity of its forms.*

**148.** - *TASSEL.* SAWYERS. Perhaps a copy. Musée des Beaux-Arts, Strasbourg

makes its appearance at any given moment will discover that, most often, the causes are psychological, to be found in the nature and temperaments of people. Only thus can we learn why they do what they do, often enough without being aware of the reason.

CLASSICISM AND THE BAROQUE. Psychological analysis—i.e., analysis of the causes that influence an artist's mind and steer him in a specific direction—is necessarily complex. First of all, there are what we may call internal causes, those pertaining to the nature of a given individual or to human nature collectively. Human groups, just like individuals, and for the same reasons having to do with heredity, geography, climate, and perhaps other factors, disclose specific dispositions or tendencies. Now, these tendencies

283

*The complexity of seventeenth-century French art is illustrated by the engravings of Stella, an artist from Lyon. The one on the opposite page is allegedly Classical, being falsely described as based on a Poussin. Actually, its violent contrasts point to Caravaggio's influence, while the other engraving is related to the current of rustic realism.*

**151.** - *CLAUDINE STELLA.* RUSTIC SCENE. Engraving after Jacques Stella, the artist's uncle

**152.** - *Opposite page: CLAUDINE STELLA.* THE PASSION: THE DENIAL OF ST. PETER.
The engraving bears the note "after Poussin," but actually it was done after a work by Jacques Stella.

predispose groups and individuals to specific forms of expression. It is certain that, in our problem, France manifests rational, Classical tendencies; no one really contests this. Even so, we must not say, "France is Classical," but rather, "The French temperament is dominantly Classical," for the human group we call the French nation is very complex. The moment we move away from the central point, the point of concentration we choose as the center, we find transitional forms. In the south, particularly the southeast or the southwest, near Marseille or near Toulouse, the Baroque tendency asserts itself as we move closer to the countries where Baroque art developed in the seventeenth century. On the eastern frontiers, Bellange, Deruet, Callot disclose a similar tendency. The region of Lorraine is contiguous to the Germanic world (Fig. 147).

The same phenomenon could be observed in Lyon, a great crossroads where, needless to say, the psychological components are very different from those of Paris. Evidence of this in the sixteenth century is the engraver's art, with eastern influences that reached Lyon via Switzerland.

However, there are also external causes that spring from historical, social, and political circumstances. The monarchy emanates from Northern France, and is primarily based there. There it was born and there it was built up. Its language is the *langue d'oil*. Both openly and secretly, it backed the Northern barons in the Albigensian crusade in their terrible assault on the Counts of Toulouse. Sprung from the Counties of Orléans and Etampes and their dependencies in the Ile-de-France, its capital was first Orléans and then Paris; it shuttled between the Loire valley and the banks of the Seine. Always it stayed in these peaceful landscapes, watered by gently flowing rivers under delicate plays of light, a region—above all—of temperateness and proportion. The great provincial centers are often in the South where, under a warm sun, amid violent contrasts of lighting, the language sings and a certain excess of enthusiasm is normal. Caravaggism and the Baroque simply do not go with the Touraine—the atmosphere there is too peaceful! However, they are at home in the regions of ardor and exuberance around Toulouse and Marseille.

The French south, and especially the southwest, endured with inarticulate bitterness the official preponderance of the north and the eclipse of its own *langue d'oc* culture. As late as the seventeenth century, royal edicts were trying to stamp it out and to impose what had in Northern eyes become "French" culture. The *parlements* of Toulouse met all such efforts with a resistance that throws light on Southern hostility to the official aesthetics. Normally—apart from more or less accidental historical circumstances—every people in every time and place clings to certain dominant ideas which it feels to be vital for its development and which, broadly speaking, constitute its policy. Thus, every social stratum possesses not only an explicit body of doctrines but, also, tendencies that it feels to be necessary for its preservation and growth. Literature and art reflect these in classes, regional groups, and religious groups. Every collective body inevitably has some conception of itself, of its mission, and of life in general, that is reflected in all its activities, in its practical, routine activities no less than in its spontaneous literary or artistic activities. Thus, every geographically founded separatism brings in its train a cult of the regional language and literature.

The seventeenth century provides us with a major example of a collective entity's putting up literary and artistic resistance in defense of its own identity and policy. The example: Catholic self-defense against the Protestant Reformation—an example not without repercussions in the matter of the Baroque! Throughout the Middle Ages, Catholicism had developed unhampered; its only adversaries were non-Christian religious bodies centered outside Europe. But, in the sixteenth century, a new and competitive collective body made its appearance inside the Christian European world—Protestantism. This had a considerable effect on art, as Emile Mâle has admirably demonstrated in his iconographic studies. He pointed out the importance of the aesthetic policies laid down by the Council of Trent. It was primarily an iconographic policy, for the tendency of a group asserts itself most immediately in the choice of subjects it urges upon an artist. When Russia today compels her painters to glorify Lenin, she shows us in the most elementary, most brutal way that politics can be an important determinant of art. Similarly, when a given religion lays down a line of iconographic orthodoxy to its painters, it is employing art as an instrument of policy.

Besides dictation to the artist in the matter of his choice of subjects, there is another variety of influence that the collectivity exercises in a more subtle, because unconscious, way. For example, Protestantism represented a new spirit within Christianity, a spirit different from the Catholic spirit. In art it was manifested primarily as a demand for austerity. The means of expression were purified, and all evidences of luxury—appeals to sensibility or sensuality through incense, decoration, gold-leaf, theatrical effects, etc.— were banished from the churches. Protestantism opposed to Catholicism the inner meditation of the individual in all his nakedness.

What became the attitude of the Counter Reformation? By innate preference, but also in a polemic spirit, it took precisely the opposite attitude. It put renewed stress on just what Protestantism attacked—appeals to sensibility, luxuriousness of ecclesiastical trappings, spellbinding effects of atmosphere, direct appeals to emotion through portrayals of lurid martyrdoms and of the mystic saints in throes of ecstasy, eyes lifted to heaven.

Thus, there was such a thing as a Baroque "policy" pursued by Catholicism in the seventeenth century. Instead of appealing to the purity and austerity of reason, the Baroque appealed to obscure and tumultuous vital powers that lie beyond reason. Only this policy accounts for the fact that the Italian genius of the Renaissance, so explicitly Classical in spirit, at the close of the sixteenth century suddenly turned to the Baroque, seemingly the opposite of the Classical in every way.

The French national temperament tends to Classicism, but France is at the same time a Catholic country. Thus, Baroque art did spring up there, especially in the churches of an ultramontane order, the Jesuits. In Flanders, on the very battleground of Protestantism, the Baroque gained complete victory, most notable thanks to the genius of Rubens. There, the Protestant threat was much more immediate than in France. We must not forget that Antwerp, though Catholic, was for a time drawn into the orbit of the rebellious Protestant Northern provinces, the orbit of Holland.

In France the problem was different. There was Gallicanism: France, "the oldest daughter of the Church," wanted to be a Catholic nation, but she wanted to be Catholic in her own way, a way that reflects her own individuality. This is why seventeenth-century French art, to the extent that it was a Counter Reformation art linked with the art of the ultramontane Jesuits, yielded to the allurement of the Baroque. But Gallicanism, the monarchy, and official French aesthetic policy were all resolutely hostile to this foreign intrusion, and continued to support Classicism and rationalism. We witness an extraordinary spectacle: while Catholic Europe in general is adopting the policy of the Baroque, France stands apart, doggedly sticking to a Gallican policy that encourages a distinctly, much more purely French art.


ABSOLUTISM SUPPORTS CLASSICISM. To interpret the parallelism between art and thought in a rigid manner would be to arrive at the notion that every generation is all of a piece. However, historical analysis discloses that every generation is torn by inner conflicts—since it is always made up of distinct groups. Only when a firm political doctrine is successfully imposed does all evidence of conflict disappear. Any such doctrine implies a definition of man—a definition reflected primarily in literature and the arts, for their task is precisely that of supplying a clear and intelligible image of man. In part consciously and in part unconsciously, Louis XIV continued and reinforced the policy of

Richelieu in this respect, which had been to assign them this role. The monarch's aim—an orderly nation and a great nation (made great in the attainment of order)—favored the rule of reason, subjecting the creative forces of a people to a single, uniform discipline, demanding the coherent, logical subordination of all elements, and predisposing every individual to accept a centralized authoritarian government the more willingly for being able to recognize in it the form of his own inner life. When La Bruyère said, "A wise man wants reason to govern alone and forever," he was merely echoing Richelieu's thought, "Man must support the sovereign rule of reason." Terms like "govern," "rule," and "sovereign" of themselves suggest the extent to which such an intellectual and artistic policy was bound up with a concern for authority. Reason is the monarch of the soul. Whatever strengthens this conception is to be exalted, whatever threatens to undermine it is to be suppressed.

French literature found in Boileau, and French art in Le Brun, two leaders imbued with the ideas that the monarch was endeavoring to make prevail in the state as a whole. In favoring these men, Louis XIV did not act as an innovator. Strong governments in France have always furthered the natural French propensity for Classicism and turned it to their account. Charlemagne, Louis XIV, and Napoleon are each associated with a self-consciously Classical period of French art. Napoleon said of architecture that its purpose is to proclaim the grandeur of the sovereign and to "serve his conceptions of policy."

Thus, in seventeenth-century France, whatever forms of art opposed the monarch's ideal for the state were ipso facto regarded as subversive, to be rejected and suppressed. What were those forms? To begin with, the brutal, violent realism that Caravaggio had just launched so magnificently. There was in it no recognition whatever of the prevailing order and its hierarchy of values. But there were still other types of art that tended to negate or upset that hierarchy, either by countenancing the freedom of individual expression to an anarchistic degree or by giving voice to anti-rationalistic—hence disintegrative —sentiments. All Mannerist, Baroque, and Romantic tendencies were frowned upon. Order had to prevail. In other words, seventeenth-century French painting tended to turn its back upon the popular brutality of Caravaggism as, later on, upon the imbalance of the Baroque. The academies were charged with the task of enforcing these principles and served as policemen of art and literature (Figs. 149 and 150).

Perhaps now we can better grasp the significance of Bernini's adventures in France. The French monarchy—and officially approved French artists—set the highest possible value on Italian art. Why? Because Italian art, as artists of the Renaissance had created it, seemed to be the very type of Classical art. The men of the seventeenth century regarded Italy, the Italian Renaissance, and Classicism as synonymous. And when Louis XIV made up his mind to employ the services of the greatest architect and sculptor of the epoch, he commissioned Bernini.

However, facts are always ahead of ideas. Italy had continued to develop since the Renaissance and was now dedicated to the art of the Baroque. When the most famous living Italian artist arrived in France, his patrons were due for a rude awakening! They made the unexpected discovery that Bernini's tastes were not Classical, but Baroque. He was given a triumphant reception, an official welcome fit for a king, he was treated as an itinerant monarch of art. But when the time came to put cards on the table, it was realized that there had been a misdeal.

The cornerstone of the Louvre colonnade did get laid, but the work was put off, and

We must keep in mind that one of the greatest Baroque sculptors of the seventeenth century was a Frenchman, Puget, a native of Toulon. The work shown here discloses anti-Classical features: the mass is broken up, the body is twisted, the forms flow dynamically, the contours are wavy....

**155.** - *PUGET.*
ST. SEBASTIAN.
Sta. Maria di Carignano,
Genoa

Bernini went back to Italy all but dismissed. For a time, an Italian assistant was entrusted with the task of completing Bernini's project, but he, too, was let go after a time, and in the end a wholly different solution—a truly French solution—was arrived at. Whether the author of the project finally realized actually was Perrault (or d'Orbay hiding behind Perrault's name), the fact is that French artists were used, artists whose orthodoxy was unimpeachable. The same thing happened at Versailles. Bernini's equestrian statue of Louis XIV was received with deep respect, but it was nevertheless relegated to the far end of the Swiss Guards' pond. It was offensive because it contradicted the spirit of Versailles art. Mademoiselle Beaulieu is our source for another such episode. She tells us that Bernini was asked to submit a plan for the altar of the Val de Grâce, upon the recommendation of the Dowager Queen. But his design was not used.

Of course, in Bernini's case we are dealing with a non-French artist. But a French artist was no less a victim of the monarch's distrust of Baroque art—Puget. He had been educated largely at Genoa, a Baroque city if there ever was one. Back in Marseille, his fame grew steadily though there were local difficulties. His *Milo of Crotona* was sent to Versailles where, however, it immediately inspired the kind of opposition known in court circles as a "cabal." Kept in various dark corners, it only emerged after the king, to whom it had been recommended, had given explicit orders that it be displayed where it could be seen. Toward the end of his career Puget went to Versailles, but only in the effort to gain support against enemies who were frustrating his projects in Versailles. There were complicated intrigues to prevent him from seeing the king. When, after a hard struggle, he finally did see him, all he got was a few words carefully calculated to appease his irritation and to persuade him to go back to his province.

Lafage had a similar, though less glamorous, experience. He was a draftsman, a native of Toulouse, probably born there in 1656. He died in Lyon in 1684. Like Puget, he went to Italy, where he became familiar with Baroque art. His teacher was Pietro da Cortona. He finally went to Paris to cash in on his reputation, and it seemed that he would be well received; but he encountered there such incomprehension and hostility that he left the capital in a rage. Mariette's *Abecedario* contains a passage that is very symptomatic of the conflict between the French provinces, which encouraged the Baroque, and the France of Versailles, which encouraged Classicism. "Lafage came back from Paris very dissatisfied with the reception he had been given there." Bernini and Puget might well have said the same thing. "He had supposed that he would find a great number of admirers there and that he would not be able to handle all the commissions for drawings he would be given." What he found, instead, was semi-indifference and some outright opposition, particularly from Le Nôtre, though the latter had supported Puget. Having already designed some marvelously "orderly" parks, he could offer himself the luxury of one Baroque statue set among the trees; but he could not stand Lafage's passionate manner of drawing. "Monsieur Le Nôtre, for all his good taste, displayed no desire to have drawings by this master, when Lafage offered him his services as a draftsman" (Fig. 156).

This was what estranged them. "He asked him to draw, it is said, or rather to make a fair copy of [*mettre au net*[1]] his ideas for the flower beds, and this displeased Lafage a great deal. He was so stung by it that he complained loudly, going so far as to insult M. Le Nôtre's taste."

---

[1] The expression *mettre au net* is itself typical of the Classical temperament, and Lafage was incapable of obeying such an order, utterly contrary to the Baroque spirit.

*Seventeenth-century France also gave birth to a Baroque draftsman, Lafage, of Toulouse, whose line is torrential, jagged, impassioned, and robust.*

**156.** - *RAYMOND DE LAFAGE.* SELF-PORTRAIT. Drawing. Royal Library, Windsor Castle.
(By gracious permission of H. M. The Queen)

THE SEVENTEENTH CENTURY PRIOR TO LOUIS XIV.   To be convinced that these seemingly aesthetic conflicts had a political source, it is enough to take note of some dates. Actually it was the fall of Fouquet that marked the moment when the French monarchy—that is, Louis XIV—became conscious of its destiny and set out to put an end to the confusion in which French art was floundering, uncertain of its choice between realistic or Baroque tendencies—between the brothers Le Nain and the Caravaggists (Vouet began as a member of this group), on the one hand, and the Classical tendencies, on the other. The Classicists gained ascendancy only with Le Brun—just as much an appointee of Louis XIV as Colbert was in another domain. It is worth noting that Le Brun was a Parisian, that is, that he was remote from the provincial tendencies. The fall of Fouquet and the rise of Colbert have more than merely anecdotal significance. Fouquet—and this was one of the reasons for his conflict with Louis XIV—represented a conception of life and government opposed to the young king's. At Vaux-le-Vicomte, the visitor will notice a kind of profusion that brings to mind the Baroque; and it is not surprising that Fouquet favored Puget and Colbert opposed him. For Colbert fully shared the views of Louis XIV. He was hostile to Puget as a former favorite of Fouquet, of course, but also because he represented views incompatible with his own.

Opposed temperaments invariably prefer different styles, because style and taste are profound expressions of a man's nature. Fouquet and Louis XIV had different political views, but, above all, their temperaments were incompatible. In Fouquet there survived the spirit of the earlier part of the century, before the monarchy had become aware of its incompatibility with the realism of Caravaggio and the disorder of the Baroque. Of the Baroque, it chose to keep only so much as unequivocally suited the royal authority, namely, the pomp and luxury.

Actually, what is often called "the century of Louis XIV" did not begin until 1660. Until then, the seventeenth century in France had been no more than a continuation of the sixteenth. Although the essential characteristics of the Grand Monarch's reign had been drawn up in outline earlier under Richelieu, French art at the time had been livelier and had reflected the most varied tendencies (Figs. 151 and 152).

We must not forget that the brothers Le Nain were admitted to the Royal Academy of Painting as soon as it was founded. When Champfleury, in the nineteenth century, wrote the book that brought back to prominence these painters who were consigned to oblivion under Louis XIV, he referred to them as "the Laon painters." He looked upon them as provincial artists—as indeed they were. When they arrived in Paris they registered with the Flemish artists in the parish of Saint-Germain-des-Prés, which did not fall under the jurisdiction of the Parisian Académie de Saint-Luc. And yet these provincials who looked upon themselves as half-Flemish representatives of Northern realism were admitted to the Academy under Louis XIII the very day it was founded! There is little doubt that twenty-five years later this would never have happened.

Georges de La Tour, who came from the Eastern provinces, and who was suppressed by the official policy of Louis XIV, had also held a prominent place in Paris under Louis XIII. Don Calmet tells us that in 1646 he was painter-in-ordinary to the king, and that Louis XIII admired his *St. Sebastian* so much that he had all other works of art removed from his bedchamber (Figs. 157 and 178).

THE ROLE OF THE PROVINCES.   Thus, as late as the middle of the century, the French monarchy had not yet taken an anti-realistic and anti-Baroque line, nor had its tendency to centralize power of government been extended to the provinces. A little later, however, its political and intellectual independence were alike threatened, and to an ever-increasing extent. With a perspicacity that is not sufficiently well remembered today, Philippe de Chennevières (whose pen name was Philippe de Pointel) wrote in 1847, "During the first half of the seventeenth century, Paris certainly did not have painters superior to those of the provinces. And in the fifteenth and the sixteenth century, did Paris have stained-glass workers comparable to those of Normandy?" He went on to say, "History, which is a systematic science despite itself, has always displayed far stronger tendencies to unification than reality." The observation is worth keeping in mind, to put us on guard against oversimplifying facts. Reality is always complex.

The French provinces displayed great vitality, and gave in to outside pressures only very gradually. The absolute monarchy demanded centralization: everything was to converge

*La Tour belongs to the Caravaggio tradition not only for his night scenes, but also for his interest in the common people. This beggar, who represents an apostle, belongs to a series of which—as I mentioned in a previous work—there was a complete set of copies at Albi.*

**157. -** *GEORGES DE LA TOUR.* FIGURE OF AN APOSTLE. Private collection upon the king, everything was to emanate from him. Provincial life, centered around the local *parlements*, contained latent possibilities of conflict with the central government. Above all, the provinces were middle-class in outlook, all the more so because under Louis XIV the nobility left the provinces—a development that eventually brought about the fall of the ancient régime. Louis XIV brought the nobility to the apogee of its splendor, but he did so by basing himself on the aristocracy alone, cutting it off from its regional functions and concentrating it around himself. He thus created a head that had no contact with the rest of the body. The head thereby lost its essential reason for being. Under the rule of the local *parlements*, the provinces continued to develop and resisted as best they could the steady encroachments of the centralized royal power. This struggle went on with growing intensity throughout the eighteenth century, and paved the way for the Revolution. The provinces refused to comply with directives emanating from Paris, and were tacitly hostile to the official art championed by the capital. In Toulouse, the *parlement* sought to preserve both the *langue d'oc* and native artistic tendencies—in fact, it sought not only to preserve them, but to strengthen them.

Whenever two powers are locked in struggle, the losing side tends to develop, in a sort of overcompensation, increasing consciousness of its individuality and tends to exalt whatever enhances its powers of resistance. In its struggle against Paris, Toulouse found its most discreet and most effective allies in its regional language and literature and in its native artists.

Artists in the provinces were essentially dependent on the city bourgeoisie. Thus, in Toulouse, every artist aspired to appointment as municipal painter. The *Capitouls*—as the municipal magistrates of Toulouse were called—were the artists' partrons and models, and made them treat subjects that exalted the glory of the *Capitoulat*—sometimes at the explicit expense of royal power. On one occasion these *messieurs de Capitouls* commissioned a painting commemorating a procedural victory over the Queen. They had compelled her to carry the Dauphin on the crupper of her own mount when they made their entrance into the city, instead of letting him ride his own horse. In this way they stressed their determination to defend their historic rights and privileges.

The provincial schools inevitably expressed a regional sensibility and spirit that conflicted with the Royal Academy and the monarchy's will to unification. Even when they paid lip service to Paris and Versailles, their deep-seated instincts were opposed. Centralization of the monarchy took a long time, and Paris absorbed the cultural autonomy of the provinces only by gradual stages. The provincial schools—like every other sort of "irregular" tendency—were relegated to oblivion. Today, after several centuries, they are barely emerging from it—and it is high time they did. The spiritual fiefs fell under constant pressure, one by one, in the same way that the political fiefs were eliminated. Artists gradually threw in their lot with the Royal Academy, just as the nobles threw in their lot with the court at Versailles.

We have become so used to identifying French art and French thought with Parisian art and thought that we find it hard to do justice to the immense role the provincial cities have played in French history. We acknowledge the existence of local schools when we study medieval art, both the Romanesque and the Gothic. But once we have rounded the turn into the Renaissance, we speak only of the capital.

Originally, and for a long time thereafter, France had three visible centers of attraction —we might almost say three capitals. Besides Paris, the most recent of the three, there was

*Sébastien Bourdon, a native of Montpellier, occasionally imitated Poussin; but he can also be regarded as a member of the Nordic Bent (gang) of Rome, and as a precursor of naturalism.*

**158. -** *SÉBASTIEN BOURDON.* ROMAN LIME KILN. Alte Pinakothek, Munich

Lyon, once pre-eminent, and Toulouse, center of the *langue d'oc* country. Getting back to the seventeenth century, we must admit that no history of French painting will be complete until we have studied the regional centers that still possessed a degree of cultural autonomy—Nancy in the east, Aix-en-Provence in the southeast, and Toulouse in the southwest. By the eighteenth century they seem to have given up and to have accepted the hegemony of Paris. But this does not mean that they vanished—became extinct! After the monarchy collapsed and the nineteenth century exalted the sense of individual originality and rebellion against Classical rules, they awakened from their slumber. Lyon and Marseille again founded—I nearly wrote "fomented"—powerful schools.

As a result of the interdiction cast by the centralized state and the royal academies upon both non-Classical aesthetics and regional centers, the two kinds of outcast tended to become allies. The local schools that opposed Paris favored Caravaggism or the Baroque.

DAME JEANE DE JULIARD,
DE MONDONUILLE, FONDATRICE
ET SUPERIEURE DES FILLES DE L'ENFANCE DE NÔTRE SEIGNEUR JESUS CHRIST,
DECEDÉE A COUTANCE LE IV. JANVIER. M.DCCIII

Georges de La Tour, like Bellange, was a native of the Eastern provinces. Tournier went from Montbéliard to Toulouse, after a stay in Narbonne. Puget, the century's great Baroque sculptor, was a native of Marseille. The brothers Le Nain had a hard time becoming part of the life of Paris, and in our thoughts they have remained associated with their native Laon. Not so Le Brun—it would occur to no one to locate him anywhere in France except Paris, or to link him with any of the French provinces.

During the first half of the seventeenth century, the various tendencies coexisted more or less peacefully. Conflict only broke out when the Academy set out to create and impose a new doctrine. The Academy, imbued with the spirit of Louis XIV and toughened by the empire-building doctrinaire Le Brun, gave the second half of the century the public image of France as the incarnation of Classical art. What Le Brun did to French art is paralleled by what Boileau did to literature. The early part of the century, with writers like Saint-Amant, Tristan l'Hermite, Dassoucy, Scarron, and Cyrano de Bergerac, displayed a tumultuous richness, often with strong provincial roots. This literature went in for realism and for Baroque effects.

PRE-CLASSICISM AND POST-CLASSICISM.   There is one painter who sums up these various tendencies better than any other—Sébastien Bourdon, a native of Montpellier. When he painted for his own pleasure, he executed realistic, somewhat truculent scenes or humorous genre pictures. Being very adaptable, however, he also assimilated the Classic strain in Rome and in Paris and went so far as to turn out pseudo-Poussins. His unsteadiness well reflects the century before Caravaggesque realism and Baroque vehemence had been anathematized and banished to the provinces. Of these two tendencies, one might be called pre-Classical and the other post-Classical. Without trying to give a definition of Classicism, we may say that it reflects an easy accord between reality and reason—between nature and the mind—the former being explored according to the postulates of reason under the assumption, moreover, that it is naturally predisposed to be compatible with reason. Consequently, realism marks a stage prior to Classicism—a celebration of the raw material of life, as yet not oriented to reason or processed by it. The Baroque, on the other hand, marks a stage beyond Classicism, inasmuch as it acknowledges that art is not the mere reproduction of reality. The order that reason imposes on reality seems to the Baroque artist inadequate, drab, and lifeless. He aims at a more violent, a more intense and dynamic transformation of reality. Rational elaboration tends to a fixed order, whereas Baroque elaboration tends to disorder, at least to what seems disorder, possibly a more mobile order (Figs. 146, 147, and 158).

Realism may thus be regarded as art in the raw, as yet unelaborated Classically. The Baroque goes beyond Classical elaboration, being carried beyond reason along paths alien to reason. This is doubtless why, as has so often been observed since Wölfflin and Focillon, the early stages of an art usually tend to institute a progressively developed realism, which is subjected to Classical elaboration at the mature stage; then, as the evolution approaches its end, there come the Mannerist and Baroque stages.

*Some provincial works are amazingly realistic.*

**159.** - *JEAN III DE TROY.* JEANNE DE JULIARD, LADY OF MONDONVILLE. Private collection, Toulouse

in their small-size portraits of the *Capitouls*, executed on parchment yearly for the *Annales*. Here, for more than a century, they remained faithful to the technique Chalette had brought with him, a precisionist technique completely Northern in spirit and recalling Antoine Le Nain. Obviously, in these special official portraits, the *Capitouls* were unwilling to sacrifice their likenesses to any aesthetic considerations, and probably cared little for *tenebroso* art. They probably insisted on accuracy, a demand that the Flemish tradition was best fitted to meet. Thus, for several generations, the official painters of the *Capitouls* practiced two manners. One was the approved manner, unchanging and precise, used for the official miniatures; the other was the manner used in their paintings, in which they could indulge all their Caravaggesque leanings.

But besides Caravaggism, there was the Baroque. The artist who is willing to give up the play of harsh contrasts can give himself over to the limitless freedom of the Baroque. Such artists continually evoke Spain, Valdès Léal and Alonso Cano, Murillo and Herrera—murky clouds, red-copper skies, vehement gesticulation, swirls, banderoles. This current probably began with Ambroise Frédeau, who was born in Paris but who may have lived some time in Spain—at least one would like to think so. Perhaps all he needed to have realized himself more fully would have been to meet El Greco. He made a serious breach in the solid technique that Chalette had implanted, and through it blew the swirling winds of the Baroque. François Fayet, a native of Reims, was swept off his feet by it, as—later on—was André Lébré (Fig. 154).

Through his pupil Jean-Pierre Rivalz—in whom he neutralized the influence of Poussin—Frédeau influenced a painter of the next generation, Antoine Rivalz. The last name was a pivotal one in the history of the School of Toulouse. The whole seventeenth century converged in Antoine Rivalz, and the eighteenth century derived in its entirety from him. In this most important Baroque artist of Toulouse, all the resources of the school combine and culminate. He reflects and amplifies Baroque sweep and energy. Line, form, drapery, composition, all wind in and out, twisting and turning with supreme ease. The Caravaggesque contrasts are there, too, but harmonized as glowing *chiaroscuro*. Even the Classical tradition—chiefly in its architectural aspects—has been assimilated and swept up in masterly style. There is even the direct apprehension of reality in his *Apothecary*, which might be placed halfway between Le Nain and Chardin (Fig. 160).

Around Antoine Rivalz gathered the prominent Baroque artists of Southern France. He was a friend and to some extent a pupil of the draftsman Raymond de Lafage, the lyrical Bohemian of seventeenth-century French graphic art, as well as of Marc Arcis, the only great French Baroque sculptor after Puget. His bust of Louis XIV is perhaps the most grandiose of all. As a matter of fact, does not the work of Antoine Rivalz bring to mind Puget's oil portraits? Was he not pretty much a Toulouse counterpart to the great Baroque artist of Marseille? I should like to believe that, on his way to Rome, Rivalz stopped in Marseille, where, as a tradition has it, he was encouraged by Puget. Rivalz and Puget—the leaders of a Southern art then at odds with Le Brun's triumphant academism—were they not in the end to conquer Paris after all, through the instrument of Fragonard (Figs. 155 and 161)?

Rivalz did more than concentrate in his art all the various attainments of the School of Toulouse before him. He also turned it toward the future. He inaugurated the eighteenth century, in a sense, by extending the Baroque impetus beyond composition and form to the execution itself. His brush moves with remarkable freedom and lyricism, its very visible trace an effort to set down the warmth of life even in the material substance of the work.

Moreover, Rivalz founded the academy of Toulouse, successful in this where several had failed. He supported it and obtained official recognition of it by the municipality. The whole eighteenth-century School of Toulouse studied at this academy—Ambroise Crozat, Despax, Cammas, and, above all, Subleyras.

Without a break the chain extends beyond him: to his son, the Chevalier Rivalz, and the latter's pupil Joseph Roques who takes us down to the nineteenth century, to his disciple Ingres and the end of the School of Toulouse.

Ingres, born at Montauban, studied at the Academy of Toulouse and, a few years later, became the pupil of David in Paris. With him, a lengthy provincial history ends. Heir to a tradition that had long upheld a *tenebroso* intensity—the poignant rule of shadow, contrast, and passionate movement—in the teeth of the overregular clarity of Classicism, Ingres capitulated to the master of the Academy and submitted docilely to his teachings. The violent muddy currents of the Garonne were deflected into the cold, untroubled waters of the school of David. The last and most famous offspring of the Academy of Toulouse became, by a historical paradox, the intransigent authoritarian head of that very official art against which Toulouse had fought for so long. Before Ingres, there had been Gros, the son of a Toulouse painter, who, after a heart-rending inner conflict, had made the same sacrifice to alien gods. However, his original Southern fieriness was to fertilize Romanticism despite his own renunciation of it. Thus ends—or seems to end—the conflict that long opposed the School of Toulouse to the official school.

And yet the genius from Languedoc did not really capitulate. One need not go far to discover in the personality of M. Ingres the same seething ferment that had once exalted, in Toulouse, an alternating (and sometimes simultaneous) surrender to the sharp contrasts of Caravaggism and the vehemence of the Baroque. Bourdelle, another native of Montauban, knew what he was doing when he molded the bust of Ingres so as to suggest a storm cloud. Nor were Ingres' contemporaries far from the truth when they repeated Préault's witty remark that Ingres was "a Chinaman who stopped off in Athens and got lost." Ingres is as ambiguous as the other Languedoc artists who tried to be Classicists. In him there are combined—or, rather, there come to grips—purity of line and lapses of taste, discipline and fire, harmony and extravagance, plastic serenity and stormy private passions.

MARSEILLE AND THE SCHOOL OF PROVENCE.   In 1947 I had the good fortune to organize an exhibition devoted to the School of Toulouse, one of a series sponsored by the Louvre at the Orangerie. It was a striking demonstration of this provincial school's markedly individual character. At that time I announced a project for a similar show to be devoted to artists of Marseille and the Provence. The project was carried out by my successor, M. Bazin, and was just as convincing as the other. There the tide of the Baroque threw up not only Puget but also the Parrocels. Nor did it die out. In the eighteenth century, when the Classicism of Versailles finally collapsed, the great painter who destroyed it once and for all—without the compromises and half-measures of Boucher—was Fragonard, another representative of Provençal art. He imposed upon Paris an essentially Baroque type of painting, both in its principle and in its execution. When we look for Baroque painting in the nineteenth century, we find it in the powerful dynamism and violent contrasts of Daumier—a native of Marseille. Moreover, when we think of Daumier as a painter of the South—abstracting him from a French school situated in Paris—we perceive more clearly the nature of the affinities that link his clashing blacks and whites with the manner of Monticelli and that of Cézanne—at least the early Cézanne. The latter, too, was a pure Phocaean, a Baroque artist of the Midi. In this manner we trace the outlines of another provincial school, which long remained faithful to the Baroque ideal.

And what about Caravaggism? It, too, is found in Provence. The most prominent painter at Aix in the seventeenth century was Finsonius, and Finsonius was a follower of Caravaggio, a counterpart, if you like, to Tournier in Toulouse. Thus, Caravaggism and the Baroque were combined in the southeast, just as they were in the southwest (Fig. 150).

There can be no doubt that many factors contributed to this result, and that at least some of them—not the least important—are of a kind that one would never suspect of having repercussions in art. So true it is that the entire psychology of the human group, as well as the whole psychology of the individual, is involved in the act of artistic creation. Politics, a major social factor, inevitably plays its part, and its invisible pressure sometimes proves to be as powerful as intellectual influences.

*Marc Arcis, a sculptor of Toulouse, seems to stand halfway between a Classicist like Warin and a Baroque artist like Bernini.*

**161.** - *MARC ARCIS.*
BUST OF LOUIS XIV. 1677.
Baked clay. Musée des Augustins,
Toulouse

**162.** - *GIORGIONE.* LANDSCAPE WITH A PAGE. Probably an early work. E. Suardo Collection, Bergamo

### CHAPTER III

# ART AND THE NATION

THE historian of art who employs psychology must be prepared, like the archae-
ologist or the geologist, those other explorers in depth, for new and unexpected
revelations the farther his investigations progress. It is the over-all spirit of a century, the
soul of an age that he discovers first, but, before long, the evidences reveal variety
and contradictions underneath the apparent unity. At this level, he is in a good position
to study the behavior of groups—the political, social, or religious history of the age—
interesting not only in and for itself but for the reflections it will inevitably have left in
art. However, further research uncovers something like "national constants" running
through all the material so far unearthed. Climate, geography, natural resources, and
human experience in time combine in the modern era to mold a national state or character—as in antiquity they combined to mold the city-state. This is a psychological
quality or factor to be discerned in all collective activities and events, and in art no less
than the others.

307

# I. A CITY-STATE:

# VENICE AND THE SCHOOL OF VENICE

Venice was a city that, like those of antiquity, achieved national status. It played an important historical role uninterruptedly from the Middle Ages to the eighteenth century.

THE ORIGINAL CONTRIBUTION OF VENICE.   Venice is an Italian city, but it is more than that—perhaps something altogether different. The main characteristics of its art are not found in the art of the rest of Italy, which was perhaps less influenced by Venice than were other European countries whose pictorial vision Venice transformed.

The schools that aimed at a more rigorous definition of beauty and at strengthening the traditional disciplines turned to Florence, to Rome, and to Bologna. In these latter cities, seventeenth-century Classicism and nineteenth-century Neo-Classicism found inspiration and models. By contrast, every effort to throw off the ascendancy and excessive restrictions of Classicism turned to Venice, which was looked upon as the traditional antidote or counterweight.

When the eighteenth century wanted to throw off the yoke of the Renaissance—which, over the years, had been gradually transformed into a type of academism—it took the Venetian School as its model, even before it went back to Rubens and the Flemish School. Moreover, although Veronese and Titian exhibited greater freedom than the other Italian masters, they were regarded as legitimate—they were Italian, after all. And yet their influence paved the way for the more revolutionary and decisive achievements of Rubens and Rembrandt.

Watteau, who launched the new tendencies at the end of the reign of Louis XIV, had seen works by Rubens at Valenciennes, his native city in Northern France. Later he went to London, but he never went to Italy. And yet in his art he continually—it seems, instinctively—looked toward Venice, copying drawings by Veronese and Campagnola when he stayed with the financier Crozat, for example, and—very probably—admiring Giorgione's *Concert champêtre*, when it was stored with the Duc d'Antin, then *surintendant des Bâtiments*, whose town house was next door to Crozat's.

During the famous Quarrel between the Ancients and the Moderns, which at that time was dividing both artists and men of letters, the modernists liked to cite Venice as a debating point in opposing the champions of strict orthodoxy, who, in their turn, had cited Italian art as faithful to the Classical past. Venice already in those days was appealed to by revolutionaries of art. Much later, in the nineteenth century, the Romantics, who reviled Raphael (in the face of Ingres' admiration), spoke of Veronese and Titian as their gods. Delacroix went to see their paintings in the Louvre no less often than those of Rubens, when he felt the need to commune with the old masters. Like Watteau, he never set foot in Italy, though he always wanted to and several times planned the trip. The only time he left France, he visited Flanders.

Whereas Rome and Florence were looked upon as depositaries of the Classical ideal bequeathed by antiquity, Venetian painting always was a source of new impulses in

*Venice, like all the great Italian ports, was influenced by the constant restlessness of the sea. This may have aided its liberation from Renaissance Classicism.*

**163. -** *TINTORETTO.* CHRIST AT THE SEA OF GALILEE. National Gallery of Art, Washington, D.C.
(Kress Collection)

France. It had the same revolutionary effect throughout the Western world, and its influence inaugurated a new stage in the history of painting.

From Venice, from Tintoretto and Bassano, El Greco received the initial impulse that was to be so fateful for the Spanish School. Velázquez stayed a time in Venice. The composition in his *Lances*, as Angulo Iniguez has shown, owes a great deal to Veronese's *Christ and the Centurion*. When he went back to Italy to buy works of art, he acquired many Venetian masterpieces.

The art of Flanders, too, was greatly influenced by Venice; we know how much Rubens and Van Dyck owe to the Venetian masters. And in Italy itself, the subversive movement of Caravaggism that developed in the seventeenth century had been anticipated by Bassano, as Isarlo confirms.

Thus, Venice seems to be, if not the sole, at least a major source of the transformations that gradually broadened the field of Western painting.

In what respects is Venetian art, while sharing in Italian tradition, to be distinguished from it, even treated as something apart? How can we account for the disturbing role that it played in the fortunes of Classical art? It is undeniable that Venice, like any other Italian school, respected form and even exhibited a sense of form, but the peculiar Venetian contribution was to concentrate especially upon the pictorial elements that form *suppresses* or *opposes*.

Whereas form enables us to apprehend the spectacle of the world by ordering it, by conforming it to the expectations of the intellect, it diverts us from direct contact with the world, from any merging of our sensibility with it. Now, it was just this immediate contact that Venice coveted and impatiently set out to rediscover. Venice was willing to reconcile it with the demands of form, but it was also—on occasion—willing to sacrifice form for its sake. This was the very contact that Western painting began to seek, once its infatuation with the Renaissance began to wear thin and some notion of the sacrifices that this infatuation had entailed became clear. Venice instinctively cultivated those faculties that the whole of Europe was trying to awaken or reawaken with realization of the limiting effects of the Renaissance.

ESCAPE FROM ITALY.   Venice was far more open to the outside world than the other artistic capitals of Italy. The other Italian centers lived primarily on a reconstructed past that went back almost uninterruptedly to ancient Rome. They were very much more self-centered and self-contained than Venice and rather less open to the rest of the world. Being a port, an important maritime city, Venice has always been ready to let herself be carried away by "the moving gulf that trembles in the wind," as Alfred de Musset put it (Fig. 163).

The port cities of Italy were always receptive to outside influences and little inclined to orthodox local rationalism. Thus, Naples allowed the somber contrasts of Spanish painting to enter her art. Genoa welcomed Rubens and Van Dyck within her walls. Both Naples and Genoa gave expression to forces that ultimately disintegrated Classicism and led to the rise of the Baroque. Although in Rome the Baroque was primarily confined to the animation of form, Genoan, Neapolitan, and Venetian Baroque tended to break it up, to supplant it with something else entirely—with the sparkling contrasting plays of light, for instance.

Our study of forms and of their evolution has shown that, from the remotest antiquity onward, familiarity with the sea has suggested dynamic forms, liberated from the essential geometric structures to which the landsman clings. The maritime cities tend rather to free themselves from subjection to the rigors of geometry. Being trade centers, inevitably they are crossroads where the most diverse people, often from distant lands, come together and learn something of one another. They are open to every passing wind of the spirit, and whenever forms, whether intellectual or plastic, come into contact, they tend to contradict and abolish one another. For this reason, new movements often begin in maritime cities. Venice's position was quite exceptional. Whereas papal Rome asserted itself by resisting, first, Byzantine power, later on, the German Emperors, Venice was, on the contrary, charmed by foreign influences and marked by them. Venice served as a window of the West opened toward the East. There Eastern products, works, taste, and art were carried by ship. More than any other city, Venice was impregnated with the spirit of Byzantium and reflected something of its splendor and brilliance. At the same time, Venice lies on the road from Germany to Italy, near the Brenner Pass. Long before Goethe visited Venice in 1790 and composed epigrams "lying in a gondola," learning to appreciate "the treasures of the South"—long before Wagner listened in 1857, in the Palazzo Giustiniani, "to the powerful, coarse call of a gondolier" cutting through the silence of the night (thereby inspiring the aria in the second act of *Tristan and Isolde*)—long before Nietzsche there let loose (as he tells us) "the songs of his appeased soul into the blue sky, like a flock of doves"—long before any of these men, Dürer visited Venice, first in 1494/95 and again in 1506. The Fondaco dei Tedeschi with façade decorated by Giorgione is sufficiently eloquent of the importance of German establishments in this city. And, conversely, the native artist Jacopo de' Barbari left Venice for Nuremberg, where he stayed from 1500 to 1504. In short, Venice was open to Northern, and more especially German, influences just as it was open to Byzantine influences. Now, was not Byzantium precisely what Italian art had to overcome in order to assert its own genius? And was it not the romantic virulence of Germanism that, more than any other single element, contributed to the devaluation of the Renaissance ideal? Venice's singularity—so great that at moments it seems almost cut off from the mainland—is accounted for by its very special location and far-flung trade contacts, which brought it in touch with civilizations very different from Italy's.

Venice thus set out to cultivate those very features of art that the Italian Renaissance was elsewhere eliminating in order to maintain its integrity and even survival. We should not be surprised, then, to find Venetian artists everywhere undermining the primarily formal system that the Renaissance proposed and imposed on Europe. Instead of gratifying the intellect's love of rigid rules, Venetian art appealed and abandoned itself to sensibility. It was an art of the senses, appealing to sensuality and sensibility alike (Figs. 165 and 166).

*Overshrill rendering of textures and sovereign stylization of form (note the treatment of the hair) here achieve a certain balance.*

**164. -** *CRIVELLI.* MARY MAGDALENE. Rijksmuseum, Amsterdam

*The poetry of Venetian art sublimated sensuality. Sumptuous fabrics and treatment of flesh celebrate womanhood. Music and musicians are also frequently evoked.*

**165. -** *GIOVANNI BELLINI.* YOUNG WOMAN AT HER TOILETTE. 1515.
Kunsthistorisches Museum, Vienna

**166. -** *Opposite page: CARPACCIO.* ORCHESTRA (detail of ST. GEORGE BAPTIZING THE GENTILES).
S. Giorgio degli Schiavoni, Venice

APPEAL TO THE SENSES.    Venetian painting is an attempt to get back to the visual perception of material things. The ambition of the Renaissance was to represent reality by clear, sharply defined forms that speak to the mind and imply an act of intellectual comprehension. To represent reality by rendering appearances as they are directly perceived by the senses is to take up the very opposite attitude, to submit to the physical datum. This was what the Northern Primitives had already done. Now, Venice was not, of course, the only Italian city to keep up continuous trade relationships with Flanders, but it alone was predisposed to assimilate Flemish art. In Venice, Antonello da Messina found the environment most congenial to appreciating and developing the elements of the Nordic vision that he introduced.

This predisposition had still other causes. Although many aspects of Venetian art are

*Assimilating the achievements of Italian and Flemish art, fifteenth-century Venice succeeded in combining visual rendering of light and materials with the intellectual rigor of form and perspective. In the sixteenth century, Giorgione added expression of the inner life.*

**167.** - *CARPACCIO.* ST. JEROME IN HIS STUDY. S. Giorgio degli Schiavoni, Venice

**168.** - *Opposite page: GIORGIONE.* DAVID (believed to be a self-portrait). Perhaps a copy of a lost original.
Duke Anton Ulrich Museum, Brunswick

accounted for by its special geographical position as a seaport and by its relations with other lands, its economic and social constitution affected its artistic destiny no less than its political destiny. Unlike the other great Italian cities, Venice was never dominated by a court and was not subject to a nobility in the same sense as elsewhere. It was ruled by a patriciate whose wealth derived from maritime trade and the manufacture of textiles. The reader will recall that the same conditions prevailed in Flanders.

The effect on art was analogous. To a scale of rigorously defined values, which are difficult of achievement and which are inevitably set up under princely and aristocratic constitutions, Venice preferred the more physical pleasures of the senses. It was fond of exploring the world as it presents itself to our eyes and hands, not as it is fashioned by the laws of the intellect. In other words, Venice liked nature and the opportunities for discovery and enjoyment it affords our bodily organs. It loved wealth and sumptuous living, and saw in them the sign of an accomplishment elsewhere looked for in perfections of an intellectual order and in austerity of taste (Fig. 167).

Venice inherited its taste for physical things from Byzantium no less than its attitude to form. The characteristic Byzantine spirit was to cultivate the material and the spiritual

*With such a tradition, the Venetian School was predestined to express and celebrate nature...*

**169.** - *CAMPAGNOLA.* LANDSCAPE. Engraving. Boymans-Van Beuningen Museum, Rotterdam

for their own sakes, for their distinct resources, but never to combine or confuse them. To the Byzantine, matter was brilliance and glow; form was rigid, hieratic order. Venice linked these separate conceptions, subordinating them alike to sensory appeal. The result is a highly individual art, deeply indebted to and linked historically with the School of Padua. Its origins go back to the Vivarini family, and its first triumphs were with Crivelli in Venice and Mantegna in Padua. The initial impulse was to create exaggerated, hyperbolic effects of physical substances. The consistency and hardness of rendering recall marble, and the appeal is to the tactile sense as much as to the eye. Its very compactness secures for it an extreme firmness of linear contour, which often suggests fragments of a ruin. It is an arbitrary approach, exalting matter and form at the same time.

Crivelli, no less than Mantegna, possessed this particular range of talent. A Northern artist, he created still lifes remarkable for their sensory appeal: the little table with objects in his *Annunciation* is strongly reminiscent of the Master of the Aix Annunciation. But, at the same time, he imposes on heads of hair the spiral forms of a seashell or a regular, seemingly mathematical, abstract waviness. Handled in this way, the sensory elements do not encroach upon the formal elements; on the contrary, the two enhance each other (Fig. 164).

316

*...from the very first it produced an exceptional line of landscape painters.*

**170. -** *CANALETTO.* THE TOWER OF MALGHERA. Engraving. Bibliothèque Nationale, Paris

The artificiality that this treatment involves could not be sustained indefinitely. Optical perception takes in not only the physical substantiality of things but also the luminous atmosphere, which is an immaterial datum. The latter, by its very nature, does not lend itself to formal treatment; on the contrary, it envelops forms, is interposed between the eye and forms of things—in other words, it absorbs them to the degree that it is present.

Transition to the next stage was effected by Giovanni Bellini. One aspect of his work evokes the implacable, concentrated hardness and sharpness of materials that we find in the works of Mantegna, his brother-in-law. Another aspect of it, however, opens the door to what is most apt to abolish matter. Compare the two men's superficially similar versions of Christ on the Mount of Olives. Mantegna turns nature into stone, and Bellini seemingly does the same, but in the latter's version we detect the presence of softening, dissolving agents. The early-morning breeze ripples the awakening water; the rising sun colors the sky and the clouds with changing nuances. Bellini is following Leonardo da Vinci's injunction to "portray landscapes with wind and water, at sunrise and sunset" (Colorplate I).

Bellini may seem to us to be wavering between two opposed tendencies, but already,

317

like Antonello da Messina and Carpaccio a little later, he is blazing a new trail that will lead to fulfillment in his pupils Giorgione and Titian.

With these other artists, life seeks to liberate itself from the matrix of form. Antonello, like many a Nordic artist, paints gliding shadows and reflections; note the imperceptible transitions on the flagstones of his *St. Jerome*. Carpaccio, too, paints vividly gesticulating figures, walking, sometimes running. He was only a little older than Giorgione, who died before he did.

SENSUALITY AND SENSIBILITY.   Giorgione really launches the new era in painting of revolt against form. Is it not striking that the term "moving" can refer to both physical movement and spiritual movement, emotion? Giorgione found the secret of movement in light and its transitions. He used it to dethrone the conventions of form.

In this sense Giorgione can be called Caravaggio's ancestor. Light is an intangible, ever-shifting thing, whereas form is a fixed definition. The two are antithetical. When Venice blazed this trail—the only other pioneer having been Leonardo—the reign of the formalists was finally shaken (Fig. 162).

By the same token, Venetian art asserted itself as a sensuous art. From the fifteenth

*Sensuality was at the basis of Venetian realism. However, the Venetian School went on to make more and more technical discoveries. It is possible to follow the growing boldness and lyricism in the painting of Titian, going far beyond the imitation of visual appearances.*

**171. - TITIAN.** CHILD WITH TWO DOGS. Boymans-Van Beuningen Museum, Rotterdam

century on, it had tended to sensuousness, delighting the eye with shimmering pigments, caressing colors, and lively subjects. Pursuit of the picturesque even went so far as to seek out the exotic. Gentile Bellini, sent to the court of Mahommed II in 1479, brought back a new taste for Orientalism, which was shared by Carpaccio and enchanted the whole Venetian fifteenth century.

Beginning with Giorgione, the Venetian School went much further. To form, which delights the mind, it definitively preferred its rival, color, which delights the senses. To the exact rendering of real materials, it preferred the exploitation of the riches inherent in painting itself. To the picturesque it added the painterly, and it was the first school to create an art based upon impressions far more than upon elaborate rules. In short, the beauty that it pursued was not an intellectual conception but a visual enchantment; it sprang from feeling for voluptuous flesh rather than from study of the body's harmonious proportions. Moreover, landscape took on new and greater importance by its juxtaposition with human bodies composed of pure volumes (in keeping with traditional Greco-Roman inspiration). Painting veered off in a new direction, with tangled vegetation swallowing up outlines and dim, thick masses lending themselves to variations of luminous density (Fig. 169).

For all its sensuality, this art appealed even more to the sensibility. The shock of the physical is but the start of a delectable tremor that ends by affecting the innermost being: every sensation is transmuted into an emotion, an inner state. A transition is effected from

**172.** - *TITIAN*. SHEPHERD AND NYMPH. Museum, Vienna

drawing, form, cerebral elements to color, atmosphere, affective elements. It was to such qualities that, to a degree that varied with each artist, Venice always gave special stress. Valéry's beautiful metaphor in *Le Cimetière marin* seems to have been made to express this quality of Venetian art:

Comme le fruit se fond en
    jouissance
… Dans une bouche où sa
    forme se meurt.
[Like a fruit melting in
    enjoyment
… its form dying in the
    mouth.]

In Venetian painting we can almost *see* traditional form melting in enjoyment. For this reason, the feelings aroused by Venetian art are not invariably passions in any Romantic sense. Although the climate of these works is more voluptuous than dramatic, the means employed do anticipate those employed by Romantic painters. They do not speak to the intellect

*Beginning with Titian and Tintoretto, free, dynamic treatment, aiming only at an equivalence to reality, became traditional in Venetian painting.*

**173. - FRANCESCO MAFFEI.**
THE VISITATION.
Parish Church, Arzignano,
near Vicenza

320

and cannot be translated into ideas. They touch the soul and play upon the senses and the nerves by means of their color harmonies, by their creation of a luminous atmosphere, an insinuating movement that reaches out and wraps itself around the heart. The result is an indeterminateness and irrationality that encourage the viewer to lose himself in reverie. Thus, Titian brings together a sumptuous blonde nude, a young nobleman looking at her while lightly touching the keyboard of an organ, and the gentleness and sweetness of nature caught at an early evening hour.

Had not Giorgione done the same in his *Concert champêtre*? Like Watteau later, he

*What liberated Venice from concern for realistic appearance and "dematerialized" Venetian art was continuous pictorial invention. In time it was ready for Tiepolo's swirling lights and figures in the void.*

**174. -** *TIEPOLO.* THE POWER OF ELOQUENCE. Sketch for a ceiling. Private collection, Zurich

blends feminine presences, whispers of love, and evocations of music with the deep shadows of evening (Fig. 242).

The art of painting discovers that it can translate, that it can communicate the vibrations of the soul, and, hence, the secret particularity of the artist's feelings. The individual, who was so insistently present in the work of Nuno Gonçalvès, at last emerges from his inner exile. Painting as the vehicle of intimate confidences, as vehicle of individualism, now becomes a fact. Just as naturally as we turn from Giorgione to Watteau,

*Preoccupation with the immaterial led in Venice to a kind of Surrealism. Ghislandi evokes what is enigmatic in the obscure and indefinable human figure; Piranesi, the mystery of life and death.*

**175.** - *Opposite page: VITTORE GHISLANDI.* PORTRAIT OF TWO NOBLEMEN (detail).
B. R. Pedroni Collection, Bergamo

**176.** - *Above: PIRANESI.* THE CAPRICES: THE DEAD MAN. Engraving

we turn from Titian to Rembrandt, and in the end we arrive at Delacroix's conception of musical painting taken up and expressed so persuasively by Baudelaire. After Delacroix, Gauguin and Van Gogh loom on the horizon—that is, the kind of painting called "expressionist." The opposition formulated at the beginning of this book is now fully exemplified. Italian art, like all Classical art, was dominated by architectural principles; Venetian art, like all Romantic art, was dominated by music and its peculiar method for generating states of mind. Incidentally, music remained an obsession with Venetian artists: from the fifteenth century on we find angels singing or playing instruments in church paintings. De Brosse said the last word on Venetian music: "An inconceivable perturbation." In music, too, Venice established relations with Germany as early as the sixteenth century; the German Schütz, in particular, played an important role in Venice (Figs. 166 and 242).

DISCOVERY OF THE "PAINTERLY." This new resonance was picked up by the immediate successors to the Venetian Renaissance masters—by Rubens, for instance, who said of Titian that, with him, "painting found its perfume." What Rubens called "perfume," Delacroix and Van Gogh later on called "music." Painting, besides gratifying the taste and intellect with clear, harmonious forms, can exercise a power of suggestion that communicates the immaterial and the ineffable.

Such a mutation required a technical transformation, a new instrument. Now that the chief purpose of painting was no longer to embody intellectually conceived volumes, as in Classical art, nor to produce an exact illusion of what the eye perceives in the physical world, as in Flemish art, it had to break away from form, on the one hand, and from the rendering of materiality, on the other. This technical transformation was primarily the work of Titian, Veronese, and Tintoretto.

Now the actual substance of painting comes into its own. Instead of serving to render plasticity by modeling, or concrete reality by an imitation that gives the form of any substance except itself, paint becomes an end in itself. It begins to be realized that there are beauties and emotions inherent in the materials of painting. More and more, painting will be content with a degree of optical coincidence that, from a distance, reconstitutes the essential features, forms, and substance of objects. But once the painter has achieved this coincidence, at the lowest possible cost—just enough to make it possible to identify what is represented—he is free to concentrate upon manipulation of the pigment itself with reference both to color and to brushwork (Figs. 171 and 172).

The effects obtained will range back and forth within the extremes of roughness and smoothness of paint, thinness and thickness, and we will be made increasingly aware of the degree of liveliness in the artist's execution. The pigment itself will reflect the impulsive life behind the brush, the nervous system behind the hand that held it (Fig. 173).

This far-reaching revolution in the painter's values gave rise to a sense of the "painterly." Modern painting, in the broadest sense of the term—we prefer "the painting of the modern era"—was thereby born. Velázquez, Rubens, Rembrandt—and, a long time after them, the Impressionists—now became possible; in fact the cornerstone of Impressionism was laid. This is not to say that Velázquez, Rubens, Rembrandt, and the others would not have taken the same path in any case, but without the example of Venice they would not have pursued it with the same sureness or drive.

By the end of the seventeenth century, this revolution was an accomplished fact. It spread to all schools and supplied them with a certain principle of unity, but nowhere was the victory of the pictorial element over form pushed so far as in Venice. We have only to look at the art of the eighteenth century, to examine Tiepolo or Guardi, for example, to see how the brush stroke explodes form, replacing rigid contours with odd jagged lines or lines only roughly parallel, and consistent volumes with scintillating spots of color.

We have just said that the revolution begun in Venice eventually made Impressionism possible. Actually, we can find there Impressionist treatments in fully developed form, as in certain of Guardi's scenes of Venetian canals and outer lagoons, where the only remaining concrete objects are a black gondola and the horizon line. The rest is nothing but modulations of light and color, just as in canvases by Monet or Sisley.

THE SOUL OF VENICE. In developing pictorial technique to the point where it could subtly render emotional modulations, the purpose of the Venetian painters was not merely to produce optical mirages. They sought to express states of mind. What were these? The same as those affected by the Romantics—juvenile melancholy exalted by the intensity of desire and the precariousness of life and multiplied by the obscure associations an indeterminate deep-lying nature can provide. Occasionally we find an insatiable ardor, a need to become part of universal life and to plunge into it as into an abyss of violence and intensity. Tintoretto, at moments, seems to anticipate Victor Hugo with his fondness for the enormous, his gigantic swirls, his harsh contrasts between light and shadow.

The colored light that, in the eighteenth century, sparkles in the works of Guardi and Canaletto suggests that its true counterpart is *chiaroscuro*. As it moves away from reason, the sensibility sometimes comes close to secret, unconscious harmonies beyond all logic. Bellini, and, later, Giorgione—in his *Tempest*, for instance—displayed a fondness for mysterious subjects about which nothing much can be understood or explained, but which are nonetheless very affecting. Panels by Hieronymus Bosch had long since been housed in the Palace of the Doges. Their presence symbolizes the contribution of Nordic artists who revealed to Venice the fascination of the unforeseen and the unknown. And whenever we encounter it elsewhere—exceptionally—in Italian art, the influence of Venice is never very far to seek. The *groteschi*, those strange, swarming chimerical fantasies exhumed (paradoxically enough) during the Renaissance's love affair with intellectual lucidity—ambiguous forms in which animal and plant features are blended—were discovered among Rome's buried treasures by two Venetians: the singular Pietro Luzzi, nicknamed "The Dead Man," and Giovanni da Udine, a collaborator of Raphael. It is noteworthy that the former worked with Giorgione on the Fondaco dei Tedeschi and that the latter was apparently his pupil. Similarly, two centuries later, the man who conjured up a rational clarity and sense of harmonious proportion hitherto found only in ancient monuments—and who projected it into a universe where the colossal and the unusual were often close to nightmare and madness—was the great Piranesi, another Venetian. In the same eighteenth century, G. B. Tiepolo, the last great master of the city of the Doges, usually appreciated only for his dazzling brilliance, was also capable of expressing the strange and the mysterious. His *Scherzi di fantasia* and his *Capricci* (the same title, *Capricci* or *Bizarre*, had been used a century earlier by the engraver Giovanni Battista Bracelli) renew exploration of the fantastic in Italian art and anticipate Goya (Figs. 175 and 176).

In this connection, too, Venice seems to be situated on the frontiers of Italian painting—on the edge of another world, as it were, which attracts it and almost intoxicates it. It was imbued with the Orient without being an Oriental city. It was imbued with the North, particularly with Germanism, without being a German city. Thus, it was in close contact with cultural influences of which the Italian soul in general was unaware or which it excluded. It was not just close to them; it was steeped in them and surrendered happily to their attractions, but at the same time kept a sense of their foreignness. Whatever is felt as "foreign" is always to some extent felt as "strange": the two terms and what they denote are closely related. The Venetian genius is certainly Italian, but being situated at the frontier, it familiarized itself with what was "other," and, no doubt, acquired a taste for it.

Thus, it is not surprising that Venice was the chosen city of the Romantics, right down to Maurice Barrès, who was recalling many predecessors when he wrote, "On the sands of the Lido, what is this gathering of shadows? Mickiewicz, George Sand, Musset, the aged Chateaubriand himself are all out there looking for the hoofprints of Byron's horses...."

# 2. A NATION:

# FRANCE AND THE ART OF THE PORTRAIT

THE School of Venice embodies the soul of a city. The soul of a nation is more complex. How can we grasp its elusive unity? Once again, art provides us with the most flexible and the most subtle approach. French art is the imaged likeness of the race; it rests upon a balance between man and nature. Farther north, man is fond of losing himself in nature; farther south, he is all too liable to forget nature and think only of himself. France, an attractive, fertile land, where the predominantly agricultural economy indicates harmony between the people and the soil, has been perhaps the only nation to keep the two terms in easy balance throughout the development of her art.

For this reason French painters have exhibited equal affection for the portrait and the landscape. From the outset, the national sensibility has been given as full and as spontaneous expression in the one genre as in the other. Even in the cathedrals, alongside the rows of saints sculptured at the entrances we find garlands of field plants on the capitals of the columns.

For all that, man plays decidedly a greater part than nature. In Northern art, portraits are often provided with a background of landscape. In French art, on the contrary—and this may be significant—the human figure is treated as self-sufficient. At the same time, perhaps under the influence of Romanticism and foreign influences, French painters seldom fail to animate their landscapes with some human presence. Claude Lorrain could dream his dream of an enchanted castle marvelously slumbering in its green surroundings bathed in light, yet he expressed solitude in this painting by adding a feminine figure at once lost in the tangle of things and at their very core, the point of our awareness of them. To Dutch artists like Ruisdael, for example, solitude is conceived as a natural scene in which no human being appears. To a French artist, it is man alone with nature. In 1831, Corot painted a landscape that shows a woman lying near a spring, reading (perhaps echoing Lamartine's line, *Je lisais au murmure de la source éternelle,* "I was reading to the murmur of the eternal source.")

The Frenchman's gift of humane sympathy for his fellow man springs perhaps from the gentle climate of his country with few regions cut off from the rest. Moreover, he is an individualist; whether as a portraitist or a moralist, he is interested both in his own image and in the image of others. It is not surprising that his art and his literature alike are a series of portraits more than anything else.

THE PORTRAIT AND THE NATIONAL SOUL.   Do these faces all have something in common, something like a portrait of France? We should hardly expect the features to be much like those of other peoples. There will be neither the passive placidity of Flemish or Dutch faces, nor that sudden flash of restlessness which, rising from the very depths, sometimes crosses them—under Rembrandt's brush, for example—and of which a more burning and harsher version appears in Spanish painting. We should not expect the hard energy of Germanic features either, nor the harmonious impassiveness of Italian faces. We find most often in French portraits an active face that feels, experiences, and still searches. Eager to the point of betraying curiosity, dreamy to the point of melancholy, meditative to the point of gravity, lively to the point of breaking into a smile, images of the French face unvariably record some aspect of inner life.

THE RHYTHM OF FRENCH HISTORY.   However, French portraiture varies over the epochs. Although it is tempting, at first, to stress its uniformity, on closer inspection we find that duality is a more appropriate rule. If I had to give a concise definition of the French soul, I should say that it is made up of a smiling gravity. Neither term suffices without the other. But according to the period, now gravity and now the smile is more prominent. Persons familiar with only the one or the other side of the French character have arrived at some highly erroneous formulas concerning it, sometimes regarded as the last word outside of France. The eighteenth-century smile enjoyed such universal prestige that it was sometimes looked upon as summing up the entire French contribution. The rest of the world readily believed that French expression was characterized by a somewhat dry, superficial, casual wit. This idea became so deep-rooted that, in the end, the French began to believe it themselves, and, at the close of the nineteenth century, France partly fashioned herself in this likeness of herself come from outside. It is enough to cast a quick glance over these successive limnings, however—so reflective, so pensive, so withdrawn, and yet so gentle—to grasp where the misunderstanding lay. Suddenly we stop seeing only smiling mouths, only serious expressions. These faces are open to the world and then closed to it again. At moments, a man is outgoing; he projects onto his fellow men his personal charm and love of life as though eager to share it, while at other moments he jealously keeps his innermost being to himself, letting it mature in its own good time, meditating on the purpose and responsibilities of existence.

There even seems to be a sort of regularity to the dual rhythm. Possibly the secret of France's unbroken creativeness in history lies here. Thanks to it, the nation is adept in the art of alternatively relaxing and renewing her inner strength. Whereas other races use up all their energies in the pursuit of their own truth, and then must go through moments of exhaustion, France alternates regularly between grave, concentrated, sometimes tense periods and pleasant, hedonistic, unconstrained periods. Her evolution is marked by an elasticity that preserves her from the sudden breaks that are the lot of more strenuous nations, and that gives France her most striking characteristic—diversity in unity. The fervent faith of the Middle Ages was followed by the sensual refinement of the Renaissance, the grandiose tension of the seventeenth century by the *joie de vivre* of the eighteenth. Such violent upsurges as the Revolution and the Empire seem to bring out in turn the virile and the feminine aspirations of the race. To ignore either is to run the risk of partiality. The former gives France her pensive, resolute, or intransigent face, as well as the

warlike face she sometimes takes; the latter her courteous, sociable, amorous face. Let us look at each in turn.

Individualistic and intelligent, the French man likes to reflect upon the meaning of life, the purpose of his existence, and the means of achieving it. He believes that every man is morally responsible for the direction his life takes; a little from personal pride, and a little out of concern for logic, he attaches great importance to his "conduct." He likes to conform to general rules, which he accepts after weighing them carefully, and on which he bases his conception of duty. Every people seems to be dominated by a type dear to it, which does not express it entirely, but which seems to embody its chief qualities: thus, the Spanish type is a passionate mystic, the German a power-hungry warrior, the English a sailor and trader. The traditional image of the French-man is the peasant and soldier, accustomed to tasks that require energy, a high sense of obligation, and I should add—contrary to stereotype ideas—a sense of discipline freely accepted, thought out, and well understood. Such seems to be the male type of the race, as evidenced by the well-balanced, serious faces, deeply imbued with a sense of responsibility, which French art has portrayed (Figs. 179 and 183).

In the Middle Ages, a new type made its appearance, which for a long time shared the characteristics of the two others—the *bourgeois*. Who can fail to be struck by the close affinity between the features of an anonymous peasant portrayed by Le Nain and a magistrate such as the Chancellor Séguier painted by Le Brun—or such a soldier, descend-ant of an old family, as we see in Nanteuil's portrait of Turenne? What is common to these figures is a self-possessed, thoughtful gravity, the firmness of the intelligent eyes. The robust nature of the peasant, the equipoise of the magistrate, and the loyalty of the soldier shown in these three portraits are combined in Poussin's self-portrait. At the same time Poussin embodied in his image the rectitude of the figures recorded by anonymous medieval artists on the portals of the cathedrals, the candid look of Chardin, the firmness and directness of Delacroix (in the latter's self-portrayal as *Man with Green Waistcoat*). The *Jeremiah* by the Master of Aix, Fouquet's *Saint Stephen*, the *Knight in Armor* of the School of Avignon, the *Jacques Hurault* of the museum at Le Mans, Nanteuil's *Maréchal Fabert*, and many other works disclose the same sense of the human task as noble. The same national characteristic gave rise to the moralists of French literature and accounts for the predominance therein of studies of character rather than fantastic inventions or metaphys-ical flights. Here, the sensibility is no harp that vibrates under a thousand light touches and whose music passes away like the wind blowing across its strings. The French sen-sibility resists the erosion of time, being rooted in deep convictions—that is, in the revela-tion of what it believes to be enduring, more enduring than itself—the eternal. Life passes, but when it has been linked with something permanent, it takes on continuity, it

*The earliest French painting was a portrait, that of Jean le Bon. A composed and penetrating feeling for human nature is asserted from the outset.*

**177. -** *Opposite page:* PORTRAIT OF A MERCHANT. End of the fifteenth century. Northern France.
National Gallery of Canada, Ottawa

**178. -** *Above:* KNIGHT IN ARMOR (detail of THE ADORATION OF THE CHILD).
End of the fifteenth century. School of Avignon. Musée Calvet, Avignon

acquires the mobility of life itself. The flashing smiles of La Tour's figures convey the melancholy of the vanished moment, but the slow and humble gestures of Chardin preserve the potential permanence of things which only the meditative eye detects. At the same time, behind these thoughtful foreheads, these eyes that look on life unblinkingly—determined to see it as it is and to be equal to the duties it imposes —we perceive a secret gentleness revealing the extent to which virile strength has been impregnated with feminine charm throughout French history. Indeed, occasionally, it has dominated it entirely.

## ALTERNATION OF VIRILITY AND FEMININITY.

If French rationalism were left to its own devices, the result would undoubtedly be a certain dryness. This danger has always lurked in French Cartesianism. It is, perhaps, because the French feel that the more vibrant and spontaneous feminine temperament is an indispensable corrective for or counterweight to the inadequacies of rationalism that they assign so important a role in their lives to women. Woman represents the sensibility of France; she introduces it into social life through her characteristic activities, and she awakens it in men by arousing their love. If the French sensibility is neither too tumultuous, nor too intense, if its moderation lacks the outbursts and exaltations of certain other races, it does possess the gift of love—love of life, love of nature, love of human beings. Whenever the country runs the risk of succumbing to an overlogical temper, by some marvelous instinct it reacts by centering all social life around woman and by conferring upon her the role of regulating sensibility. Toward the end of the twelfth century, in the heyday of Gothic art, the trouvères and troubadours launched a period of female domination in reaction to the warlike coarseness of the preceding years. There was Marie de France, the novels of the Breton cycle, and the *Roman de la Rose* (*"où l'art d'amour est tout enclose"*), then the *Cité des Dames* of Christine de Pisan. From the twelfth to the fourteenth century, "courts of love" favored the spread of sociability and gentility. In the fourteenth century, a period of wars and inner dissensions, the spirit of chivalry gave way to bourgeois positivism, which gained ascendancy in the fifteenth century under certain Valois kings, like Charles VII and Louis XI—but the following century once again revived the courtly life. Social life was once more centered around women, they were again exalted by artists and writers, and, early in the seventeenth century, the first salons made their appearance with all their preciosity. Similarly, after the reign of Louis XIV, which strained toward more grandiose achievements, the eighteenth century restored the power of woman. The Revolution in turn ended in the feminine relaxation of the Directoire, just as the period of Napoleonic wars ended in the feminine obsession with the Romantic.

In every one of these periods of feminine pre-eminence, French life was intensely social. Men and women polished and cultivated their attractiveness, displaying only their most pleasing aspects. The portraits from these periods show features directed not inward but outward: the mouths are animated and smiling; the faces, gestures, and bodies of women provide sources of the artists' inspiration. Yet every time woman is reborn in art, she appears essentially unchanged. Womanly grace provides a somewhat disturbing link over

*A certain virile, serious, and even pensive human type asserts itself in French portraiture at an early date.*

**179.** - PORTRAIT OF JACQUES HURAULT. Sixteenth century. French School. Museum, Le Mans

331

*The virility of French art is always counterbalanced by a lively and loving treatment of woman, which comes close to daydream and remains constant over the centuries.*

**180.** - *Opposite page: SCHOOL OF FONTAINEBLEAU.* LA RICOLINA. Sixteenth century.
Communicated by M. Wildenstein

**181.** - *Above: COROT.* REPOSE. Musée d'Art et d'Histoire, Geneva

centuries that otherwise seem to have nothing in common. Those three elegant ladies with pretty childish faces in a drawing of c. 1400 are very like the group of affected ladies whom Bellange drew three centuries later (both drawings are in the Louvre). A century later, these ladies turn up again, chattering under Watteau's shady trees. Diana, nude, bathing with her companions, has scarcely changed as she moved from sixteenth-century Fontainebleau to the canvases of Boucher, and she is still recognizable in the painting by Corot. This feminine image, which, like a graceful herald, announces the periodical return of the pleasures of life in French art, is its familiar genius to a degree unknown in the art of other nations. Affectionate and sprightly, enveloped as though in a light veil of sensuality, attractive and yet chaste, this image has neither the rather cheerless sculptural grandeur of an animated statue, typical of Italian treatments of woman, nor the too carnal physical abundance typical of Flemish treatments. Whether smiling or pensive, woman in French portraits is as much soul as body, the two linked effortlessly, the visible sign of a gentle world propitious to men (Figs. 180 and 181).

Between these traditions, one virile, the other feminine, which are we to choose? According to whether historians looked upon the one or the other as the more authentic, they denounced the temporary eclipse of either as a deviation from French tradition. But the Renaissance did not really kill off Gothic art; nor did eighteenth-century art destroy that of the reign of Louis XIV. The conflict is more apparent than real: every time one of the two traditions seems to be giving way to the other, it is merely retreating temporarily to gather new strength.

In fact, when we take a closer look, we can see that in periods when one was triumphant, the other was never entirely absent. It moves into the background, but it has faithful adherents and is just waiting for its moment. Occasionally the two traditions combine. Poussin, the most complete embodiment of French genius, was faithful to both. Contrary to the general opinion, scarcely any other artist has expressed the attractions of the feminine body with greater sensual intensity. His Thetis, his Flora, with their muscular, slightly squat, but nervous and agile bodies, are the younger sisters of those nymphs of Ronsard brought to life in the paintings of the School of Fontainebleau, and older sisters of Boucher's chubby girls. At the same time, no artist was more Cartesian, more logical, more convincingly balanced than Poussin; none has more fully rendered the gravity and virility of the seventeenth century as he did, once the fires of youth had given way to the serenity of mature age (Figs. 213, 214, and 215).

BETWEEN NORTH AND SOUTH.   Not all features of French art can be accounted for by internal factors. The evolutionary rhythm that I outlined above is not exclusively the result of internal forces. Outside influences have, if not provoked, at least accentuated the variations in its inspiration. Situated geographically and spiritually between the Low Countries and Italy, France, as was only natural, looked to the North or the South according to the aspirations and political contingencies of the moment.

Now, the portrait was chiefly cultivated by Northern artists. The middle-class realism of the Flemish and Dutch cultures predisposed them to record the most characteristic human features. On the other hand, the Italians were fond of conceiving man with greater intellectual breadth, and they often re-created physical forms and proportions in more universal terms. For this reason, French artists influenced by Northern art were first of all portraitists: those who took their cues from Italy treated man as one of the principal elements in the over-all architecture of painting.

In the fourteenth century the art of the portrait was virtually nonexistent in Paris and Avignon, the two main centers of French painting. The portrait of Jean le Bon, painted c. 1360, is no more than a placid profile of the type usually engraved on coins and medals. The Italians for a long time favored the profile view, because it brings out the plastic qualities of the face. In the fifteenth century, the Flemish Primitives were exerting greater and greater influence; the Dukes of Burgundy secured continuous contact between their possessions in Flanders and in France. This influence even reached the School of Avignon, where it supplanted the Italian influence. This development accounts for the appearance of portraits in three-quarter view, with accentuated volumes, subtly modeled shadows, and carefully observed details like meticulously rendered wrinkles and unshaven beards. Nicolas Froment, like the Master of the Aix Annunciation, went to the extreme of veracity while Enguerrand Quarton was still pursuing a more ideal vision in the face of his crowned Virgin. At the end of the century, the figure of the Knight in Armor, his eyes

*When a French artist keenly scrutinizes the features of a face, he discloses his debt to Northern realism.*

**182.** - *SCHOOL OF FOUQUET.* HEAD OF DONOR (detail of a PIETÀ). Church of Nouana (Indre-et-Loire)

lowered beneath his white hair, combines realistic sharpness and concern for harmony with spirituality. Union of these elements was henceforward to define the French portrait (Fig. 178).

The Flemish impact was even stronger in Northern France. On the banks of the Loire, Jean Fouquet achieved an original balance between the two tendencies. In his work, the living truth was expressed less by accurate rendering of features than by intensification of inner life. Fouquet was the first to create forms with smooth, rounded, simplified volumes, of a sculptural purity inherited from the medieval stone cutters. We find that same purity again, just as daring and intense, in the works of Georges de La Tour in the seventeenth century. At the court of Bourbonnais, the Master of Moulins preserved this moving purity of the forms with less power but greater delicacy. All these masters were still too close to the then waning Middle Ages not to express the profounder rather than the more pleasing aspects of French art. They reflect the firm convictions of epochs of great spiritual unity. Religious faith animates all these faces, and, the better to render the fervor of their inner lives, the eyes are often shown half closed, the glance veiled. Even feminine suavity becomes solemn because of this presence of religious faith (Fig. 182).

Intensity and grandeur are characteristic of epochs when every individual life is multiplied by collective aspirations. In such epochs there can be no question of sociability replacing public life. What is pursued is contentment rather than pleasure. The sixteenth century reversed this order with a generally more relaxed attitude. The figures grew slack and spiritless. Clouet's *Charles IX* expresses indolence, his *Francis I* sensual weariness. As though the word had just been whispered around, the smile makes its appearance, curling the lips of Elisabeth de Valois and the features ascribed to Rabelais in a portrait by Corneille de Lyon. The faces become more friendly, more affable, more at ease in the world; they are trying to please rather than to be intensely themselves. At the same time, the nude female body began to haunt artists' imagination. Italian influence regained the ground that it had lost to Flanders, but it is to be noted that the portrait remained the domain of Northern painters. Clouet and Corneille de Lyon, though steeped in French sensibility, were of Northern origin. Until the seventeenth century, the tradition of the portrait was kept up by the Flemings Pourbus and Philippe de Champaigne, and artists such as Vouet, La Hire, and Le Sueur perpetuated the other tradition, derived from Italy and the School of Fontainebleau, of calm, harmonious beauty of body and face. Significantly, under Louis XIV, when Italian influence gained unmistakable predominance, the portrait was relegated to the minor techniques like drawing or engraving; and its brilliant return with Rigaud, Largillière, and others coincided with a brisk revival of Flemish influence. Even before then, Sébastien Bourdon and Mignard had been inspired by Flemish masters, and the aristocratic melancholy that clouds the eyes of their models is none other than Van Dyck's.

SKETCH OF THE FRENCH FACE. However, prior to the partial eclipse of portraiture under Louis XIV, the first half of the seventeenth century created some of the most admirable portraits of French art, perhaps of all art. We may recall that, in 1661, the year when Louis XIV assumed personal rule, Poussin had only four years of life left, Philippe de Champaigne was almost sixty, Corneille was fifty-five, and Pascal was to die the next year. Descartes had been dead for eleven years. Voltaire was to confuse several generations yet unborn by grouping these men and events under "The Century of Louis XIV." The extent to which the first half of the seventeenth century had a character all its own cannot be stressed too strongly: it was one of the most individualistic in our history, and it came right before a period of great collective unity. Religion itself was strongly marked by individualism: the harsh doctrinal disputes engendered by Protestantism made religion a matter of individual conscience for many, and, even among the most faithful Catholics, "mystical individualism often took the place of Catholicism," as the Abbé Bremond observed. After the pagan hedonism of the court of Francis I, men became passionately interested in the problem of human fate, occasionally—as in Pascal—reaching the extreme of metaphysical anguish ("The eternal silence of eternal space terrifies me"). The questions that men of this earlier seventeenth century addressed to themselves are reflected in the mirrors that they held before them: their portraits.

The history of the portrait follows a curve parallel to that of individualism. It received enormous impetus at the end of the sixteenth century, when the Wars of Religion were raging, Protestants taking up arms against Catholics. It reached full flowering early in the seventeenth century, the period of powerful personalities meditating intensely upon themselves: Pascal and the recluses of Port-Royal, Descartes, Corneille. Only with the advent of Louis XIV did the great collective certainties of a state-imposed discipline gain dominance, and then the art of the portrait showed signs of weakening. Between the generation of Philippe de Champaigne, born in 1601, and that of Rigaud, born in 1659, there is a sixty-year void peopled only by minor artists like Lefebvre, Nocret, and François Lemaire. The art of the portrait shrank to the proportions of more modest media, with engravers like Edelinck and draftsmen like Nanteuil. It seems that its function was now to record and multiply the effigies of prominent men. It served not so much to gratify the need for psychological exploration as the need for official commemorations. The portrait lived on its laurels and remained faithful to traditional formulas: certain drawings by Nanteuil preserve the austerity of Dumonstier, and certain figures of pages in Le Brun's portrait of the Chancellor Séguier bring to mind the art of Mathieu Le Nain. Not until the end of Louis XIV's reign did Rigaud, who was only two years old when it began, and Vivien, who had been four, create a new type of portrait. In this new type of portrait, impassive, inscrutable figures are hidden behind elaborate robes and wigs indicative of the sitters' social status. However, as early as Rigaud and Largillière, the smile reappears, announcing a new phase of individualism and hedonism—the eighteenth century (Fig. 186).

At the beginning of the seventeenth century there are no smiling portraits. Inspired primarily by moral ideals, men find in them precisely what they supposed they had sacrificed to them—joy in living, or, rather, contentment. The faces are characterized by the same kind of beauty as those of the Middle Ages, the beauty of perfect inner sincerity. When we compare these with portraits from the end of the century, those by Rigaud and Largillière, we are struck, in the earlier examples, by the comparative immobility of the features, the absence or subordination of hands and gestures; everything is expressed by the face, the extremely keen glance sufficing to reflect the figure's inner life. Their thoughtful gravity discloses that they are familiar with the great problems of human fate, and above all with that of death. La Tour's *Repentant Magdalene* before the mirror, feeling a polished

skull and taking stock of the imperceptible difference between it and her own beauty, marks a transition from the frivolous Venuses of the School of Fontainebleau to profounder questionings. The *Dead Nun* attributed to Philippe de Champaigne, with its ultimate serenity (like that of many other funerary effigies), illustrates the firmness with which men and women of the age faced, in death, a familiar problem. All these figures are unmistakably contemporaries of Pascal: they convey the recently discovered balance between human grandeur and the humbleness of the human condition (Fig. 301).

This transformation, a sort of adolescent phase in the growth of a race to maturity, is not perfectly smooth, is not without a certain hidden melancholy characteristic of deep religious and philosophical doubts. Firmness and resolution are veiled with sadness, a thoughtfulness that can be read even in the eyes of beings very close to nature, such as the peasants portrayed by Antoine and Louis Le Nain, simple village fiddlers oddly caught up in the last lingering strains that they have just produced. It is still more apparent in the pensive aristocrats of Sébastien Bourdon, and in that strange solitary nymph who, with her silent lyre, is the only figure in Claude Lorrain's *Enchanted Castle* (Fig. 185).

Thus, the French School of portraiture is made up of many strands: varied certainly, it possesses astonishing coherence when viewed in proper historical perspective.

THE PORTRAIT AND THE INDIVIDUAL SOUL. Even in the most collective-minded periods, the individual was always there, more or less aware of his possible autonomy. The psychologist and historian thus arrive at two different readings of the portrait, according to whether they focus on salient individual cases or on the common substructure in depth.

THE DISCOVERY OF PSYCHOLOGICAL LIFE.  The process of discovering the individual, to which Nuno Gonçalvès gave the most impressive early expression in art, was slow and gradual even in France, where it reflected a national aspiration. The oldest portraits have an aloof, reserved quality; the fascinating human flame is slow to be lit and take fire, only really beginning to sparkle in the eighteenth century, to burn steadily in the nineteenth. Whereas medieval faces seem cold and withdrawn, utterly beyond our reach, separated from us by a thick layer of centuries-long silence, in a nineteenth-century portrait man seems to be present whole and entire, clutching at life through art like the hand of a drowning man going down for the last time.

The increasing fullness of the individual personality in the development of French painting has a character of regularity and inevitability not exhibited so clearly in any other nation's art. Having no great solitary geniuses like El Greco or Rembrandt, the French School was not disturbed by sudden prophetic illuminations misunderstood by contemporaries and only recognized centuries later. Elsewhere, such artists had, as early as the sixteenth and seventeenth centuries, expressed in their portraits an inner torment that did not achieve collective expression until the nineteenth century. In France, portraiture developed more evenly.

In the Middle Ages, when the art of the portrait was just beginning, only the individual's outer shell seems to have been shown; his uniqueness is missing—his soul is elsewhere. Usually depicted as absorbed in some divine spectacle, frozen in contemplation, he appears as though empty of all reaction, whether intellectual or emotional. This is not to say that medieval portraitists were devoid of penetration. They were as adept in practical psychology as portraitists at any other epoch—perfectly capable of scrutinizing the human face and bringing out significant features. But they seem never to have caught their sitters in action, as it were. They patiently record the sum total of a life in terms of its most permanent traits, and the structure and appearance of a face is rendered in terms of the most familiar expressions. In order the better to grasp those features, they cut or carved them out of hard, immobile, petrified flesh, as rigid as it will be in death, at the moment when an entire existence can be read at a glance, like the total of a bill on a bank slip. Respect for religion may account for some of the fixity of expression; the donor possibly did not as yet quite trust portraiture, was not, as yet, ready to become the subject of painting. Happy, only too proud to be shown as a self-effacing supernumerary in the presence of divine personages, he held his breath and was present only as a kind of signature affixed to his act of donation. But it is possible to exaggerate the religious factor: the individual portraits that show the human figure most intimately present us with faces just as frozen, expressions just as remote. The convention was so deep-rooted that even where the donor is shown with many other figures (whose faces do express vivid emotions), he alone—the portrait subject—remains impassive and withdrawn, his inner life inscrutable.

This impassiveness has deeper causes. We must recognize here a principle that goes beyond the individual case and even beyond art, a principle that governs the development of any civilization. When a new culture is in process of forming, the mind as yet inexpert and unskillful seeks only to establish its grip on what is fixed, material, measurable, immutable. It has an instinctive aversion for all that changes and evolves, that does not last long enough to be carefully observed and finally understood. Its conscious attention goes to the constants of life, not its variables. It could be shown that the history of any intellectual discipline is a progressive conquest of what Bergson summed up in one word—*le mouvant*, what changes. And it could be shown that a given art or civilization has reached the end of its development—or is about to reach it—when it gives itself over wholly to the expression of movement and change. Even the sciences are subject to this evolutionary law. At first they take only solid, visible realities as objects of investigation, then gradually they concern themselves with mechanics, with movement, with fluid and inconstant processes in nature, like light and electricity. In the end, they conceive the world as an infinite scattering of invisible atoms, and then they are ready to take up the most immaterial, the most ungraspable domain of all—the psychic life. Even here, they deal first with concrete manifestations, with psychophysiology. The same is true of philosophy, which starts from fixed abstractions, then gradually takes up evolution and transformism, and ends up with the relative, the intuitive, and the indefinable.

To get back to painting, is there not a similar pattern of development in its history? Setting out first to identify objects and determine their forms—stylizing them, if need be, in order the better to fix appearances—it proceeds to discover light, modeling, and shadows. To begin with, it assumes an average, constant, almost abstract light; only later does it render the variations, the changes, and the nuances of light. In an earlier chapter, we saw how, almost simultaneously, effects of penumbra or artificial light began to be rendered in the seventeenth century, first by Caravaggio and then by countless imitators, gliding shadows by Ruisdael, and sunsets by Claude Lorrain. Only a little later, painting sacrificed precision of forms to the approximations of virtuoso brush strokes; ultimately, it dissolved the same forms in the universal fluidity of Impressionism. In a parallel development, the artist became more and more concerned for movement, instability, instantaneousness. There is really nothing mysterious about this evolutionary principle governing all branches of human thought, the total cycle of which reflects the cycle of every single civilization. We may add that, as a rule, every civilization marks an advance of the same kind in relation to the preceding civilization, reflecting a progressive improvement in the sharpness and subtlety of our intellectual means.

Nowhere, however, is the law more apparent than in psychology and its pictorial counterpart, the art of the portrait. Although man discloses, on the practical plane, a very keen, instinctive, empirical knowledge of his fellow man's motives even in the early centuries of a civilization, his intellectual analysis of these motives often remains very elementary. Thus, a statesman may give evidence of keen understanding of motives while a chronicler of the same epoch gives a most puerile account of them—nonetheless failing to shock his contemporary readers. The commentator may lag behind the actor for a very long time—look at Plutarch, for instance.

Now, the portrait is a comment on human nature, too, and, hence, it displays the same initial awkwardness in dealing with psychological life. The living element in a face, that part of it which, more than any other, is resistant to uniformity or fixity, is the complex, fleeting play of the features. The early painters relate the expression of the features to some specific point, and, moreover, never show the sitter looking at the viewer. Their treatment is still hesitant. Of the facial characteristics, they are most concerned for the eyes, for their moist reflections and luminous flashes rather than for the expression as a whole. They dare not focus the sitter's eyes on whatever obscure point best reveals his soul. But as portraitists freed themselves from these constraints, they were inevitably led to concen-

*Already, in the seventeenth century, a sense of harmony between man and nature gave expression to the romantic charm of solitude.*

**185.** - *CLAUDE LORRAIN.* THE ENCHANTED CASTLE (detail). Collection Sir A. T. Lloyd, Great Britain

trate on an indefinable, unique part of man—his individual personality. Eventually, pursuit of the most ungraspable aspects of life induced them to set down only what they glimpsed of invisible inner worlds.

GROWTH OF INDIVIDUALISM AND SOCIAL COMPULSION. Progress toward individualism, like that toward concern for change and process, has not been governed only by laws intrinsic in the development of portraiture or even of painting as a whole. It also reflects the transformation of society itself, which, as it grows older and more refined, assumes more and more individualistic forms. At first, society is subjected to collective disciplines, then gradually liberates itself from them, sometimes even to an excessive extent. However, the evolutionary graph outlined here is something of an oversimplification. Every now and then, an upsurge of individualism reacts against what is excessive in collective oppression and disturbs it—sometimes at an early stage. That happened in the sixteenth century. The development of portraiture reflects such fluctuations. As we have observed, its fate is bound up with that of individualism, for it implies a concern for the isolated individual, for the closed world that he constitutes, for the particulars that separate him from the mass. Not only has the portrait allowed an ever-increasing place for the individual, historically speaking—just as society has—but its very extension and popularity have depended on the strength of individualistic feelings in a given epoch. History confirms this amply over the centuries. At first, the Middle Ages rested upon a great principle that was more than merely collective—it was unanimous, the principle of religious faith. Catholicism constituted the framework of a gigantic spiritual administration, which assigned a place and rank to all things, from the loftiest theological conceptions to the rhythm of daily occupations. Nothing could live that was not integrated into this whole. Any assertion of nonconformism entailed excommunication, rejection from the community. Portraiture as an artistic genre was consequently unthinkable. Artists almost never signed their works, and, in their wildest imaginings, did not conceive that the personality of a model could be a sole and sufficient object of art. The portrait did not appear until the fifteenth century, when social bonds grew looser and men set out to discover by their own unaided resources a new principle of existence (Fig. 177).

This was accomplished in the sixteenth century, which was dominated and determined by two major factors. Both were manifestations of individualism, of liberation from the very constraints that had made for strength and uniformity in the Middle Ages. One of these was the rise of Protestantism, which replaced docile religious obedience with the rights of the individual conscience, making the individual mind the judge of collective opinions. The other, humanism, marked the triumph of the individual artist and thinker, who now regarded the exercise of his faculties as a means of enjoyment and self-improvement. No longer conceived as a tribute to God, the arts were now dedicated to the loftiest human pleasures—but purely human pleasures. It is not surprising, then, that the sixteenth century assigned a very high place to portraiture—indeed, there is scarcely anything but portraits to represent French painting in that epoch. Not only did everyone want to have a likeness of himself drawn or painted, but, for the first time in Western civilization, artists appeared who practiced nothing but portraiture: Clouet, Corneille de Lyon, and many others who remain anonymous.

At first glance, a number of portraits appear hardly distinguishable from those of the preceding century. The figures, painted in three-quarter view, have fixed and vacant glances and disclose the artists' inability to capture the momentary, fleeting aspects of life. And, yet, many such portraits show that one important advance has been made. The three-quarter view affords glimpses into the inner life of the figure represented, and its extremely expressive mobility makes it possible to follow complex palpitations of the soul wherever eyes, mouth, or hands are touched by a spark. The gestures are losing their immobility, becoming animated in the proper sense of the word. The eyes suddenly look out at the viewer and meet his glance; the mouth attempts to smile, the corners curling upward, experimenting with so unstable a position; the hands are shown more frequently and, sometimes, the whole body is shown.

The first half of the seventeenth century—which, as we have seen, is not to be confused any longer with the second—is obviously a continuation of the sixteenth century. However, it also betrays symptoms of a fresh rise of collective discipline such as would eventually stifle the frenzied and somewhat premature individualism of the sixteenth century. At bottom, the seventeenth-century Fronde was no more than the last upsurge of that exceptional century, which had progressively undermined not only the order but the very existence of French society. But the collective spirit that the second half of the seventeenth century gradually imposed lacked the deep foundations of the Middle Ages. It was just a shade weaker. Although it called upon traditional religious feelings with which the passionate energies of the individual and the example of outstanding personalities had been associated more recently, religion was now too undermined from within to provide the fundamental principle of coherence and unity. It strengthened the absolute monarchy, but the latter was not founded upon it. The new authorities repressed the individualism of the beginning of the century. Jansenism was condemned. Religion, particularly in the hands of a Bossuet, now became an instrument of moral, social, and intellectual co-ordination. Society found a principle of unity in its own existence—in a concept of the state as embodied in the monarch. All the collective forces of that society centered around him as the this-worldly replica of the supreme center, God. Individualists disappeared or were relegated to a minor role. The arts were subjected to the same unifying principle and placed in the hands of Le Brun, who acted as the monarch's deputy. However absolute this revival of collective unanimity may seem, it was precarious, for it was founded on no principle transcending historical man, but upon reason, a human faculty, however strongly its origin in Godhead may have been (and was) urged. In the later seventeenth century in France, we are somewhere between the ages of religion and the age of individualism.

What happened to portraiture under these circumstances? At the beginning of the century, as might be expected, it extended and fulfilled the promise of the sixteenth century. Artists such as Philippe de Champaigne and Bourdon realized their sitters, raising in each portrait the problem of the closed cycle of human destiny, with its familiar thoughts, convictions, and even anxieties. The expression of the eyes became insistent and the hands animated, frequently making expressive gestures.

The moment that Louis XIV assumed personal rule and a solid architecture began to be imposed upon society, French portraiture went into decline, as noted above. We may add that even the drawings of an artist such as Nanteuil disclose a timidity, an absence of animation, that is very nearly a throwback to sixteenth-century drawing.

*In the seventeenth century, man is seen above all as a performer of social functions—an attitude reflected in the portraits of the period.*

**186.** - *RIGAUD.* PORTRAIT OF THE MARQUIS DE DANGEAU. Palace of Versailles

*Eighteenth-century painting is considerably more relaxed. Tradition still demands majesty in court portraits, but the newer tendencies favor simplicity. The individual is becoming more important than society.*

**187. - *TOCQUÉ*. PORTRAIT OF MARIA LESZCZYNSKA. 1740.**
Palace of Versailles

Toward the end of the Grand Monarch's reign, however, when the ideal it furthered was about to crumble away—and not a minute before—there appears a brilliant group of great portraitists led by Rigaud and Largillière. This revival of portraiture affords us glimpses into the splendor of the century at its close, an image that already hints at decline. To be sure, still powerful social imperatives continue to take precedence over the individual: these pompous, important figures are men of state who exist only in and by their social functions. Rigaud does not paint Louis XIV but the Grand Monarch; not Bossuet but the prince of the Church; not Dangeau but the courtier. He portrays social types wearing their robes of office and posed against backgrounds descriptive of their service to the state. The art of the portrait conquers new territory in these works, a territory not located within man and not used for communication of his innermost self to others, but located outside man in hangings, pillars, throne room, desk, etc. descriptive of his official function. The individual's personal characteristics have no place here. Man is no longer shown either against a background of nature or alone with himself on a neutral ground. Instead he is shown as a member of society—ceremonial robes and professional gestures placing his exact function within an all-encompassing social entity, the state (Fig. 186).

PROGRESS TOWARD INTIMISM. The individualism of an earlier age might seem a closed chapter, yet development toward individualism continued, and the eighteenth century marks a new stage in that development. What do eighteenth-century portraits express? They still express a strong sense of solidarity with the body social, but on a more restricted, intimate scale. Persons are identifiable now by the little group they belong to—a circle of acquaintances, a particular salon. The individual is not stifled, for social life, unlike societal life, does not require the sacrifice of individuality. On the contrary, its purpose is to enhance individuality for the pleasure of all. One might say that, whereas the seventeenth-century portrait is a reflection of official life, the eighteenth-century portrait is a reflection of private life (and the nineteenth-century portrait a reflection of intimate life).

Most instructive in this respect are some portraits of Maria Leszczynska. In 1740, Tocqué

**188.** - *NATTIER.*
PORTRAIT OF MARIA LESZCZYNSKA.
1748. Palace of Versailles.
According to Madame Tocqué,
Nattier's daughter, "the Queen gave him
explicit orders to paint her
in nonceremonial dress."

represented her in the great Rigaud tradition: draped in an ermine robe adorned with fleurs-de-lis, standing on a marble floor against a background of columns and hangings that tell us that this is the palace of Versailles. Her crown rests on a cushion to which she points in a symbolic gesture. Eight years later, Nattier (Tocqué's father-in-law) painted "the good Queen." This time she is depicted as rather less hemmed in by the official portrait tradition as practiced by a Belle or a Van Loo. The columns are concealed, the drapery is less overpowering, and, although the crown is still there, in this portrait the Queen turns her back to it. She is shown seated, one elbow resting casually on an open book. She wears ordinary dress, the lace kerchief over her bonnet loosely knotted at her neck. Nattier's daughter reports that he was not permitted to make more than a simple portrait, the Queen having ordered him to paint her in ordinary dress. In the Versailles museum there is still another version of this portrait, showing the central figure only, with scarcely any décor and no crown at all. In the Salon of 1748, the Queen was also represented in the famous pastel by La Tour as a simple *bourgeoise* of Paris, seated in an armchair, fiddling with her fan, talking, and smiling. In this last portrait, she has escaped all reference to the pomp of her official status. It is as though a mask had been torn off to reveal her as she really was—as her friends must have known her. These few works sum up the whole philosophy of the eighteenth-century portrait (Figs. 187 and 188).

At the beginning of the eighteenth century, a curious transitional type of portrait made its appearance. Has anyone noticed how many times Largillière, Watteau, Desportes, Lancret, etc. painted individuals hunting or in hunting costume? It is as though the artists remained faithful to the tradition of painting the model in a costume indicating his rank or function, but they seize upon the one costume that suggests relaxation, leisure moments, the individual pursuing his own pleasure away from stifling official duties. Increasingly we find formal attire, open shirts, casually arranged foulards, unbuttoned vests disclosing rumpled linen, heads covered with turbans or madras handkerchiefs instead of the much more formal wig. The décor behind the figure disappears altogether, or gives way to a glimpse of a room or of the outdoors. Clearly, these portraits are conversation pieces of a sort, for, as yet, there are no monologues, no self-questionings in front of the mirror. "I get inside them without their realizing, and I get out all there is to get," La Tour used to say of his models. Of course, he did no such thing. The eighteenth-century portraitist recorded man, not as he was, but as he showed himself to others. The subject still obeys an essentially social discipline, but now reduced to the obligation to be agreeable. The subjects invariably smile, and their eyes sparkle; the painter takes approximately the same interest in his subject as someone who is telling a story takes in his listener—the latter, like the former, calculating the pleasure to be derived from this particular meeting of the minds (Fig. 189).

The eighteenth century did not aim at depth in portraying faces but at vivacity and brilliance. It may be noted that, very often, the artist enhanced the charm of a woman's face with a few flowers. Also noteworthy is how many portraits of women were painted in that period and—this is a novelty—portraits of children as well. Whereas the nineteenth century was often fond of aged subjects with faces reflecting long experience of life, the eighteenth, to a remarkable degree, preferred rather childish or youthful subjects, reflecting ages when human beings are at their most attractive perhaps, but before they have acquired a very strong personality or a clearly formed inner life. Titian, El Greco, Rembrandt, and other artists who have portrayed the depths of the human soul rarely, if ever, painted childish faces. Indeed, they were most fascinated by faces reflecting deep experience of life.

THE NINETEENTH CENTURY REVEALS INWARDNESS. As the eighteenth century closes, we are given a rude shock. Portraits like David's *Marketwoman* and *Old Man*, or Géricault's *Madman*, are as remote as can be from the facile charm of the preceding century. For some decades now, the eye had glided with pleasure from face to face without making too clear a distinction between them—much as we take in a pleasant arrangement of variegated flowers. Now the eye is obliged to look longer and harder at individual faces—for every face raises its own problems. We have reached the nineteenth century. The Revolution hastened the emergence of a new society, and, by doing away with traditional usages, accentuated the contrast between the two centuries. Man is no longer shown in his familiar surroundings. Rather, he is shown alone with all his inwardness; his ties with society are broken. He will no longer be defined by his social function but, often enough, by his opposition to society, or locked within himself as in a refuge from society (Fig. 190).

As always when man withdraws inside himself, anxiety rises like a brisk flame. Individualism and anxiety go hand in hand; they are found whenever a civilization, if not a nation, having exhausted its means of sustaining a collective discipline, can no longer protect its members against themselves. When we look over the ground that we have traveled, we may note how greatly collective discipline has shrunk, slowly, inexorably, since its peak in the thirteenth century. The faith of the Middle Ages gathered and sustained the entire soul, heart, and mind. Hence, the prodigiously well-sustained balance of Gothic art, which simultaneously gratifies the senses with its realism, reason with its austerity, constructive logic, and consistent symbolism, and the sensibility with the loftiness of religious feeling. In the seventeenth century, the common bond among men had been reduced to intellectual adherence, to a mere matter of conviction. Everyone confined himself to applying or strengthening universally accepted principles. In the eighteenth

*Eighteenth-century individualism rebels against the traditional stiffness of portraits, preferring naturalness, spontaneity, even casualness.*

**189.** - *MAURICE QUENTIN DE LA TOUR.* SELF-PORTRAIT. Musée d'Art et d'Histoire, Geneva.
Madame Roslin claimed to have portrayed herself making a rectangular copy of La Tour's originally oval picture.
She was his pupil. Could this pastel be that copy?

*With the nineteenth century, personality comes into its own.*

**190.** - *LOUIS DAVID.* MAN WITH A HAT. Royal Museum of Fine Arts, Antwerp

century, community was further reduced to ordinary sensualism; collective beliefs had lost all constructive value. Men shared a common state of mind—but this state of mind was skepticism—and a common way of life—but this way of life consisted in the destruction of the very principles on which it rested. As early as 1697, at the threshold of the eighteenth century, Bayle formulated a keyword for it: "Man's mind is more fertile in objections than in solutions." The celebration of the senses that flowered and sparkled everywhere was itself an assertion, in the most selfish and materialistic form, of the pre-eminence of the individual.

As the nineteenth century opened, men's minds were beset by doubts, their senses weary; and mankind found itself on its own at last. Materialistic, practical concerns spelled life for the majority, while the rest cut themselves off from a society incapable of communicating any spiritual impulse. A kind of intoxication with solitude was experienced and cultivated by many poets, thinkers, and artists of the period. Alienated from the world around them, questioning the purpose and meaning of life, they were overwhelmed by uncertainty and sadness, a *mal du siècle* that Musset defined as "an appalling sickness." In the past, only a few powerful minds had been able to carry so full a burden of existence upon their shoulders, unaided. Now this was the lot of every thinking, feeling being. It must be admitted, historically speaking, that the resulting anxiety has been favorable to the art of portraiture. Had not the geniuses who sought to form a conception of life independent of prevalent solutions been ardent devotees of the portrait —men like Rembrandt and El Greco? The keenest, most restless, and poignant of these artists—Rembrandt, Van Gogh, Degas—never wearied of searching their own faces, and they all made a number of self-portraits. It is true, not only of artists but of entire epochs, that, when a civilization reaches its final stage and skepticism gives way to anxiety, portraiture becomes a feverish obsession. In periods of individualism, when the intellect is rejected by the currents that might catch it up and inspire it, it falls back upon itself, devours itself in solitude. When there is no altar at which to worship, no matter what sort of altar, there is nothing left but the mirror. Which, after all, have been the great epochs for searching, tormented, emphatic portraits? In Egypt, the eighteenth dynasty, when traditional beliefs collapsed; in the Classical world, toward the end of the Roman Empire, when religions were fading away and springing up like mushrooms at the same time—a sure sign of decay. In France, the sixteenth century, when the medieval faith was breaking down, the eighteenth century, and the nineteenth.

RESISTANCE AND DECLINE OF THE HUMAN FIGURE. However, not all artists were affected by the new anxiety. Some of them preserved elements of the eighteenth-century spirit. David, for instance, was sufficiently popular, sufficiently authoritarian—and sufficiently narrow-minded as well—to remain untouched by the mounting sense of uncertainty and to permit himself to believe that he was in possession of some truths. He clung to principles, as did Ingres and the Classicists who survived in this perturbed world, and who, like David, remained insolently objective in their portraits. Ingres, more violent and more deliberate than David, still was one to believe in principles at any price. But these artists were anything but typical of the epoch. Ingres has a great many affinities with the eighteenth century. He is at once a rationalist and a sensualist. In his portraits of women he was primarily interested in a feminine type corresponding to his personal tastes, and he also revived the atmosphere of eighteenth-century canvases: the inner vacuity, the smile, the desire to please, the sensualism. Even the soft inclination of heads and the swelling dovelike necks bring back a pose created by the eighteenth century. Influenced by Ingres, Chassériau continued this tradition of worldly charm in his portraits of women, which he bathed in a new melancholy.

Far more numerous were the artists who succumbed to the new century's mood of depression. These are restless artists characterized by harsh energy, like Géricault and Millet, or, more often, by a strange discouragement such as weighs upon Delacroix's *Bruya*, Carpeaux's self-portrait, Ricard's *Chenavard*, Carrière's *Daudet*, and even Courbet's *Polish Woman*. Cover that woman's face so you can see only her eyes, and you will discover that Courbet—for all his revolt against Romanticism in the name of a vocally strenuous realism—did not escape the fate of his century. His best portraits—of Berlioz, Champfleury, and of himself as a young man—instinctively give expression to the restlessness that he himself, stupid fellow, was quite incapable of feeling. What resignation, what discouragement is written on so many faces in nineteenth-century portraiture! Most of them are bowed, or at least not fully erect. They make use of a gesture familiar to their contemporaries but never pictured before them: they lean their heads on their hands, physically translating the weariness that overwhelms them. And what a revelation, to rediscover at the end of the century, in portraits by the very man who made the most forceful attempt to restore order and intellectual discipline to painting—in Cézanne's portraits—the same weary resignation, the more poignant because it proceeds from the very rock that artist hoped to make himself in an age that he considered weak. Weary resignation hovers about the heads of his figures, sometimes leaning on their elbows, and lingers in the eyes of that somewhat stooping old worker, at once so self-possessed and riddled with doubts (Fig. 192).

At the same time, the evolution toward the immaterial mentioned at the beginning of this chapter was approaching its term. Already, the eighteenth century had been less interested in the internal and external structure of the face than in the breath of life that gave it animation and made it vibrate. We have here the pursuit of something ungraspable, as yet unnamable—life itself. The nineteenth century pursued this immaterial element in its subtlest, most fleeting aspects—not the life that animated the eighteenth-century masks, physical at bottom for all the spiritual trimmings—but the inner life of the individual. The cycle is now complete: the nineteenth-century painter can use *only* the fugitive play of expression that the Primitive artist avoided. The eyes that he paints are not those of the eighteenth century—hard, shining, moist little globes—but mere openings, mere holes in the head—blurry shadows with flickering lights behind them. Only Ingres and the Classicists—in this respect, too, heirs to the eighteenth-century spirit— seek to render the physical substance of the eye as well as that of flesh. To the others, the eyes have become the hypnotic focus of the painting—all else is blurred or effaced. With Ricard and Carrière, all that is left is portraits of eyes, a pair of nailheads holding down the light, floating mass of the body. *La Samary* by Renoir marks the extreme point of this development—it is nothing but a momentary glance cloaked in a form (Fig. 193).

Just when we had achieved this amazing degree of intensity in the portrait, art suddenly —whether from weariness or from inability to continue developing in this direction—

*Romanticism is the expression of youthful ardor and energy.*
  **191.** - *DELACROIX.* Presumed PORTRAIT OF HIS NEPHEW DE VERNINAC. 1833. Private collection

*In the end, the fires of Romanticism burn away physical appearance and expose man's inner anxieties.*

**192.** - *CARPEAUX*. SELF-PORTRAIT. Musée des Beaux-Arts de la Ville de Paris

*At the end of the century, personal melancholy becomes a kind of exhaustion, which is even reflected in matters of technique.*

**193.** - *EUGÈNE CARRIÈRE.* ALPHONSE DAUDET AND HIS DAUGHTER (detail). 1891.
The Louvre, Paris

turned away from preoccupation with the inner life. The Impressionists were utterly unconcerned with it; theirs was a purely perceptional conception of painting. The Impressionist portrait painter records only what is striking, what is most picturesque or most characteristic. The expressive silhouettes drawn by Toulouse-Lautrec give us the secret of a particular pose or gesture rather than any revelation of the human being making them. Other artists restricted their ambitions to even less than this, aiming at no more than skillful, aesthetically pleasing combinations of line and color. The desperate effort of the nineteenth century to capture the human figure ended in a general retreat, which, in the twentieth century, became an utter rout. The French portrait had one last upsurge with Vuillard and Bonnard. A new civilization was in the making, and, in it, France, like the rest of the world today, is searching for its place—and its face (Fig. 194).

★

★   ★

The magic spell of the portrait! Texts and documents can only give us clues that must be interpreted, whereas paintings give us man himself, his own time and nation living as he wanted us to see him, as he believed himself to be. A portrait is an immediate imprint of life on time.

There is no one so powerful as not to be concerned for his own disappearance, unaware of the necessity to be no more after having once been. Ruins of the past, which seemingly endure to remind us that nothing endures, have moved the most self-possessed of men to a melancholy that Romanticism did not exhaust. This mystery receives most intense expression in the portrait. We can conceive the annihilation of a civilization or of a city, but we find it hard to conceive our own. The portrait gives us an obscure intimation of it whenever the artist has succeeded in preserving the mirage that a living being creates. The most beautiful portraits are akin to the poems that arouse in us the deepest melancholy. Thus, the appearance of a being, of a face, lives on after its reality has been annihilated. Once upon a time, there was this man. Just for fun, one day, at a certain age, at a certain hour and minute of a particular year, he had an artist set down his features and expression of that hour and minute. All he parted with was his appearance, that is, what was most external in him, what anyone around could learn of him. And yet this passing, fleeting imprint survives, immutable, while his existence is long since passed away.

What permanence in this fragile image, and what a precious burden of history it preserves and protects! Like fossil remains, which perpetuate long-extinct rudimentary forms of life, portraits are fossil remains of human life in time, preserving the very wrinkles of the soul. To study them is more than a scientific historian's activity, however —gazing at them is also to experience obscure wonders analogous to what happens when a child puts a seashell to its ear. Portraits convey something more or less than is visible in them. They stir our imaginations, arouse our own inner resources in response to what is indefinable in a sitter's eye.

The faces of these ghosts somehow quicken our own experience of life in time, not only because of the intimations of mortality they hold for us, but, also, because they represent a particular shaping of human experience in visual terms. Caught up in the clock's relentless march, hung forever between a moment just past and another about to be, we can only marvel at living presences for whom there is no more past, no more future.

There they are, unchanging and unchangeable, right down to the unpredictable moment of their physical destruction— and yet, originally, they, too, were once subject to the clock, incarnations of passing moments in lives like our own, in a few days or weeks or years to be altered out of all resemblance.

*With Impressionism and its concern for optical fidelity, personality and inner life alike disappear.*

**194. - *MONET*. PORTRAIT OF THE ARTIST AS AN OLD MAN.**
The Louvre, Paris

356

**195.** - *POUSSIN.* ORPHEUS AND EURIDICE (detail). About 1650. The Louvre, Paris

CHAPTER IV

# ART AND THE INDIVIDUAL

## LIBERATION OF THE PERSONALITY IN THE SEVENTEENTH CENTURY

T HE shift in the direction of individualism that Nuno Gonçalvès was one of the first to reflect in painting, as in other efforts made to give individuality new means of expression (especially by the Venetian School), foreshadowed the course of Western culture. The various stages in this development, from its earliest beginnings to its contemporary end, are beautifully illustrated in French portraiture, which we surveyed in the preceding chapter. What happened in the seventeenth century was especially crucial for this development.

The Middle Ages raised problems of collective psychology, systematically discounting the importance of individual fates. The talent or the genius of the artist was at the service of a common faith, and it is only rarely that an individual artist's name has survived. During the fifteenth century, under the impulse of the Renaissance, a transition was effected from the craftsman—docile instrument of the collective body—to the artist. With this transition, personality began to be recognized and exploited, though not for a long time was it permitted to interfere with the social ties by which the individual was bound to other men, in matter of faith and artistic practice alike.

But, before long, European society began to break up. Most important, the religion upon which it had long been founded split in two. Man found himself in the unprecedented situation of being obliged to choose between two religions. Although, for the most part, he chose Catholicism or Protestantism on a basis of social or geographic

357

grouping, the important point is that he was confronted with the possibility, the necessity of making a choice—and in a fundamental matter. And then, one day, the Baroque, displaying a new kind of freedom and vivacity, made its appearance and routed the Classical aesthetics. Where and when the latter survived or was revived, its formalism and sense of discipline disintegrated into academism.

The seventeenth century marks a stage midway in these historical developments. It was an age of choice: choice between Catholicism and Protestantism, between Classicism and the Baroque, between humanism and individual loneliness.

These issues were fought out in the works of the greatest masters. Three of these works illustrate the key antagonisms of this conflict especially clearly. In Rubens, the united forces of Catholicism and humanism—though the stirrings of the Baroque also are in evidence —uphold the collective meaning of genius. In Poussin, Classicism at its apogee exhibits new awareness of the personal sensibility and its need to express itself. In Rembrandt, the transition has been completed; art ceases to be oriented toward universal concerns and advances boldly into the uncharted domain of inner existence.

*Song of the soul: Watteau pours out his inner music in the heart of nature. Here he shows us how he transforms this music into a painting.*

**196. -** *TARDIEU.* WATTEAU PAINTING AS HIS FRIEND JULIENNE PLAYS THE CELLO. Engraving after Watteau

*The elegant interior shown in this painting represents one of the rooms in Rubens' house in Antwerp. The canvas on the easel is a* Last Judgment *(cf. Fig. 131).*

**197.** - *CORNELIS DE VOS.* RUBENS' DRAWING ROOM. National Museum, Stockholm

# I. RUBENS AND HUMANISM

HUMANISM was a movement that began in the sixteenth century and ended in the seventeenth, in many ways a reflection of the Renaissance spirit and yet never exactly identical with it. Rubens is one of its most magnificent representatives.

Humanism marks a shift from the Middle Ages' central concern with religion in every phase of life and thought. It marks an advance toward the modern era, although it is still far from any cult of the individual such as we know today. Midway between the two epochs, humanism exhibited a certain this-worldliness of outlook (though often unconsciously), without going so far as to lose itself in the particulars of a wholly secular civilization. Humanism represented a new faith in man's powers. It marked the moment in Western history when man and nature came face to face on a new basis of equality, dispensing with the mediation of the divine.

For centuries, all reflection, all activities had been inconceivable apart from the mediation of Christian faith and institutions. The faith provided a center to which all things were related and from which they derived their sense—as the twigs and branches of a tree to its life-giving trunk. Humanity was merely the custodian of divinely revealed truth; although men might make commentaries on such truth, to question it was unknown.

Now man began to exhibit great faith in his own unaided powers, feeling himself to be at the center of things. Exalted by the range of possibilities open to him, his mind set out to conquer and pillage the treasures of this world. At this moment, a generation of universal artists was born, possessed of unusual technical skills and interested in —quite literally—everything. Leonardo da Vinci, who was as much interested in the ancient past as in the life and times around him, demonstrated as great a concern for matters of science and learning as for art—"art" here signifying all the arts. To men such as he human powers seemed of universal scope, and they set themselves the goal of becoming truly universal men.

## UNIVERSALITY & GRANDEUR.
Some writers deny that Rubens was a humanist. They are right if "humanism" denotes the pursuit of learning in the narrowest, most literal sense. But what really matters is breadth of intellectual attitude. In this nobler sense of the term, Rubens was certainly a humanist. He thought and lived naturally in terms of universals. To be sure, he was first

*Like his brother, a pupil of Justus Lipsius, Rubens was a student of ancient philosophy. He was particularly interested in Stoicism, which is here evoked by the bust of Seneca. But Rubens, as the vase of flowers shows, does not divorce thought from life.*

**198. 199.** - *RUBENS. PORTRAITS OF THE ARTIST, HIS BROTHER PHILIP, AND THE PHILOSOPHERS LIPSIUS AND JAN WOVERINS.* Entire painting and detail (BUST OF SENECA). Pitti Palace, Florence

and foremost a painter, but it would never have occurred to him to think of himself as merely a painter. He was a gentleman, a courtier, even an ambassador. Neither a man of a specific profession nor of a specific milieu, Rubens exchanged letters with the Archduchess Isabella as well as with the sculptor Duquesnoy, with Buckingham as well as with the painter Sustermans. Humanist scholars such as Peiresc, Pierre Dupuy, J. G. Gevaert, Plantin, and Moretus were his dearest friends. He never thought of himself as belonging to a single country. Repeating the words of an ancient philosopher, he wrote, "In my opinion, the whole world is my homeland" (Figs. 198 and 199).

Rubens had an infinitely open mind. He had intimate knowledge of the secret march of political events and occasionally took part in them. "In the course of his peregrinations he visited a great many different countries, becoming acquainted with *multorum hominum mores et urbes* (the customs and cities of many men). (Though he spoke Flemish, French, Italian, Spanish, and English, he did not mind using Latin when he wrote.) While painting, he would have someone read aloud from one of the authors whose work had been illustrated by his teacher Venius (who, incidentally, had been skilled in Latin verse)—

Plutarch, Seneca, or Horace. For diversion, he liked to ride. His letters show that he collected medallions, discussed archaeological problems, bought or borrowed all the new books of philosophy, history, and even astronomy, and was interested in every sort of contemporary invention: a clock without works, a magnifying mirror, and a "plan for perpetual movement" that he passed on to Peiresc.

His curiosity, if not his learning, was universal—though, if I may say so, he was exclusively universal—another characteristic of humanism. He was as completely ignorant of the mystical preoccupations of the preceding period as he was devoid of the individualistic anxieties of the following period. He lived on a plane of universal humanism. Two centuries of unrestrained individualism have given us a more restricted and a more exacting idea of the artistic personality—one that Rubens simply does not live up to. In our time he scarcely shares the popularity of the solitary masters. We think in individual terms, whereas these men thought in universals. We are attached to a certain conception of depth; they exhibit a more two-dimensional extension.

Rubens and Raphael, whose ambitions lay more in the direction of making themselves "universal men" than interesting individuals, are separated by a century, but they were animated by the same humanistic concern for subordinating the accidents of sensibility to the uniformity of thought. The scale of their labors surprises us today: their studios were small factories, with a great many pupils and helpers to execute their works for them after having been assigned a theme consisting of some general idea and a sketch. The works that the pupils and helpers turned out were then corrected by the master. Such a collective enterprise, with the master artist acting as supervisor, seems strange today. But how else could Rubens have turned out so formidable a production—the term is his own? In 1625, while he was gone for several months on a political mission, his firm went right on filling commissions. He was very much a man of his times, incapable of believing that there could be anything incommunicable in human intercourse, far more interested in broad human values than in unpredictable personal quirks and tastes, a man with an overall conception of humanity who was as yet unaware of the lonely places of the soul.

And yet he lived at the same time as his older contemporary El Greco and his younger contemporary Rembrandt, a time when a new world was coming to birth—a world that one day would echo Gide's words, "Within yourself love only those things that you feel to exist nowhere but within yourself." The modern soul recognizes itself more readily in the poignant uncertainties of Rembrandt than in Rubens' magnificent certainties. In the same way, it is less sensitive to Bossuet's faith than to Pascal's anguish. In that anguish we see our greatness, but it would be just as correct to perceive our weakness in it. We appreciate the intimate note of confession, and find it hard to rise to the breadth of universal expression. And, yet, there is a certain magnificence in minds such as Rubens' and Bossuet's alike in their sense of balance between intellect and sensibility, their capacity for prolific achievement at a uniformly sustained level of expression, and the authoritativeness with which they stick to the essentials without being sidetracked into pursuit of the picturesque, the pathetic, or the accidental (whether in subject or treatment).

Such minds exhibit a sense of human grandeur. It was not with impunity that the age of humanism stressed man's unaided powers over the world and himself, conceiving an exalted, almost intoxicated sense of the mind and of its natural dignity. It would not be

*Rubens had a deep sense of life, which made it possible for him to renew our vision of nature. Instead of a mere spectacle, nature now appears as a mysterious power, romantic before the era of Romanticism.*

**200. -** *RUBENS.* CLEARING IN THE WOODS. Alte Pinakothek, Munich

playing on words to say that humanism contained within it a superhumanism. Religious faith did not disappear in that age, but what did disappear was that Christian humility which, in the Middle Ages, had kept mankind on its knees before God's altar. Death, like human frailty and pettiness, continued to be an object of meditation, but now humble piety took on grandiose proportions. We must not forget that in Catholic countries humanism was associated with the Counter Reformation.

The geniuses of the age of humanism did everything in a big way—their conceptions were big, the feelings expressed are big, and the execution is to scale. First of all there had been Michelangelo, an artist who left a deep imprint on the young Rubens. Like Michelangelo, the Antwerp artist would give birth to a race of giants, in whom human powers are literally enormous. Like him, Rubens requires acres of wall space—the most material aspect of his art expressing the scale of ambitions.

VITAL LYRICISM. What grandeur! We find it hard to take in today, in our era of individualists. With Rubens as also with Delacroix—though, with the latter, grandeur became a longing for grandeur—we prefer the drawings to the vast finished works. By such a judgment we doubtless display the refinement of our sensibility, but we also display our inability to understand a genius too overwhelming for us! Rubens told William Trumbell in 1621, "The more capacious the painting, the greater the courage it gives us to develop our conception with verisimilitude.... I confess that by my natural instinct I am more fitted to do very large works than small curiosities. My talent is such that no undertaking, however immense in terms of quantity or diversity of subject, has ever proved too much for me."

Rubens, we have argued, is a humanist by the sheer force of an art based upon universality and greatness. But what about its content? It is plain to see that geniuses of this type —unlike Rembrandt, Goya, or Delacroix—tell us nothing of their inner lives, their personal complexities, troubles, or secrets. With admirable authority, they delineate certain broadly human feelings inherent in all of us, the elements of our common existence. It might be said that Leonardo magnifies the powers of the intellect, Raphael the harmony of reason, Michelangelo the tension of energy, and Titian the serenity of the gratified senses. What about Rubens? Rubens was the last of these artists (the spirit of humanism seems to have taken a century to pass from Italy to Flanders, where it produced the last of its prodigies), and he, too, concentrated on one of the essential human truths, the most fundamental of them all—life itself, the joy of living.

In this he was faithful to the genius of Flanders, merely giving free rein to an impulse latent in Northern painting for the previous two centuries, ever since it began. The Flemish Primitives expressed love of life, but they had the somewhat naïve notion that it was enough to give as accurate as possible a reproduction of what provided their enjoyment, namely, the spectacle of nature. Conscientious, patient treatment, however, tended to render appearances too stiffly, and thus to empty them of that vivacity that had attracted the artist in the first place.

The vivacity subsisted—it was merely not exploited. Rubens made the transition, addressing himself not to the spectacle of nature, but to its living presence, its vitality. He paid tribute to this aspect of nature, treating it as a poetic force. At this point, we may discontinue discussion of his place in a historical evolution and focus on what remains of enduring value in his work.

It would not be hard to show that Rubens brings together and orchestrates a number of great forces, all of which are universal and expressed by him with unmatched resonance. His Flemish blood, to begin with—characteristically more generous than delicate—bears along with it wave after wave of a vitality that here attains its plenitude. Then there is in Rubens the eternal Baroque, throbbing with a powerful steady beat, all the stronger for the contrast it implies with Renaissance weariness. Then there is the spirit of the Counter Reformation, conscious of how all this newly unleashed vitality may be an instrument of appeal to the masses, in winning them back to the Church. Finally, there is Rubens' humanism, which endows all these sometimes inexplicit aspects of his genius with a grasp of the Classical tradition. Rubens at once contains all this and heralds it—his genius and his eloquence are put to the service of these great themes. It should not surprise us that little space was left for personal, individualistic concerns. Driven by such grandly conceived forces—at once natural and historical—his only concern is to let them attain their

Thanks to his sense of universal life, Rubens is able to transcend arbitrary boundaries of forms and to suggest a complete fusion of people, thing, light, space.... He uses the Venetian technique, with its rapid brush strokes and sparkling accents. In his preliminary sketches he applies it with greater freedom than in his finished paintings. The result is a world as homogeneous, throbbing, and surging as the ocean.

**201. -** *RUBENS.* ALL SAINTS' DAY. Study. Boymans-Van Beuningen Museum, Rotterdam

Rubens is a master of composition; he learned this art in Italy. But instead of distributing and balancing his masses in a static architectural pattern, he subordinates them to dynamic currents. The resulting effect of irresistible movement is further stressed by continually recurring curves, volutes, and swirling spirals.

**202.** - *RUBENS.* JUNO AND ARGUS.
Wallraf-Richartz Museum, Cologne

366

maximum scope, their fullest possible expression in his art. Rubens' achievement is the best single instance of the fact that great works are susceptible of two readings. They record a moment in the historical development of our thought and feeling, giving it a physical and enduring expression. At the same time, they embody a timeless revelation that speaks as strongly and immediately in one age as another to the mind and heart of men, conveying universal truths. The historian seizes upon the first aspect, the poet upon the second, not always recognizing that it is the same great achievement to which they are both paying tribute in different ways. Footsteps on the sands of time, masterpieces are also pictures and poems of enduring value as such. When life has departed from the body, the spirit lives on.

In judging Rubens, we must overlook neither the man who was so very much of his age—which explains him and which he helps to explain in turn—nor the Rubens of all time, whose genius reaches far beyond his historical, psychological fate as an individual and speaks to us in terms of feelings as old as the species, valid as long as it lasts. Rubens will remain the greatest lyricist of human vitality, of life grasped in its intensity. The whole of his work celebrates activity, energy, the plenitude of physical pleasures, not only the life that loves but the life that love creates, the woman who bears it and the child who renews and continues it. No matter what subject he treats. In the ancient mythological divinities—satyrs, nymphs, naiads—he saw the embodiment of natural forces. His first big pagan composition, executed in 1604, was a bacchanal, the *Drunken Hercules* in Dresden. In his religious works, he chose scenes of violent martyrdom or such miracles as the driving out of demons. He treated three religious subjects several times—the Adoration of the Magi, with deployments of crowds and displays of pomp, the Last Judgment with falling, swirling bodies of the doomed and the massed numbers of the saved—dizzying arrangements of flesh and gestures inspired by Michelangelo, and the Passion of the Saviour, with death exalting the excruciating drama. When free to follow his own inspiration, he imagined unleashed forces in conflict—human beings struggling with each other (*The Amazons, The Capture of Tunis, The Rout of Sennacherib*, etc.) or, in his hunting scenes, with beasts.

THE RENDERING OF LIFE.   Great painters know how to subject even the most material elements of their art to the feelings that they express. In respect to composition, for instance, Rubens studied the Classical conception in Italy, but he found the symmetry and implacable stiffness too expressive of stability and immobility. It could not serve as vehicle for his ardent sense of life. He was driven to animate it, transform it, revolutionize it. He remains faithful to the principle of a few guiding lines that give the painting its unity and clarity as well as its harmony, but, in his works, these lines are unstable, and they break the balance for the sake of movement. Whereas the Italians had been fond of the middle axis, which lends symmetry, he replaced it with the diagonal—an ascending seesawing form. The majority of his paintings are composed along diagonals (Fig. 202).

Frequently, his composition is not based on any fixed lines but on a movement continued through the painting, sweeping the elements along with it. He creates currents of movement similar to those that catch up things that fall on water and swirl them about. Every element in the painting is swept up in the same feverish movement, bodies often being twisted like coiled springs—here again his example was Michelangelo (Fig. 201).

His animated transmutation of reality extends to material things. Divided between his Flemish temperament and his Classical Italian education, he never dared liberate himself from the ancient idealistic approach to the human form, but he frequently tried to escape from the coldness and inertia of overprecise contours. To copy the plastic beauty of statues, he felt, would be to reflect their rigidity. Here, too, his genius reconciled apparent opposites. "Distinguish matter from form," he says in his *Fragment on Antiquity*. The task of form should be to establish proportions and harmony in the spirit of ancient sculpture, but the matter so enclosed in form must remain free, carnal, living. Here is the passage in its entirety: "Knowledge of antiquities is important for the ultimate perfection of painting, but let its use be judicious and let it not smell of stone in any way whatever. Distinguish matter from form; you may produce something hard, difficult, the thorniest part of anatomy, but if you have failed to imitate the flesh, all you have done is to color marble statues." Flesh seems clay under the hands of this sculptor. It is everywhere with its gentle warmth, its tender flexibility, and the painter, fearing to stifle its living vibration, does not delimit its contours by clearly traced lines but—following the example of the aged Titian—he often blurs them with a kind of halo that prolongs the warm, light flesh colors and makes them radiate. In this way he captures "the ungraspable, trembling feature of nature that Raphael's drawing never renders," which, according to Baudelaire *(Salon de 1845)*, characterizes the drawing of the great colorists. Far from confining flesh to precise forms, he makes it bulge or fall in creases and wrinkles; thereby it takes on a life of its own, escaping from stiffness of line.

There is one last area of painting still to be caught up and transformed in the surging tide of vitality: execution, or technique. To the Primitives, the colors themselves were no more than a means for imitating the materials they saw around them. Titian inaugurated modern painting, however—the painting of Velázquez, Rubens, Fragonard, Delacroix, and all artists who, unlike David and Ingres, rejected the bondage of Classicism—when he demonstrated that technique is not merely a means for imitating or reproducing, but a means of expression and suggestion that, properly used, can communicate a particular emotion or sensation, as a musical instrument does.

Rubens grasped this teaching perfectly. His colored pigment does not present the smooth, enameled, anonymous surface of his Flemish predecessors; it is a soft wax that records all the movements of his brush—its excitement, its impulsiveness, its moments of relaxation. His brushwork provides a subtle graph of the pulsations of his hand and heart. It discloses the traces of creative struggle, in much the same way as the trampled grass of a field preserves the marks of battle (Figs. 201 and 203).

Rubens' drawing follows suit. No longer do we find short, straight, angular lines that check the eye, as in drawings of the Northern Primitives, nor is it the firm, pure immobilizing of movement as in the drawings of Italian artists. It is a rapid wavy line, a line of life that, like a river choosing its own course, follows a meandering, natural impulse.

His coloring consists of unequivocally intense tones full of healthy vitality. Instead of unifying them to create harmonies, he orchestrates them into a symphony where they all have equal brilliance, accentuated by a few grays. His very name, Rubens, is identical with a Latin word—it might even be one of those erudite pen names such as the humanists loved to take—meaning bright red, vermillion (Colorplate VI).

FROM THE PHYSICAL TO THE SPIRITUAL. Does his enormous emphasis upon physical vitality keep Rubens from rising to spiritual heights? On the contrary, it is thanks to it that he expresses some of the sublimest emotions to be found in the history of painting. (Delacroix somewhere praised his "sublime ideas"!) He invariably finds the striking physical detail (analogous to the poet's concrete image) that stirs us deeply, such a detail, for instance, as the drops of water on the naiad's skin in *Marie de Médicis Landing in Marseille*, which evoke the immensity of the sea, or the torn flesh in the *Coup de Lance*,

*With unfailing sureness, the agile brush of Rubens jots down the swift movements of the mind, the eye, the hand....*

**203.** - *RUBENS*. SAINTS. Sketch. Dulwich Gallery, London

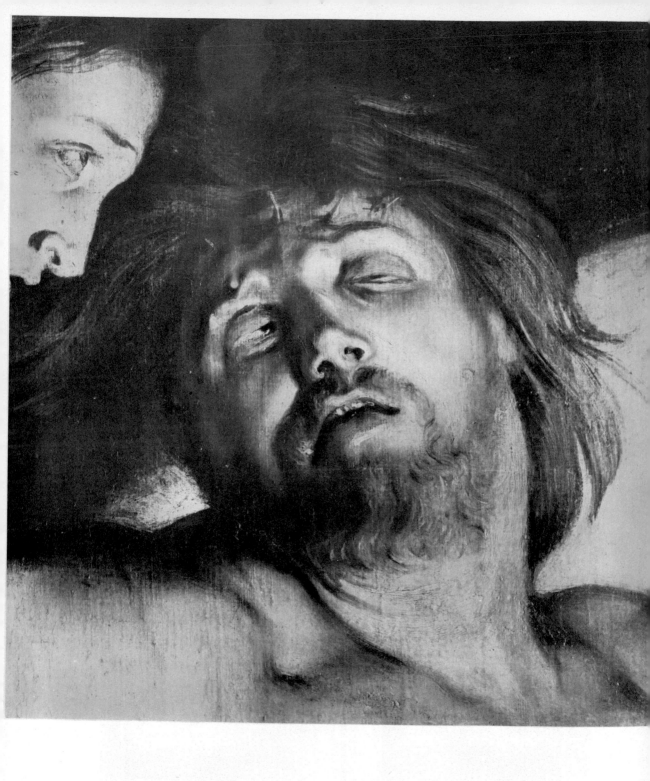

or St. Dominic's striking gesture in the painting at Lyon, covering the earth with his cloak to protect it from the divine wrath. In his figures of the dead Christ he attains great profundity of feeling. He invests them with such physical truth that the soul is deeply stirred. He expresses death in the horrible heaviness of the corpse which, robbed of the breath that animated it, is going back to the earth, slipping helplessly to the ground. He shows the Cross being raised, carrying so heavy a burden that under it the strongest men grow tired—as once Christopher grew tired from carrying the Child Jesus. Sometimes it is a minor detail, like the clot of blood that stops up the nostrils in *Christ à la paille*. *The Communion of St. Francis* alone is enough to show us what heights of spirituality his physical power can sometimes achieve (Fig. 204).

With advancing age, Rubens' inner voices are heard more distinctly. In 1630, four years after the death of Isabella Brant, his first wife, Rubens, who was fifty-five, married the sixteen-year-old Helene Fourment. Physical passion was transmuted into love, and few songs are as warmly caressing as his portrait of Helene and her children.

In 1635 Rubens purchased the medieval Steen Castle in Antwerp, where he spent most of his remaining years far from the busy life of court and society. It would seem that, to powerful, sensitive beings, the approach of death brings unwonted serenity: man turns with sympathy to that universal, diffuse life within which, a tiny ripple in the stream, he will in his turn be engulfed. A strange closeness grows up between him and nature. Events lose their importance, and behind them now lies revealed the background that they had masked, which now alone matters. Titian, Poussin, and Delacroix all know this twilight peace; already a little aloof from men, passions, and events, they measure the greatness of an apparent silence in which they perceive the rustling of another world (Fig. 205).

In the vast landscapes that he executed late in life, Rubens discovers and fully expresses a more hidden but no less powerful and grandiose cosmic vitality, which is eternally serene. Life is diffused among rolling clouds and rays of light that shoot through space— and in rainbows—the whole surging expanse of earth punctuated by paths leading off into the distance and by the ups and downs of topography.

> Le vent lit à quelqu'un d'invisible un passage
> Du poème inouï de la création....
> L'hosanna des forêts, des fleuves et des plaines
> S'élève gravement vers Dieu, Père du jour....[1]

[The wind reads to someone unseen a passage from the great poem of creation.... The hosanna of the forests, rivers, and plains rises gravely toward God, the Father of light....]

A muffled life, agitated by tremors, seems to emanate from the permanent principle of things, beyond all man's efforts to leave his mark upon them.

[1] Victor Hugo, *Les Contemplations*, I, 4.

*Rubens intuitively stresses physical details capable of producing the most expressive spiritual resonance. This feature of his art, which is often overlooked, is illustrated here by the uprolled eyes of Christ, His muscles wrecked by pain, the bristling thorns on His head, and the woman's compassionate glance.*

**204. -** *RUBENS.* THE DESCENT FROM THE CROSS (detail). Museum, Lille

*Nature in its entirety, the rolling fields, the flight of birds, are thrown into the dizzying vastness of space, opening onto infinity.*

**205.** - *RUBENS.* THE FARM AT LAEKEN (detail). Buckingham Palace, London.
(By gracious permission of H. M. The Queen)

*The Kermess* sums up in itself the whole sense of Rubens' achievement. It could serve as symbol for his entire work. At first it appears to be nothing but an unleashing of the vital energies of Flanders. There are drinking, shouting, loving, dancing, all of it in furious, surging, ebbing movement, all the elements mingling and tangling with one another as insistently as the bubbles in boiling water. But gradually the composition trails off, and as we move closer to nature, the groups become thinner. The turbulence decreases, the air grows fresher, the scene more limpid and calm. There is now only the hushed field at evening. The last strapping fellows are making so much noise that they cannot hear the silence that the night is bringing. One more step and we are in the plain, which heaves gently like the chest of someone fast asleep. The human agitation has been absorbed in the slower but vaster rhythm of the universe that closes it in as silence encloses the sharp cry of the two birds hustling off into space.

# 2. POUSSIN, CLASSICISM, AND THE "MODES"

PRAISE of a really great man, especially when proffered by a man less than great, can be a subtle way of making the former appear less, of cutting him down to the latter's size. Since there is nothing to be gained by frank attack upon the great—their powerful complexity and aggressive lucidity remain untouchable—a much cleverer tactic is to praise them for qualities they never possessed, so that posterity is bequeathed a harmless image of them. The great man has been transformed into a monument—and monuments, of course, are the work of those who come after the genius being honored, but those who erect them often fail to recognize the hand that they have had in the pious enterprise....

Contemporaries are especially untrustworthy. When they finally get around to accepting their great man, they take of him only what suits their own needs, confirms his concern with their problems, and expresses the most immediate preoccupations of the age. The prestige of his genius—and he is a genius to the extent that he has expanded the field of human potentialities and has transcended the limitations of his age—now, once he is dead, is invoked to give authoritative sanction to the age's most petty concerns, in enhancement of its image of itself.


POUSSIN'S HISTORICAL FATE.  The seventeenth-century writer on art, André Félibien, was just such a monument-builder in the generation after Poussin's death. Although his authority has long been accepted, I am afraid that he only grasped as much of Poussin—both as man and as painter—as could be adapted to the immediate interests of the age. He missed altogether the Poussin who transcended the age, whose vitality and poetic powers of invention still speak to us today. At that time, learned men were chiefly concerned with art as it could be supposed to have bearing upon the Quarrel between the Ancients and the Moderns. Not so differently, in the nineteenth century, they proclaimed the absolute necessity of a choice between Romanticism and Classicism.[1] And not so differently today, we are told that we must declare whether we are for or against abstract art. But suppose, despite all these quarrels, that I choose to like whatever is valuable in both camps? Such attempts to make formal questions prey to the passing whims of public opinion are perfectly absurd.

The genius of Poussin interested his immediately surviving contemporaries only insofar as he could provide grist to their little mills and could be invoked to confirm their most conventional ideas. The primacy of drawing and the theory of drawing were all they cared about. Even faithful disciples were quite ready to fly in the face of all evidence, when to do so could support Poussin's orthodoxy—as they currently defined it. We would no longer dream of disputing the immense influence of Titian on Poussin—an influence especially notable in the figures of *putti*, which the Norman artist openly borrowed from the Venetian. But this fact embarrassed and frustrated the doctrinaires.

---

[1] Delacroix was well aware of the false perspective of his contemporaries. Piron relates that on one occasion Delacroix said, "Most of those who took my side as a rule merely took their own, and fought for their ideas, if they had any, using me as a kind of flag." Much the same could be said about Poussin and many other great masters.

*Poussin's self-portraits are far removed from the conventional idea held of Poussin's art. The first shows him with the features of a robust Norman peasant; the second, convalescing after a serious illness.*

**206. -** *POUSSIN.* SELF-PORTRAIT OF THE YOUNG ARTIST. Collection Sir William Worsten, Great Britain

The good Dughet did not hesitate to write to his crony Félibien that Poussin could not possibly have been inspired by those *putti* because—he says it quite plainly—"because it is well known that Titian was less good as a draftsman than as a colorist."

It was in this way that Poussin became a textbook embodiment of Classicism, just as Delacroix later came to be identified with Romanticism. Delacroix was annoyed when anyone called him a Romantic. He would protest, "I am a Classicist, Monsieur!" Cavalier Marin had disputed the validity of such classifications two and a half centuries earlier when he introduced Poussin to the Cardinal Barberini. What he said was, "You are to meet a young man of demoniacal fury!" But protests are of no avail. Because his imagination was nourished by his passionate sensibility, Delacroix will always remain *the* Romantic; and because Poussin revered self-control and disliked the obscure and the factitious—he said, "My natural disposition compels me to seek out and cherish well-ordered things"—he will always remain *the* Classicist. (Indeed, even *the* academic painter, if we let Le Brun influence us.)

In actual fact, these two masters, who are normally regarded as constituting the two opposite poles of French painting, are linked by profound analogies. Delacroix is far closer to Poussin than is Le Brun or David. Once we stop arguing about schools and look at artists' lifework, we see that both Poussin and Delacroix embody the fundamental balance of French genius, which recognizes as valid only works of art that express *both* sensuality and spirituality, *both* spontaneity and lucidity.

Delacroix and Poussin were equally aware of the importance of passion. Delacroix asserted "the necessity of running a fever," and the aging Poussin said, "As I grow older, I feel, as other men do not, *inflamed* by a great desire to paint well." Both knew that no work is complete unless it is built on the sacred threefold foundation of sensibility, intelligence, and will. They also knew that no work is successful unless these fortunate conditions are fertilized by the imponderable addition of genius, by the grace of the gift, "Virgil's golden bough."

The striking differences between them spring less from their fundamental conceptions, which were, I daresay, closely related, than from the perspectives created by contrasting

374

circumstances. In reaction against excesses the one insisted on rich balance and the other on balanced richness; in unlike historical situations they fought for the same cause and undertook the same regulative task. Poussin rebelled against the Mannerism inherited from the sixteenth century, which had degenerated into facile artifice, and hence he had to emphasize the salutary discipline of reason. Delacroix rebelled against the excesses of a dry, regimented academism, and hence he had to emphasize the essential freedom of the sensibility. But no one will fail to see that, in doing this, the two struggled for a superior balance between the forces of the sensibility and the forces of the intellect, which both felt to a similar extent to be the peak of their art (Fig. 216).

The most recent historians of Delacroix, reacting against partisan views born of passing historical conditions, have justly stressed the Classical aspect of his genius. Nevertheless, there can be no question of denying the preponderance of passionate, poignant sensibility in his case. With Poussin, although it is important not to underestimate his respect for the primacy of reason, it is also permissible to reject a view so one-sided as to be false, and to stress the importance of the many generous, lusty, passionate elements in his art and the poetic quality of his work as a whole.

THE RUSTIC SENSE OF LIFE.   No one can truly understand or love Poussin without being impressed by the generous vitality that is the essence of his art. Nothing could be less abstract than Poussin's painting, nothing farther removed from the pedantry with which he was identified in his own day and for a long time thereafter. He was no intellectual, never a professor like Le Brun. Basically, he was a peasant, and he always remained close to his origins, to their hereditary and natural virtues. It was not some philosophical theory that taught him respect for reason, but spontaneous instinct, something in his blood and bones. That was the source of moral health in the people from whom he sprang. His country origins cast far more light on him than the theories he indirectly gave rise to and occasionally repeated on his own account, in response to the demands of the age.

How should we define his Classicism if not as concern for measure, balance, and "judgment in all things," a certain gravity and unshatterable self-control—all of which

In the painting, the inscription reads:

NICOLAVS POVSSINVS ANDELIENSIS ACADEMICVS ROMANVS PRImus
PICTOR ORDINARIVS LVDOVICI IVSTI REGIS GALLIÆ ANNO DOMINI
1649 Romæ                                      ÆTATIS SVÆ 55

*Nobility comes with age. But these two self-portraits, painted a year apart, show the artist's evolution in his treatment of form and composition. In the first, the inscription on the spine of the book reads, "On Light and Color." In the other, the frames in the background create an entirely abstract geometry.*

376

**208.** - *POUSSIN*. SELF-PORTRAIT OF THE ARTIST IN ROME IN 1649. State Museums, Berlin
**209.** - *POUSSIN*. SELF-PORTRAIT OF THE ARTIST IN ROME IN 1650. The Louvre, Paris

*Poussin's spontaneity, the directness and sharpness of his vision, are most strikingly disclosed in his wash drawings. They are very similar to those of Claude Lorrain, where everything is rendered in terms of light.*

**212. - POUSSIN.** LANDSCAPE. Wash drawing. The Louvre, Paris

rather than in interpretations of them. According to Félibien, "he avoided company as best he could and slipped away from friends by himself to the vineyards and most remote places of Rome, where he could examine ancient statues at his leisure, enjoy pleasant views, and observe the most beautiful effects of nature. It was in such retreats and during his solitary walks that he made quick sketches of things he encountered."

He went off by himself—his quest for solitude foreshadows the age of individualism, when the artist would come to rely entirely upon his own resources. He wandered off alone through the Roman countryside in the morning when nature was still in her pristine freshness, the light making long streaks through the still slumbering heavy foliage. He gave up the pencil—which compels an abstract definition of forms and contours—and, like Rembrandt, used a watercolor brush instead. By spots of shadow on the white paper he sketched his incomparable visions of trees and paths through the underbrush, among the most direct and thrilling in the history of art. The period of the draftsman was not to come until later (Fig. 212).

With figures, too, of which ancient and Renaissance masters provided him with abundant examples (and from which he occasionally profited), he felt the need to draw from the living source. "Wherever he happened to be, he studied," Félibien relates. "Even when he was walking in the streets, he would watch the actions of the people he saw, and when he discovered any unusual actions, he made notes of them in a book that he kept by him for the purpose." The mind can always erect its superstructures later, once the materials have been hewn out of the bedrock of reality.

If Poussin discloses his peasant origins in his very Classicism, respect for reason, and meticulous probity, what are we to say of his sensibility, with its controlled strength, of his spare, laconic poetry? *"Je fais profession de choses muettes"* ("I sing the praises of silent things"), he used to say.

When we consider these matters, the accusations of Poussin's dryness and coldness collapse. We feel that his sensibility is consonant with his sturdy, muscular physique. The analogy that comes to mind is Colas Breugnon rather than the pedant or the academician. He is very much a creature of flesh and blood, a strapping fellow with a touch of crudeness. His letters confirm this impression. He speaks of a "hogshead of wine" that he is planning to drink with his friends, or "a barrel of good wine, two years old," or a pastry of venison so big that, "clearly, all the baker kept for himself was the horns." He uses picturesque local idioms: *"Qui chapons mange, chapons lui vient..."* ("Capons come to the man who eats them"). He was fond of this one: *"Avec le temps et la paille se mûrissent les nèfles"* ("Given time and straw, fruit ripens"). Besides quoting the wisdom of the fields, he occasionally takes a heartier line: "That ignorant fellow Jacquelin ought to be strung up by his genitals" [*génitoires*—an old-fashioned word]. Referring to Scarron, "With all due respect, he is a wonder-worker, for he has a round arse and makes square turds." And so it goes....

REASON DOES NOT EXCLUDE LIFE.  Bernini said that "Signor Poussin" was "a painter who works with this"—pointing to his forehead. Bernini was right, but we must not forget that a head given to reflection, however serious, is not incompatible with richness of temperament or warmth of sensibility, nor with a fresh, lyrical sense of reality. Poussin himself recognized the two aspects of his nature when he remarked, "The pretty girls you will have seen at Nîmes, I am sure, will not have delighted your mind by their sight any less than the beautiful columns of the Maison Carrée, considering that the latter are but old copies of the former."

Poussin takes us away from the academism in which his imitators have for so long floundered (misrepresenting him in the process), helping us to realize what "Classicism" really was and reminding us that its roots lay in humanism. As cultivated in the sixteenth century, humanism was a fresh sense of the fullness of life, quite as appreciative of warmth and color as of the sublimations of the spirit. (Nor is it always remembered that these men of the early seventeenth century in France retained a great deal of what had survived from the previous century.) His humanism is reflected in his wholesomeness, in a balance and composure typical of the peasant.

Poussin had pretty nearly the entire gamut in his grasp: sensuality, sensibility, and reflection, but let us consider his sensuality first. A nude was never to him merely a harmonious, perfect form. When Félibien wrote of him that he did not paint the female body "as it is actually seen," he was not telling the truth. He was carried away by his own convictions. If proof of this is asked for, look at Poussin's drawings, which are more direct and candid than his paintings. He was fond of real bodies with milky complexions, figures "suave and tender" *(souefs et tendres)*, relaxed in languorous sleep, throbbing with voluptuousness. However, in his *Bacchanalia* with the plump, drunken *putti*, love is closely associated with wine and childhood, and this joyous trinity is supplemented with music and dance. "Dances, bacchanals, festivities," Poussin tells us, were represented by the ancients "as of a jolly nature" (Figs. 213 and 214).

Toward the end, sickness, coupled with mistrust and a progressive withdrawal into himself, gradually dissipated the jollity of his youth. Bacchanals were now things of the past; even to have evoked them would have been to shatter the majestic melancholy of his declining years. But this is not to say that he lost his love of life. Though he could no longer dance and sing, he could listen in contemplative silence to its most secret murmurings, to the yearly rise of the earth's juices in growing things, their germination and flowering. At this serious time of life, the religious sense awakens, and life seems less the hurly-burly of human affairs than a cosmic force. The old man perceives the rhythm of its law in the slow, eternal cycle of the seasons. During the last four years of his life, the brush already slipping out of his grasp, Poussin made a mighty effort to set down, in its awesome simplicity, the progression of spring, summer, autumn, and winter. He brought to this task the spirit of the anonymous medieval sculptor making his contribution to the great cathedral. Life is no longer seen as loving mistress but as the mother to whose womb the artist will shortly return.

Poussin's art unfolds as a development from the one pole to the other. Fondness for life and fondness for reason contribute to it in varying degrees, but, even when reason appears to have gained the upper hand, life is always present. After the early works of his maturity, in which warmth of feeling predominates, he does seem for a time to have succumbed to a kind of formula—of his own invention or derived by others from his invention. This most austere and disciplined period in his work reached its culminating point when he came back to France, thereafter to have less and less time to himself, to be alone and think and realize the profoundest depths within himself.

THE SCULPTURAL VISION.  Let us consider Poussin in his most austere period, the Poussin whom some critics find "cold," the Poussin who turned his back, as upon some sin of his youth, upon the pictorial freedom and joyfulness he had encountered in Venice. He does indeed, in this phase, display a propensity for constrained coldness, for deliberate dryness. He comes close to being an academic painter, anticipating such neo-academicians as the followers of David. What was the reason for this? It was a considerable preoccupation with sculpture and sculptural effects, much encouraged by the narrowly plastic character of ancient art. To this preoccupation he sacrificed the delights of color and brushwork. Does this reflect the influence of theories of Classicism? I believe that, even in this period, his dogmatic intentions are merely superimposed on a very old tendency in French painting—which Classicism encouraged, but which had asserted itself much earlier

*The roots of Poussin's warm sensuality, which blends woman with nature, color with matter, are found in his vibrant wash drawings.*

**213.** - *POUSSIN.* SLEEPING BACCHANTE. Drawing

**214.** - *POUSSIN.* SLEEPING VENUS AND EROS. About 1630–33. Museum, Dresden

—the sculptural tendency. Delacroix—to whom we must constantly make cross reference, as an artist whose genius has many affinities with Poussin's, and who is the most perspicacious commentator on Poussin—saw clearly the difference between him and the nineteenth-century academicians. Poussin, he observes, "did not imitate the material aspect of ancient bas-reliefs and statues, as has been done in our own day." However, "his passion for sculpture" led him to "a systematic abandonment of color." This statement must be qualified (and Delacroix himself, later on in the text, suggests that on some points his ideas would have to be qualified). Poussin abandoned color only during a specific phase of his career. Delacroix was referring primarily to Poussin's paintings in the Louvre, which were at the time hard to see properly, on account of the accumulation of old varnishes, and were, in addition, defaced by the darker undercoatings having come to the surface. No one who really knows Poussin will deny his color sense or his fondness for color, warm in his youth and at the end of his life, transmuted into profound symphonies that unify the atmosphere of his paintings. Delacroix was closer to the truth when he criticized "the excessive pursuit of form," which, according to him, accounts for the occasional stiffness of Poussin's paintings and the fact that "the figures are but loosely linked" in them (Fig. 146).

It will be said that the failure is typical of the peasant who lets himself get involved with theories and fashionable worship of antiquity. But the matter is not so simple. As we have said, the French taste for sculpture is older than French Classicism. Ever since the Middle Ages, it has reflected the Frenchman's fondness for concrete reality. He likes the feel of volumes in the hand, volumes which he can finger, stroke, and weigh, and which, in painting, give an opportunity for illusionistic effects. It has long been observed that the French genius is essentially sculptural, that Romanesque and Gothic art found their most accomplished expression in sculpture—indeed, to such a degree that in the art of those periods sculpture is indistinguishable from architecture. And it has been said that French painters, until Rubens revealed to them the meaning of painting for its own sake, "saw" everything in sculptural terms. They defined form in terms of simplified volumes, disencumbered of details and surface accidents such as might have provided brushwork effects. The *Avignon Pietà*, with its sharply chiseled features, seems carved out of some particularly hard wood. The figures of Fouquet and Georges de La Tour appear almost to have been turned on a lathe; their smooth, compact volumes bring sculpture to mind (Figs. 140, 182, and 301).

Poussin was merely a painter in the same tradition when, after sketching in the composition of a picture, he experimented with figurines modeled by him in wax, put wet cloths over them, and then arranged them and studied various lighting effects. We know that as soon as he arrived in Rome he formed a close friendship with the sculptors Duquesnoy and Algardi. That we are dealing here with an atavistic fondness for the concrete rather than with the effects of any abstract theory is sufficiently proved by the following evidence. What nineteenth-century artist revived Poussin's method? Was it one of the painters imbued with the Classicism of antiquity or of the Renaissance, such as David or Ingres? Not at all: it was the most rustic, the most peasantlike of all French painters, François Millet, also—incidentally—of Norman stock. Like Poussin, and no doubt for the same reasons, Millet liked to make clay models of the figures he was intending to paint and then sketched them, arranging them to test the images he had in mind.

*Poussin's most intellectual conceptions are always rooted in his innate sensibility. As he grew older this spontaneous vision was transfigured into austere beauty.*

**215. -** *POUSSIN.* TWO HEADS (fragment). Cut from a WORSHIP OF THE GOLDEN CALF (?).
Cecil Liddell Collection, Great Britain

THE EARTH'S JUICES. Perhaps we are a little less inclined now, like Bernini, to point to the forehead as the key to the real Poussin; we should do better to point to the heart. Let there be no equivocation about it: however great the role of intellect in his art, the source of his most original contributions to painting was a spare, laconic, but powerful personality.

I would like to stress two of these contributions—one, because often overlooked, his rendering of the textures of terrain and foliage, the other, because essential, the pictorial harmony that he achieved between the soul of man and the soul of nature. This latter contribution antedates Romanticism by more than two centuries and makes him one of the great pioneers in the expression of human individuality.

Poussin's art marks an essential stage in the progressive conquest of matter, the suggestion and rendering of it in art. In this regard, Poussin played a major role in the development of modern painting. The fifteenth century had discovered techniques for rendering material textures, but it had not gone beyond frozen, petrified, or mineral effects of opacity and translucence, as exhibited in stone and metal. Even though Van Eyck and his followers achieved some quite subtle effects of transparency and reflection, their textures remain essentially stiff and solid.

The sixteenth century saw further technical advances. Skin and drapery acquired greater pliability. Leonardo, Correggio, Andrea del Sarto, and the Venetians reached a point at which light was no longer rendered with implacable limpidity but with soft shadows and *chiaroscuro* effects that made possible subtler treatment of moving, living things (Figs. 48–50).

The seventeenth century saw the development of unusual effects of light carried to the extreme by Caravaggio. Rubens achieved further effects of drapery, and Rembrandt achieved unusually warm and radiant flesh tones. But Poussin made the greatest single advance. He annexed to painting the whole range of plant and earth textures. Foliage, rotting leaves, clay banks, damp soils and dry soils, rutted roads, wheat fields rustling in the wind, moss-covered rocks, barkless tree trunks, the surface of standing and running water—and more. The Dutch artists, Ruisdael included, observe nature very attentively, and their eye is perhaps subtler than Poussin's. But they do not share his intimacy with the substances of things, his profound sense of the soil, which Gilles de La Tourette was the first to bring out. Poussin had a great need to be in direct physical contact with things. "I have even seen him scrutinize stones, lumps of earth, and pieces of wood," Félibien tells us uncomprehendingly, "the better to imitate rocks, gardens, and tree trunks."

An earthy man, he celebrated the earth and its fruits. To him, the human being was the most precious fruit, and, although he saw it in the sun of the mind, he did not neglect its fleshly substance. Not until Courbet was nature again felt so intimately or perceived so sharply with all the senses. The affinity between Poussin and Courbet was strikingly illustrated when I deliberately hung paintings by them next to each other, when the Louvre reopened after the Liberation (Fig. 211).

This sensory, sensual experience of nature was without precedent in the history of art. Through Poussin, the French peasant made his contribution to world painting, with conquest of the tangible matter of things. The discovery of the fluid, the liquid, the immaterial, which Corot and the Impressionists made in the nineteenth century, marked a final stage in the exploration of reality in which Western painting was engaged from the fourteenth century down to the twentieth. In the history of that exploration, Poussin opened an entirely new chapter (Fig. 68).

What is, however, essential in Poussin, is his poetry. It is just as new and effects a revolution no less bold. Even though it rises to spiritual heights, its source is not in the spirit. It is rooted in the earth and nourished by the earth's juices. This is why Poussin's plants are so beautiful, so alive, so *true*. His painting is poetic in the sense that it conveys an accord between man and nature in terms of feeling, reveals their kinship of soul. The keenest commentators on Poussin, those who have had the deepest insights into his genius, have emphasized the importance of this contribution: nature is no longer a mere background for human activities, the place where they occur; it is an extension, an amplification of them, a wave emanating from them or an immense shadow cast by them. Man and nature are now different incarnations of the soul, just as the facial features and the gestures of a given figure are different expressions of the inner life.

---

*In his large landscapes illustrating mythological subjects, Poussin achieves perfect balance between his sensibility and his genius for order.*

**216.** - *POUSSIN*. THE FUNERAL OF PHOCION (detail). 1648. Collection Lord Plymouth, Great Britain

Delacroix noted the "happy mixture of ideal figures with poetic yet true landscapes, a genre that he created." Paul Jamot praised Poussin's "philosophical and poetic genius, which looked in nature for correspondences with human thoughts and passions," and carried his analysis further: "In his compositions, the trees, the waters, and the Classical heroes who move about them are so closely united with the sky that man and nature may be said to form one great symphony."

DESCRIPTION AND SUGGESTION. On this point, too, the teachings of Poussin's contemporaries, who had a narrow-minded, doctrinaire conception of his work, must be thrown overboard. Were we to listen to his disciples and to Watteau's, these great artists were as unlike as two artists ever were. Occasionally, the contrast between them has been advanced as an argument against the unity of the French genius. But it is enough to look at them to realize that they are related, that each complements the other. The mysterious accord between man and nature expressed by Poussin is also expressed by Watteau, though, in the latter, it takes on a certain mobility, a certain feminine sharpness. In both artists, however, the action of the human figures, for all the precision with which it is portrayed, seems no more than one musical theme within a vaster and more varied orchestration of the landscape.

When I tried to demonstrate this at the Exhibition of French Art held in London in 1932, by hanging Poussins and Watteaus together, the works of these two artists harmonized with each other perfectly, contrary to conventional expectations. They blended and revealed, each in its own register, the intimate affinity that we have been discussing, to show that Poussin and Watteau embodied the French genius, one in the major key and the other in the minor.

The awareness that human life is closely related with other growing things, and that the relationship among them is one of harmonious balance or spontaneous agreement, could have been born only in a happy, hospitable land such as France, to which the Comtesse de Fels justly dedicated her essay on Poussin. Needless to say, Poussin did not discover this accord, but he was the first to give it conscious expression. Once this is realized, we understand Poussin's originality and we see the truth of Delacroix's prophetic statement: "It has so often been said that he is the most Classical of painters that the reader may be surprised to find that, in this essay, he is treated as one of the most daring innovators in the history of painting." The tradition of Classicism rooted in the Renaissance, which, in the seventeenth century, was revived in France (Poussin contributed to the brilliance of that revival), was interested merely in description—description of the external signs of the passions and emotions. They are portrayed in the figures, their facial features, and the movements of their bodies, and are intelligible to anyone. Such paintings are a little like the theater, where the inner conflicts of human beings are expounded by "actors," in the most literal sense of the word, that is, by what these persons do, by their "actions." Leonardo da Vinci was one of the first to undertake a study of the mechanism of externalization: what can still be seen of *The Last Supper* and what we know

388

*The admirable X-ray photographs made in the laboratory of the Louvre show that in the execution of his works Poussin started from a vibrant modern technique, which he disciplined in the final stages.*

**217. 218.** - *POUSSIN.* HEAD OF THE VIRGIN (detail of THE VIRGIN APPEARING TO ST. JAMES THE GREAT). 1629. Direct photo and X-ray photo. The Louvre, Paris about *The Battle of Anghiari* disclose a systematic attempt at psychological analysis through modification of appearances. Then a real science, that of the correspondence between the movements of the soul and those of the muscles, was developed. Poussin applied it with consummate mastery, and the academicians enthusiastically refined it. Le Brun systematized and codified it meticulously in a treatise that became the basis of the official teaching of the Ecole des Beaux-Arts; it is based essentially upon knowledge and reflection.

However, Venice revealed a diametrically opposed approach to painting. The Venetian artists trusted instinct, inspiration, and they also trusted the intuition of the viewer rather than relied upon methodical reflection. To borrow Bernini's expression, "we work with that," the Venetian artists pointed to the heart when they said it—to the heart, as Musset said, "where genius lies." The purpose was still to convey a spiritual content to the man viewing the work of art, but now not to make him understand it but to make him feel it. Here, the intellect no longer plays the leading part for either artist or viewer; heart speaks to heart. Although the Classical conception of painting may be compared to the theater—which, incidentally, it imitates with a conventionally organized depth articulated by "flats" and an open space delimited by the proscenium—the comparison does not hold for the other conception of painting. We are not watching a show; we are experiencing an emotion together. A better comparison is with music, which magically transforms the atmosphere around us. We have seen that Venetian painting was intimatily associated with music. And this is why the landscape takes on new importance: the purpose is no longer to analyze the play of the actors who are the figures, but to plunge into a certain *ambiance*. This *ambiance* is nature, which, according to the gentleness or anger of its moods, its aloofness or its tenderness, envelops man, weighs upon him, elates him, or terrifies him. The Venetians realized this from the outset. Titian discloses three major sources of their wizardry in his various versions of Venus, which bring together women, music, and nature. Titian captured and distilled the secret of the new sensibility with which painting was to be endowed: the purpose was no longer to expound and develop a subject, but to make the viewer experience it by evoking a living presence. The Venetians were introducing into art all the elements of the subsequent theory of *Einfühlung* (empathy), so dear to the Germans. But the revelation they had of these new powers of painting remained empirical. Giorgione and Titian knew from experience the landscapes that enchanted and comforted them and most fully corresponded to their obscure inner expectations. They delighted in re-creating such landscapes, reducing them to an enchanting harmony, a magic spell, the better to communicate them to us. But their landscapes are always the same landscape, possessing the same resonance, because clothed in but a single color, that of each artist's inner life, his soul.

MODULATION IN PAINTING.   Dreamy in Giorgione, voluptuous in Titian, nature is hallucinating in El Greco, nostalgic in Ruisdael, pantheistic in Rubens. It is all of that in each of these artists, but never more. Invested with the power to incarnate the inner life of the artist, it can be the vehicle of only one soul, the artist's. Poussin, on the other hand, takes command and tells us what to do. It is not his own soul that he infuses into the landscape; it is the soul which he has invented for it and which he endows his human figures with at the same time—a poetic soul which he makes the center of his painting and around which he constructs the painting.

Poussin, a highly cultivated man, chose as his masters the Bolognese and Roman painters, but his personal sensibility was delighted by the Venetians, particularly in his youth. The rational man in him admired the range of the Classical method, but the peasan in him was deeply moved by the Venetians, who revealed the power of nature to arouse our feelings. He was too imbued with the Latin cult of order to let any conflict arise. Rather, he applied his clear, firm mind to the task of understanding why and how his sensibility was moved, with a view to gaining control of its mysterious powers. Once gained, such control would permit him to direct them as he chose. He did not turn his back on the powers of reason—rather, he gave them a new field for their exercise. His aim was to enrich the human mind by subjecting to it the sphere of the emotions.

Thus, he developed his theory of "modes," which I have treated in detail elsewhere. He realized from the outset that his undertaking consisted in endowing painting, the art of the visible, with the resources of music and poetry. Moreover, he was reassured to discover that ancient artists had been familiar with the emotional magic that he meant to introduce into painting. They had used the term "modes" for variations in an artist's manner that act subtly upon the sensibility and induce it to attune itself to an explicit subject. A mode in painting is comparable to a particular tone of voice in speech— modulation that influences our understanding. As Poussin remained faithful to a theatrical conception of painting, his notion of mode might be compared to background music accompanying the actors in a play or motion picture. He sees well that the land- scape complements the human elements, that it possesses the power to amplify the latter in a confused way, as waves enlarge and extend the shock of the stone thrown into the water, that it provides the *ambiance* within which an action takes place. But he analyzes it and discovers in it a play of suggestion born of combinations of lines, colors, and lights. The painter must learn to use them and to influence the viewer by their means. In his own words, he adds to painting—which already has the power "to represent"—the power "to arouse and to give birth to" emotions. He adds to it the power of suggestion.

Among the many examples provided by his works, we might choose his *St. Matthew and the Angel*. When treating the same subject, Caravaggio and Rembrandt concentrated on the two figures, which they presented full length and down to the waist respectively. The whole canvas is filled with them and the dark space closes up again behind. The Apostle listening to the divine promptings of the angel is the sole subject. How does Poussin approach the same subject? By varying the expressive gestures of the two figures? This is what we might expect from a pure Classicist. But Poussin goes to the opposite extreme. He makes the figures small, swallowed up in an immense landscape. Does this signify that he wishes to minimize the importance of the subject? Not at all! It fills the entire space—and what a space he has created! The river reflecting the sky's immensity takes a slow, winding course that forms a pathway into infinity. And, so as to make it impossible to misunderstand his intentions, he puts the saint and the angel at the point where the river begins its solemn progression into depth: they are placed this side of the limitless opening into space. It is almost as though the river took its source in them, from their encounter, but that is merely one way of looking at the picture. The river is going

*For Poussin, a work is stylization of the sensibility. The definitive composition merely expresses the initial emotion in intellectual terms. Polyphemus symbolizes the profuse splendor of eternal summer; St. Matthew symbolizes progress toward the infinite—each is an aspect of nature.*

**219.** - *POUSSIN.* LANDSCAPE WITH POLYPHEMUS. 1649. The Hermitage, Leningrad

back to its true origin—into the immense heights where God rules. The gravity of the colors, the slow and majestic solemnity of the lines further dignify the river's slow ascension to the universal source (Fig. 220).

When Poussin treats a pagan subject, as in the *Landscape with Polyphemus,* he similarly plunges his figures into a natural landscape, but now nature appears teeming with life. The picture is an exaltation of vegetable, terrestrial vitality, crammed with bushes, plants, trees, earth, and rocks. In the distance, the giant sits peacefully atop one of two mountains. The work is a flute-song celebrating summer's beauty (Fig. 219).

★
★　★

Poussin's greatness consists in this, that in him thought does not gain the upper hand over sensibility, nor sensibility over thought. They fertilize each other. A river not fed by perpetually flowing springs would be no more than a succession of stagnant ponds; without firm banks it would be no more than a swamp. Both the flow and the constraint are necessary, and when the two are balanced we have greatness.

If Classicism is understood to mean the repression of sensibility by an implacable reason, then the term does not apply to Poussin. However, if it means the conscious orchestration of all the resources of being, so that they animate and control one another, then Poussin is the greatest French Classicist.

He remains a figure of the past if we see in him no more than an end product of Renaissance rationalism, but he belongs to the future if we recognize the new possibilities with which he endowed art. These were immense. Thanks to them, the individual, for so long prevented from communicating his private feelings, was enabled to do so in all their uniqueness. Artists will now be less obliged to follow one or another well-beaten path, stifling their own inner lyricism, their own uniqueness and originality.

**221. -** *POUSSIN.* TREES IN THE WIND. Wash drawing. The Louvre, Paris

# 3. REMBRANDT:

# THE EXPLORATION OF INNER DEPTHS

WE all talk about Dutch realism, and, ever since Taine's day, it has been a common-place that the art of Holland is confined to the faithful observation of appearances. This is just what we expect of a nation of burghers and practical-minded merchants. And, yet, this widespread view leaves out of account the greatest Dutch artists, making them seem mere exceptions that prove the rule. Ruisdael is first and foremost a poet, though he is also a realist, and the same is true of Vermeer. In Rembrandt, the supernatural element of poetry bursts its bonds and takes its place in the very foreground of painting. Now, who will deny that these three painters are profoundly representative of their country and their race? It is true that they are head and shoulder above the common run, but, this being so, perhaps we should revise the traditional view and say that in Holland the mediocre artists are realists and nothing more, just as in Italy the mediocre artists are academicians and nothing more.

Actually, if you really look around enough, you must realize that in Holland everything opens out toward the immaterial. When you leave the four walls of your room, the moment you open your door, you are overwhelmed by the infinite wind-swept spaces, by the limitlessness of earth, sky, and water. How could Holland be a purely materialistic country? Paul Claudel understood it very well when he wrote, "Nature did not provide a set horizon line, but merely welded an ever-changing sky to an earth that runs off, in every direction, into the void."

Paintings are like mirrors in a certain sense—and do we not often see mirrors in paintings by Northern artists, reflecting the semidarkness of their rooms? When we look at them from a distance, they appear to be no more than coldly exact reflections of the reality around them. But anyone who scrutinizes them close up finds in them the revelation of his own face and features, his own eyes. They open into an inner darkness, which is just as infinite as space. Rembrandt did this. With brush, pen, and etching needle, he was able to evoke the infinite at least as vividly as the Dutch landscape painters, who showed us their land dissolved in plays of light and passing shadows.

PROMOTION OF THE INDIVIDUAL. To be sure, art before Rembrandt expressed the inner life. But Rembrandt was the first to perceive and explore it as the expression of an individual being, of a self, the first fully to realize how much the artist can draw from his own inner resources. Increasing numbers of artists after him, down to our own day, have devoted themselves to self-questioning of this sort, to laying bare the secrets of their souls. We put this to the credit of Romanticism, but the Romantics knew very well how much they owed to Rembrandt, and they looked upon him as a precursor. Musset's Fantasio exclaims, "Alas! The things people tell one another are always the same things. The ideas they exchange are almost always the same in all their conversations. And yet, inside these isolated machines, what hidden alcoves, what secret compartments! It is a whole world that each man carries around with him! A world that remains unknown, that is born and dies in silence! What a lonely unknown land is the human frame!" Two centuries earlier, Rembrandt had divined the same profound truth and made himself the first painter to reveal in art the terra incognita of personality. Rembrandt marks, in the history of art, a turning point related to a turning point in the history of ideas, even of Western civilization as a whole. This upgrading of individuality was to become the distinctive characteristic of the following centuries, and, indeed, eventually to be inflated to excessive proportions.

Throughout the Middle Ages—and throughout antiquity as well—no man had sought deliberately to set himself apart from his fellow men, although outstanding talents and achievements were, of course, recognized. But no one deliberately set out to cultivate his innate originality. To the strongly rationalistic sense of community in ancient Greece and Rome Christianity added the sense of community in faith and works. All men lived in communion with one another and, as individuals, were absorbed in the collective body. Great artists contributed their particular gifts, but they used their gifts to repeat the same truths and treat the same subjects, in accordance with an ordained, unchanging iconography. Similarly, the loftiest medieval thinkers were not so much guided by their private experiences of the faith as putting their special faculties at the service of dogmatic elaboration and explication. The mystics were the only individuals who shut themselves off and pursued private experiences within themselves; but, although they could urge others to reproduce such experiences for themselves, they could neither account for them nor communicate them. This is why El Greco, who was undoubtedly influenced by St. John of the Cross, was the only artist to assert and cultivate individual resources of originality prior to Rembrandt.

In the meantime, however, a great event occurred in the West—the emergence of Protestantism. The historian can touch upon these religious problems only with the greatest caution, but he must evaluate their consequences. When we compare Rembrandt and Rubens, the two greatest seventeenth-century artists in the Low Countries, and bring out the striking contrasts between them, we realize how different an inspiration each received from his religious affiliation. Of Rubens, Claudel wrote, "With his entire work we shall pray to God. For the Protestant prays alone, but the Catholic prays in the community of the Church." This is why Rubens remains so powerfully a humanist, his unique glow imbedded within the bricks and mortar of a larger ecumenical community. He does not seek to particularize himself save by his exceptional powers, nor to set himself apart from others save by the range of his inspiration. Like Raphael, he scorned overindividualization, and, in consequence, has been felt to be rather incompatible with our own epoch. Rembrandt is very different: everything is by him personally re-thought, re-experienced, imagined and rendered solely in terms of his own personal resources.

*The quest for inner life which drove Rembrandt to portray himself time and again at first merely reflected his lively interest in fleeting expressions.*

**222.** - *REMBRANDT.* SELF-PORTRAIT OF THE YOUNG ARTIST IN 1630. Alte Pinakothek, Munich

The Protestantism from which he sprang plays a great part in this: it has been said that, "the Bible in his hands, each Protestant is pope." The hierarchical discipline of the Roman Church was rejected by Protestantism; every believer is brought face to face with the Scriptures, either alone or in the circle of his family. He reads the Bible in his own language, for himself, not in the universal medium of Latin. It is up to him and to him alone to discover what the Scriptures mean and what their teachings are. He has turned his back on Catholic unity, which is strengthened by collective rituals. The artist in Protestant lands is no less encouraged to employ the resources of his own imagination. The result is a proliferation of ever-new versions of the sacred story—not least among them being Rembrandt's powerful and poignant visions.

Another circumstance had important consequences for Rembrandt's art. The religious split had separated the Northern Low Countries from Rome, not only from the Papacy but also from Latinity, from the solid rational discipline that the Church had inherited from the Empire. Now, it so happens that the demarcation line separating the two religions runs along the frontiers of the traditionally Latin countries. France hesitated, but in the end she allied herself with Rome; the part of Flanders still occupied by Spain remained similarly within the fold. But Holland, Switzerland, Germany, and England deserted Rome. Except, perhaps, for England, these countries had never been deeply penetrated by the Latin spirit. Thus, the seeds of Protestant individualism were planted among peoples who had never been greatly influenced by the deep-seated rationalism of the Middle Ages and antiquity, who had never been subjected to the solid armature of a universally conceived logic. Thus, they were less trained than the Latin, Catholic countries to escape from themselves, to disregard their own inner promptings, and to mistrust their feelings. At the same time, they lacked effective means for ordering and elucidating the data of their inner life.

THE INNER EYE. Is this to imply that Rembrandt was simply the product of historical circumstances? Certainly not, but these were the conditions that he inherited and responded to with all his wealth of genius. Nobody could have predicted the achievements of Rembrandt from knowing the soil in which he was rooted and the waters that nourished his genius, but there are no fruits of any sort without a slow process of growth to maturity; and it is this that we must examine now. Although, from the outset as a painter, he was teased by the promptings of his inner life, he did not, by any means, discern their message all at once. The exceptional number of self-portraits, done at every period of his career, shows clearly enough where he looked in search of truth and the meaning of life. But what does he see in the mirror—himself? No—the play of features. His face serves as an experimental field for the study of expressions. In the earliest self-portraits, both paintings and etchings, we see him concentrated and attentive. Suddenly, everything becomes

*The mature Rembrandt no longer projects himself outward. He knows that his riches are entirely within himself, in his innermost being, which can be reached only by a descent into oneself, as into the central fiery core of the planets.*

**223.** - *REMBRANDT.* SELF-PORTRAIT OF 1655. Kunsthistorisches Museum, Vienna

animated: he is laughing, crying out as though in pain, lifting his eyebrows in astonishment, frowning in anger. Actually, his quest of the self is still in the groping stage. He still believes that the inner life is to be read in the expression indicated by muscular movements; he is still faithful to the tradition masterfully launched by Leonardo da Vinci in a series of drawings that dissect psychological life by capturing changes in facial features. Yet, even at this stage of his development, Rembrandt was painting figures of motionless old men shut up within themselves, thinking their own thoughts (Fig. 222).

This was the way his future lay, but he had found it instinctively—he did not understand it, as yet, nor make the discovery fully his own. Houbraken, who was not quite Rembrandt's contemporary, praised those of his works in which "the emotions of the soul aroused by the most various events are expressed with so much art and clarity in their essential traits...." The Rembrandt of this period was so well understood by the contemporary public thanks only to this misunderstanding: they looked to the outward appearance for a secret that exists only in depth. And it is true that Rembrandt, in the period when Amsterdam society was showering commissions on him, studied man primarily in his visible manifestations. The portraits are mode of acts, gestures, and expressions cultivated as on the stage of a theater, where it is important to be intelligible to the eye. The first *Anatomy Lesson* of 1632, showing Professor Tulp, is a dazzling set of variations on the theme of attentiveness. For ten years, down to the tumultuous *Night Watch*, which is a sort of torchlight procession of such figures leaving the stage, he painted many portraits in this style. The same animated gestures characterize *The Shipbuilder* of 1633,

in which the male figure is seen turning toward his wife as she comes in, one hand on the door and a letter in the other, and *The Mennonite Preacher* of 1641, where the man is shown turning away from his book to address his wife (Figs. 224 and 225).

Rembrandt in this stage of his career is wholly concerned with surface appearances. In his self-portraits, he appears gay, scintillating, greedy—above all greedy: sensual mouth, avid nostrils, the eye impatient to take in everything. He is the fashionable young painter, happily in love with Saskia, whom he married in 1634.

We are in the first half of the century. Holland has only gradually withdrawn from the Flemish community and is becoming aware of her separate destiny. It has perhaps not been sufficiently stressed to what extent the first generation of Dutch painters—the School of Utrecht and Frans Hals and his group, who painted smoking rooms and military scenes—still expressed a communal sense of life. In 1636, Rembrandt, when he portrayed Danaë greeting the shower of gold with open arms—or when he executed his still life of game and *Samson's Wedding*—was not far removed from the sensual ardor of Rubens. Rembrandt, the great Protestant painter of biblical subjects, reflected more than a little what we think as "the spirit of the Counter Reformation," and was capable of treating great religious and artistic themes that appealed to the collective imagination of an earlier age. The very vastness of his canvases is evidence for this. The *Night Watch* of 1642 has a Baroque resonance: this turbulence, this dissymmetry, these figures that come forward and step out of the canvas before our eyes—all this is remarkably compatible with the art of Catholic Flanders. In his prosperous period, Rembrandt not only externalized himself; he also multiplied himself in imagination. He loved to dress up in fancy costumes. He portrayed himself wearing a turban, as an Oriental leaning proudly on a stick, and as a soldier with a plumed helmet and steel breastplate. In one etching he posed as an exotic potentate with an ermine collar and golden chain, an unsheathed scimitar at his shoulder. In 1636, he portrayed himself as a mercenary in sword and armor, with Saskia sitting in his lap, holding up a tall glass of Rhine wine in front of an overladen table on which a peacock is enthroned. To use a modern psychological word, Rembrandt was the perfect example of an extrovert in this phase of his career, or, in older terminology, of the outgoing type. And, yet, Rembrandt was, even at this time, slowly moving in an opposite direction, as though he mistrusted his own success.

EXPLORING THE INNER DEPTHS.   Around 1637/38, Rembrandt discovered the sense of mystery and the supernatural. He painted the angel of light lifting the lid of the tomb and Christ just about to get to his feet, the two figures portrayed amid a strange assemblage of glinting armor and weapons, the soldiers in their consternation falling over one another. There is also a painting in which we see the Magdalene discovering with amazement that the tomb is empty, turning to receive fullface the light of the rising sun. Christ the gardener, clothed in white, is standing behind her, raised from the dead. And he painted several landscapes with shadows, glowing lights, storms, and ruins, occasionally peopled with faces of an insistent spirituality.

A number of crucial events came one right after the other. In 1642 Saskia died. Rembrandt withdrew into himself. He became estranged from his public; his admirers, one by one, deserted him. Now he began to have financial difficulties, and they grew increasingly worse. In 1656 he went bankrupt, and his property was put up for public auction in 1658. Now Rembrandt began a period of loneliness. Turning his back on everyone, he advanced alone in the unknown, anticipating the centuries to come.

His ever deeper descent into the inner depths can be followed in his self-portraits. At first, he shows himself a strong, massive figure (looking rather like Balzac) in a rough homespun gown (Fig. 223). Then his skin becomes furrowed with wrinkles and the firmness of the flesh gives way to puffiness. The eyes, which formerly seized voraciously upon everything within their range, become dreamy, focused seemingly on something that lies behind appearances. Overnight, as it were, he has made himself the most inner-directed of painters. In one self-portrait he is no more than a reflection, the outer glow of a fire slumbering in the depths.

The problem of solitude is formulated—the problem which henceforth will increasingly haunt the imagination of all thinking, feeling men and women. Possibly the most lucid comment on what took place in Rembrandt at that time is to be found in modern philosophy. According to Karl Jaspers, solitude alone can give us access to *Existenz*. It is only in solitude that being, having escaped from the web of conventions, including the intellectual conventions that govern interhuman relationships, apprehends itself, the only reality it can really know. The nineteenth-century artists felt this, and were the first to try to explain it. Delacroix wrote: "Everything is subject; the subject is yourself." (We may observe that "subject" is taken here in the sense of Kantian subjectivity—Kant's philosophy was then gaining ground in France.) "It is your impressions, your

*In middle life Rembrandt became aware that a man may have to die to the world in order to awaken to the light that comes from the soul—for instance, the light of the Resurrection....*

**226.** - *REMBRANDT.* THE RESURRECTION. 1639. Alte Pinakothek, Munich

*In his drawings Rembrandt reduces reality to a few expressive indications. His aim is to keep his spiritual visions free from descriptive clutter.*

**227. -** *REMBRANDT.* WOMAN SEATED AT A WINDOW. National Museum, Stockholm

feelings in the presence of nature. You must look into yourself and not around you."
Baudelaire, who was always so close to Delacroix, expresses the same idea:

... le monde
Hier, demain, toujours nous fait voir notre image.

[Yesterday, today, always, the image that the world presents is our own, of us.]

At that time the current of ideas whose birth we have witnessed was coming to a head. Until then, it had been supposed that everything can conceivably be known and explained, that this knowledge is inevitably identical in all men, and only as such true. Truth was supposed to lie in what everyone saw with the same eyes as well as in what everyone thought according to identical conceptions and identical logic. Now it was becoming apparent that, on the contrary, every individual thinks in his own way because he is a unique being. It was understood that the individual discovers his own being, his own nature, in the sensations aroused by things around him and in the ideas he forms of them. At the end of the eighteenth century, in his *Destination of Man* (translated into French as early as 1801), Fichte asserted, "In every perception you perceive only your own mode of being." Charles Villers, his French translator, commented, "We do not feel anything that is outside of us, and we are conscious only of our own feelings." Does not this formula define the principle of Rembrandt's art, as well as all subsequent art of the Romantic type? For, to the degree that he believes this, the artist is no longer compelled—indeed, is no longer able—to conform to a model existing outside himself and conceived as identical for all, whether visible reality or an idea of beauty. Actually, the artist can no longer find a model that exists prior to him. He must create *his* art, externalize *his* vision. Rembrandt, two centuries earlier, acted in accordance with this belief: the artist, instead of faithfully reproducing the outside world, must make visible his own peculiar way of seeing things, emphasizing (not suppressing) what distinguishes his work from nature as schematically reduced to observations and concepts common to all men. With this development, the work of art becomes an act of pure creation and marks the birth of a new order, a new kind of vision.

THE GIFT OF THE HEART.   What Rembrandt might well have feared in his solitude and estrangement from his contemporaries would be the bitterness of contemplating an unshared truth, peculiar to him and hidden from the world. It must have been tempting to withdraw into oneself, "to escape into the interior," to take pride in being incommunicable. But what he found as he penetrated into his own inner depths was an incandescent core, a subterranean source of fire quite capable of transcending loneliness and the misunderstanding of men. The inner flame he found was love. Rembrandt was not merely driven by the desire of every explorer to communicate his discoveries to others, to transfer them from the personal to the universal plane. He was also possessed with the generous impulse to love his fellow men, nature, and God. He is all love, affection, pity: he radiates warmth and light. This, perhaps, is why he is so great, even among the greatest, for in him goodness is not much different from beauty. Possessed of an irresistible need to give, he never shrank from the chancy enterprise of transmitting to others what was most unknown, what was unique in himself. The enterprise required a new language,

But the more harshly life treated Rembrandt, the more of himself he gave to the world. Every one of his works glows with light, warmth, and beauty—and with something more. We reach with Rembrandt a point beyond painting—goodness, the soul itself. Alone he retraced the path of the great mystics, a way that leads through the darkness of night into the unknown, where another kind of light appears, a light whose source is not in nature. It springs from the soul, the human soul and the divine soul, the soul of that Christ who, in the work of Rembrandt, is revealed to eyes other than those of the body, as to the pilgrims at Emmaus.

A point beyond painting.... Tauler, a mystic of the late Middle Ages, said, "The spirit is transported above all the powers to a kind of immense solitude about which no mortal can speak adequately. It is the mysterious darkness where the boundless Good lies hidden."

*In his last period, after concrete reality had been dissolved into the penumbra, Rembrandt's technique achieved complete fusion. Nothing disturbs the mystery of the spirit.*

**230. -** *REMBRANDT.* SIMEON AND THE CHILD JESUS. 1669. National Museum, Stockholm

# THE FLOWERING OF PERSONALITY
# IN THE EIGHTEENTH AND THE
# NINETEENTH CENTURY

## I. WATTEAU: SONG OF THE SOUL

B Y a variety of circumstances, Watteau was projected beyond his time and place. A subject of Louis XIV, he nevertheless belongs to the period of reaction against the *grand règne*. Though an artist whose greatest fame lay in the future, his work renewed ties with the art that preceded the Classicism of Versailles. A Northerner himself, he contributed more than any other to an eventual break with the Classical tradition and with the Academy. The ambivalence of his historical position made him more aware of himself, and within himself he perceived a disquiet only partly due to poor health. He was thus compelled to create for himself an art to his unique measure, and, thus, to be a pioneer of Romantic individualism.

WHO WAS WATTEAU? Especially in France, you would suppose, no artist is better known than Watteau. His name has become a byword: we speak of "Watteau charm" and "Watteau grace." But fame that comes down to a name and familiar image—of dolls dancing an exquisite minuet—is deceptive. It makes Watteau seem to embody the most dazzling, but also the most superficial aspects of the eighteenth century. It masks, if it does not also obliterate, the man he actually was—one of the profoundest, most revolutionary artists France has produced. A widespread cliché in France is to call him "the painter of the *fêtes galantes*." We expect to find his name linked with Boucher, Madame de Pompadour, and Fragonard, who—as every French schoolboy knows—are leading representatives of the age. Unfortunately, the historian must get his dates a bit straighter than this. Watteau was born at Valenciennes in 1684, at the peak of Louis XIV's reign, and he died just thirty-seven years later. He died of consumption in 1721, the year of Madame de Pompadour's birth. Fragonard had not been born—that event occurred twelve years later. Thus, all but the last six years of Watteau's life were spent under the reign of the Sun King.

If the reign of Louis XIV is all but entitled to claim him for itself, the nineteenth century is entitled to claim him as one of its precursors. Though he lived in the early eighteenth century, he was a great Romantic—if, that is, we understand by Romanticism effusion of the individual soul and the gift of communicating its most hidden secrets. Yet, the nineteenth-century Romantics did not know Watteau. His very existence had been obliterated, it seems, by David's students, who chewed up paper into wet wads and threw them at *The Embarkation for Cythera*, which then hung at the Ecole des Beaux-Arts. This was the painting that had earned Watteau admission to the Academy in 1717. On the other hand, Ingres, a pupil of David and his successor as leader of French Classicism, copied Watteau's drawings and paintings for his own pleasure and instruction. It is also a fact that early in the nineteenth century, Watteau's *Gilles,* now in the Louvre, was exhibited in the Place de la

Bourse for a long time without finding a buyer. The dealer had scrawled in chalk above it:

> Pierrot would be so happy
> If only you liked him a little.

Denon, who was then director of French museums, finally got the message and bought the painting for himself for 150 francs. In 1845, the famous collector Dr. La Caze, who eventually gave it to the Louvre along with the rest of his pictures, bought it for 800 francs. Although these were gold francs, it is clear that the good doctor got quite a bargain! In the second half of the nineteenth century, there was a sharp rise in Watteau's fame. In 1851, the famous lines by Baudelaire were printed:

> Watteau, ce carnaval où bien des cœurs illustres,
> Comme des papillons, errent en flamboyant,
> Décors frais et légers éclairés par des lustres
> Qui versent la folie à ce bal tournoyant....

A little later, the brothers Goncourt, who were infatuated with the eighteenth century, created a charming, witty image of Watteau that was to remain the last word for some time: "Elegance ... fantasy ... grace ... feminine seductiveness ... superb clothes ... Thélème[1] partout et partout Tempé[2]." Such were the words they used. Yet the following was added: "I don't know what elusive, ungraspable harmony lingers behind the laughing words." Now, this elusive, ungraspable harmony is precisely what holds our attention today. A few have even suggested that it is an undertone of tragedy. Consider, for instance, this recent opinion, a twentieth-century one. Jean Cocteau in his Propos, where he records a conversation with Louis Aragon about the Dresden Museum, says, "Watteau is still protected by a trap for fools. Just as with Mozart, there are still many persons who find Watteau frivolous, an operetta painter.... Watteau was no less a prodigy than Vermeer. His grace is the obverse of the terrible.... The dust of powdered wigs he stirs is really a threatening storm cloud; he charms as others frighten.... I see lurking in his misty atmospheres a great deal of violence, behind the graciousness there is a powerful fist... the iron hand in the velvet glove." But is this latest verdict any more final than the others? Although Cocteau's vision touches upon a very profound aspect of Watteau, and might be called a post-Romantic vision, is not Cocteau really the last of our great Romantics? His version of Watteau was born with Michelet in the nineteenth century. It is the modern version. In the space of one hundred years, Watteau came to look utterly different. Whereas people once evaluated him in terms of marivaudage[3], now they speak in terms of serious drama. We may still ask which, if any, was the true Watteau.

To begin with, he was more than the gifted inspirer of artists such as Pater and Lancret, creators of delightful marionettes with plump yet delicate bodies dressed up in fancy costumes employing every color in the rainbow. His disciples, like the eighteenth century generally, certainly owed a great deal to his example, but they clung to and improved upon only the most conspicuous, superficial aspects of Watteau's art. He stands at the

---

[1] The "Abbey" of Thélème is an invention of Rabelais, at the urging of whose character Gargantua one Brother John set up an institution for men and women, who would be free to behave precisely as they pleased. — Transl.

[2] A valley in Thessaly celebrated by Vergil for its ideal beauty. — Transl.

[3] The refined, delicate comedy of the eighteenth century, as typified in the plays of Marivaux. — Transl.

Every human figure painted
by Watteau, every line he
ever drew, is an emanation
of his own personality. His
is vibrant as music, sharp
and emaciated like a body
exhausted by excess of
emotion.

**231. -** *WATTEAU.*
THE VIOLINIST.
Drawing. Museum, Rennes

*This early work by Watteau is descriptive. It portrays troops laboriously making their way through northern France, unconcerned with military glamour.*

**232. -** *WATTEAU.* THE LABORS OF WAR. The Hermitage, Leningrad

threshold of the eighteenth century like one of those flower-decorated arches which—as his own paintings show—used to be a feature of village holidays. The eighteenth century did not grasp the spirit of Watteau—perhaps because it was a rather unspiritual century. Its sensibility was all on the surface, pleasure-bent, and convinced of the primacy of the senses. It had to wait for Jean-Jacques Rousseau to discover its own deeper resonances—a discovery with which, incidentally, the century culminated. Now, Watteau is one of the very most spiritual of painters. Perhaps this was why the eighteenth century neglected all but his least essential aspects.

The eighteenth century merely touched the surface of Watteau; his roots run much deeper than his contemporaries suspected. He is not strictly an eighteenth-, seventeenth-, or nineteenth-century artist. He belongs to the entire French tradition. He is one of those who turn up now and again, and, singlehandedly, incarnate the art of an entire people, who by their appearance give it a new look, a different orientation. At the same time, of course, we must "place" Watteau historically. For the greater part of his short life Watteau was a contemporary of Louis XIV, but contemporaneity does not necessarily imply conformity or harmony. Watteau represents the last years of the reign, a period when the country was enormously weary of the long rule and beginning to raise its voice in criticism. With Watteau, the sun of the eighteenth century, which at its high noon gave off only the light of "clear, distinct ideas," was near its setting. Claude Lorrain heralded this sunset, and Watteau did not just celebrate the twilit hours of early evening in all their delightful freshness; he also took note of the advancing shadows of approaching night—when the soul would find itself alone and confronted with new, still-indistinct anxieties (consciousness of which a century later would take the form of Romanticism). He is the twilight of the *grand siècle* and its apotheosis. Melancholy, as are all twilights, he was the distant harbinger of the nineteenth century's sensibility (Fig. 234).

WATTEAU'S BACKGROUND.   Watteau was a Frenchman, but a Frenchman of recent vintage, for it was only in 1678, six years before he was born, that Valenciennes became French under the Treaty of Nijmegen. He was thoroughly French, nonetheless, for the province of Hainaut had always been French-speaking and culturally oriented to France. Watteau was not a Fleming, as his contemporaries liked to call him; he was a Walloon. Moreover his lack of admiration for Louis XIV could only have been enhanced by memories of his native city's subjugation in the course of a war that had not ended with that conquest, but continued to be prosecuted with mounting bitterness.

*In the fictitious world of the theater Watteau discovered the path leading from realism, celebrated by the Flemish artists, to the dream dwelling within him.*

**233.** - THE DEPARTURE OF THE ITALIAN ACTORS. Engraving after Watteau. Bibliothèque Nationale, Paris

In 1702, Watteau went to Paris. In 1709, he competed for the Prix de Rome. He took the second prize only, which did not include the privilege of a trip to Italy. Somewhat resentful, he went back to Valenciennes. This was the moment when Louis XIV, in a desperate move, decided to resume the war against his enemies rather than to fight with them against his grandson, Philip V. [We call it the War of the Spanish Succession.] The Maréchal de Villars attempted to save the situation. 1709 was the year of Malplaquet. When we look at Watteau's portrait of Laroque, for example—the officer with the broken leg whom Watteau probably met while the former was convalescing at Valenciennes, and whom he painted surrounded by nymphs—we must keep in mind that Laroque received his wound in that terrible battle which contemporaries called a "massacre." No fewer than twenty thousand of the enemy and about ten thousand French lost their lives on the battlefield—enormous figures at the time! Watteau traveled the roads of northern France and saw the ugly side of the heroic battles (Fig. 232). Indeed, he began as a painter of military scenes, and he never—like Van der Meulen, for example—portrayed an army in all its splendor, with strutting kings and generals on horseback. Rather, he shows us unglamorous, common troops dragging themselves along the roads with makeshift equipment, pots and pans hanging from a stick, tattered uniforms, men carrying their guns under their arms, followed by a sad procession of women and children. This was the seamy side of the Grand Monarch's wars, and it is more evocative of a rout than of a victory. And this could hardly fill him with admiration for Louis XIV. If, as modern psychoanalysis asserts, the sovereign symbolizes the leader or the father, Watteau had an additional reason for despising the Grand Monarch, a portrait of whom is being unceremoniously packed in a crate in the *Gersaint's Signboard* (Fig. 234). Watteau's own father, a tiler by trade, was not a poor man (as has been asserted by some—we have documentary evidence that he owned two houses). He was rough, quarrelsome, much given to drinking, and was often in trouble and involved in several lawsuits. There can be no doubt that Watteau had a hard time as a child, and the fact may account for his precocious withdrawal into himself. Some psychologists ascribe tuberculosis to early traumatic experiences, and we know that it was of consumption that Watteau died at the age of thirty-seven. In any case, hostility toward his father accounts for the fact that he left home and went to Paris in 1702, in a spirit of seeking refuge there, according to Gersaint. Conflict with his father, retreat into himself, melancholy, and poor health were all crucial in determining his character.

In Paris he settled in the quarter of Saint-Germain-des-Prés, which enjoyed extraterritorial rights and was not under the jurisdiction of the corporation of Paris painters. The city limits of Paris then ran more or less along the Rue de Seine, and Saint-Germain-des-Prés (the "Prés" being "prairies" or "fields") thus fell outside the city limits. Foreign artists who lived here could sell their paintings without being subjected to the very strict regulations of the city guilds. At the fair of Saint-Germain the Flemish painters had their own stands, as we would call them today. There was also a chapel where they assembled. Watteau frequented this Nordic milieu, where he met Wleughels de Spoede of Antwerp. He lived in the house of La Chasse, situated on the Carrefour de la Croix-Rouge, where the little old Rue du Dragon runs into the Rue de Sèvres. The squat rickety old house stands between the two streets where they end. Nearby, in the Rue du Vieux-Colombier, Watteau frequented taverns where the Northern painters met. In this way he escaped the grip of the French tradition as it had already been laid down by the Academy, especially

*Watteau opens up a new world—not only that of the eighteenth century but also that of modern individualism. In this painting he symbolically stores away the dead glory of Louis XIV.*

**234. - WATTEAU.** Fragment of GERSAINT'S SIGNBOARD. 1720. State Museums, Berlin.
Gersaint's previous shop was under the sign of the Grand Monarch

under Le Brun, dictator of the arts in the name of the crown. On the contrary, Watteau was associated with the movement of reaction against Le Brun. He denounced the Italian influence and advocated a return to Northern painting, to Flemish painting, to Rubens— works by whom Watteau had admired as a child in Valenciennes.

BREAK WITH THE "ESTABLISHMENT." Watteau was in touch not only with the artistic opposition, but also with something very like a political opposition. At an early date, probably in 1704, he entered the studio of Gillot, a painter who was connected with the theater and found inspiration in Italian comedy. Only a few years earlier, in 1697, the companies of the Italian actors had been expelled because they were too irreverent, having gone so far as to make fun of Madame de Maintenon, the clandestine queen, whose secret marriage with the king had taken place the year Watteau was born. The Italian comedians were gone, but their memory was still fresh, and both Gillot and Watteau liked to treat them as subjects, in a sort of defiance to the royal orthodoxy (Fig. 233).

Just how did Watteau indicate his opposition? Well, among other things, it should be noted that he shows no sign of the Cartesian influence. To be sure, Descartes was no contemporary of Louis XIV, having lived before the latter's reign, but Cartesianism, however distorted, left a very deep imprint on the rationalistic spirit of the period. Like all great monarchs, Louis XIV was bent upon establishing a rule of order, discipline, and expansion of power, none of which can be achieved without an appeal to reason and the

*Here Watteau has completely found himself: lovers in fictional costumes, flowing water, dying flowers, hovering mists....*

**235. -** *WATTEAU.* THE SHY LOVER or COUNTRY EASE. National Palace, Madrid

invocation of rules. Louis XIV realized the dangers involved in fantasy and freedom of expression. This was why the official painting subjected the expression of emotional life to rules formulated by a kind of mechanics of passion—and Descartes had much to do with their formulation. In Watteau's day, Le Brun had just died but his influence still prevailed in the Academy and, thus, in official art. And Le Brun, as we have mentioned above in connection with Poussin, left behind him a theory of the expression of passions, formulated not only in lectures but also in a treatise illustrated with engravings. Le Brun ruled out all possibility of a spontaneously flowing sensibility creating its own expression at the moment it manifests itself. Rather, the sensibility of the artist was subjected to a kind of official vocabulary and an official grammar that tolerated no mistakes or exceptions to the rules.

Le Brun's tradition, even though the eighteenth century did away with it, survived longer than many of us realize. The eighteenth century, it is true, made the reconquest of the senses, but it did not go so far as to do away with rationalism, at least not before Rousseau. If you consult the article on painting in Diderot's *Encyclopedia*, you will find that Le Brun's theories have remained intact: the art of expressing passions is still demonstrated there by passages from his works and by illustrations of his drawings. It is best to give a sample. Here is one, picked at random: "Hate or Jealousy. This passion is depicted by a wrinkled forehead, frowning, lowered eyebrows, and a gleam in the eye, where the pupil is half hidden under the brows and turned toward the object [of jealousy or hate]. The mouth is closed in such a way that the clenched teeth can be divined." And so on. The artist was anything but free to express the human passions. Soldiers in the armies of the period could scarcely have been put through any less strenuous drill with their muskets. Furthermore, the passions were carefully distinguished and subdivided in exhaustive detail. The rules for the expression of ordinary admiration were different from those of "admiration mingled with surprise"—which if sufficiently intense becomes "veneration," and at a still higher level, "rapture." Now, perhaps, we can understand what Caylus meant when, in a famous and often quoted lecture at the Academy of Painting, he accused our poet-painter of lacking "expression"! (Caylus was a friend of Watteau's, but he was eventually a recruit to the ranks of Neo-Classicism.) It is true that Watteau's faces practically never wear expressions in anything like the sense understood by Le Brun and the Academy—but this is not to say that his painting does not overflow with expressiveness. Here we have the crucial difference: eighteenth-century painting still supposed that it had to follow the syntax and vocabulary of a book of rules, whereas Watteau simply ignored this mechanical approach to the life of the emotions—actually a serious hindrance to the pure effusion of feeling. Although no painting is more vibrant, more musical, more deeply moving than Watteau's, we never catch his figures mimicking some state of mind or feeling. The expressiveness lies in the spontaneously flowing movement of the work as a whole, in its irresistible, spellbinding power. Caylus simply could not and did not understand, as so he said: "As for his *expression*, I cannot say anything about it, for he has never ventured to render any passion." And he said this of Watteau, the poet par excellence among painters, whose works all throb with passionate feeling! And Caylus went right on: "His compositions have no object. They express no passions and are consequently devoid of one of the most stimulating elements of painting, namely, action."

Thus the two traditions that Poussin had so marvelously reconciled and linked became, after him, irretrievably separated—and in being faithful to Poussin's example, Watteau had to come into conscious antagonism with those who thought of themselves as Poussin's most direct descendants.

Close but not obvious ties link Watteau with Poussin, something that can be more clearly grasped in the instance of Poussin's famous contemporary Claude Lorrain. Here the relationship is somewhat more obvious. Claude liked to linger on a beach to paint the sunset, but since he had to make concessions to the requirements of his epoch, he would put some sort of historical scene in the foreground, almost as an afterthought. (There is even a tradition that he did not paint the foregrounds himself, but left them to an assistant.) All he cared about was being on the beach in the evening, watching the sea at its calmest hour, the waves running in to expire in the sand at the moment that the sun sank below the horizon. He expresses a kind of sumptuous, gentle melancholy, a poignant but magnificent sadness. This is Claude Lorrain's special beauty, his personal poetry. Like Watteau, he was more concerned with the music of things than with their mechanics (Fig. 185).

It was in the same sense that Watteau summed up and gave new depth to a tradition that, although it originated in Venice, had its representatives in France, too. *L'expression*, whose absence in Watteau's works Caylus deplored, is actually omnipresent in them. This is why the systematic, critical eye could not find it there for so long a time. It is in Watteau's skies, in the light that shimmers silkily in accord with the rippling waters of a pond. It is in the shadows cast by trees and in the red of the setting sun. It is everywhere, diffused throughout his pictures. It was in Watteau's innermost being and passed from there to the landscape, from the landscape to the figures inhabiting it, and from them it finally passed into our own innermost being. Where did Watteau find the courage—and the encouragement—to escape the academic grip, to ignore it, actually? His background was provincial, and we have already seen how the official views have distorted our picture of the seventeenth century by focusing on Paris and the academic, official painters. We know that the provinces clung to their autonomy, making repeated attempts to evade Le Brun's authoritarianism. Very little attuned to the spirit of the Grand Monarch, Watteau looked elsewhere than to the Academy for inspiration. Coming from the northernmost provinces, he hastened the disintegration of Classicism. Whereas the seventeenth century generally had glorified Italian art and worshiped Raphael, he looked up to Flemish artists and to Rubens. His contemporary d'Argenville tells us that "Rubens and Van Dyck, whose colors had enchanted him, were his true models." This Walloon was known as the "Flemish painter" to his contemporaries, and the same d'Argenville felt it necessary to point out that "he is reputed to be French, a subject of the King." Moreover, instead of going to Rome like other painters, he went to London at the end of his short life, ruining whatever health was left him in the foggy climate. He thus brought to the English School certain elements that it was eventually, in the nineteenth century, to give back to France in more developed form, with Turner and Bonington (Figs. 239 and 240).

REVISING SOME HISTORICAL CONCEPTS.  Watteau obliges us to put some of our most traditional conceptions aside. Despite his dates and the powerful regime he lived under, he was really a throwback to an older tradition, in his own day momentarily eclipsed. He would have been more at home in the sixteenth century, when the sensibility was so much less constrained—indeed, occasionally quite outrageously remote from that order and balance of which official seventeenth-century art was so fond. He recalls a host of sixteenth-century themes, deriving from the Middle Ages, that had still been very much alive under Louis XIV's predecessor. Among these are the cult of woman and the celebration of love, in nature, to the accompaniment of music. A tribe of aristocratic shepherds had inspired French poetry ever since the thirteenth century, from the *Roman de la Rose* through the pastoral genre and the courtly novels contemporary with the Précieuses, down to the famous *Carte du Tendre*. The same medieval current in England produced Shakespeare's sonnets, Hilliard's refined miniatures, and passionate Elizabethan music. We must not be surprised that an Englishman, Horace Walpole—who was a familiar figure in the salons of eighteenth-century Paris—first perceived Watteau's true ancestry and influences. He saw Watteau's works as "a kind of unreal pastoral," and observed that "his genre resembles that of his compatriot Honoré d'Urfé," whose famous *Astrée*, illustrating the loves of the shepherd Céladon, was published between 1610 and 1627, to the delight of an entire generation. Woman and nature, love and music had indeed been primary themes of inspiration until the moment when Malherbe appeared on the scene and Boileau set himself up as the regulating authority in poetry. Although Watteau's Northern origin suffices to account for his affinities with Flemish art, his infatuation with the past is somewhat less obviously accounted for. To begin with, Watteau was a pupil of Gillot, an artist who was inspired by the Italian comedy. Now, the Italian comedy came to France in the age of the court of the Valois. Do not the first paintings in which it is represented date from the sixteenth century? Gillot's engravings often bring to mind Jacques Callot who, like Bellange, belonged to the Lorraine group. Under Louis XIII those artists were frequently preoccupied with the irrational, and the same school eventually produced Claude Lorrain. As a border province, Lorraine was especially resistant to Versailles' centralizing tendencies. But what about Watteau's second teacher, Claude Audran? A great decorator, he served as "concierge" of the Luxembourg palace, i.e., he watched over its collections of art. Through him, Watteau came to be housed in one of the dependencies of the palace, before which stood those lovely gardens whose poetry even Caylus felt—though Watteau felt it more intensely. "He was always making drawings," Caylus writes, "of the trees in that beautiful garden which, being less well tended than the gardens of other royal establishments, supplied him with an endless number of vistas... sometimes by differences between the same view seen from different spots... and sometimes [here Impressionism rears its head, but timidly] by differences between the morning and evening sun on the same spots." So we must note how contact with nature—a contact otherwise all but lost in the seventeenth century—served Watteau as a link with the sensibility of an earlier age (Fig. 243).

Audran was also in charge of the mural paintings in the Luxembourg palace, which included, most notably, the great series of the *Life of Marie de Médicis* by Rubens. Watteau was in a position to see it as often as he liked. His native tendency to go back to the example of Northern artists, in preference to the Italians, was thus encouraged (Figs. 237 and 238).

At the same time Audran was himself a painter, the cultivator of an old genre called "grotesque." The genre, though it goes back to the Romans, owed its survival to a sixteenth-century rediscovery of some Alexandrian pictures that decorated the Baths of Titus or, perhaps, the Golden House. This was anything but an orthodox seventeenth-century interest, and it contained Venetian strains. True Classicists had repudiated the genre from antiquity on. What indignation sensible Romans had for it under Augustus is well conveyed in Vitruvius' bristling words. "How is it possible," he wrote in his *Treatise*

**236. - WATTEAU. THE VALLEY OF THE BIÈVRE AND THE CHURCH TOWER OF GENTILLY.** Drawing in red chalk. Musée Fabre, Montpellier

*on Architecture,* "that reeds could actually support a roof or that candelabra could hold up the cupola of a little temple with all its ornamentation, or that a fragile plant stem could support a seated figurine? And yet, although people realize that these fantasies are completely false, they do not criticize them; they even take pleasure in them. This happens because the intellect is dimmed." And he added that one must not "judge paintings before one has discovered lucid, well-founded reasons that clear up difficulties."

The passage reflects eternal antagonism between the logical spirit of rationalism and good sense, on the one hand, and the spirit of freedom, fantasy, magic, and escape, on the other. The latter reached Rome from Alexandria or perhaps even from ancient Mesopotamia, and, via Rome, reached France. There it flowered, for example, at Fontainebleau, to which Poussin advised young painters to go for their own instruction. Engravings by Enea Vico particularly contributed to the popularity of this manner; du Cerceau sometimes imitated these closely and gave currency to the style. It must be kept in mind that early in the eighteenth century descendants of artists who had painted under Francis I could still be found in the workshops of Fontainebleau.[1]

THE BACKWARD LOOK. What elements did Watteau borrow from sixteenth-century traditions of art? To begin with, his proportions: his figures are tall and slim, and do not correspond to the normalizing, Classical canon of the seventeenth century. Rather, they bring to mind the Mannerists. Nor must we forget that he worked in the house of the financier Crozat, an extremely wealthy individual who was often ironically referred to by his contemporaries as "the poor man." He owned an admirable collection of drawings, including four hundred drawings by Parmigianino! Thus, the heritage of Mannerism reached Watteau in works by Primaticcio, Parmigianino, and their rivals. The same elongated quality is also found in his compositions involving imaginary décor, in which

[1] In August 1804, Mlle. du Bois d'Arneuville, a descendant of Ambroise Dubois, lived at Fontainebleau. There she married Colonel Lagorsse, who had been in charge of the guards of Pius VII during the latter's forced residence at the Palace!

*We admire the realism of some details, for instance, this dog hunting fleas; it comes from the pictorial world of Rubens!*

**237.** - *WATTEAU.* GERSAINT'S SIGNBOARD (detail). State Museums, Berlin

**238.** - *RUBENS.* CORONATION OF MARIE DE MÉDICIS (detail). The Louvre, Paris

flexible stems and reeds support architectural elements. There can be no doubt that it is evocative of femininity.

More than any other French artist—within the oscillation between the virile and the feminine strain, as we have said—Watteau contributed to the eventual revival of the feminine strain, which had been well-nigh nonexistent under Louis XIV (Fig. 235). He thus resuscitated the tradition of the court of the Valois, where men had made a great effort to adjust themselves to feminine refinement and sensibility—a tradition that, at the beginning of the *grand siècle*, was still upheld in the *Salon bleu* of Arthénice, by Madame de Rambouillet, and even—why deny it?—by the Précieuses. Molière might have been describing a Watteau when he has Madelon, in the *Précieuses ridicules*, explain that declarations of love "should usually be made in a path of some garden, when the rest of the company has moved on a bit...." The lines are in the tradition of pastoral poems and amorous intrigues by which Watteau is related to the beginning of the seventeenth century, and through it to the sixteenth-century tradition of the "courts of love." When, in 1585–88, Nicolas de Montreuil wrote *Le premier livre des Bergeries de Juliette,* "in which, through the love affairs of shepherds and shepherdesses, one may observe the various effects of love," he seems to be outlining the subject matter of Watteau's art. This tradition continued throughout the seventeenth century. Honoré d'Urfé's *Astrée*, published between 1610 and 1637, was read by La Fontaine—the freedom and independence of whose verse often heralds Watteau. La Fontaine wrote the libretto for an opera based on *Astrée*, calling the latter an exquisite work. Referring to d'Urfé he wrote:

> I read his novel as a little boy
> And I still read it now my beard is gray.

In 1691 appeared his five-act tragedy based on the same work, with a musical score by Colasse—when Watteau was seven years old.

Madeleine de Scudéry in *Clélie* created the *Carte du Tendre,* the map of an imaginary land

*There is, however, an undercurrent of Northern realism in Watteau's poetic world: the curiosity of this indiscreet fellow is very… Flemish*

**239. -** *WATTEAU.* L'INDISCRET. Boymans-Van Beuningen Museum, Rotterdam

of the heart that brings to mind Watteau's *Cythera.* She died in 1701, not quite twenty years before Watteau, and her novels continued to be popular in circles other than Versailles. Her *Mathilde* was reprinted in 1702 and 1706; her *Ibrahim*, as late as 1723! Similarly the inaccessible island of *Polexandre* published by Gomberville in 1632 brings to mind Watteau's *Enchanted Island*, which anticipates the island of Cythera. This was the background Horace Walpole recognized so much more readily than Watteau's own countrymen, and called attention to.

Watteau's fondness for Van Dyck is related both to the Flemish influence and to his nostalgia for the pastoral art of the reign of Louis XIII. The costumes his figures wear are rarely those of his own day—they go back to the age of Van Dyck. Watteau kept trunkloads of gleaming silks and satins, cast-off theatrical costumes in the tradition of the Italian comedy. He asked friends to wear them when they posed for him. No doubt they gratified his personal taste, which is in many ways close to Van Dyck's. Watteau may be closer to the latter than to Rubens, though it is certain that in the works of Rubens he found a certain romantic quality, particularly in the landscapes. His own landscapes break with the academic tradition and go back to that of Rubens, reviving his immaterial trees, fluid with life, rising up into the sky like smoke. The great Antwerp artist, who

*Occasionally Watteau discloses his realistic vein by his affinity with Chardin, which is apparent here both in the treatment of the interior and the still life it contains.*

**240.** - *WATTEAU.* A TASK FOR EVERY AGE. Private collection

was fond of introducing medieval castles into his landscapes, had already conveyed something of the pre-Romantic quality which is more strongly marked in Watteau.

However, our painter found more of this pre-Romantic quality in Van Dyck. Here he encountered echoes of his own most intimate being. His real affiliation was with that race of refined, elegant, sad young men, seemingly in poor health, who never laugh. Dressed in satin, they stand silhouetted against darkening skies. Night is falling and one can almost hear the sound of the hunting horns blowing the mort in the distance.

Watteau in a sense goes back to Ronsard, the poet of woman and nature, though he lacks Ronsard's robustness and sunny good health. Watteau more nearly reflects the refinement of the Elizabethan epoch, and, like Van Dyck, he adds to it the melancholy of good things that have passed. What Claude Lorrain merely suggests, Watteau seizes upon and develops. Claude has taken us to the very edge of dry land, where water and light, those fluid elements, come into their own. Watteau has a boat waiting, to set sail for distant islands bathed in a dreamy, spectral sea. All the pretty screens with which Classical reason shut us off from the mysteries of the sensibility collapse. Now, the bland, ordered constructions of the architects fade away in the leafy shade of a dimly discernible undergrowth; dogmas of eternal, immutable truth vanish in the ever-changing cycle of the days and seasons. Watteau's figures move away from the viewer and often turn their backs. In what is a true pictorial innovation, they seem slowly drawn away from us into the openings in the verdure by the ineffable appeal of Cythera in the distance, swept away like leaves upon a stream. They are on the point of vanishing into the horizon as night slowly falls. Verlaine expressed it very well:

> ... ces instants sereins
> Qui m'ont conduit et t'ont conduite,
> Mélancoliques pèlerins,
> Jusqu'à cette heure dont la fuite
> Tournoie au son des tambourins.

[Those serene moments which led me on and led you on, melancholy pilgrims, to the time which, when it goes, swirls to the sound of tamburines.]

But whither are they all headed,

> avec des airs de nonchalance
> et des mouvements d'aile

[so carelessly, with such wing-like movements], to quote Verlaine again? They are inexorably, like the painter, headed "for other climes, for other loves," for the end of all things, death itself.

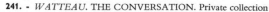

**241. -** *WATTEAU.* THE CONVERSATION. Private collection

TEMPERAMENT, SENSIBILITY, IMAGINATION. Watteau's short life seems to have been one protracted bout of feverishness: his own poor health, his burning devotion to art, his unappeased longing for love. This feverishness has a name: the Romantics called it "consumption"; physicians today call it "tuberculosis." Some of the latter[1] have investigated its effects on the patient's sensibility and whole personality. They have singled out the artists and poets who are related by their common malady, grouping Watteau next to Van Dyck, and beside Van Dyck—who died at forty-four—stand Parmigianino and Purcell who died at thirty-three, Mozart at thirty-five, Chopin at thirty-nine, Keats at twenty-six, Laforgue at twenty-seven, Giorgione at thirty-three, and Le Sueur at thirty-nine. How can we briefly define the character of these men who died so much before their time? All of them were gripped by great hopes, by an adolescent's expectations and desire to live. They did not so much burn themselves out as burn to be burned. The flame that consumed them came from within. And all their sleeping and waking thoughts were for love—life is love to an adolescent. They whisper with Laforgue:

[1] Following Dr. Roger Amsler's *Psychologie du tuberculeux dans la littérature contemporaine*, Dr. Vincent Rolle in 1945 published a comparative study on *A. Watteau, J. Laforgue, K. Mansfield*. A complete bibliography would have to list several other writings on this subject.

*The transition from reality, which Watteau uses as his point of departure, to dream, into which he escapes, is illustrated by these two paintings. In the first, Watteau or his double in contemporary dress pays awkward court to a cold beauty. In the second, the couple in theatrical costumes is well on its way to Cythera.*

**242. -** *WATTEAU.* VISTA IN CROZAT'S GARDEN AT MONTMORENCY. Museum of Fine Arts, Boston

> Jupes de quinze ans, aurores de femmes,
> Qui veut, enfin, du palais de mon âme?

[Skirts of fifteen, dawning women, which is to take at last the palace of my soul?]

I think that Watteau throughout his life carried this palace of his soul within him, although I do not know whether he ever populated it with anything but dreams. Watteau, usually looked upon as a great ladies' man, was actually—as all his biographers tell us—melancholy, shy, withdrawn. It would be a mistake to suppose that his life resembled that of his pictures: his paintings were all dreams. Watteau was sickly and lonely. The island that haunted him throughout his short life, that he yearned for with all his heart, that he could not wait to reach, he called his "Cythera," but it turned out to be death. Laforgue will have a similar figure of speech: "My pale island is at the pole, but at the last of poles...." These young men were consumed with desire—desire that never achieves possession. In women they grasp only the charm and femininity, not the flesh. They are made drunk with the silks and satins and the rustling gowns. Their desire remains at the stage of expectation, it never knows the satiety that can come with possession. But at the same time they are haunted with the obscure feeling that they are about to die, that they will not have the time to live. Like Mozart, like Chopin, they desire that which will come, but they are infatuated with everything that passes away. All they have not yet achieved takes on the quality of a mirage that slips away from them, that can never quite be captured, that fades into the distance even as they start toward it. Michelet perceived this keenly. "As for the Journey to Cythera which these gentle young pilgrims are making for the first time, he stays behind, saying goodbye. What he paints is only his dream, his hope of going with them. He sees them off, but he himself stands on the shore. His life was altogether different: it was one continuous departure, will to be off, preparations for the journey." So soon farewell: when it is barely morning, it is already evening, of which Laforgue was always singing:

> Ah! ce soir j'ai le cœur mal, le cœur à la Lune,
> O nappes de silence, étalez vos lagunes...."

Farewell to the day, and farewell to the season, too.... Not only is the sun setting, the summer is over and done. Watteau's scene is always set at dusk, but also it is always autumn:

> Complainte de l'automne monotone,
> Automne, automne, adieux de l'Adieu
> Est-il de vrais yeux?
> Nulle ne songe à m'aimer un peu....

Without carrying the parallel with Laforgue too far, we might quote, right after his farewell to the day and the season, his farewell to the figures who are leaving:

> Tu t'en vas et tu nous quittes;
> Tu nous quittes et tu t'en vas....

And in his *Légendes* he finds Verlaine prompting the conclusion, "Since sooner or later we shall die...."

I once tried to sum up this attitude of the soul in a formula, and I said that Watteau was one of those men who of the future know hope, of the past melancholy, but of the present nothing. What a pleasant surprise it has been to find Novalis (who was one of the fevered

*Watteau's landscape seems to be made of shadows and mists. It still has something of Leonardo's dreaminess, and foreshadows Corot's reverie.*

**243.** - *WATTEAU.* THE VILLAGE BRIDE (detail of the landscape). Soane's Museum, London

ones) giving a similar definition of his hero, Heinrich von Ofterdingen: "His whole soul was nothing but a tender *lied*, a direct expression of Nostalgia and Aspiration." This is Watteau in a nutshell. And this dual movement of the soul was subtly analyzed by a poet who loved Watteau so much that he dreamed of composing a drama around *The Indifferent* —I refer to Pierre Louÿs. He noted in his diary, referring to himself, "For I live little in the present; the past charms me and the future attracts me. I live in dream and recollection."

Watteau was one of those beings who avoid—or merely ignore—the blaze of noon, that overpoweringly brilliant noon that Valéry saluted in *Le Cimetière marin*. Their aspirations for what does not as yet exist are transmuted without any intervening transition into a farewell to what is passing away, perhaps is already no more. All of them, like Watteau, seem characterized by a feverish intensity, at odds with the precariousness of their lives. They shiver and they burn. And, for this reason, they rank first in the history of those who ushered in the reign of the individual and his secret life in art. Watteau's painting is not at the service of any collectively recognized iconography. It is neither a vehicle for the expression of the sacred themes of religion, nor one for portraying the pagan myths of traditional Western culture. The subject scarcely matters in his painting; the purpose of his art does not reside in his subjects, nor does he rely upon them for support, as Poussin did. His subject is merely a pretext for expressing his own feelings and communicating them to others. As we look at his pictures, we feel the artist himself putting one dry, emaciated hand, as nervous and burning as the hands of his figures, on our shoulder and silently pressing it. These works are the effort of a man to express what is most essential in him by means other than the customary language. Is not just this the truest, the most difficult kind of Romanticism? Watteau's figures in their exquisite satins, singing their carefree madrigals, are there only for the purpose of providing his feverish fingers with puppets to act out on the stage of his soul his innermost desires, regrets, and yearnings. And, as if painting alone were not equal to this task, he continually evokes music, as Giorgione did. Moreover, his painting itself becomes music (Fig. 231).

This is the role that Delacroix later assigned to painting. But Watteau's own personality was remote from the brash heroics of his illustrious descendant.

He is of a race of poet-painters, individual members of which turn up in all ages. Watteau proves his membership in it, above all, by succeeding in being himself, by making his art a dream image of his inner being. Whereas, in daily life, he *lived* it out, in his art he *saw* himself and enabled others to see it. He had no use for the expressions and passions whose absence in his work was deplored by Caylus. His work is otherwise animated,

filled by a presence that leaves no room for anything else—his innermost being. This presence is insistent, as obsessive in his pictures as the headiest of perfumes. To every viewer an individual being is revealed so intimately that the viewer's own innermost being is touched and responds according to his affinities with the painter's. Although the self revealed is strikingly integrated, it is also sufficiently nuanced and complex to arouse unlimited echoes.

Watteau is unquestionably a painter of joy, who pursues life as prolongation of his own dreams, his own capacities for the subtlest and most vibrant of pleasures. But he is a painter of sadness, too, because he senses the fragility and ephemeralness of life, which is an undoing as well as a doing, whose glory fades as rapidly as the great fiery ball of the sun sinks below the horizon (though we must look right at it to see how rapidly it sinks). The word for this in the language of words is "twilight." It applies equally to the half-light of morning and of evening. Watteau, too, signifies both dawn and dusk.

*Art is perhaps a mask, but, as in the Italian comedy, it reveals the character of those who think they can hide behind it.*

**244.** - MASKED MAN: SCARAMOUCHE.
Engraving after Watteau in Julienne's compilation

*The individualist aesthetics was formulated by Delacroix and Baudelaire. The poet was so impressed by the painter that he imitated the cut of his beard after meeting him in 1845.*

**245. -** DAGUERREOTYPE OF
DELACROIX IN 1845.
Bibliothèque Nationale, Paris

**246. -** PORTRAIT OF BAUDELAIRE
drawn by himself in 1848 and etched by
Bracquemond. Bibliothèque Nationale, Paris

# 2. FROM THE AESTHETIC
# OF THE INDIVIDUAL TO THE MULTIPLICATION
# OF THE SELF

IN the nineteenth century, the vague aspirations that great artists like Watteau had expressed by means of their personal genius alone and unaided gave rise to a formal aesthetics —the aesthetics of individualism. The hitherto prevalent doctrines, far from stressing what distinguished men from one another, had on the contrary been solely concerned with what we all have in common. The older theories had stressed the importance of a model to be imitated with perfect fidelity; and this model, being the same for all, had universal value. The older literary theories demonstrate this no less than theories of the fine arts.

Some painters, for instance the Flemish Primitives, saw nature as an objective datum, and tried to reproduce it as faithfully as they could. This visual conformity with physical reality was not incompatible with the aim of expressing spiritual realities, but the latter reflected a single religious faith, the as yet uncontested foundation of society.

Prior to the philosophers of ancient Greece, aesthetics had been a matter of instinctive feeling; ever since they appeared, however, theoreticians had sought to define it according to concepts of beauty. This beauty was conceived as a kind of superior, invisible reality, an immaterial model of perfection that artists had to seek out and find among the confused reflections of it provided by nature. Though abstract, the model was conceived as external to the individual, the same for all men by definition, hence objective.

A principle of identity was at the bottom of this traditional aesthetics: identity essential between visual appearances and intellectual concepts of those appearances.

*In this Classically austere studio Delacroix received Baudelaire for the first time.*

**247.** - DELACROIX'S STUDIO IN THE RUE
NOTRE-DAME-DE-LORETTE.
Engraving. Published in *L'Illustration*,
July 25, 1842

RISE OF AN INDIVIDUALIST AESTHETICS. As the medieval epoch came to its close, its characteristic collective solidarity began to disintegrate and a new sense of individualism gradually made itself felt. Man became increasingly aware of his own autonomy as a separate person. The ancient ideal, according to which artistic perfection consists of making truth visible or of rendering intellectually conceived types of beauty, gave way bit by bit to a pursuit of differentiation on the part of the artist—more accurately, to a desire on his part to give expression to what differentiates him from others. There is scarcely a better way to define modern times than this. It devolved upon the nineteenth century to carry out the revolution that had long been a-borning and to be the first age to give full scope to the previously ignored force of individualism.

Henceforth, art would be less and less a science consisting of technical rules for reproducing a model whether in nature or in the conscious mind. What had been held together so long as a single art—thanks to factitious rules and discipline—now broke up into as many arts as there are creators. Every artist now turned to himself and himself alone for authority: he began to explore the strange universe that he carries with him, inside himself, and he began to make discoveries about himself. He acquired a new sense of himself as the vehicle of something which had never existed before him and would never exist again after him, his own inner uniqueness. Art now seemed to him the sole possible means of giving permanent expression to that unique self.

Actually, every great painter, like every great poet—indeed, like every inspired man—has in all times and places pursued the goal of communicating to others his own inner riches, his own unique insights. Genius did not await its theoreticians to discover the freedom of the self. But, prior to the nineteenth century, this matter had not been fully understood, recognized, and explicitly formulated. For this reason the new ideas had always run into difficulties, when they opposed the contemporary official theories of art.

Delacroix and Baudelaire must be given credit for having clearly expressed these ideas for the first time. The poet was here the painter's disciple. It seems certain that Baudelaire met Delacroix in 1845, shortly after he had published the first *Salon*. He may well have seen him before this at the meetings in the Hôtel Pimodan, which will be referred to below. But it is probable that Baudelaire, who at the time was cultivating famous men and had given Delacroix prominent mention in his *Salon de 1845*, called on him in the studio at No. 54 Rue Notre-Dame-de-Lorette to which the artist had just moved. "Thanks to the sincerity of my admiration I was able, though still very young, to enter that notoriously well-guarded studio." What is important is that there are many indications, scattered through various of Baudelaire's writings and private papers, to confirm that this meeting crucially influenced his aesthetic ideas. After Delacroix's death, Baudelaire himself, in a letter to the editor of *L'Opinion Nationale,* repeated, as he says, "the words I once wrote almost as the master dictated them to me." He also observes that "to begin with" they discussed "the vastest and most profound questions." (It is interesting that Delacroix somewhere notes how Denis Diderot had once taken a young visitor into his confidence, being impressed by his intelligence.) This explains why within a few weeks of this meeting Baudelaire's ideas on art—until then hesitant, based primarily on immediate impressions— were formulated as a coherent intellectual ensemble perfectly attuned to Delacroix's ideas. In the *Salon de 1846* he was able to formulate what a contemporary called "the catechism of modern art." Indeed, this *Salon* contains the statement of a new aesthetic dogma, the same as that professed by Delacroix, as can be seen from the latter's numerous articles and his *Diary* (Figs. 245, 246, and 247).

What was that dogma?

To begin with, since the painter must by definition look at the visible world and make use of it to express himself, what place is he to assign reality or nature in art? That of a model to be reproduced? Obviously not. Just as the writer uses words common to all in order to communicate ideas that are his alone, the painter will make use of images common to all in order to suggest what he alone feels. What he will try to express visually is "the invisible... the intangible," according to Baudelaire, who goes on to develop a concept of supernaturalism, which he opposes to traditional naturalism. "The entire visible universe is nothing but a store of signs and images, a kind of nourishment that the imagination must assimilate and transform." Baudelaire here merely paraphrases Delacroix's own words, "Nature is a dictionary. . . . Even in the presence of nature, it is our imagination that makes the painting." Thus nature is reduced to a storehouse of images, a sort of dictionary compiled by the artist himself, in which he makes his own choice of words he needs to express his ideas. This view gives new and added importance to the imagination, now empowered to use nature as a means to its own ends, reducing the world to a mere list of signs to be combined at will.

A famous film by Cocteau showed the Poet confronting a mirror which reflects all there is to see and in which no one expects to find anything but things previously known. But the Poet senses a mystery behind the passive surface reflecting the familiar world, a mystery that he is determined to fathom. Suddenly, he leaps forward and breaks through the mirror: the usual mirage is dispelled, and the Poet dives slowly down into the obscure depths, into a world existing beyond the appearances he has left behind. When, eventually, he comes back to the surface, like a pearl diver, he is laden with the treasures he has found. Where did they come from, those treasures, if not from his own innermost depths?


THE INNER UNIVERSE.   External reality is no longer the artist's ultimate goal, but his point of departure—and remains indispensable as such. Delacroix told Huet that he did not possess a pure imagination and that all his creative visions originated in actual observa-

*In this painting, which shows the poet jeered by the madmen who surround him, as well as in the painting showing Christ deserted by His own disciples, Delacroix portrayed the solitude of the genius.*

**248.** - DELACROIX. TASSO IN THE MADHOUSE. 1824. Formerly Collection Sir Kenneth Clark

tion. Nature now serves as a springboard by means of which the artist takes off into the realms of private fantasy.

We can follow Baudelaire as he does this, in the poem *La Chevelure*, "*toison, moutonnant jusque sur l'encolure.*" He spread it out with his fingers, breathes into it, "*je la veux agiter dans l'air comme un mouchoir,*" and suddenly "*l'alcôve obscure*" is thronged with an uprush of memories which had been "*dormant dans cette chevelure.*" The imagination has taken wing, and the poet is possessed of an "*éblouissant rêve de voiles, de rameurs, de flammes et de mâts*" beyond which lies "*la langoureuse Asie et la brûlante Afrique.*" As the poem unfolds, we follow, line by line, the quick flight of the imagination, whose point of departure had been familiar sensations imposed by reality. But these sensations take on new and richer meanings in the soul of the poet, stirring up multiple echoes, until he—and we with him—is carried away to another world.

What is this other world that the imagination can attain to, taking reality for springboard? It is an inner universe, situated within ourselves, that has no landmarks and no language of

432

**249.** - *DELACROIX*. THE AGONY IN THE GARDEN. 1826/27. Watercolor.
Formerly Koechlin Collection; The Louvre, Paris

its own but only such features and tongue as our expressive power can give it. It is the spirit. Hitherto, the term has been used in a different sense, today almost obsolete in French usage.

For it is indeed the creator's own spirit that the work of art now attempts to communicate to the viewer and to add to his experience. Delacroix anticipated Baudelaire when he envisaged the work of art as a kind of "bridge between souls," and went on to say that "the principal source of interest springs from the spirit, and it flows irresistibly to the viewer's spirit." Baudelaire in 1855 used the following words to describe the great Romantic's *Lion Hunt*, "Never have more beautiful, more intense colors reached so deeply into the spirit through the channel of the eyes." From spirit to spirit, through the channel of the eyes—this is the outline of a new aesthetics. The program, however, still needs to be worked out in practical terms.

The goal of art is thus to manifest the inner universe that man holds in his depths, whose secret Hamlet had pondered when he examined Yorick's skull—a passage Delacroix was fond of quoting.

Delacroix saw clearly the difficulties in any such enterprise. Every man is inaccessible to other men, an impenetrable mystery. Delacroix painted several versions of Tasso meditating in a madhouse, utterly absorbed in his own thoughts, oblivious to the screaming madmen around him. Baudelaire, meanwhile, created the allegory of the albatross condemned never to fly again, "amid taunts and jeers." Delacroix was haunted by "impressions that I experience alone in my own way." There is a threshold to be crossed before we can gain access to the invisible and inexpressible reaches of our innermost being. Art must break through the barrier, breach it, if the inner sources are to be tapped for mankind. As early as 1824, Delacroix set himself this goal: "You can add another soul to those who have looked on nature in their own way" (Figs. 248 and 249).

German thinkers in this period were stressing the opposition between the non-I, or external reality, and the I. Armed with visual impressions borrowed from the outside world, art will, nonetheless, acquire the ability to reveal the essence of the inner world. Every man has his own individual way of feeling and of seeing—a way that reflects his innermost being. Proust was later to write, in *La Prisonnière*, "The universe is true for all of us and dissimilar to each of us.... It is not one universe, but millions of universes, almost as many of them as there are eyes and minds that awaken every morning." The task of the painter will be to portray this universe, to provide an image of it.

Our sensations are not merely passive records. Initially, they bring us an echo of the outside world, but, before they have run their course, they have acted upon our nervous system, giving it a shock that awakens resonances peculiar to it. Similarly, when we strike bronze bells with a hammer, each gives off a sound peculiarly its own.

The realist seeks primarily to be faithful to his own sensations insofar as they reflect a reality outside himself. Henceforth, in reproducing the artist's sensations, art will rather be concerned with revealing the particular expressive features that these sensations take on in each of us. "The imagination alone," Delacroix says, "shows us things where others see nothing, and it shows them in a different way." But how can the artist make others see things in a different way?

THE KEYBOARD OF SENSATIONS.   The elements that the artist borrows from reality must be compelled to render what was only within the artist himself. How can we make a tree express the mysterious sadness of the woods? How can familiar images be made to express something that only the artist feels when he sees them?

Art can not only imitate things, as has been supposed for so long, but also suggest them. In music, the minor mode predisposes the listener to melancholy, the major mode to

*The theme of struggles in which man and beast unleash their utmost energies is particularly suitable for the feverish hatchings of Delacroix.*

**250. -** *DELACROIX.* LION THROWING AN ARAB TO THE GROUND. Drawing. Private collection

exaltation. Lines and colors have a similar effect. They can both describe emotional states and reflect them. If the artist succeeds in imprinting his own emotional states on them, they will inevitably awaken an echo in the viewer. Poussin's theory of the modes was based on this insight (Figs. 254, 255, 256, and 257).

This emotional impregnation may be instinctive to some extent. A person's handwriting unconsciously reflects his temperament and inclinations; this circumstance is at the basis of

*Only two fragments survive of this painting, whose composition is given in the sketch. Here Delacroix placed the passions of his soul under the sign of music.*

**252.** - *At left: DELACROIX.* PORTRAIT OF CHOPIN. 1838. The Louvre, Paris

**253.** - *Above: DELACROIX.* Sketch for GEORGE SAND LISTENING TO CHOPIN PLAYING THE PIANO. The Louvre, Paris

graphology. Psychologists have also tried to discover hidden relations between the handwriting and the drawing of great artists. Certain Raphael and Rembrandt drawings containing written characters reveal such relations. And, even though color does not lend itself to a similar study, it is just as eloquent as line. Delacroix knew this better than anyone, but he added, "It affects us without our knowing it, so to speak."

"Without our knowing it"—the concept of the unconscious makes its appearance here! Neither Delacroix nor Baudelaire employed this term, although the Germans were just beginning to; nevertheless, the unconscious is involved here. Until then, the most important thing in a work of art had been supposed to be what it represented. At this time, the artist's manner of representing things came more and more to be regarded as the important thing. As the artist became increasingly aware of his powers, he extended them. To an ever greater extent, he was concerned with exploiting the suggestive resonance that plays the same part in images as the intonation of the voice plays in speech. The viewer is affected by it: "We are exposed to mysterious shocks that our spirit... withdrawn in its most immaterial reaches, receives almost without being aware of it," Delacroix wrote. But the artist can become aware of them and he can deliberately organize the effect he wants to produce. Between two widely separated poles—the positively charged pole of the creator and the negatively charged pole of the viewer—the art of the former can produce a spark in the latter. As he learns the tonal qualities of every sensation and becomes able to control more and more of them, he will associate or combine them to reinforce their separate actions, and play upon the harmonious relations that he set up between them.

**251.** - *DELACROIX.* PORTRAIT OF GEORGE SAND (unfinished). 1838. Museum of Ordrupgaard, near Copenhagen

*Developing the principle formulated by Poussin, Delacroix combines line, light, form, color to endow the feeling embodied by the subject with its greatest communicative force.*

**254. -** *DELACROIX.* CHRIST ON THE WATERS. Private collection

The artist and the poet now began to dream of a "total art," capable of acting upon the innermost reaches of the spirit, capable of awakening its inexpressible affinities with all of the inexpressible things there are. Delacroix imagined symphonies performed while the audiences are shown paintings intended to "supplement the impression." Baudelaire outlined a still more ambitious program of synesthesia in the famous line, *"Les parfums, les couleurs et les sons se répondent."*

This artist-poet and this poet-artist trained themselves to anticipate, on the keyboard of sensations, the notes that would arouse in other spirits echoes of the incommunicable they perceived within themselves. They made this incalculable discovery for themselves and were the first to formulate consciously what they had done. Their discovery became the basis of modern art: that it is not what a sensation refers to in the outside world that matters but what it evokes in the self. The artist treats it not as a fact, but as a magic formula for producing a particular effect. He hurls it at us like a stone, computing and harmonizing the ripples that it will produce, in ever-widening circles, in our nervous system. He knows what color or line or word he must use to arouse the precise tone of joy or sorrow that he is after.

Combining the effects of drawing, palette, and composition, he exploits the whole keyboard of sensations artfully, harmonically, until our spirit is touched at the ineffable point of junction and fusion. The poet's task, whether he expresses himself in words or visual images, becomes to select, with his special powers of intuition, the right suggestive elements in reality and then to arrange them as effectively as he is able. The bouquet of sensations so composed will give off a fragrance of his own feelings capable of being communicated to others.

In his article on the Exposition universelle de 1855 Baudelaire analyzed the method with great insight. In a passage of his poem *Les Phares* he had written:

> Delacroix, lac de sang hanté des mauvais anges,
> Ombragé par un bois de sapins toujours verts,
> Où, sous un ciel chagrin, des fanfares étranges
> Passent, comme un soupir étouffé de Weber.

And here is his own comment on these lines: "Lake of blood: his red; haunted by evil angels: his supernaturalism; a woods forever green: the green complementary to the red; under a troubled sky: the stormy water scenes he paints; the flourish of trumpets and Weber: ideas of Romantic music suggested by his color harmonies."

Ideas of music! This is where it was all leading! This new aesthetics is indeed closely related to music, since it seeks to reach the viewer's innermost soul and compel it passively to mimic the creator's, thereby communicating the latter's impulses, his own most secret

255. - *DELACROIX.* THE DELIVERANCE OF PRINCESS ROWENA. 1860.
Private collection; on loan to the Museum of Bern

*In these paintings treating two successive themes of the Passion and executed ten years apart, Delacroix comes close to Rembrandt by his ability to create an effect of mystery with the help of shadows and to suggest intense feelings by the play of line and light.*

**256.** - *DELACROIX.* THE ENTOMBMENT.
1859. Private collection

emotions. You cannot escape from music. It is the only art that divests itself of all representation and is nothing but modulated time, the movement of inner life itself. Thus it will for a moment attune itself to the spirit that it covets, like a horseman making up to a horse that has never been ridden, and who, having soothed it, suddenly jumps on the animal and compels it to be no more than a docile, sensitive instrument of his will. *La musique du tableau!* Since Delacroix, this metaphor has been more and more often invoked, for it best expresses the new talents that painting called upon (Figs. 251, 252, and 253).

CREATIVE POWER.   It is now demanded of forms, colors, and lines that they arouse the sensibility, that they be recognized as evocative powers analogous to sounds. "Poetry comes close to music through a mysterious, unknown prosody," Baudelaire wrote, and Verlaine demanded "music above all else." This is why color, which is more affecting than the other elements of painting, took a pre-eminent place in Delacroix's art. In Classical painting, the artist's major instrument had been drawing, for it is most suitable for defining forms in a primarily intellectual way. Referring to the direct action of color upon the sensibility, Delacroix said, "You come into a cathedral, and, although you happen to be too far from the painting to know yet what it represents, still you may already fall under the spell of its magical harmony."

Magical harmony…. Here the creator is indeed restored to his superhuman role, his true greatness! It is no longer enough to study diligently, like the realists, not to cultivate one's mind by the ordinary disciplines of knowledge. No truth accessible to all men any longer suffices—neither native skill nor acquired learning. The true nature of poetic creation is finally revealed as the possession of supernatural powers.

The development toward individualism terminates in the modern conception of creative genius. The Abbé Dubos, a great French aesthetician whose value is often slighted today,

**257.** - *DELACROIX*. PIETA. 1848.
Museum of Fine Arts, Boston

saw this coming early in the eighteenth century. He wrote prophet-
ically, "Lines of poetry should be
able to stir the heart and arouse the
feelings they suggest.... A poem, no
more than a painting, can produce
this effect so long as its sole merit is
regularity and elegance of execution.... These are but the means to
bring into play beauties of a superior
order.... But to be able to invent,
one must be born with genius." One
must possess "the divine enthusiasm
that transforms painters into poets
and poets into painters." Delacroix,
a century later, said much the same
thing. "Who says art, says poetry.
There is no art without a poetic
goal." Nor would Baudelaire have
disagreed.

This accounts for the fact that the
old conception of art, which aimed
above all at an ideal perfection,
more and more gave way to a conception of art as a creation, whose
primordial value is originality. Leibniz, that great genius, had already found in the
aesthetic act a power "to produce something that resembles the works of God, though on
a smaller scale." The purpose is not, however, to reflect God by copying his creations, as
the realists do, nor to discover their secret beauty, as the idealists try to do. The German
philosopher stressed the fact that works of art must not be "mirrors or images of the universe of created things ... but also images of the Godhead itself... capable of imitating
certain elements of 'the system of the universe' in the form of architectonic samples, each
mind being like a little Godhead in its own compartment." This bold new idea was hardly
more than outlined by Leibniz. Romanticism brought it up to date and made it its fundamental dogma, so that Lamennais could say, "Art is to man what the creative power is
to God," and Baudelaire spoke of *l'Homme-Dieu*, the "Man-God."

In order to stimulate in the poet and the artist this mysterious, to some extent divine
power to create, the nineteenth century looked for stimulants capable of transporting the
individual beyond himself. No single development was more alien to the Classical spirit.
Man's ambition is indeed insatiable, for no sooner had he, after centuries of effort, taken
full possession of his personality, than he strove to go beyond it. This is a development
that must be treated with proper respect for the secrecy which it was at first embarked
upon.

441

*Toward the end of their lives, Delacroix and Baudelaire, in spite of certain similarities, present the contrast between will crowning personality and surrender to impulses threatening to ruin it.*

**258. -** *At left:* PHOTOGRAPH OF DELACROIX TOWARD THE END OF HIS LIFE

**259. -** *At right:* PHOTOGRAPH OF BAUDELAIRE TOWARD THE END OF HIS LIFE

LE CLUB DES HASCHISCHINS. Théophile Gautier tells us that, late one bleak December afternoon in 1845, he took a cab to the Ile Saint-Louis. He went there, he says, in response to a mysterious summons. "I arrived in a distant quarter, an oasis of solitude in the very heart of Paris, that the river, by throwing its arms about it, seems to protect from the encroachments of civilization (Fig. 260).

"Although it was no more than six o'clock, it was already pitch dark.... The rain-soaked pavement glistened under the street lamps like a body of water reflecting an illumination. A cutting north wind whipped your face with icy particles, and its guttural whistling provided a treble to the bass lappings of the swollen river against the arches of the bridges.... Along these deserted *quais,* among the bunched mass of dark buildings, I was looking for a house. By standing up on his seat my coachman managed to read a half-tarnished plaque bearing the name of the old town house.... I lifted a sculptured hammer to knock, the use of bells having not as yet penetrated this remote region, and I heard the doorpull creak several times to no avail. Finally, yielding to a more vigorous pull, the rusty old latch gave, and the massive door began slowly to turn on its hinges." The name deciphered with so much effort was that of the Hôtel Lauzun or Pimodan, at 17 Quai d'Anjou. The place was as romantic as one could wish, and, precisely because of its isolation, the Ile Saint-Louis was chosen as place of residence by a number of artists and writers. The Quai d'Anjou at that time sheltered both Daubigny and Daumier. The Hôtel Lauzun itself had had many famous tenants, ever since Roger de Beauvoir had earlier in the century reclaimed it from the corporation of dyers. When he found it, he tells us, "it was an old Venetian palace on the banks of the Seine.... Here the noises of Paris did not carry, and here the bloodstream of the capital did not pulsate. Life passed this place by." In his *Stances* he added:

> ... C'est tout un monde
> D'oubli, de solitude et de splendeur profonde...
> Une tombe dorée au bout du vieux Paris.

[It is a whole world of oblivion, solitude, and hidden splendor... a gilded tomb on the edge of the oldest quarter of Paris.]

He had left it in March 1845, a few weeks before Baudelaire, who, since the fall of 1843, had occupied a strangely decorated little flat on the top floor. (This was the last prosperous period of Baudelaire's life.) The main floor consisted of a number of sumptuously paneled and gilded rooms containing paintings executed by pupils of Le Brun and Le Sueur, the decorations apparently having been the work of Lepautre.[1] The tenant who succeeded Beauvoir on the main floor was the painter Boissard de Boisdenier. Today, he is remembered only for his astonishing masterpiece, the *Episode de la retraite de Russie* in the Museum of Rouen. He was a pupil of Gros and a friend of Delacroix, and he often invited his acquaintances to private concerts in the salon of the Hôtel Lauzun. Music lovers gathered there to hear Bach, Mozart, Beethoven, and Mendelssohn. In his diary, Delacroix refers, now and again, to these evenings. Boissard himself took part in the chamber-music recitals, and Balzac, Delacroix, and Théophile Gautier were among the guests. Gautier himself became a tenant in the building a little later, in December 1849 (Fig. 261).

But what else was going on there? Gautier speaks of a "mysterious invitation composed in enigmatic terms understood only by the members to whom it was sent." Now, musical evenings scarcely demand such mystery. Delacroix puts us on the right track. He says that on May 22 he listened to Boissard de Boisdenier playing the violin, and adds that Boisdenier played "with the consent of those present, under the influence of hashish... something he had never tried before."

Perhaps we may learn more about this if we go back to our first guide, Théophile Gautier. Let us pass through the courtyard with him; we come to the grand staircase, which had already known so many avatars, its original stone demolished and replaced with wood, although in our own day it has finally been reconstructed.

We go upstairs and find ourselves before the doorway of a room hung with portions of Utrecht velvet. We walk in. "When one stepped inside that room, one was carried back two centuries in time. This house seemed to have stood still, like a clock nobody remembered to wind, its hands forever fixed." One was still in the seventeenth century (Fig. 265).

*Baudelaire lived here, Delacroix lived here, and here were held the meetings of the Club des Haschischins.*

**260. - PARIS, QUAI D'ANJOU;
FAÇADE OF THE HÔTEL LAUZUN**

[1] According to the convincing attribution of Mr. Fiske Kimball, former Director of the Philadelphia Museum, which has recently acquired some of these panels. It is greatly to be regretted that they no longer form part of this admirable ensemble.

443

*This unpublished painting by Boissard de Boisdenier, known only by one work, casts some light on this enigmatic artist.*

**261.** - *BOISSARD DE BOISDENIER.* RETREAT FROM RUSSIA.
Collection Mr. and Mrs. G. Seligman, New York

In the first drawing room, around a table, there was quite a gathering. In front of each guest, Gautier relates, was placed "a greenish paste or jelly, about an inch thick, and a silver-gilt spoon alongside it." The guests at this *dawamesk* were then served (according to both Gautier and Baudelaire) "a cup of coffee in the Arab manner," i.e., without sugar. Only afterward, according to a ritual familiar to students of hashish—for that was what the guests had been given—was supper served. The action of the coffee combined with that of the meal soon provoked the first effects of the drug. This was the moment for the guests to move into the grand drawing room. The effects of hashish are described in great detail in an article, "Le Club des Haschischins," by Théophile Gautier in the *Revue des Deux-Mondes* for February 1, 1846. Baudelaire, too, analyzes them in his *Paradis artificiels.*

"I felt a red flash under my eyelids," says Gautier, and, suddenly "everything was bigger, richer, more splendid. Reality served only as a starting point for magnificent hallucinations." Various other states ensued—calm, gaiety, terror—until the moment when Gautier (as any caricaturist might have foreseen) found himself bearing

*As for this unpublished Delacroix, it is no doubt the figure of Grief, which Baudelaire bought, sold, and bought back several times, and which was a haunting feature of the little flat the poet occupied in the Hôtel Lauzun.*

**262.** - *Opposite page:* DELACROIX. HEAD OF MAGDALENE. 1843. Collection Alfred Daber, Paris

*Romanticism dreamed of titanic visions. Everything was amplified and multiplied in a kind of intoxication of the imagination, reflecting the artist's obsessions.*

**263.** - *JAMES WARD*. GORDALE SCAR, YORKSHIRE. The Tate Gallery, London

an elephant's head on his shoulders. When he left, it took him no less than "ten thousand years" to walk down the stairs, he relates, for his sense of time had been affected no less than his vision.

THE MULTIPLICATION OF THE SELF.   We could go on stirring up the ashes of the past and might recount many more anecdotes and historical facts of this nature. But it is time to stop and ask what they actually tell us about the nineteenth-century mind and sensibility.

The fact that the taste for stimulants, especially for drug-induced "artificial paradises," appeared at this time is not simply a historical accident. Nineteenth-century man was really trying to go beyond his familiar self. Prior to the discovery of hashish and opium he had resorted to such simple means as wine and tobacco. Evidence of this is given by Balzac in 1838 in his *Traité des excitants modernes*, which he appended to the reissue of

Brillat-Savarin. No one kept a sharper eye for novelties than Balzac, yet his treatise lists only five rather anodyne products—alcohol, sugar, tea, coffee, and tobacco! Today, these artificial intoxicants scarcely strike us as dangerous, but, at the time, people were somewhat more easily impressed. Balzac warns that he is a danger to his hosts, for he can drink any amount of wine without reaching satiety and without feeling any ill effects. It is all well known what enormous quantities of coffee he consumed in the course of a day as a stimulant to his pen. Moreover, he recounts his earliest experiments with tobacco, which, as he describes it, produces effects comparable to those of hashish. When you have smoked five cigars, he says, "your brain acquires new faculties... you really soar away into the realms of fantasy." Of our own first experiments with cigars we would doubtless be less lyrical. But, then, the Romantic era is a thing of the past....

What these Romantics were seeking—and, perhaps, were rather ready to find—was a certain multiplication of the individual faculties, and, above all, stimulation of the faculty they held dearest, i.e., the imagination. In earlier ages, reason had been deemed the most valuable faculty, and this judgment persisted down to through the Encyclopedists of the eighteenth century, though they began to give "sensibility" a somewhat more respectable place than it had held in previous centuries. Beginning with the nineteenth century the imagination supplanted reason as the leading faculty, and so it had to be stimulated by every possible means.

A man as composed in his personal life as Delacroix, and as self-controlled, had a passion for tobacco, despite a persistent throat ailment of which he finally died. Nor, on occasion, was he averse to stimulation by wine. "In a state of half-drunkenness," he says, "certain men, and I am one, acquire a lucidity of vision far superior, in many instances, to their lucidity in the sober state."

What was Delacroix looking for, if not a kind of multiplication of himself, as it were, a heightening of his powers like the mathematical squaring, cubing, etc. of a number? But where Delacroix remained on the whole a highly self-controlled person, Musset (among others) went on to excess and eventual self-destruction.

The effect that the Romantics first sought in wine, they later found in certain narcotic drugs. Baudelaire, too, had begun by using wine as a stimulant to his imagination. In *Le Vin*, a series of poems published after 1850 but written earlier (surprisingly enough, published in a magazine called *The Family Magazine*), he celebrated in turn *L'Ame du Vin*, *Le Vin des Chiffonniers*, *Le Vin de l'Assassin*, *Le Vin du Solitaire*, and *Le Vin des Amants*.

> En toi je tomberai, végétale ambroisie,
> Grain précieux jeté par l'éternel Semeur,
> Pour que de notre amour naisse la poésie
> Qui jaillira vers Dieu comme une rare fleur!

Poetic flights of the imagination like the above—in the nineteenth century men sought these inside themselves, in the innate capacities of personal genius, but they were not above recourse to artificial stimulants to heighten, intensify, and extend the range of those capacities.

It is always fascinating to remark how the most unrelated elements within a given age run parallel. Nineteenth-century science, too, was at this time beginning to address itself to the interrelatedness of physiological and psychological factors in the human organism. In 1830 the great French psychiatrist Moreau de Tours published his *Physical Influences on*

*Disorders of the Intellectual Faculties.* The Romantic artists and poets who were then looking for stimulants more effective than alcohol may well have been led to the narcotic drugs by Moreau de Tours, for the Club des Haschischins was founded in 1845, the same year he published a pioneer work on *Hashish and Mental Alienation.*

However that may be, at this time literary circles began to experiment with hashish. Baudelaire took note of this development in March 1851, in his *Alcohol and Hashish as Means of Multiplying the Individuality.* The very title of his article reveals the goal of the Romantics—the multiplication of the self. Whereas the Classicists devote all their efforts to integration of the individual within patterns of social and artistic uniformity, the Romantics pursued the diametrically opposed goal of expanding the private self and cultivating the extremest ranges of its uniqueness.

However, by July 1858, only hashish seems to have held Baudelaire's attention. In his *Poème du Haschisch* he says that the effects of this drug are far more powerful than those of wine. The original title of the poem—later discarded—is significant: *De l'Idéal artificiel*— "On the Artificial Ideal" (Fig. 266).

In January 1860, he discovered opium, although he was not the first to have done so. He then wrote his *Mangeur d'Opium*, which contains a biography of Thomas de Quincey and an analysis of the latter's *Confessions of an English Opium-Eater* (which had been published in 1822).

Both hashish and opium are products imported from the Orient, which fed the Romantic imagination in so many ways (hashish is simply Indian hemp), and constituted one of several foreign influences that were revolutionizing French art and literature in this period. It was merely one of the many ways in which the dominance of reason in art and letters was being overturned, the expression of a desire to become *amens*, as the Romans would have said with revulsion. The German writer E. T. A. Hoffmann first popularized the custom of seeking in wine and drunkenness an imaginary transcendence of the self. Edgar Allan Poe, who wrote in English, came a generation later, and similarly cultivated alcohol as a source of inspiration and exaltation. Thomas de Quincey launched the fashion of consuming opium, the East India Company being the leading European trafficker in it at this time. German-language and English-language influences were thus of major importance in the search of hitherto unknown inner states as well as literary influences in the narrower sense.

AN EXPERIMENTAL ROMANTICISM. Just how significant were these experiments? The Romantic artists and writers were scarcely lacking in imagination, even without recourse to hashish. Shortly before his death, P. d'Espezel questioned the authenticity of these confessions, but careful scrutiny since has shown that they were sincere enough. To be sure, we must not suppose that the Club des Haschischins became

*At night, in the phosphorescent glow of the sea, the waves turn into sirens, chimeras. The ship looms like a monstrous head. Everything takes on a fantastic shape, everything becomes a hallucination in the over-stimulated human brain astern.*

**264.** - *GUSTAVE DORÉ.* ILLUSTRATION FOR THE RIME OF THE ANCIENT MARINER.
Woodcut by Jonnard

ART AND THE INDIVIDUAL

an established institution. It seems to have met only a few times, but the point is that it did meet. In his preface to *Les Fleurs du Mal*, Gautier paid tribute to "the scrupulous accuracy" of Baudelaire's *Paradis artificiels*, and, although he hastened to point out that he had attended the meetings "rarely and only as an observer" and never took the drug "for any length of time," he admitted that he had tried it himself, "as a physiological experiment." It appears that Gautier was telling the truth when he says that he made "about ten experiments." Now, just what did the Romantics gain from these experiences?

Gautier and Baudelaire describe the effects of the drug in the same way, and sometimes use almost the same images. Could it be that Baudelaire copied Gautier to some extent? And that both were influenced by the psychiatrist Moreau de Tours?

Baudelaire's account is very convincing. One day I wandered around the rooms of the Hôtel Lauzun reading *Les Paradis artificiels,* trying to evoke the atmosphere of those bygone times. I recognized in the decoration of the *petit salon* the original source for Baudelaire's account of the young woman who takes hashish in her château in the country. The story is undoubtedly a transposition of Baudelaire's own impressions during a meeting of the Club on the Île Saint-Louis. Gautier refers to a hallucination "experienced by a woman in a *cabinet de glaces* decorated with a gilded trellis and festooned with flowers, easily recognizable as the boudoir of the Hôtel Pimodan." This is a verification of the authenticity of Baudelaire's notes.

Of course, even if his account were wholly imaginary, it would still cast light on his artistic motives and tell us what he hoped to gain from the drugs. The deeper desires and ambitions of the age are here seen through a magnifying glass. According to Gautier, the hallucinations induced by hashish "create nothing. They merely develop the individual's particular dispositions and heighten them to the limits of his capacity." These accounts help us grasp the hidden motives of the Romantic soul.

To begin with, what was pursued was the exaltation of the individual faculties, as Baudelaire said, a multiplication of the self. Do we not have here the essence of Romanticism? To transcend normality.... Whereas the Classicist was governed by centripetal aspirations in search of a central point of balance common to all mankind, the Romanticist was centrifugal. All his efforts were in the direction of expanding individual energies, exploring peripheral zones of possibility beyond habitual experience. He was an explorer of the unknown. His stress on individual expression reflects the same effort to escape from the normal and habitual (Fig. 263).

Now, how are we to reconcile the deep exploration of the self with such a flight from the self as is implied by recourse to alcohol and hashish? Actually, the contradiction is more apparent than real. Romanticism was a negation of humanism, of its concept of a norm for humanity. What occurred was a joining together of drugs with the other forces of individualism in antagonism to normality. When Baudelaire spoke of "a development of mankind toward poetic excess," was he not defining Romanticism? According to Gautier, hashish "develops the particular dispositions of the individual by a process of extreme exacerbation"; according to Baudelaire, it provoked "an exacerbation of the personality." Clearly, individualism was moving into a phase of exaltation and exploitation of the self—a phase that lasted right down to Maurice Barrès.

*It was in a room like the one shown here that Baudelaire, under the influence of hashish, thought he saw the figures in the paintings come to life and assume fantastic shapes.*

**265. -** THE GREAT MUSIC ROOM, ROOM IN THE HÔTEL LAUZUN, PARIS

EXALTATION OF THE SELF. To ask how this came about is to analyze Romanticism. First of all, the reliance on sensation. The Classical ages had had little respect for sensation as such. The eighteenth century was the first to enshrine psychological sensationalism as the very basis of life and thought.... But the Romantics went further. They attempted to transcend the range of normal sensation. Beginning with the pursuit of intensity, they ended in the pursuit of the anomalous, the alien. Chemically, this can be achieved by the use of hashish. Its initial effect is to increase the vividness of sensory perception. According to Gautier, "the senses become extraordinarily keen and subtle." But carried to the limit, intensity inevitably leads beyond normality, to disturbances of the personality, of the senses themselves.

An elementary sign of this is confusion among the senses, an actual realization of the famous Baudelairian notion of "correspondences." Poets are sometimes accused of indulging in idle fictions, of fabricating literature. But the poet's knowledge may be based on his actual experience no less than the scientist's, however subjective (as opposed to objective). What the hostile reader sees only as words and rhetorical formulas may very well be a record of actually experienced, all but concrete, facts. When Baudelaire wrote, *Les parfums, les couleurs et les sons se répondent*, he was not simply indulging in fantasy but recording an experience he had under the influence of hashish. He actually set down this observation while under the influence of the drug: "Sounds have a color, colors have music." This is the notion of correspondences realized physiologically. Gautier made the same point: "Hashish eaters perceive mysterious correspondences between frequently disparate images." Note that he employed the same term.

So much for the Romantic exploitation of the senses. What of the effect of all this on the intellect? According to the Romantic doctrine, the mind, too, lends itself to an intensification of its powers to an anomalous degree. One of the first effects of hashish is indeed increased intensity. According to Gautier, "what you see is your own self, more powerful, more sensitive, and immeasurably more excitable." Carried beyond a certain point, intensification becomes anomaly—derangement of the overworked organism. What occurs on the plane of perception also occurs on the plane of intellectual comprehension, namely, a fusion of normally, customarily distinct matters of reflection.

At the basis of all Romanticism is an exaggerated expansion of the self, to which the Germans have given a name: *Einfühlung* (empathy). The self makes a desperate attempt to go beyond its own limits and to become identical with the universe. The Romantic poet, the Romantic painter is forever identifying with the surging ocean, the passing cloud, the forest, the single tree. Mysteriously, he has been transmuted into a sonorous echo of nature, while at the same time he is the very soul of nature. Nature is within him, and he is within nature. By means of this essentially poetic phenomenon, the self is exalted to a degree where it has become limitless, where it loses itself in the all. And this sense of identity with the universe—*Einfühlung* or empathy—is physiologically accelerated by the use of hashish.

Gautier tells us of one of his experiences with hashish, that as he looked at the decorations in the Hôtel Lauzun, he became one with a figure in a painting, one with the flowing river, one with the rustling foliage. "I merged with whatever object I looked at and myself became that object." (Victor Hugo's definition of poetry was not so different.) Baudelaire expressed the same thing more precisely: "Behold, you are a tree moaning in the wind, singing your verdant melodies in nature."

This peculiar state which begins with the exaltation of the self and ends in the transcendence of the self—in something very like the atomizing of the self—where does it lead? To Baudelaire's Man-God. Has there ever been a better definition of Romanticism? "Man has been promoted to Godhead," Baudelaire elucidated. What it means is that he has successfully realized the dream of the German Romantics—the transcendence of humanity, the emergence into unknown realms of being, even an investiture with new powers: those of *creating* the unknown.

Here we are at the very heart and core of the Romantic aesthetics. Classical man had sought to deepen his understanding of the known, rather in the Leibnizian spirit of an essential harmony between man and the universe. He had tried to get ever closer to cosmic stature by discovering within himself the power of giving objective realization to this balance. Such was the law of Classicism. The Romantic man, however, started from a dialectically opposed premise. His whole aim was to get out of the narrow rut of ordinary experience, and in escaping from it to conquer the unknown, to penetrate the dark regions that lie beyond the light of reason.

The Romantic's means of escape lay in the power of the imagination. This was the power that enabled him to go beyond the known, the routine, the normal, and to discover experiences never before experienced or even dreamed of. Romanticism was the first in a number of developments that, in our own century, culminated in Surrealism. Indeed, the word itself—"Surrealism"—is but a variant of Baudelaire's "supernaturalism" (Fig. 264).

FAILURE OF THE "MAN-GOD."   The goal of poetry and art will now be increasingly that of conquering hitherto unknown territories, both within the individual and in realms outside. When they cannot be discovered, they will be invented. The Surrealists, too, relied upon artificial aids to creation—automatic writing, for instance. The hallucination provoked by hashish was merely one of the more deliberate excesses of the Romantic imagination. When Victor Hugo, in his eulogy of Baudelaire, said, "You have given us a new thrill," he summed up a program that Baudelaire's successors would attempt to carry out by any and all means, however illegitimate, however abnormal.

This historical experience is at the same time a human experience highly instructive of our understanding and our conduct of life alike. It has yielded some magnificent flowers, and some poisonous ones as well; but, pushed to the extreme, it has ended in failure. And what is true of Romanticism, is also true of its corollary, hashish. What accounts for the failure? To begin with, this kind of experience can only lead to illusion; Baudelaire said as much in respect to hashish. What reason is there to believe that it takes one out of oneself, that it produces a state of genius, that it promotes man to the status of a god? What has been multiplied is not man, not the world, not the self, but only the self's intoxication with its own vanity. Baudelaire admits this, recognizes the deception. What has been enlarged is merely man's belief in his own value; the man who takes hashish "is held in thrall, but unhappily for him, only by himself.... Man cannot escape his physical and moral nature!" All that he finds at the end of his cult of experience is a mirror, a mirror that presents his image larger than life, but still a mirror. Dedicated to the cult of self-pride, he is inevitably thrown back upon himself in his own inner prison. He has lined the walls of his prison with distorting mirrors, but they all give back to him but one image: himself alone.

And what is the cost of this failure? A kind of higher dispensation decrees that multiplication of the self in the end destroys it. Exaltation of a single human potentiality has led to the destruction of all potentiality to create.

Baudelaire tells us what it is like to have a hashish hangover. The will founders. "You are punished for the inspired prodigality with which you have scattered your personality to the four winds. Trying to be God, man now is fallen lower than his real nature."

When we look beyond the little experiments with hashish, we glimpse the fate that lay in store for the Romantic cult of the superhuman, of the man-god. It is symbolized in Nietzsche's appalling descent into madness. It is symbolized in Baudelaire's sudden stumbling, that tragic day, in the church of Saint-Loup at Namur when his final Calvary began. Prodigious master of the word that he was, this was the beginning of a long agony when, though his mind may have been intact, he was stricken with aphasia, and could utter only unintelligible moans and curses.

Baudelaire had lucidly foreseen the inevitable consequences of Romanticism. Nor was he alone to do so: it is interesting to note how many pioneers in the transcendence of the self grasped where they were headed, Edgar Allan Poe, the alcoholic, no less than Baudelaire, the drug addict. They recognized that when man seeks rashly to get beyond the human condition, he sacrifices the most precious parts of his own self: lucidity and will.

Baudelaire chose to desert the real world for the world of illusion, and paid dearly for it. We know that, in his last years, he struggled desperately to recover, to regain command of himself, to climb back up the slippery slope. He sought salvation in self-discipline, in judgment, in self-control. He concluded *Du vin et du haschisch* with these words: "I cannot understand why rational and spiritual man uses artificial means to achieve poetic bliss, considering that will and enthusiasm suffice to raise him to supernatural realms of being."

HUMANISM, CORRECTIVE OF INDIVIDUALISM.   A view of the individual as limited to nervous stimulation cannot be anything but extremely misleading. The self is first and foremost will. Maine de Biran, at the beginning of the nineteenth century, had stressed this point. Baudelaire had forgotten the lesson and had to relearn it the hard way. If only he had paid more attention to Delacroix! For Delacroix, who shared the attitudes of English dandyism, which, at its best, implied perfect self-control, never had recourse to artificial means of inspiration. There is an anecdote about Balzac, related by both Gautier and Baudelaire, telling how he exhibited the same distaste. "Offered *dawamesk*, he examined it, sniffed at it, and handed it back without touching it. The struggle between his almost childish authority and his unwillingness to give in to it was strikingly reflected on his expressive face: love of dignity won the upper hand. ... No doubt Balzac thought that there could be no greater disgrace and no sharper pain than abdication of the will."

Delacroix's case was similar to Balzac's. Love of dignity won the upper hand. Such was the case of all men who weathered the Romantic era; Alfred de Vigny, for example.

Delacroix had a broader, a more total view of the individual. Baudelaire shared that view, but only after perilous experiments and in awareness of the risks he was running. To Delacroix, the initial electrifying impulse that charges the creator and sends off the sparks does indeed come from the inspired sensibility, from enthusiasm, but the sparks are actually produced only after reason has intervened lucidly and coldly (Fig. 258).

Delacroix is not just a "Romantic." He incorporated Classical elements in his work. To him, composition, the architectural aspect of art, was necessary to co-ordinate the painter's own original findings, in order to endow them with utmost effectiveness. His entire doctrine is summed up in this sentence, written at the age of twenty-two, in a letter to his friend Pierret: "Composition gives wisdom and steadiness to a terrain shaken and set on fire by volcanoes. There lies the integration that, alone, makes for greatness!" For Delacroix believed, as he said again in 1850 when he was much older, "It is the union of the two faculties of imagination and reason that produces exceptional men."

Thus, individualism had already glimpsed the dangers inherent in itself. In its aspect of blind self-indulgence, of surrender to the pleasurable sensations that can be extracted from one's own nervous sensibility, it destroys personality even as it exalts it. Delacroix saw this from the outset. True individualism means an equal and parallel development of the faculties of emotion and the faculties of control. An artist must be both lucid and inspired. Delacroix said it over and over again: what we need is "an immense passion endowed with a formidable will.... One must be coldly resolved to seek out the means to express passion in the most visible way." And, conversely, "the very great men, I am wholly convinced, are perhaps those who have preserved, at an age where the intellect attains its full strength, some of the impetuosity and the impressionability that characterize youth."

Baudelaire, for all his weaknesses and painful mistakes, came to share this view. Referring to Wagner, he said, "Everything implied by the terms 'will, desire, concentration, nervous intensity, explosion' can be felt and sensed in his works. I do not think I am deceiving myself or anyone else when I say that these are the principal characteristics of

*After the meetings at the Hôtel Lauzun, Baudelaire often wandered in the streets trying to get over the effects of the drug. This watercolor by him is an ironical comment on the aggrandizement of his self.*

**266. - BAUDELAIRE.
WATERCOLOR IN WHICH HE
PORTRAYS HIMSELF UNDER THE
INFLUENCE OF HASHISH.**
Collection Baroness
de Goldschmidt-Rothschild

the phenomenon we call genius."

Delacroix and Baudelaire thus paved the way for the late-nineteenth-century reaction against Romanticism, the first symptoms of which in France are discernible in the Parnassian movement. At that time, the repeated attempts to attain genius by a hypertrophied individualism, but the cultivation of disorder and self-conscious pursuit of the unknown, were checked and opposed by a sort of mathematics of the mind. Baudelaire, in certain features of his work, anticipated that very reaction we associate with Mallarmé and Valéry. Although they believed that art had the right to end in obscurity, if necessary, they did not believe that it springs from obscurity. To this later generation, the essence of the creative mind did not any longer seem to reside in unforeseeable elements of personality or accidents of inspiration, but in the most responsible part of the self—in lucidity.

If Valéry, like Mallarmé, admired Edgar Allan Poe and Baudelaire, it was because they had reacted against a condition whose danger they sensed in their own poetic experience. Of course, the reaction did not stop a continuing pursuit of the irrational that is very much all around us still today. Romanticism found other ways of circumventing the problems of individualism.

Baudelaire in the end condemned the heightening of personality by recourse to artificial paradises. It is a conclusion that goes beyond any mere concern with narcotic drugs, being true to human experience. Can man transcend himself by using any and every means of escaping his limitations? Is there anything of value outside himself? Is it possible to escape our given conditions of existence? Quite possibly the answer is yes to all these questions, and quite possibly it is art—as I suggest at the end of this book—that resolves them.

Delacroix, and, after him, Baudelaire, in formulating the new aesthetics of individualism, foresaw the dangers it would create for civilization and they deserve our admiration for their farsightedness. They realized that in order to extract from the individual the freshest and most productive resources for enriching the common heritage, it was indispensable not to let him be sidetracked into egoism and anarchy.

Intoxicated by increasingly heady experiments upon themselves, poets and artists have occasionally gone so far as to endow their own egoism with a sacred quality. Concerned solely with self-expression, they have not always bothered to make contact with those to whom they address themselves. But societies have a deep instinct of self-preservation, and in our own day we seem to be witnessing the beginnings of a reaction against individualism, a reaction born of increasing awareness of its excesses and its possible dangers to the collective body.

The teachings of the man who created this doctrine have not been sufficiently heeded, sufficiently respected. The individual has the right to exalt himself and delight in himself only on condition that the freedoms he thus arrogates are counterbalanced by exacting discipline. The gifts of sensibility and creativity are all but meaningless unless lucidity and concern for order are cultivated no less intensively.

Otherwise the individual risks becoming a monstrous parasite on the body social rather than what he should be: the indispensable leaven of progress and social renewal, the man who gives other men a richer, nobler image of what they could be.

*Raw impulse projects beyond rational thought.*

**267.** - *GEORGES MATHIEU.* CAPETIANS EVERYWHERE. 1954. Musée d'Art Moderne de la Ville de Paris

CHAPTER V

# ART AND THE IRRATIONAL

Aʀᴛ, as we have seen, not only reflects the changing ideas of man over the centuries; it also can give expression to the inner life. This is why it progressively gained greater importance in recent generations. For many centuries art's role was often reduced to mere illustration of clear, rational ideas; but that was in ages when the rational mind was in the saddle. Today we are fascinated by anything and everything that lies outside or beyond the comparatively circumscribed domains to which reason gives access. It is true that scientific thought occasionally displays a certain reluctance to readjust its basic concepts in keeping with its own new requirements, but the realm of the imprecise, the realm of unknown or dormant possibilities which lurk within the human breast has become the very element of art. As never before, the artist today is at one with his age, and art is our favorite instrument for exploring our unknown inner resources—an instrument notable for the effortlessness with which it today adjusts itself to the most unforeseen developments. Art has been ready for the tasks that confront us in the twentieth century. Its rise and status have paralleled the collapse of rationalism and a growing concern for gaining a more comprehensive grasp of reality. More effectively than anything else to date, art gives immediate access to unconscious realms of being.

# 1. FROM THE RATIONAL TO THE ABSURD

*The absurd is born of the confrontation between man's voice and the world's unreasoning silence.*
*Albert Camus*

THIS growing importance of art has accompanied the rise of individualism. The nineteenth century, in its exaltation of the individual and its attempts to expand his powers, brought about dissolution of the traditional identification of creativity with the conscious reason. This did not come about easily or overnight, for it was long and bitterly resisted. The nineteenth century believed firmly in science and progress, believed it was *the* century of science and progress, successor to the Age of Enlightenment and, before that, to the Age of Reason. The range of knowledge had enormously expanded; nineteenth-century man felt himself in a vast wild forest never trod by human foot, tangled, complex, labyrinthine, and did not doubt that his ax—i.e., his intellect—would suffice to reclaim it and master it. He went at his task with the confidence in the powers of logic; he was like the men who constructed orderly, geometric paths through the gardens and woods of Versailles for Louis XIV. (It was in the nineteenth century that Haussmann imposed his orderly plan of boulevards upon the haphazardly winding little streets of Paris.) Time and industry should suffice, it was felt, to achieve order and clarity, and to banish forever the strange and the unknown. Although the nineteenth-century mind recognized the existence of problems in all branches of knowledge, it felt that these were purely temporary and would sooner or later be cleared up.

Few seemed to recall the words of Pascal, "The eternal silence of infinite space terrifies me...."

THE AGE OF THE ABSURD.   In our own century, man is no longer convinced that he occupies the very center of the world's stage. In a second Fall of Man, he has been driven from the earthly paradise. The center I refer to is not the earth as center of the universe— Galileo had long since accomplished that displacement in men's minds. I refer to moral certainty, man's conviction of being at the very core of things, the unique source of clarity in the world, the light-bringing dispeller of darkness. All this has gone. Under our feet there is no more solid ground, and we are pitched to and fro on a stormy sea. Around us, our eyes no longer perceive the three fixed dimensions of space, but only gathering shadows. Clinging to the raft of existence, we are, at every moment, threatened by the immensity of events and the instability of every certainty we still clutch at. Overwhelmed by its own perceptions, the intellect wrestles with the irrational and the absurd, more than a little convinced that human existence is a purely empirical business without any cosmic assurance to sustain it or buoy it up. Life and the universe are incommensurable: no common scale any longer relates man to his physical setting. The predicament produces a

*This temple swept away by the unleashed elements symbolizes the debacle of Greco-Roman reason.*

**268. -** *ANDRÉ MASSON.* THE RIVER HERACLITUS. 1940. Galerie Simon, Paris

specifically intellectual malaise—called "nausea" by a French existentialist. Silenced now is that music of the spheres that Cicero was sure human ears would be able to hear, had they not been dulled by habit! Vanished now, the mirage of a supreme harmony which the moving universe used in all its parts to sing! Now all is silence, save for inhuman stridencies and demented howls—as appalling to logic as to our senses—which we keep one ear cocked for, while shuddering inwardly lest we actually have to hear them (Fig. 268)!

The illusions that sustained mankind in the past have all been torn to shreds. The universe whose master we one day aspired to be is no longer recognizable; the planet which was our familiar home now appears alien. Nothing is what it seemed; all our attempts to understand are frustrated. The busy mind continues to explore—always in depth, always descending to ever blacker, more lightless reaches, its only reward the intensification of the initial dilemma. Science, upon which all the successive rationalisms of Western culture had always pinned their hopes, today soars to ever dizzier heights of mathematical improvisation, but, whether exploring the infinitely great or the infinitely small, it runs head-on into the irrational.

Reason, it seems, serves a function like that of the atmosphere around our planet: it provides mankind with a zone of immediate intelligibility, to step outside of which is to gasp for breath, to lose protective covering. The expansion of human powers demands a terrible cost. Nor is retreat to the interior, withdrawal into one's shell, much safer. The protective layer extends only so far; beneath it is the fiery magma of the unconscious in continuous eruption, a zone where reason is quickly turned to cinders and smoke. Psychoanalysts sink mine shafts into these bottomless depths, to inform us how our thoughts and acts are in fact determined by hidden forces in contempt of all our conscious controls (Fig. 287).

In this unstable, fluid predicament, is it yet possible for the human will to assert itself? Is it yet possible for modern man to make of himself what he believes and wishes himself to be? Today he goes Ulysses one better: not only does he unplug his ears the more clearly to hear the Sirens singing, he also cuts the ropes that lash him to the mast, the more swiftly to fall into the abyss that yawns. He runs headlong to welcome the most unlikely fates, cheerfully entering into pacts with the absurd (that satanic perversion of logic) and the antirational. The question is, do such attitudes constitute a new chapter in human achievement, or do they signify a surrender? This is the big question of our times, whether a plus sign or a minus sign precedes the coefficient of our culture. A whole technique of the absurd has been elaborated to free man from the bondage of reason, to give him "the new thrill" of negating it. Encouraged by its growing popularity, art has done yeoman prop-aganda service in support of such attitudes, aggressively and only too visibly spreading the new gospel. Though it is not safe to open all cages—some birds die—no matter! The experiment proceeds. Dadaism and Surrealism were the first movements explicitly to excommunicate the rational. There is widespread respect for the art of children and madmen, beings who have not yet attained to reason or have lost it. Nonfigurative painting does not seem intelligible to the public, nor is it intended to be, in any traditional sense (Figs. 267 and 273).

Meanwhile, as contemporary society gets on with its labor of dismantling the façade of logic (which up to now had served to hold back the forces of disorder and destruction), it simultaneously offers us relapses into barbarism in the name of progress, ruins nations to insure their prosperity, wastes the world's resources on the pretext of securing them, and slaughters people by the millions to insure their right to happiness. Drenched in blood, covered with rotting corpses, bombed to bits, the world after two monumentally destruc-tive wars pauses dazed and takes stock—if only to catch its breath before embarking on yet a third.

At this point, the mind stops. What are we to make of this bewildering predicament in which we find ourselves, this unprecedentedly convulsed and confused situation? It is as though mankind had gone through some monstrous mutation inconceivable even so few as fifty years ago. Many efforts have been made to formulate a philosophy to the scale of this mutation, but they all seem to come down to self-doubts, to intellectual panic, anxiety, and despair. Absurdity has become an absolutely indispensable term (Fig. 292).

Waehlens, an expositor of the German philosopher Heidegger, says, "We are caught up in a sort of whirlpool, and we can feel the existents slipping away one after another. They do not disappear in the material sense, but—something much worse—they evaporate on the plane of being and value.... We feel suspended in the void. All solid reality fails us. Everything is collapsing and we cannot stop it, cannot cling to anything whatever. Being is crumbling away, foundering, and we are disappearing with it."

And what about absurdity? What is the absurd? It is the sense of how anything what-ever, no matter how long it has proved serviceable, no longer meets the test of a customary reason; it is conceived of as "against common sense." One way of summing up our age would be to describe it as an extensive, prolonged assault on common sense. Once more, the question is: are we dealing with a capitulation of the human mind or with an impend-ing mutation? With a collapse of intellectual pretensions or with the discovery of fresh

*Long before the Surrealism of our day, art skirted the zone of the unintelligible. Furini uses the theme of St. Lucy to conjure up a livid shoulder emerging from the darkness and a pair of eyes without a face.*

**269.** - *FRANCESCO FURINI.* ST. LUCY. Spada Gallery, Rome

*In the same seventeenth-century Italy, Salvator Rosa imagined monsters born of delirium and nameless creatures.*

**270.** - *SALVATOR ROSA.* THE TEMPTATION OF ST. ANTHONY.
Rambaldi di Coldirodi Gallery, San Remo

perspectives? A bankruptcy or a renascence? Periods of renascence in human history have often proved stormy, even painful, but it is by means of them that mankind renews itself, secures its right to go on living (Fig. 294).

ONCE UPON A TIME.... A volcano erupts, a cliff crumbles and falls into the sea, a tidal wave sweeps over the ocean vastness, the land is convulsed with earthquakes. These disturbances, as we call them, are caused by slow, invisible shifts, enormous shudders of the earth's crust. In this way, the planet patiently, continuously, goes on shaping itself over the millions of years, recasting and making unrecognizable features we think of as familiar or even eternal, merely because we are not given the time to know them as they were before or will be after. Now, is mankind really so different from the earth, save in being much, much younger—indeed, still fairly close to its beginnings? Today it is merely going through a particularly troubled adolescence, having in its childhood naïvely supposed that the world was cast in its own image. Just as the child and the primitive ascribe to animals their own ways of thinking and feeling, so until quite recently mankind ascribed to the world a soul identical with its own.

Knowing himself, his own nature—but nothing more—man reconstructed the world in his imagination, endowing it with a rationality analogous to his own. From a distance, this mirror image is much more plausible than close up. Close up, the illusion of a humanized space vanishes. The surface of the mirror is cold, unfamiliar, and impenetrable—the image was a mirage. Man thought he knew the world, but all he had done was to recognize it.

For centuries now, man has been gradually ridding himself of the anthropocentrism and anthropomorphism that, for a time, had seemed so natural and self-evident. Originally, he had imagined in every thing or phenomenon a double of himself—a spirit, demon, troll, or fairy. No eagle and no ox but was inhabited by a god, no spring that did not house a naiad, no oak without its hamadryad.

> Ecoute, bûcheron, arrête un peu le bras...
> Ne vois-tu pas le sang, lequel dégoutte à force,
> Des nymphes qui vivaient dessous la dure écorce?

[Listen, woodsman, stay your arm a moment.... Don't you see the blood you are spilling? There were nymphs living under that tough bark.] In his imagination, primitive man clothed the inhuman aspect of things in human forms. He sculptured the totem pole or the statue of the idol in his own image. He replaced the alien universe with forms resembling his own, which he could sway by his prayers and win over to his side.

Then came an age when man asked, Why so many images where one would be enough, a single immense image to the scale of the infinite? Why not one God—the creator, single Idea, the soul of the universe? "And God created man in his own image." Man conceived of God as a being different from him only in His perfection and infallibility, a being in whom our own potentialities are actualized, a being whose goals are unfathomable but reassurnig because logical and just. Now all seemed order, certainty, reason; the age of the gods was followed by the age of God.

After the age of God came the age of reason. For century after century, man had applied himself to the task of simplifying, of reducing mystery—the unknown—to an indispensable minimum. Mystery subsisted in God, in His inconceivable greatness, but in all other respects mystery gradually capitulated to reason. But it had long been recognized that mystery is to be found in man himself, in his body, that enclave of the outside world in his own substance. In the action of instincts, passions, sudden and unforeseeable impulses, disturbances of all kinds, the body stealthily introduces the threatening unfamiliarity of the physical world into the very soul. How then is man to feel safe and sound? What armor can he devise to protect his integrity? With the appearance of reason, mistress of herself, imposing her own law and order in a code of logic, man believed he had found just such a shield and buckler. With the passing of time, he found it more reliable than God.

The God of the Middle Ages had overwhelmed man with the unfathomable mystery of His nature and threatened at any moment to be as impenetrable as the universe it was His function to explain. The God of the seventeenth century was more humane; He was essentially identified with divine reason. Descartes respected Him, but very nearly did without Him, reducing Him—as the constitutional monarch of heaven—to countersigning the decrees of logic. "We must never let ourselves be persuaded save by the evidences of our reason."

From this position, it was but a step to doing without God altogether. The eighteenth century was divided, either clinging to a vague notion of a "Supreme Being" or denying the existence of God. That century was unwilling to grant that the universe has a soul— "soul" evoked too many obscurities of feeling. It was incompatible with that age's fond belief in a mechanistic explanation of the universe. Like an old scrap of paper, God was thrown into the dustbin of history. The world illumined *a giorno* (after all, this was the century of the Enlightenment!) was now governed solely by the light of reason, that reason which was deified as goddess only at the close of the century, in the new public festivities organized by the Revolution. If the law of the world is identical with that of the human mind, man becomes master of the world, capable of understanding it, of discovering its deepest secrets, of controlling and exploiting it. All science has to do is to jump into the saddle of this clockwork Pegasus and set off to storm heaven and earth alike. Once God is no longer seen as the originator of all things, then perfection does not lie behind us, but in front of us: the limitless perspective of rational progress was opening out to mankind.

But reason is only a framework, a technique; without substantial content it is mere formalism, without living flesh a skeleton. It needs a matter to mold, and this matter is provided by experience. The Christian ages knew only one kind of experience, that of God; faith and reason exercised their powers and made their inferences only on this basis. The modern age shifted its attitude to experience from causes to effects, from the creator to the creation, from God to nature. No longer concerning itself with the revelations of religion, it puts its faith in empirical observation. Down to this point, reason had been turned in upon itself; now its movement became centrifugal, as it set out to conquer the unknown. (What a threat is implied in Claude Bernard's succinct formula, "The fact judges the idea"!) At first, reason took no heed of the risks it ran. Intoxicated with self-confidence and its new autonomy, it still took for granted that what it would find behind the enigmatic appearances of things would be another rational order like its own, a Nature to its own measure. All that was needed, surely, was to get rid of the screen of appearances that stood like a dark cloud between reason—the armature of thought—and its double or counterpart, the hidden armature of the universe. Alas! In getting past the cloud to the things themselves, the most self-confident explorers were due for many a rude shock. The recent history of the physical sciences reads like an adventure story, with every advance dearly paid for, every heroic victory counting its disasters.

THE MODERN CRISIS. More and more surrounded, more and more oppressed by the fog into which its confident investigations had led it, reason gained acquaintance with the unknowable, the ineffable. And yet, at the very outset, Kant had brilliantly anticipated the future in the *Critique of Pure Reason*. He suggested that reason does not necessarily reflect the inner nature of things, that it provides us only with categories and forms that enable us to devise a mental image of the world, but not to grasp the things in themselves.

Was, then, the universe impenetrable to reason? Was man merely adrift in a frail boat of intellectual clarity amid ever-increasing threats of shipwreck? In the end, was the would-be conqueror of the unknown merely delivering himself into its hands? The opening moves in the great chess game were made in the nineteenth century. Classical culture clung with all its strength to the credo of rationalism, but the Germanic, the Anglo-Saxon, and the Scandinavian peoples, less loath to summon up the forces of darkness, opened assault on the shaken Latin spirit. The first contact with the unknowable was made when Romanticism discovered the long-banished enemy of reason in man's own soul: every man carries an unknown world within him. Check to reason! Henceforward its powers will end at the frontiers of inwardness, increasingly recognized as the essence of personality and located outside the domain of logical explanation, accessible only to the sensibility. Every man carries the secret of his soul within himself, and only genius can give us a glimpse of its supernatural flashes. And what of nature—has she no soul? a soul that only the magic of art can express? What Baudelaire glimpsed still eludes the explanations of physical science:

> La Nature est un temple où de vivants piliers
> Laissent parfois sortir de confuses paroles ...

[Nature is a temple whose living pillars sometimes utter obscure words....] But science took no notice of these literary fantasies. The mysteries capitulated to it one after the other; it explained, explained, explained.... It even invaded its adversary's territory, undertaking to reduce psychology to physiology and consciousness to an epiphenomenon, a mere bubble on the surface of biological facts. Rationalist science felt itself on the threshold of universal triumph.

At the very moment science was setting off in pursuit of the adversary far from its own bases, its own fundamental assumptions began to crack up and fall apart, letting the omnipresent irrational be glimpsed at the very shrine of reason itself. Our latterday initiation to the absurd began with certain scientific developments that occurred the moment that investigation went beyond traditional areas of experience. It was discovered that as soon as one left the normal range of experience, i.e., the zone of phenomena perceivable by our senses, the age-old principles of reason lose their efficacy. No sooner had the telescope transported us far beyond the limits of natural vision to the threshold of the ultrahuman, into the infinitely great, than the old logic, as though deprived of its habitual air, began to gasp in bewilderment. Einstein's theory of relativity aroused passionate polemics forty years ago, but it is fully accepted today. It is confirmed by facts that it alone can account for. Now, the theory is based on notions and principles that Le Roy qualifies as scandalous in the eyes of the traditional reason. How can we visualize the curvature of space-time? How can we conceive more than three dimensions, as the theory demands? And is it any easier to conceive of functions without differentials, numbers greater than infinity? The intelligence here bumps right up against limitations that it had never suspected; from here on, only an increasingly abstruse recourse to mathematics can give us a clue as to where we are, where we have just been.

Nor are we a bit more at home in the zone of the infinitesimally small, which the microscope has opened up to us. Here, too, the mind must set aside its most traditional, most basic notions. Confronted with the atom, the mind can no longer resolve all difficulties by imagining an infinitely small particle, as Lucretius did. Actually, there is no longer such thing as matter at all: analytic investigation has swallowed it up, volatilized it, and, today, matter is seen as only a momentary localization of energy. Only fifty years ago, scientists laughed heartily when Bergson predicted that before long they would have to give up ready-made concepts. Today, physicists have given up a great many. Thus, this infinitesimal corpuscle, the ultimate reality that constitutes the substance of the whole world, cannot be visualized at all. Not just because it is invisible, not just because it is too small to be perceived by any instruments, but because it is unobservable, because it does not possess the property of spatial expansion. According to Louis de Broglie, its localization in space is "a borderline case, with a probability equal to zero." More than that, it has no individuality, it is not a determinable unit in any group. It is nowhere and everywhere within the system from which it is inseparable—it is an act, "a quantified value of energy, which cannot be visualized in the framework of space," in de Broglie's words. Thus Planck's famous quantum theory is evoked, doing away with the old adage, *Natura non facit saltum*, and the notion of discontinuity, also absurd in the scale of habitual human experience, is introduced.

Louis de Broglie concludes, "The elementary entities float in space and time as in an ill-fitting garment, not made to their measure. Individuality fades out in the mysterious process of interaction; determinism itself, so dear to the physicists of bygone times, has had to give way." And much else has had to give way with it—the very foundations of Classical reason, the principle of causality (now blurred by the universal interdependence of phenomena), the principle of finality (which was discarded even before this), and last, but not least, the most sacred principle of all, the principle of identity. Since the statistical studies of Fermi-Dirac appeared, we are compelled to deny the individuality of certain categories of elementary corpuscles. Dirac has also revealed the existence of electrons that cannot be observed directly, but whose presence played a part in the very real—only too real—invention of the atom bomb. As for the principle of noncontradiction, which Hegel had already undermined, it has been supplanted, at least in the mind of the philosopher Stéphane Lupesco, by an axiom of fundamental contradiction.

*The solid vault of reality has collapsed; a dizzying infinite void opens up, streaked with hoarfrost.*

**271.** - *RAOUL MICHAUT. MATIN CRISSANT.* 1960. Private collection

A NEW CONCEPTION OF REALITY.   However, there is no reason to panic. We are witnessing the bankruptcy not so much of reason itself as of the old conception of reality. The traditional form of our reason is what has been discredited, and reason itself only to the extent that our mind clung to it. The familiar world of matter, three-dimensional Euclidean space, and the laws of mechanics, which we believed to constitute the very nature of reality, have collapsed. For many years, Bergson denounced the illegitimacy of founding reason on the concrete visible world: he showed how the forms, methods, and categories of reason had assumed the existence of counterparts in the visible world, whereas close analysis of that world fails to justify any such assumptions. The visible world is mere appearance; what we have for so long called the real world corresponds to no reality at all.

Far from having failed, human thought has gone through this ordeal with flying colors. Since the traditional realistic, representable images lost the support of science, and the universe has proved to be impossible of visualization, thought has become more flexible, more abstract. It has given up attempts to imagine the world, since the images that it used to conceive have proved fallacious and obsolete. Instead, we rely on pure symbols, figures, or algebraic letters; indeed, mathematics has become a sort of acrobatics of abstraction.

Actually, the mind has moved on to some of its most prodigious triumphs. For, in this universe where it gropes blindly through the intermediary of numbers, it has proved capable of many discoveries achieved solely on the basis of exact computations. The diffraction of electrons, the pressure of light waves, and Dirac's positrons were all deduced as pure intellectual concepts before being verified experimentally. In the same way, the eclipse of May 29, 1919 verified Einstein's theory of the deviation of light rays in the neighborhood of the sun. Thus, human thought, at a moment when it was being shaken to the roots, attained some of its most brilliant successes.

To be sure, the old conception of reason collapsed with the old conception of the universe, but reason will no doubt subsist, rid of the restricting definitions with which it was formerly hedged around. Reason and the universe have begun to disclose a common mathematical nature. We can no longer imagine the world or construct a visual model of it, but we can compute it. In other words, we have reached the stage of absurdity where the mind can compute, discover, and foresee things unimaginable and assimilable in terms of reason! We might say without aesthetic sophistry that nonfigurative art, which does not represent the world as we perceive it at the sensory level, but seeks to create equivalents for it with the aid of abstract or instinctive signs, has reached an analogous stage.

TWENTIETH-CENTURY MODERNISM.   Everything is interrelated in a given epoch: the seemingly most original manifestations in different fields are rooted in the same soil. If it is scarcely contestable that Impressionism is a corollary to Bergson's philosophy and Proust's novel as well as to the new physics,[1] it will come as no surprise to discover that the literature and art of our epoch perceive intuitively the same difficulties that

---

[1] At least I tried to prove this in "L'Impressionnisme et la pensée de son temps," *Prométhée-Amour de l'Art,* February 1939.

*It was Cubism that first launched a concentrated attack on reality. The formal laws of the intellect supplant the laws governing the physical world. The debris of the latter are pieced together again like fragments of a broken mirror on the ground.*

**272. -** *BRAQUE.* **VIOLIN AND PITCHER.** 1910. Museum of Fine Arts, Basel

*With the advent of Surrealism, the intellect, too, is thrown overboard. The fragments of reality preserve their familiar appearance for the eye, but their arrangements are absurd, and the intellect is forced to surrender to the unconscious.*

**273. -** *DALI.* THE SOURCE OF SOUNDS. Private collection

contemporary science encounters in coming to grips with the facts. Some people are still fearful of being taken in by modernism in the arts and devise elaborate theories as to how artists, in combination with dealers and publishers, are engaged in some monstrous swindle of the public. Although it may be true that modernism has been exploited in this way, its source lies deeper. The initial impulse was, beyond doubt, profoundly sincere and corresponded to an almost organic need of our time. Inveterate skeptics should take the trouble to be really skeptical, and remember that a man is most easily fooled by his fear of being fooled, that credulity is often the result of a determination not to be taken in. Actually, authentic avant-garde art and literature are scarcely more bewildering than modern science, though it is possible to respect the latter more readily because its effects can be admired without understanding its underlying principles. But these principles are governed by the same historical necessities. They, too, reflect the crisis of rationalism, they, too, proclaim the bankruptcy of traditional reason, and they, too, are in process of recasting it. The result of all this cannot as yet be foreseen. We are all under the sway of the law of the epoch, which is the law of the absurd—using this term objectively and implying no pejorative connotations.

*There is another type of Surrealism. Like the first, it renounces reason and reality, but lets the hand be guided by uncontrolled impulses. Miró practices it with a great deal of humor.*

**274. -** *MIRÓ.* MRS. MILLS. 1929. Galerie Pierre, Paris

471

Impressionism in art and symbolism in literature simultaneously destroyed man's blind faith in concrete reality. Symbolism, according to Gide, "had little use for the transient forms that the Idea takes on in time." It reduced reality to mirage, an external wrapping of true spiritual substance. It saw in reality no more than "the visible signification of an idea." At the same time, Impressionism was dissolving reality into an ungraspable blur of successive, momentary appearances.

Before long, the whole of the visible world—everything the public at large still called "reality"—was to lose all prestige, ceased to be tangible. Fauvism recast it, turned it upside down, reduced it to no more than a soft clay in which traces of the creative thumb are set down. Around 1910, the Cubists went further: they dislocated reality, broke it up. Out of its scattered, least glamorous fragments, and in accordance with laws which were no longer those of verisimilitude and logic, they reconstructed painting as a perfectly arbitrary original object. Like modern scientists, the Cubists supplanted faithfulness to appearance with almost mathematical harmonic relationships. Like modern science, Cubism is abstract. Picasso, the *dinamitero* of traditional respect for nature in painting, employs a highly lucid, refined intelligence to denigrate the appearances of the visible world. He reduces them to seeming incoherence, but also subjects them to a new logic, entirely internal and arbitrary, which superimposes an impossible universe upon the traditional universe and creates visual absurdity (Fig. 272).

Whereas Cubism still made use of intellectual calculation, Surrealism, which succeeded Cubism around 1920, has no use for it whatever. Surrealism went over to the enemy—the absurd. The Surrealists do not see life as the assault of a militant reason upon the irreducible mystery of the world. Intellectual anarchists, they concluded a pact with mystery and the absurd, became handmaidens of the unconscious. Paul Dermée was very clear about this: "The poet must repudiate reason." It is the exact opposite of Richelieu's "Man must recognize the sovereign rule of reason." Eluard went still further and declared, "I shall reinforce my delirium." A lengthy cycle of history is comprised between the two utterly opposed formulas (Fig. 293).

The nineteenth century had been content to toy with danger, to cultivate a sense of thrill to be gained by confronting reason with absurdity, and drew upon the irrational and the obscure throughout the periods of Romanticism and Symbolism. Then, taking a detour around the real problem—reason itself, now under suspicion—the intelligence attempted a serious exploration of its very opposite, the living ungraspable reality which is too fluid to be caught in the finest meshes of traditional reason. More and more territory was reclaimed from the latter in the name of intuition. That was Bergsonism.

When the 1914 war broke out, something snapped in the noble, rational edifice erected by the nineteenth century in the name of progress. By the very eve of the war, international courts had been created to settle all conflicts in a rational way, and yet the war came notwithstanding. The unleashing of blind passions could hardly fail to show cracks in the façade of prosperity, the perfect ordering of society. Entire nations were ruined, millions slaughtered in the name of the most venerable moral values—Right, Fatherland, Justice. At the close of the First World War, Dada sneaked up behind a totally discredited traditional reason and with shouts of pure glee toppled it over into the quicksands on the brink of which it had for so long been standing.

It was at this point that Surrealism came in, as an attempt to organize and codify the absurd. In the spirit of such precursors as Rimbaud and Lautréamont, it publicly celebrated Black Masses to the memory of reason and frenziedly cursed everything reason had blessed. To this end it developed two techniques. The first ruined, in terms of language as well as vision, every trace of logic and organization, going back to the original incoherence of word and line. Submitting passively to the dictation of the unconscious, it produced states similar to dreams where nature puts logic to sleep by physiological means. Making use of automatic writing, it recorded the most elementary, the most irrational pulsations of being. Klee, Miró, and Arp expressed all this in images. The other technique is more insidious; it respects the appearances of reality, even insists upon them, but it is as deceptive a tribute to nature as the hollow trunk of a tree which has been struck by lightning. Writers maintained the legibility of the sentence and painters the illusion of the object, but they did so only to bring out, by contrast, the inner incoherence and absurdity of the new and hallucinating relationships they wished to create. A real rock ended in a real lung and through it one could see the open door of a real wardrobe. According to André Breton, "every discovery that changes the nature or purpose of an object or a phenomenon constitutes a Surrealist fact." Salvador Dali is the most illustrious—that is, the best publicized—representative of this tendency (Figs. 273 and 274).

The sense of this program was made clear in *La Révolution Surréaliste* (No. 3): "Ideas, logic, order, Truth (with a capital T), reason, we give them all up to the nothingness of death. You do not know to what lengths our hatred of logic can make us go." The hostilities against reason had been opened.

Today, they are in a sense closed, because we have gone beyond this stage. Surrealism has a tense, edgy quality, because it really did cross swords with reason, and really attempted to score off it. The art known as Abstract Expressionism, which today spearheads the modern movement, occupies a region beyond this conflict. Reason is not involved at all, not even as an adversary. It is sometimes said that this art simply does not take reality into account: the imputation is not true. It remains a confrontation between man and the world, at least in the case of the sincere artists, but it no longer resorts to direct observation nor does it recognize the claims of logic. What it is in search of is direct, organic contact with the world, the expression of intensity, violence, anguish—a kind of direct plugging in of the artist's nervous system to the sources of energy. His hand becomes a recording instrument which produces visible equivalences. In much the same spirit, modern technology channels radiations coming from remote regions of the cosmos and translates them into sounds. We can listen to their "song." The latest modernists do something similar: they translate into dynamic images the energies that pass through them, from what they often call "the cosmos." Their language is brutal and incoherent, stammering or passionate, closer to a scream or even a prolonged moan than to music; but its impact is occasionally quite powerful. Between the traditional version of reality and this new one there is a difference like that to be found between a theoretical understanding of electricity and actual exposure to an electric current. But reality is there, always present, even if its familiar appearances have disappeared. This is evidenced by an interesting fact: if, in the nineteenth century, the painter's vision paralleled the daguerreotype, the canvases of today's Abstract Expressionists are sometimes just as strangely similar to micrographs. This is certainly not imitation, but coincidence; a coincidence which suggests that these unexpected creations, however irrational they may be, are not insane or even arbitrary (Figs. 275 and 276).

*With the advent of a new generation the game assumes a more violent, more tragic character. Either the frenzied impulses of the sensibility disturb the vestiges of visual appearance or the brush strokes combine accident and impulsive motions of the hand.*

**275.** - *SEBASTIAN MATTA.* LISTEN TO LIFE. 1941. The Museum of Modern Art, New York

Although there are only too many cases—it is true—where fashion seduces the credulous, or artists are taken advantage of by dealers, still the greatest audacities of the present day cannot be dismissed as jokes or provocations. No—they reflect a new conception of man, and they are dictated by our age. Whether we like them or not, we should not underestimate their significance.

NEW RELATIONSHIPS WITH THE WORLD.   Formerly man identified himself with reason, made it his headquarters, his control tower. He sought in it clearsighted motives for what he had done and for what he ought to do. Modern psychology has destroyed this confidence in reason, and by a piquant paradox, it was nineteenth-century scientism, the ultimate bastion of rationalism, that, carried away by its materialistic hatred for all spiritual realities, dealt it the first blow. To denounce consciousness and the life of the mind as mere epiphenomena superimposed on physiological reality, to transform ideals into mere bubbles rising from the surface of the brain and expressing its organic chemistry, to deny free will in the name of determinism—was this not to subject thought to material necessity, to rob reason of its traditional role of guide, and to

**276. -** *JACKSON POLLOCK.* NUMBER 1. 1948. The Museum of Modern Art, New York

reduce it to a superfluous manifestation? Once human behavior was subjected to the yoke of blind necessity, it no longer needed to be meaningful: the door was opened to the absurd.

Then came the twentieth century, which sought relentlessly to prove that human actions are not rationally motivated, but merely the effect of blind causes. Whether these causes lie in the unconscious operation of dark instincts, as Freud insisted, or in the countless social and economic necessities that surround us, turning the individual into a docile cog of the collectivity—as asserted in the dialectical materialism derived from Hegel and Marx—whether these mindless causes lurk inside ourselves or on the contrary dominate us through the power of human masses, the result is the same. Reason is no more the source of our actions, it merely interprets them post facto and is all too often duped when it does so.

How could man, overwhelmed and harassed from all sides, preserve his precarious rational balance in the midst of these seismic tremors, this breakdown of all his values and beliefs? The inevitable happened. He got used to the vertigo of living in absurdity; he began to like it, even found it stimulating. As we have seen, a century earlier he had begun to look to narcotics for a holiday from normal society, as in the club frequented by Gautier and Balzac and in the opium that fed the dreams of De Quincey, which preceded Baudelaire's artificial paradises. That this mechanical method of liberating oneself from reason has its own characteristic forms in our own day is well known.

And so it is that areas of experience which were barely glimpsed a century ago have become man's favorite, well-nigh habitual haunts. Over modern writing hovers an insidious, unreal mistiness. *Le Grand Meaulnes* first popularized it, investing unreality with glamour. Before that, Rilke had made himself adept at transporting readers to another universe, in which we move with the silent shuffle of the sleepwalker. Kafka enjoys far too wide a popularity in many countries not to reflect our secret tastes. The oppressive atmosphere of his novels springs precisely from the fact that he rejects any rational cause for the actions that unfold in them with inexorable logic. Their rigorous, ineluctable plots are constructed over a void. Starobinsky was correct when he pointed out that Kafka's work was one of the most exact prefigurations of the absurdity and cruelty that attained open expression in the free air of the twentieth century.

Thus, the accord between rational man and the world, once taken for granted, has given way today to a widespread recognition of their fundamental incompatibility. They can only coexist now, and their coexistence takes on more and more savage forms. We are like blind men, who can find their way around pretty well, but without seeing where they are going. To coexist with the world, without ever grasping it—or simply to exist, gratuitously varying the modalities of that existence—such seems to be the only possibility open to us, in the eyes of modern thinkers. A philosophy only too eager for popular acceptance has formulated the metaphysics of a profoundly altered human condition. Thus existentialism was born.

At the beginning of this century the intellect had already resigned itself to this new state of affairs, to the reasoned abdication of reason from all the claims of reason. Pragmatism, and later Paul Valéry as well, agreed to abandon the search for certainty, to occupy themselves wholly with an empirical pursuit of power, an ever more completely organized manipulation of reality.

Existentialism went further. Bringing together scattered elements drawn from contemporary philosophy—Kierkegaard, Chestov, Jaspers, Heidegger—it condensed the vast experience of the absurd into a doctrine that asserts that man is a "stranger" (to use a title of a novel by Camus) in this world, and the task of the mind that of adjusting us to the unintelligibility of our condition (Fig. 295).

All that exists is inexplicable. Only what does not really exist—only what has been freely conceived by the intellect—is explicable. "A circle is not absurd," says Sartre. "It is adequately accounted for as the rotation of a segment of a straight line around one of its extremities. But then, there is no such thing as a circle." It is a purely intellectual conception. "To exist is to be there, simply," to be impervious to explanation. "The world of explanations and reasons is not that of existence." Life is a fact whose only meaning is that which we assign it, *ex post facto*.


IN QUEST OF A DIRECTION.   What possibilities, then, remain open to the human mind? Camus tells us, "True knowledge is impossible. Appearances can be enumerated, and the climate can be felt—that is all. This divorce between man and his life, between the actor and his setting, is properly speaking the feeling of the absurd."

476

According to this philosophy, "reason becomes confused and frees itself by negating itself.... The absurd man is no longer concerned with explanations and solutions, he merely experiences and describes. An indifferent clearsightedness is at the origin of all that transpires." Human life is sterile, hence absurd, and knows that it is absurd. Man's greatness lies in the lucidity of his despair, in his ability to accept and surmount despair with lucidity" (Fig. 290).

Man's tremendous effort over the centuries to elucidate the mystery of the universe, to make the human condition ever less and less absurd, has ended in failure. Man is defeated by the very forces that he had set up to subdue. Both in his actual life and in his scientific investigations, he meets and verifies absurdity, and, today, the intellect itself bows before it. Abjectly, he acknowledges his own absurdity in philosophy, in literature, and in art.

Hovering over the gulf that yawns between the riddle of the individuality and the

*Abstract Expressionism aims at a return to the primordial and seeks to strip man of his organized existence. It often evokes degraded aspects of matter, such as are featured in modern photography.*

**277.** - ERODED WALL. Photographed by Aaron Siskind (b. 1903). Chicago

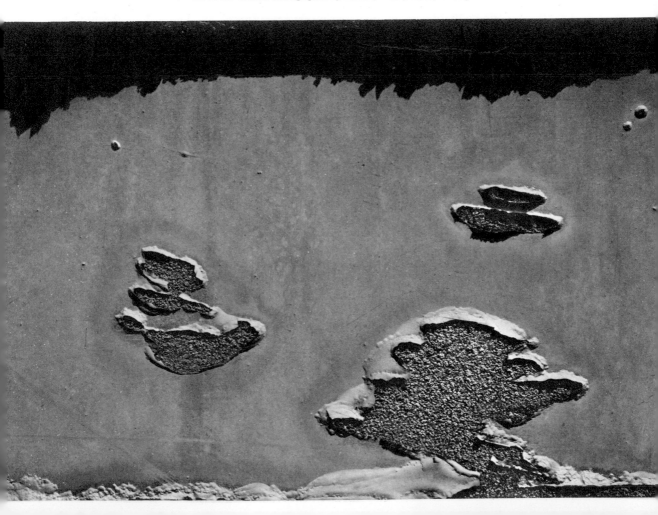

universe surrounding it, mankind fears that it is losing its way. Like some rocket in outer space that has got off the beam of its planned trajectory, it floats at random in space, with no landmarks, no means of getting back on course. The worst has happened: mankind actually, consciously, experiences absurdity—the very thing it had cautiously avoided for centuries (Fig. 271).

The situation is filled with terror, but, at the same time, it arouses boundless curiosity. To mankind everything is a sign of life; our avidity for life is insatiable. Our failure is patent: we have not succeeded in banishing absurdity through recourse to logic. But, lo and behold: already we are busy assimilating the absurd, feeding on it as best we can. Man is a tireless rodent who gnaws even at the trap in which he finds himself, in order to get free of it.

Who can foretell the outcome? Four centuries ago, mankind was compelled to capitulate, and, disavowing its most deep-seated beliefs, admitted that it was not the center of the universe nor the measure of all things. Galileo and Copernicus reassigned us to a more modest place in infinity, a mere speck in the cosmos. Must we now make a second capitulation, and resign ourselves to the reign of the absurd, developing a wholly new awareness of our relation to the world? Are we truly no more than a wisp of straw being carried no one knows where by unknown waves operating no one knows how through the blackness? Can we really be reconciled to a life without understanding? For what is understanding?—and perhaps there is nothing to be understood.

Perhaps. But since when is thought to be regarded as immutable? Why can we not regard it as subject, like living species, to mutations and periodic explosions, efforts to break out of one after another all-too-confining framework? Our all-pervading feeling of absurdity, even our seemingly morbid taste for the absurd, may be no more than symptomatic—the preliminary sign of a realization that a new vision is needed. A new reason— broader in range, more flexible, based upon more comprehensive principles, less tied to the concrete representation of things, a reason which our own still cannot conceive of, is perhaps in process of being born.

The vital instinct is incomparably wise. We are surprised and we are shocked by the progressive stifling of individuality today, by the mounting mistrust of an awareness and lucidity only so recently attained. Increasingly, we are being driven along by blind tides of collective imperatives. We do not understand what it all means. Who can tell, perhaps mankind is temporarily anesthetizing its nervous centers—its individuals—the better to assist an enormous mutation already taking place?

We are living through a fateful moment in the history of the race, whose meaning is hard to discern, slow to announce itself. Our more than ever lucid minds—so especially aware of their limitations—are gaining the ability to compute and make use of the very things impervious to our understanding. Ignorant of our goal we may be, but we are no less eager than earlier ages to go forward and meet it.

# 2. SYMBOLISM OF THE MODERN SOUL

Having rid ourselves of the traditional modes of expression and escaped from the traditional disciplines, the modern soul, uncertain of everything save its own predicament, has found that art alone provides it with a suitable language, a language of images.

This book has been written to show how the human imagination defines the forms of our inner life. The images born of our own reflection are concrete condensations of the whole diffuse, shifting content we carry about inside ourselves. The obscure currents that animate our inner life disclose a pattern, just as slivers of iron thrown onto a magnetized plate arrange themselves in a pattern corresponding to the invisible magnetic field. Art, which sets down and elaborates images drawn from our internal resources, proves a magic mirror of the mind. Anyone who attempts to explore the themes most familiar to our times may thus expect to discover in them singular revelations as to the dominant character, the most insistent concerns, the prevailing anxieties of the age. Never before has man been so powerful technologically, and never before has he felt so overwhelmed, so morally abandoned.

THE CRISIS OF THE WEST. If there were still the slightest doubt that the West is passing through a deep crisis—certainly one of the severest it has ever experienced—such a doubt would be dispelled by contemporary art were we to view it not as an aesthetic experience in terms of currently held theories, but as a visual record of the tendencies of our time. Viewed in such a way, the artist's projections are situated midway between the unconscious zone where the sleeper lives in dreams and the conscious zone where tendencies of our time take on comminatory meaning.

It is possible to make significant groupings of these scattered indications. To begin with, art has shown increasing hostility to the most familiar themes of the Western tradition and even to its patiently elaborated repertory of individual forms. At the same time it has turned with mounting enthusiasm, first to forms coming from the most remote areas of the planet (the role of Far Eastern art at the end of the nineteenth century is well known), and second, to the forms developed by culturally backward, so-called primitive peoples (at the beginning of the twentieth century, Negro art became popular; today this is true of all the arts of the so-called barbarian peoples). It cannot be denied that the aesthetic value of this type of art may be just as high as that of the Western types, but what is revealing is the fact that unfamiliarity and strangeness make it more fascinating to us. It is as though our age were in a very great hurry to strip itself of its patiently accumulated heritage, of everything it was so proud of only the day before yesterday. There is a dizzy fascination with the elementary, which in Buffet takes on forms of asceticism and poverty, but in Dubuffet becomes an irresistible attraction to the most unpleasant, sordid materials of art, worked over with infantile elaboration. Dubuffet writes, "We call *art brut* ('raw art') works executed by persons undamaged by artistic culture." The latest-comers among the abstract artists are trying to achieve direct contact with organic reality, which

479

some of them call "the cosmos," by recording their most instinctual impulses and spontaneous gestures, making use of sheer accidents in the course of work (Figs. 277, 278, and 291).

This regression to the elementary is a concrete aspect of the attraction that, since Freud and Surrealism, has been exerted upon the youngest generation by the dark forces of instinct, psychologically understood. But is it correct to use the term "regression"? It is too early to say whether we are dealing with the symptoms of cultural decline, with a civilization exhausted by its own refinement and intellectual mandarinism, or with symptoms of a more healthy disposition—a jettisoning of the past in an effort to adjust at any cost to an existence that, under the impact of science and technology, requires total recasting of our modes of thinking. It was a painter, Paul Klee, who wrote the highly significant words, "The world in its present form may not be the only possible world."

This feeling is mingled with unspoken terror. Goya was the first of modern artists—in works like the enigmatic painting in the Prado, known as *The Colossus* or *Panic*—to portray a man-monster, a "wild man" whose appearance puts a panic-stricken world to flight. Although our age deplores and despises everything that had formerly seemed a positive conquest of culture, it does not by any means think in terms of a fresh start, clearing the decks, beginning anew. The imperious notion of the negative is inseparable from the other manifestations of our day. The unconscious has often appeared naked and unleashed in open hostility to reason. Surrealism, which could have provided a much needed complement or counterbalance to rationalism, instead chose to declare war and wielded its weapons of hatred and sarcasm with deadly efficiency.

THE OBSESSIONS OF OUR AGE. As the human face, particularly in its more noble aspects, has more and more been disappearing from contemporary works, its counterpart, the animal, has come to occupy an ever more prominent place. It appears often, as though to testify to a secret obsession of our age. Between the two world wars, a great deal of interest has been displayed in the stupid brutality of the bull, from Picasso's well-known treatment of it in the *Guernica* and other works to the *Minotaur*, which was the title of a well-known magazine of those years. It would be interesting to analyze this disturbing obsession with the animal, and especially with the animal in its most brutish aspects. Sometimes it takes on the form of an insect: Ensor was fond of disguising himself and others as insects, long before Kafka portrayed man as turning into a bug. Sometimes we are confronted with prehistoric monsters mysteriously brought to life and threatening the world of the twentieth century—as in the recent Japanese films, *Rodan* and *Godzilla*. Other images show monsters looming on the horizon, curiously like Goya's *Colossus*, and like the latter, putting human beings to flight. In the United States, a science-fiction film, *The Forbidden Planet*, portrayed the interplanetary adventures of a monster, who was clearly intended to incarnate a materialized unconscious. This identification is in itself revealing. Even the imagination of children—of children even more than adults—is as fascinated with the exploration of outer space as it is with evocations of the first animals which populated our planet. Paradoxically, the two extremes meet—the plesiosaurus and the space rocket, our remotest origins and anticipation of the future. The large number of

In a letter addressed to the publisher Flammarion, Dubuffet
expresses his fear that the
author "may be incapable of
understanding the meaning of
his works." But is he himself
aware of the contemporary
currents that determine his
painting? Even if, not without
shrewdness, he exploits them
in order to be successful? In the
painting reproduced here he
reflects an instinctive desire to
return to the zero point, to discredit civilization by celebrating wretchedness—all this to be
followed by what new
departure?

**278.** - *JEAN DUBUFFET.
VENUS OF THE
SIDEWALKS. 1946.*
Engraved white lead,
asphalt,
and gravel on staff

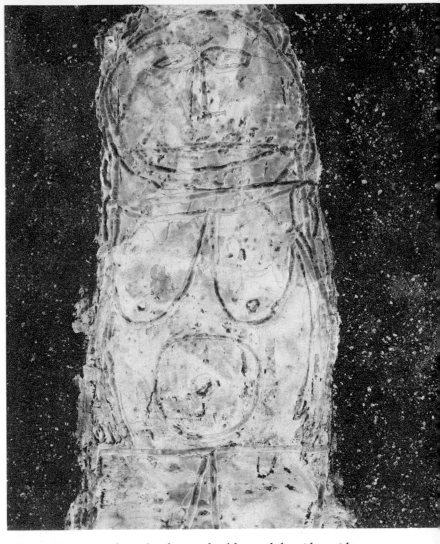

motion pictures that treat these subjects merely make them palatable to adults. Alongside
such elementary fantasies, the more refined ones created by artists reflect the same tendency to go back to the monstrous and the animal. Sculpture alone, from Germaine
Richier to Chadwick or Roszak, provides numerous examples of this: rough-hewn,
formless monsters, sometimes headless, carved out of crude, refractory materials (often
unpolished metal) disclose a secret alliance between preoccupation with the brute animal
and fascination with raw concreteness (Figs. 279—283).

From times immemorial, the Beast has been associated with another symbol, also a
reflection of unconscious fears, and also opposed to lucid thought. The Beast is symbol of
the other, the adversary, the negator and the negation, the Devil—to name him. The
Romantic epoch brought back this symbol into the modern consciousness. We may not
believe in God very much any more, but we are certainly very much concerned with the
Devil. Writers like Sartre, for example, have given the Devil a prominent place in their

Goya was a great precursor. He unconsciously anticipated the anxieties of the modern world, its terror before the unleashed forces which are beyond its control and understanding. The gigantic prehistoric monsters that appear in science-fiction films are mythological figures, imaginative embodiments of the forces that threaten our civilization. Picasso, too, expresses these forces when he represents the murderous Beast, enemy of woman's beauty and of the noble horse in a scene lighted only by the fragile candle in the hands of a little girl.

**279.** - *GOYA.*
THE COLOSSUS or PANIC.
About 1809. The Prado,
Madrid

**280.** - The prehistoric
beast in the Japanese film
GODZILLA

281. - *PICASSO*. MINOTAUROMACHY. 1935. Etching

works, and film makers as well. *Marguerite de la Nuit*, a recent film, corresponds in this respect to *Faust*, with this improvement: Satan who, we were assured thirty years ago in a noisy pamphlet, "conducts the ball," no longer requires disguise as an operatic character. Our contemporaries see him as a well-dressed figure of the present day, a man among men—when, that is, they do not pay their respects to him through the intermediary of some such figure as the Marquis de Sade. Judging by the considerable literature devoted to the latter, we are indeed preoccupied with him.

Exhibitions, and even congresses, have for some time been devoted to the demonic in art—in Italy, in Holland, and elsewhere. This was the central theme of an exhibition in Bordeaux in 1957 devoted to the fantastic, an even greater success than earlier exhibitions of the type. The posters showed the Great Goat (painted by Goya) presiding over a witches' Sabbath by moonlight.

Whatever oppresses man, whatever lies beyond his reach or threatens him, is always placed under the sign of the Devil.

In the fifteenth century, as the Middle Ages came to an end—an age like our own perhaps, if civilization is indeed approaching its end today—a new epoch was being born. Though no one was aware of it at the time, that century marked both the end of the Middle Ages and the beginning of the modern era. The reappearance of the same symptoms may mean that today, too, something is coming to an end—namely, the modern era that began with the decline of the Middle Ages. Perhaps we are at the beginning of an unknown era, only just coming to birth in much travail and suffering. If so, we, too, are unable to discern it clearly (Figs. 285 and 286).

It is important to study these symptoms and take note of the state of mind that they reflect. But their true significance will be understood only if they are related to the central problem of man, the problem that determines the pattern of his destiny and that he tries to solve by the founding of civilizations.

RESURGENCE OF PRIMITIVE FEARS. It has never been an obligation of the human condition that man must understand his predicament—not, at least, beyond a certain depth. In certain periods, however, he succeeded in creating a sufficiently coherent set of explanations to make him believe that he did understand it. These were the Classical periods, such as were realized around the Mediterranean basin. The balance and certainty that characterize the Mediterranean spirit rest upon two foundations. First, man believes in what he sees. This is realism, a realism that is today disappearing—in science as well as in art, for the sciences are no longer based on visual data, on the tangible or concrete evidences of sensory experience, formerly regarded as the essential stuff of truth. Today the sciences are largely based on abstract computations.

The Mediterranean spirit does not merely define reality in terms of sensory appearances, however. In Greece, especially, the self-confidence that man achieved, perhaps for the first time in history, in dispelling the curse of the demonic, had a second foundation. The Greeks believed that beyond or behind appearances the world was governed by exactly the same laws as those governing human thought.

With this conviction, the universe was now made to seem less disquieting, less mysterious. As an echo or twin of mankind's most notable traits, the universe appeared to be in conformity with the senses with respect to its substance, and in conformity with human reason with respect to its structure.

It is becoming harder and harder to recall that we are the heirs of this high civilization.

With the achievement of rational balance, the importance of the Beast, both in religion and in art, was notably reduced. Previously it had played a very great part in the human imagination. It had made its appearance in the earliest times, and had dominated pre-

---

*The primitives portrayed their fears under the guise of the Beast with inhuman and ferocious features. Exorcized by Greco-Roman rationalism, the Beast today again haunts the nightmares of the imagination. It borrows its carapace, its mandibles, its pincers from insects or crustaceans.*

**282.** - *WALTER R. ROGASKI.* SCORPION AND CRAB. 1951. Copper engraving.
The Museum of Modern Art, New York

**283.** - *LYNN CHADWICK.* BEAST VIII. 1956. Owned by the artist.

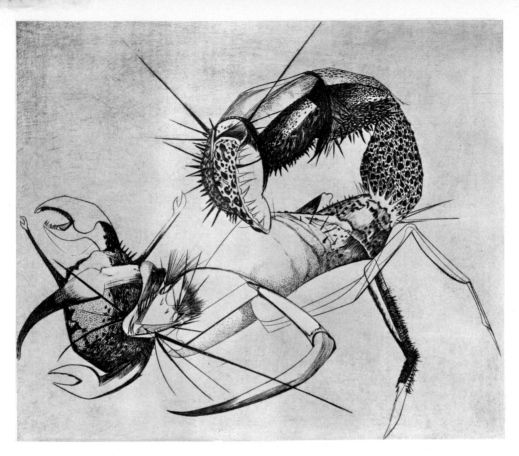

history. It held a major place in the first agrarian civilizations of Mesopotamia and Egypt. However, it was vanquished by the Hunter King, who fulfilled, in relation to it and in relation to the enemy, the function of guardian of the city. And even then, particularly in Mesopotamia, it was associated with the demon.

When the Greeks enthroned reason and realism, the Beast disappeared. The few monsters that survive in Greek mythology were all imported from the East, from Asia Minor, or Ionian Greece, which had imported them from Persia and ancient Assyria. The Greeks were interested only in domesticated, humanized animals, and were particularly fond of the noblest animal of all—the horse, which always symbolized to them the highest things —the spirit, the soul. But just as soon as mankind was again assailed by doubts and fears, the Beast moved back to the foreground of the imagination. The early Middle Ages, throughout the period of the barbarian invasions, and the Romanesque Middle Ages created a great many mythological beasts inherited indirectly from the Far East. Obsession with the Beast was once again prevalent. But it faded away in turn with the advent of the Gothic age, particularly in that age of harmony and Classicism, the thirteenth century. A new sense of balance was achieved, in some ways perhaps more far-reaching than that of ancient Greece, for this new accord between reason and the senses now also comprised the heart, that important contribution of Christianity. Between man and the world a new bond was forged through the intermediary of God—the bond of love. Reason and realism more than ever induced man to have faith in himself and faith in the world: he ceased to be afraid.

The fourteenth century came, and a slow degradation began. In the fifteenth century it was in full swing; once more man gave way to fear. And along with the ancestral terrors, the Beast came back, closely followed by the Devil. The two are inseparable. The Devil, at first portrayed as a black angel, i.e., an angel deprived of light, but nonetheless an *angel*— had gradually taken on animal features over the course of the centuries. The first signs of this transformation appeared in Romanesque art, with its rich heritage from the barbarian and Oriental bestiaries. They abound in the monasteries, especially in the sculptures of the capitals. The monks looked upon themselves, as their texts confirm, as besieged by the Evil One; they fought against him on the behalf of others, and in their eyes the Devil took on the monstrous appearances of the Beast, every sort of characteristic of repulsive, hairy animals. In the fifteenth and sixteenth centuries the transformation had become complete and was spread all over Europe. We find many mixtures of human and animal forms, in which we recognize the wolf, the goat, the bat, the vulture.... This heterogeneous and monstrous mutation reached its peak in that branch of European art which had been least influenced by Christianity and by Greco-Roman civilization—in the art of the Germanic peoples, last to have been converted to Christianity as well as last to have been touched— only very slightly—by Mediterranean civilization. Even at the heyday of the Renaissance there was an extraordinary proliferation of the Beast at the same time as a singular tendency to depict savage, hairy, half-animal men. Occasionally we see semihuman figures of this type waging combat with the unicorn, symbol of purity. But even though this resurgence of a disturbed and anguish-ridden unconscious mind was especially striking in Central and Northern Europe, it was as widespread a phenomenon as Surrealism in our own day and left as great an imprint on nearly all aspects of European thought.

Thus it would seem that European man is forever struggling to get on an equal footing

*Here man himself has been robbed of his face together with his control and lucidity. He appears in the guise of a mechanized beast—the machine, too, it terrifying because it is a blind force.*

**284.** - *JACOB EPSTEIN* (1880–1959). ROCK DRILL. Bronze. National Gallery of Canada, Ottawa

487

In periods of uncertainty and insecurity, the imagination conjures up the evil Beast and identifies it with the Devil. He has a thousand faces, each of them expressing dark threats.

**285.** - *At left: URS GRAF.* HERMIT PURSUED BY THE DEVIL. Museum of Fine Arts, Basel

**286.** - *Below: NICOLAS MANUEL DEUTSCH.* THE TEMPTATION OF ST. ANTHONY. Museum of Fine Arts, Bern

**287.** - *Opposite page: LEONOR FINI.* PHILAGRIA

*While Classicism attempted to build a new human order, some seventeenth-century Baroque artists continued to treat the late medieval theme of the danse macabre. In our own day, the image of the skeleton has re-emerged in art, placed in the most familiar surroundings.*

**288.** - *At Left: ANTOINE CARON.* DIALOGUE BETWEEN THE PRINCE AND DEATH. Seventeenth century. Max Janlet Collection, Brussels

**289.** - *Opposite page:* *LAURENT DELVAUX.* SKELETONS. 1944. C. Spaak Collection

with the world around him, where he must make a home, feed his children, and build a society. But he cannot live in peace and security until he has eliminated fear. When the caveman drew, painted, and sculptured figures of animals, it was for the purpose of controlling them; it was a magical operation whereby he gained confidence in his own powers. Art was at the service of this deeply human need.

What is the situation today? Never before has man's control of his environment been so extensive, but the new and unknown vistas that still open up are to such a scale as once again to arouse deep-lying fears. Once more man feels that he is faced with forces superior to his own. His self-doubts and anxieties stem from this sense of menace. However rational or experimental his explorations may be in intention, they have revealed and released hitherto undreamed-of forces of nature. We are crushed by the very energies that we have discovered and unleashed. Their rapid multiplication over a relatively brief period gives us the feeling of having lost our mastery of our environment. It is no longer the Beast that worries mankind. It is the unknown powers which we have released through science and which threaten to crush us, to destroy us, to annihilate us.

Analysis of the contemporary imagination as it manifests itself in its major outlet, motion pictures—which have become the seventh art—is also revealing. If the prehistoric world is associated in them with the most daring scientific inventions—inventions still in

a rudimentary stage—this is because they arouse atavistic terrors of tremendous uncontrolled forces. It is noteworthy that in the Japanese *Godzilla* series, it is the atom bomb that drives the apocalyptic beasts from the bottom of the sea to launch an assault upon modern civilization; and yet all the latest weapons prove incapable of repelling their attack. The abyssal past is not only associated with the future; the two trade places and substitute for each other; they are interchangeable. The producers of *Godzilla* used the same actors and a similarly constructed scenario in another motion picture, where, instead of huge tyrannosaurs, an enormous robot comes from outer space to wreck our cities. His metallic head, which recalls ancient helmets that imitated the beaks of hawks and snouts of animals, could almost be the sharp, angular profile of some quaternary animal (Fig. 280). We find the same strange mixture in a sculpture by Epstein (Fig. 284). Man gives a face to his terrors, borrowing from creatures which antedate our species or which we have just recently invented. Endowed with the active powers of mankind, they are devoid of any

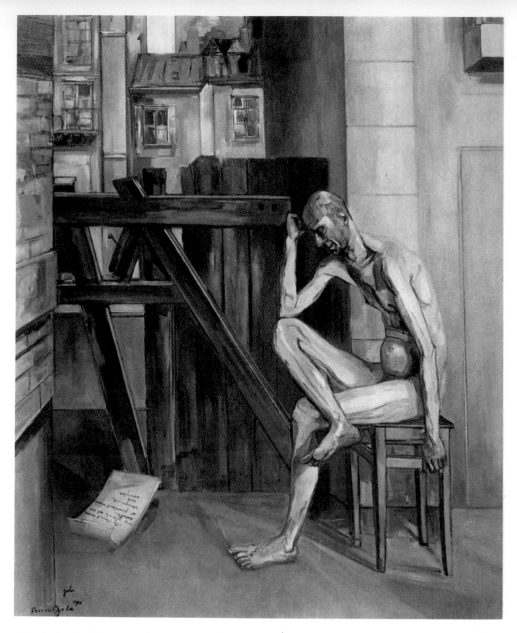

Early in the sixteenth century, during a period of upheaval, Dürer painted his Melancolia. In the twentieth century, Grüber's Job expresses a similar despair. Buffet has vulgarized such themes, and his popularity is too great not to reflect a deep yearning of the modern sensibility. America is more familiar than any other country with the horrors of a world where the machine crushes man. The mother shown here seems to be protecting her unborn child from the neutralization of the faces; this hideous uniformity has already begun to affect her.

**290.** - *FRANCIS GRÜBER. JOB. 1944. The Tate Gallery, London*

**292.** - *Opposite page, bottom: GEORGE TOOKER. THE SUBWAY. 1950. Whitney Museum of American Art, New York*

**291. -** *Above: BERNARD BUFFET.* THE ROOM. 1947

soul such as would make them comprehensible to us, and thus let us feel closer to them. In such anguished cries of fear rising out of the depths of the contemporary unconscious, we are witnessing the beginning of another reign of the fantastic.

SIGNIFICANCE OF THE FANTASTIC.   The fantastic raises a number of problems. To begin with, it may be manifested in two separate domains—in the outside world, and, perhaps more tragically, in the inner world.

When man falls under the sway of the fantastic, first of all the outside world changes its appearance in his eyes and becomes unfamiliar. In the course of our own civilization the fantastic has been cropping up insidiously throughout the modern era. The Renaissance was a reaction against the panic that seized men at the end of the Middle Ages. Resolutely, imperiously, it exorcized the fears of the epoch by restoring the universal rule of realistic truth for the senses, rational truth for the mind.

Nonetheless, the fantastic had not been defeated; it was on the prowl, and we find traces of it even in the School of Raphael, even in Raphael's own works. Though the fantastic was not completely eliminated, it was largely ignored, save for rare exceptions. It raised its head again only with the appearance of Mannerism, though the Mannerists were not so much out to shatter the security of Classicism as to refine it. Nonetheless, their pursuit of elegance led them without realizing it to a certain cult of strangeness. What was intended as no more than a subtle improvement touched off an incalculable chain of consequences (Figs. 269 and 270).

The Baroque art that followed Mannerism marked a new step forward, invoking the vital instincts and freeing art from all fetters. It was a celebration of life's irrepressibility, until then subjected to the human order. From this point onward, life itself would gain ever greater ascendancy over all conceptions of order, shattering them in the end. With the escape from rationality, life again appeared cloaked in mystery. Before long, the flavor, the thrill of mystery was deliberately cultivated: nineteenth-century Romanticism, and the Surrealism of our own day. A new vision of the outside world as incomprehensible was developed.

We must see here, too, a swing of the pendulum. Man wearies of the very order that he designs and imposes, however great the struggle to inaugurate it, initially. We are so made that even happiness tires us when it is too far prolonged. This is no doubt why the life of man has to be short. The species tires fast; we possess a sort of vice that drives us, once balance has been achieved, to upset it.

Another name for this vice is the demonic.

A world under the sway of the fantastic began to be imagined centuries ago. Everything in that world is unusual, unexpected, marvelous in the true sense of the word. Animal is confused with mineral, mineral with vegetable, and the vegetable and the mineral mixed with the human. Such are the figures of Arcimboldo, in which a human face dissolves on closer inspection into a weird assortment of disparate, unlike things. So, too, are the figures attributed to Josse de Momper, what looks to be head being transformed, by a mere shift in our attention, into a rock covered with vegetation, with paths and hovels scattered over the steep slopes. All is mirage, illusion. The evidence of the senses has lost its certainty and value; it no longer leads to truth, to reality, but to the fleeting inconsistency of the dream, to unreality.

This is still the external brand of the fantastic; it was soon supplemented by what I call the "inner" fantasy. The two are inseparable. It is via the latter that man retreats or regresses to the infra-rational zones. In the fifteenth century the figure of the Devil served the function of satisfying inner fantasy; in our own day, the unconscious serves. Indeed, one part of the unconscious is profoundly related to what was formerly called the "bestial" or "diabolical." I say one part, for another part, perhaps, enables us to transcend reason, to go beyond it and above it, and to come closer to the divine. The mystics, as we shall see, were not far behind in proving that this is so.

But very often—and Freudianism has stressed this point—to plunge into the unconscious is merely to descend to levels of near-animality, to the level where instincts are uncontrolled.

Now, our age delights in such explorations of the lower depths no less than the fifteenth century, and gets as big a thrill out of them. Today, as before, we are witnessing the release of every sort of quasi-animal instinct, breaking past the barriers that reason has erected in the form of social order and ethical values. Moral values are depreciated, and the untamed instincts are cultivated. In the fifteenth century, the same reversion had the effect of making the diabolical attractive. Today, in line with our more scientific demands, the effect is to glorify the unconscious. Science itself serves merely as a camouflage, as objective sanction for an infatuation with the cloacal by which our age resembles the waning Middle Ages.

Seen from this point of view, what I call the fantastic is something altogether different from the associational fantasying that goes on in every human mind. Coming as it does from the depths, it may well be one of the acutest symptoms of human self-doubts, of spiritual anguish, of man's perpetual struggle with the world around him and the world with him. Under the thin crust of intelligence and lucidity, which our conscious mind supposes to be *terra firma,* lurks another, permanently unsettled world.

The existence of the fantastic may well reveal one aspect of the struggle we carry on to find a place for ourselves and keep it within an alien world. This struggle cannot be reduced to a confrontation of two opposed forces; it is more complex than that. The dangers are more bewildering, more insidious; they surround us on every side. Almost from time immemorial they have been symbolized in tales of how the Devil sets his traps for mankind. They lurk at the end of both the (otherwise opposed) paths that we think between them cover all our acts. The diabolical is possessed of two natures, for the Devil is multi-form—he is diversity; he is legion. The one danger is the temptation of perpetual renewal, the other that of eternal fixity.

THE DOUBLE TRAP. Man strives laboriously (and art helps him, just as do reason and the mind in general) to construct an image of the world enabling him, to begin with, to find his way in it. This image may be scientific—that is, considered to conform to a model and for this reason to be true—and yet it never ceases to be revised, just like other kinds of images. There are many images of the world: reason with its theories, faith with its revelations, dreams with their fantasies present us with any number of them. They vary with historical period, with the age of the individual, with places. The point is, we continually interpose them between the unknown world and ourselves in order to understand it, so as not to lose our way in it.

Art is perhaps one of our sublimest efforts in this direction; it is the very model of man's attempt to invest the world with meaning, to get closer to it, through creating an image that opens a window onto it, but which nonetheless remains a reflection of man, for it always bears his imprint, that of his presence and his values.

The image of the world provided by art—like the images of all philosophies and all sciences, which pursue the same goal by different means—entails contradictory risks.

Suppose it has taken form: the day this is achieved, a culture has been constituted and asserted—a culture and a civilization. What else is a civilization, at bottom, but an image, a coherent view of the world, assumed to be total and stable? It will so appear for a time, during which the civilization that produced it will believe itself to be eternal. The seventeenth-century image of the world had this solid character, and so did the image of the age of Pericles.

At this point the Devil steps in. First he tempts us to change the form that we have created and arrived at; he suggests to us that it is monotonous, wearisome, that life is an adventure, a continual discovery, that the very form so laboriously achieved becomes a prison in the end. Then man begins to destroy the form, which is his civilization, in order to set off on new adventures, wherever the Devil calls. This is the beginning of the cycle we referred to above, which opened with Mannerism, went on into the Baroque, produced

496

## SYMBOLISM

*The animal, vegetable, and mineral kingdoms become indistinguishable in a world where each thing is in process of either dying or being born. One more step and all that is left is a mirage of potential forms.*

**293.** - *Opposite page: MAX ERNST.*
THE EYE OF SILENCE. 1943/44.
Washington University, St. Louis

**294.** - *At right: OSCAR DOMINGUEZ.*
DECALCOMANIA WITHOUT OBJECTS.
1936. The Museum of Modern Art, New York

a number of Romanticisms, and led directly to the great uncertainty in which we are living today. In current use among art critics is a highly significant term—"nonformal" art, i.e., an art that repudiates form. The Flamboyant Gothic style of the fifteenth century marked a similar effort to break out of the pattern of established structures, to use them up, to be liberated from them—on impulse, in sudden conviction that their constructive purpose had lost all meaning.

Why, then, the sages ask, do we not cling to the form that we have already and to Classical solutions?

Beware! The security that such a course seems to promise is nothing but a trap, the most deceptive of all of the Devil's temptations. One of the most eminent specialists in diabolical lore, Professor Castelli of the University of Rome, has denounced it. Stubborn clinging to patterns created by the mind, in the determination to keep them forever unchanged, refusal to evolve—just this was called the *ars diabolica* par excellence in the Middle Ages. Though less obviously demonic than the first attitude (it does not look destructive), the second is far more insidious. The Devil is always insidious: this attitude resists development in time, is opposed to life. It prompts man to call a halt at some particular high point of his civilization and to free life in rigid academism, that is, in cultural death.

The Devil makes use of both strategies. Occasionally he pretends to celebrate life and

*Man loses consistency: he wanders unaware of his fellow men in an increasingly erosive void.*

**295. - *GIACOMETTI.***
GROUP OF THREE MEN I. 1948–49.
Galerie Maeght, Paris

denounces death, prompting us to hand ourselves over to the pyromania of revolutionary freedom: flinging our cultural heritage happily into the flames, reducing civilization to some more elemental level of life itself, surrendering to unleashed instinct. This gives us the illusion of liberation, but actually we have become prisoners of life itself, our control over it lost, our right to pass value judgments on it abandoned, our capacity to discipline and shape it forgotten. We may be passing through just such a crisis today. On the other hand, if we succumbed to the other temptation, that of immobility, the Devil would cease to pretend to be on the side of Life, and would become Death. By this tactic he would have us no less in his power—only now in the name of tradition, peace, security, certainty, and perfect achievement.

Thus, it is our fate to walk a tightrope, to try to preserve a balance between regression to the formless and disorderly—which leads to chaos and nothingness—and fascination with Death in the guise of definitive marmoreal perfection, an elaborate reconstruction of some past life in which the living substance has long since dried up and blown away.

Such are the two yawning gulfs to left and to right that threaten us as we walk the tightrope and the Devil lies in wait on either side.

Where can we look for help in our predicament? Perhaps to humanism, understood as the sense of the human. It is possible that a less simple-minded attitude to life would safeguard against rash, panicky decisions.

# 3. LUX ET NOX

MAN is not merely in quest of balance; he also aspires to transcend himself. Mystery —poetry—God? We seek God throughout our lives, are in perpetual quest of his name. At all events, it is certain that we are looking for something else all through our lives—something different from the too obvious light of day, a light that does not merely illuminate appearances, but makes visible the secret that underlies them: a mysterious light not made for human eyes, a light imperceptible to those who see only with their eyes. To them this light would look like darkness, and yet would nonetheless be the sole true light, the only light capable of slaking the thirst of the spirit.

ANOTHER LIGHT.   When I was a little boy, I imagined that God and His angels were located beyond the clouds which hid them from my sight, above the firmament that served them as a floor. A little later, my ideas of this beyond became more precise. It began outside the atmosphere of our planet, outside the sphere illumined by the sun. It was the abyss that yawned just at the edge of the horizon, where those whose legs were long enough to get there would surely see the world collapsing dizzily into the sluice gates of Night. Here began an unknown region without light—for I supposed the sun did not reach there—a black translucid domain, a great, limpid, lightless peace, where eyes would no longer be needed and yet everything would be perceivable. Infinity surely started there.

Still later (I had grown up in the meantime), I lost this kingdom of shadow, for I had been taught that knowledge has no geographical boundaries, that the horizon recedes continuously as we move closer to it, and that other suns take over where our own leaves off. I lost this kingdom of shadow, but I suddenly found it again when I closed my eyes. This kingdom that I had thought so far away was within me, always there, always available; it was enough to close my eyes to plunge into it.

I open my eyes: the light of the world, a material light that our nerves can almost touch, a sensory light submerges me and submerges all things. I close my eyes: the light of the world is extinguished; darkness. But the mind's eye gets used to it, and the soul gives off its own secret light, an intangible radiance. A more mysterious, more solemn light spreads and rises gently, like a slow moonrise after the hurrying sun has been swallowed up. It calls to us from out of our own innermost depths. We are suspended between two kinds of light—such is our nature. And the one is at odds with the other, for each is darkness to the other.

These were no doubt the thoughts of El Greco, when he sat in his studio without working or sleeping, "with the window curtains drawn so tight that it was scarcely possible to make out objects." And yet, Giulio Clovio tells us in his account of a visit to the painter,[1]

---

[1] In a letter that was published thanks to the librarian of Split; but the late Antonina Vallentin was unable to find it in the archives. *Se non è vero....*

*What an introduction to Night is this painting, probably by a Flemish Mannerist but in which we can detect a Germanic, Rhenish accent (it anticipates the Master of St. Ursula at Grünewald, and even Alt-dorfer)! Its details plunge us into a darkness articulated by glimmers of light. Under the broken vault continued by a sky throbbing with stars, strange angels are flying like nocturnal birds. It is the end of the Night that is cracking apart to let new lights seep through.... (cf. Fig. 55).*

**296. 297. 298.** - *FLEMISH SCHOOL.*
THE ADORATION OF THE SHEPHERDS.
Entire painting and details.
Sixteenth-century Antwerp Mannerist.
Young Memorial Museum, San Francisco

the weather was fine, with a delightful spring sun that made everyone happy. The whole city looked in a holiday mood. But, in his darkened studio, shut away from the light of the world, El Greco sat meditating. "He refused to go out with me," adds the old Dalmatian painter, "for the light of day disturbed the inner light."

What a terrible burden of reality there is in the insolent light of the sun! It seduces us, it draws us outside; it distracts us in the original meaning of the term—*dis-trahit*: it pulls us away from ourselves, separates us from ourselves, wrenches us from ourselves, giving us the illusion that we are happier so.

But some men know. They are not unaware of reality, but they carry it within themselves like something that they have captured and subdued. When El Greco drew the curtains to shut out the sun and the season, the artificial dimness was not enough for him. He would sit down on a chair, close his eyes—I imagine him in that posture of physical relaxation and renunciation that has, for so long, been taught by the Indian yoga, hands resting on his knees, holding his breath. He plunges the visible universe into this lustral darkness behind his closed eyes, as into a deep cold well, stripping it of its carnality, purifying it, tuning it to the silence of his soul. Behind his closed eyelids the whole universe lies brooding (Fig. 305).

Stripped of everything that is not spirit, the universe re-emerges to the surface, trailing inner shadows. Abducted from the light, it will henceforth belong to Night, will rise out of it like a spectral apparition, illumined in a single brilliant fleeting spark that elongates the forms, makes them dance, and exasperates the colors. These clouds fringed with livid foam, this throbbing view of Toledo, as jagged as a fever chart, are not seen by daylight but by some ghostly light which had died and been resurrected from the tomb.

Such are the unreal, supernatural worlds of the great contemplators, worlds fed entirely on shadow. Rembrandt extracted his world from the depths where it had been resting, still irradiated by a strange, slow, phosphorescent glow. The new world he re-creates on canvas is illumined by its own light; from it emanates the light that he could no longer receive, but only give. In other painters, this world remains underground, buried in some unknown cellar of the soul, and the artist—in the instance of Georges de La Tour, for example—must light a torch or lamp to make it visible to our physical eyes. But we feel clearly that we are being conducted into considerable depths where the light of day and ordinary sounds cannot easily penetrate (Fig. 303).

The scintillation of high noon drives out the meditations of the soul, just as the sun dispels the mists. Although the sun does not disturb the reflections of the pure intellect, it interferes with the meditations of the soul. The Impressionists were never deterred by full sunlight, but then, the Impressionists never embarked, so to speak, upon any very notable spiritual adventure. Painters in broad daylight are devoid of inner mystery. The Impressionists even lost interest in the human face, although Carrière was rediscovering it at the same moment with the help of a colorless dimness. They are no more than pairs of keen, avid eyes, no more than functions of light. The soul, like a fresh breeze, stirs only at dawn or dusk, when the light is faint. Corot and Claude Lorrain loved the soul and light with equal fervor, and were inevitably fond of these transitional times of day. But, as the inner life extends its sway over an artist, he cautiously turns down the light-giving lamp and finds more and more room for shadows to absorb and disembody the material world. He dims his vision, the better to listen for precious whispers from

*David's music suddenly fills the obscure silence which has oppressed Saul, the veil of Night is lifted, and his eyes begin to pierce the darkness.*

**299. 299-a. -** *REMBRANDT.*
DAVID AND SAUL.
Entire painting and detail.
Mauritshuis, The Hague

**300.** - Attributed to *GERARD VAN HONTHORST*. ALLEGORY OF VANITY. Ashmolean Museum, Oxford

Sometimes the Night is scrutinized like the indistinct depths of a mirror, and all the eye perceives in them is the reflection of a skull in the ultimate darkness. Everything has been weighted—memento mori!

**301.** - *GEORGES DE LA TOUR.*
THE REPENTANT MAGDALENE
(upper part of the painting).
Private collection, Paris

**302.** - *MORIN.* MEMENTO MORI,
after Philippe de Champaigne.
Seventeenth century. Engraving.
Bibliothèque Nationale, Paris

the deep source. Dusk, night, silence, void, immobility—these are all required by the painters of the soul. Poetic effects require darkness, just as music sounds best against a background of perfect silence. The nightingale sings at night, and Homer was blind. Rembrandt showed his grasp of this when he painted sightless eyes and when he painted the aged Saul listening, eyes lost in the distance, to David's harp. There are lights that must be played down if we are to be made to glimpse the existence of other, purer lights. The painters of spirituality are always, to some extent, painters of darkness (Fig. 299).

THE TWO SIDES OF THE MOUNTAIN.   Man walks a Great Divide, the shifting demarcation line between day and night. On the one side appear the truths of the senses and the intellect, brightly lit for all to see; on the other side, the truths of the soul, harder to discern. It is tempting to run down the one slope or the other, pretending there is no other side of the mountain, to opt uncompromisingly for realism or for mysticism. Mankind is alternately solicited by these two seemingly opposed destinies. Incidentally, it would be erroneous to assign all light to the one, all shadow to the other: only painters who still address themselves to our eyes are compelled to remain strictly faithful to the metaphor. But we need not be so literal: the contrast is not so much between the light of day on the one hand, the dark of night on the other, as between two different kinds of light, so contradictory that each, juxtaposed with the other, appears to negate it. The light of the senses is shadow to the soul, and the light of the soul is darkness to the eyes.

All around us lie expanses of light, where all is visible, all intelligible. We need only open our eyes and our other senses to perceive what there is to perceive, need only apply our intelligence to these data of perception in order to understand. A world proliferating with objects presents itself to our eyes, our hands, and our feet, whose acquaintance we earnestly desire to make, which offers intoxicating scope for our activities. To become the master of all we perceive, enjoying it with all our senses and grasping it with our minds, dominating the visible world by our own powers—this is the dream of the West, the dream which modern science has pursued to its present-day climax. This is the dream of perfect lucidity. It is also an illusion, however, for our civilization advances, in this sense, only to discover that the horizon lies just as far ahead as ever. The light that makes all things clear will never reveal—and this is the terrible price we have to pay—anything more than appearances, the outward aspects of things and creatures. This external light tells me very little about my inner substance or secret depths, the living flesh under the visible shell, my heart and soul. I am obliged to infer the existence of these things, to make conjectures about their nature. Although I can, to some degree, verify these inferences, I can never touch these things as such. To the light, everything that is becomes an object. It is a pitiless word—*ob-jacet*: that which is not self, which lies outside me, distinct from me, which I see only by separating myself from it (for one must move back the better to see what has become too close!). The West knows well how eager it has been to pay the price of clarity, which offers us everything and gives us nothing. The things are made to seem clear only because light is reflected from their surfaces.

But is was lovely, that Western light, when it first lit up the skies over Greece! It defined forms so harmoniously and it made the marble shimmer with such splendor that centuries had to go by before a hunger it could never satisfy made itself felt. One day a warmer wind began to agitate the too calm, too limpid air. It was the stirrings of Christianity, the breath of love, and it may have come from the distant East. To get behind form, behind definitions, behind the knowledge that explains, to break down the barriers between things and creatures—to plunge inside them as the swimmer dives into the sea, to bathe in them and to become one with them—such is the aim and miracle of love. St. Thomas himself was moved to observe that love is not "an objective union like knowledge" but that it "transforms the lover into the loved." Unlike the eye, the heart does not stop short at the shimmering surface of things, nor even, like the mind, at the pattern of their structure. It plunges into the depths of their substance. Light may still serve to illumine space, to expose the goal toward which the vibrant arrow flies—but the goal is somewhere beyond light: to pierce through the outer envelope of things and be drenched in the warm blood of life itself. St. Francis was fascinated by birdsong and by the red and blue of flowers, but he loved them: he loved his "brother Sun and brother Wind." His love went ever farther, ever deeper; he loved, as well, the invisible God who created and animated them. Beneath the surface of appearances he sought the central eternal fires that would consume him. When the Christ appeared to him in all His glory, the effulgent rays of light broke open the wounds of the saint's stigmata, making them breaches through which the inner being—a being that bleeds—was touched.

"THE NOCTURNAL UNKNOWN."   Thus, the ordinary light of day came to appear insufficient to our needs. It became a mere medium for spanning the bridge between souls of which Delacroix wrote, a mere instrumentality in the hands of a force stronger than and alien to it.

One step further, and love brings us to mysticism. We cross the shadow boundary and find ourselves in Rimbaud's nocturnal unknown. Whereas clear knowledge postulates that we are distinct from the object, to know and to be are fused in love. Love wants to be what attracts it. But is it possible to be more than we are? Can union and total fusion with the other be truly realized, save inside ourselves? Henceforth, I shall have no use for the outside world, no use for light. All I have now to do is to imagine what I am. It is enough to close my eyes, to cut myself off from the world, to fall silent, and feel within myself the life that is within us all. Close the doors and windows; let no chink of daylight seep through. Let our eyes get accustomed to the dark, where the organ of visual perception is useless, where the eyes of the intellect stare vacantly. How can we cast our eyes upon what is behind the eyes? In this pitch blackness we grope at a loss until suddenly we feel, underfoot, a narrow staircase leading down to the inner depths. All we have now to do is keep on where it leads, step by step getting farther and farther away from the daylight. We are making our way through our own blackness. We may discover that the way narrows as we advance, the heat becomes more stifling, the air thinner; we may miss the broad expanses of light. But gradually we will experience the three successive nights of the mystics, the three nights that San Juan de la Cruz described as stages in our progress toward God. These are: (1) the night of the senses, when we close our shutters to the outside world, (2) the night of the intellect, when we stop standing at a window open to the world, through which we thought we could watch everything that is, and (3) the night of the soul when we have been racked by anxiety by the deep descent, rendered well-nigh hopeless by the ever-deeper darkness. We are now in a bottomless cave, where we seem to have left everything behind, where we seem to have dug our own tomb. "A painful and laborious night," says San Juan de la Cruz, who is our guide, but a night that reassured him when he realized that "the sublimity of divine wisdom so greatly surpasses the capacity of the soul that it appears as darkness."

This secret knowledge had long been promulgated in the East, especially in India. The existence of God is far more convincingly and certainly knowable within us than outside us. To *look* for him, we may raise our eyes to heaven, like the saints of Guido or Bernini; but to *find* him we should close our eyes like the figures of La Tour and Rembrandt. Once we quit Maya—the world of light and illusion—we must first cross through the I, the individual self. We must sink a mine shaft into our own ground, and at first, all we find is ourselves. But at a greater depth, we have left behind the ground, the earth itself. We reach the vast surface of an immense subterranean sea that stretches to infinity and is the common ground of being for all humanity. Every man who has thus put behind him his own substance, his individual I, attains the *atman*, the universal I, whose existence his own I had obscured. And yet the individual selves of all human beings constitute this underground sea, indeed, flow into it like so many rivers. The *atman* is at the same time each of us and all of us together—it is Being, God, the infinite substance in which we all participate. There is a passage in the Upanishads where the king sets this question: "The sun has gone down, the moon has set, the fire is out, words are absent; what is the light that illumines this figure?" and he is told, "It is the *atman* that is this light." Here is the underground spring whose freshness and murmuring the mystics felt rising within themselves: "the well of living water" of the Gospel, the water that quenches every thirst, the water in which—fused at last with the object of his knowledge—man is dissolved again, a molecule lost in the infinitude of Being. Thus, at the end of Night, Light is reborn, a supernatural light no longer of space and time, but of the infinite, the absolute. This light is not a light that comes to us, but a light that we ourselves give off as an inner radiance, a sort of phosphorescence. It was recognized, at least symbolically, at a very early stage of civilization. When the prehistoric sorcerer took the neophyte out of the solar day farther and farther, down into the deepening dark of the cave and on to its central hall, he found himself in the presence of mysterious new lights.

Prior to the year 1000, the Sufi Al-Hallaj—eventually crucified for his daring ideas in Baghdad (though the city was a center of Greek and Eastern culture)—wrote in the *Divan*: "The dawn that I love rises in the night at its most splendid and it will never set." This was the source of a current of mysticism that, in the eleventh century, reached Western Islam and Spain, perhaps preparing the soil for such later Christian mystics as St. John of the Cross and St. Theresa of Avila. Seville was the home of Aby Medin; Murcia of Ibn 'Arabi. A little later, Alexandria sheltered Ibn 'Ata Allah, and Fez Ibn 'Abba de Ronda. The last of these, in the fourteenth century, summed up the message of them all when he declared, "The night has advantages that do not exist in the day."

*Light arising from the shadows destroyed forms in the art of Caravaggio and his followers (cf. Fig. 56). Light asserts forms in the art of La Tour by simplifying the modeling. In the figure shown here light expresses the spiritual intensity withdrawn behind closed eyes.*

**303.** - *GEORGES DE LA TOUR.* ST. SEBASTIAN (detail). State Museums, Berlin

THE PAINTERS OF SHADOW. Can painting draw upon this night of the soul? Is not darkness its very negation? Is it sufficiently flexible to participate in this strange domain and yield up its secret to us?

Certainly there have been painters of the night, to begin with all those who, like Honthorst (his nickname was *Gherardo della notte*) were influenced by Caravaggio. The latter has often been denounced as the most brutal of all materialists. However, the most recent studies by Italian historians have shown that he was a sincerely religious artist. The public he painted for, however, was professing new and almost revolutionary ideas, under the stimulus of the Counter Reformation's effort to replace the Church's traditional attitudes with new attitudes capable of standing up to the threat of Protestantism. Thus San Filippo de' Neri created a new sense of religiosity, which rapidly became more popular than the old. It has been established that Caravaggio painted primarily for the followers of the latter, and that his pictures were intended for their oratories. His fondness for portraying humble people, for darkness, for violent effects of light is to be accounted for less by some taste for brutal, shocking realism than by the vigorousness of his faith and a desire to touch the viewer with freshness and immediacy. It is a fact that his *tenebrosismo*, as he matured, went in less and less for violent effects and achieved, in the end, an emotional and spiritual power that sometimes brings Rembrandt to mind. This is particularly apparent in Caravaggio's last paintings. They were for a long time so seldom seen, hanging as they did in Sicily and Malta, and were to be seen in such poor light, that it is only quite recently, with restoration to their original state, that due importance has been assigned them (Fig. 304).

Caravaggism may well seem a strange method of attaining to spirituality. However, as early as Gentileschi and even more clearly in the instance of Saraceni (a colleague of the Lorrainer Leclerc, who probably initiated La Tour to the possibilities of an art of darkness), the attainment is unmistakable. With La Tour, the first French Caravaggist (Tournier was another), the night begins to yield up its secrets of the inner life. I once suggested that La Tour should be called the "Master of the Lowered Eyelids." Not a single one of his figures (save possibly in the earliest works)—so much alive, so much preoccupied with their own thoughts—raises his or her eyes to us. They scarcely look at each other, even. Their eyes look inward, contemplating the secrets of life. Even the little newborn babe seems preoccupied with the mystery of his arrival in the world. St. Joseph is shown fast asleep, dreaming; St. Francis is shown in trance, wrenched from his earthly condition to confrontation of another world. St. Sebastian, wounded, in agony, is at the threshold of quitting this world forever. St. Alexis—who has crossed that threshold—is not of this world at all. And finally, the skull next to which the Magdalene is shown repenting is possessed of a life of its own, as though come back from the grave to bear witness to the mystery.

All La Tour's figures look down, modestly veiling their eyes, and thereby reflect an inner flame of meditation. In the shadow and the silence, the only lights are uncompromising, unflickering, supplied by torch or candle—the latter sometimes screened by a trembling hand, apart from that inner light which is screened by the downcast lids.

*At the end of his short life, Caravaggio himself began to sense a mysterious presence in the shadows which, until then, had served him only to brutalize form.*

**304.** - *CARAVAGGIO.* THE RAISING OF LAZARUS. National Museum, Messina

Sometimes the light vanishes altogether and the eyes close. Those of the newborn infant, for example, tight closed against a still uncertain consciousness of life. Those of St. Joseph, closed to all but dreams. Those of the hurdy-gurdy player, closed because he is blind. Those of St. Sebastian because he has lost consciousness. Those of St. Alexis are closed upon nothingness, and those of St. Francis upon the revelation of God's presence to him. Occasionally the night closes in upon its own void: the skull of Fig. 306 has mere shadows for eye sockets.

If La Tour, like Honthorst, chose to be primarily a painter of the night, it is because too much light prevents disclosure of spiritual mysteries—it can only disclose matter. La Tour scorns the picturesque, even scorns action: all he portrays is silent meditation. The real action is going on in the souls of the individuals portrayed, which gives off a mysterious radiance. Light, so to speak, falls silent and effaces itself. Failure to grasp this inner life is to misunderstand the painter entirely. The painting showing St. Francis in ecstasy (Museum of Le Mans) was long supposed to be a portrayal of him after death; it was interpreted according to materialist standards. To understand the saint's closed eyes and his lifeless appearance, we have to recall the Counter Reformation and such characteristic developments as Loyola's spiritual exercises. The methods of prayer then inaugurated taught that to achieve the deepest meditation one had to shut oneself up far away from distracting light and noise in a dark cell. There one was to light a single small candle ("I shall give myself just enough light to see the topics I am to meditate on"), and then to concentrate the imagination firmly on death (second day, first exercise: "I shall recall what I have seen of the horrors of death"). Georges de La Tour's Magdalene and St. Francis are shown meditating on the insignificance of the human condition in semidarkness with a skull (Fig. 301).

Thus, darkness came to be utilized in connection with spiritual adventures, and its virtues deliberately cultivated. This is a development remote from primitive man's use of darkness to symbolize evil. The darkness assists St. Francis to achieve ecstasy, to transport him beyond himself, beyond the normal sphere of possibility. This ecstasy is the same as that in which Plotinus had seen the supreme degree of human attainment: a soaring toward God beyond all physical reality. Such a journey to the end of the Night need not necessarily bog down in quicksand—contrary to what Céline supposed. Properly guided, it can raise man to a vision of the very brightest things, to an effulgence remote from earthly lights.


"THE DARK NIGHT OF THE FIRE OF LOVE." Painters, too, began to discover the reversibility of light. The light of day, which had once been regarded as symbol of all that escapes the grip of the material, physical world, was disavowed in its turn, because, after all, it, too, is empirical. The soul must hold it at a distance, and cultivate darkness if it is to be liberated. The soul must rid itself of the eyes of the body if it is to discover its own light, its true light. But how? San Juan de la Cruz, who was a very great mystic, would have us embark forthrightedly upon "the dark night of the fire of love without other light or guide save that burning in my heart."

Was Rembrandt's light any different? Rembrandt, like La Tour, was the painter of meditation in darkness. Look at his *Philosophers*—seated near a tiny window in some little cell in which they have withdrawn, and inside which falls no very illuminating shaft of

daylight. Even so they sometimes have their eyes closed—
they, too—the better to withdraw within themselves.

Rembrandt was perhaps the
only painter able to illumine the
mysterious darkness of which
Tauler spoke, filling it with a
fire in which blaze the flames of
affection, love, and goodness.

We have arrived at what Claudel
has called the boundary between
two worlds. He relates that in an
old Chinese fairy tale a man who
was wandering around in a fog
suddenly came to a stele in a field.
On it was inscribed, "This is the
boundary between two worlds."

Man has indeed transcended
himself. Having at once penetrated to the innermost reaches
of his own existence and to a region beyond this world, he finds
himself at the boundary between
Being and Nothingness. Nothing
can be more easily mistaken for
death than the advanced mystic
states. Indeed, the mystic is dead
to the world, someone who dies
the better to realize his ultimate
inner resources. Naïve psychologists have inferred, from the fact
that mystic ecstasy outwardly resembles sleep, that it is a kind of
sleep. Minds similarly incapable
of freeing themselves from Western prejudices have concluded
that the Indian nirvana is identical
with nothingness. Now, it is quite
true that the mystic in trance is so
utterly shut within his innermost
substance that he looks as though

*It devolved upon El Greco to create another light, which is not for the eyes. Like a throbbing, electric* moiré, *it runs in swift waves on the veil of the night.*

**305. -** *EL GRECO.* THE ANNUNCIATION. St. Vincent Museum, Toledo

[Tragic is light. O joy! I am deaf. I no longer hear the slightest sound, save only my heartbeats in the night....]

These are the heartbeats for which the two joined hands in Rembrandt's *The Jewish Bride* are anxiously feeling: the living heart inside the human breast.

*When the eyes are lost in reverie, there remains only the heart, throbbing deep within the breast.*

**308. -** *REMBRANDT.* THE JEWISH BRIDE (detail). Rijksmuseum, Amsterdam

# ACKNOWLEDGMENTS

The author and publisher wish to thank the libraries, museums, and private collectors for permitting the reproduction of the works of art in their collections. Photographs have been supplied by the owners or custodians of the works of art reproduced, except for the following, whose courtesy in furnishing photographs is gratefully acknowledged:

Copyright A.C.L., Brussels (Figures 127, 129, 190; Colorplate III); Alinari, Florence (4, 7, 51, 56, 95, 115); Alinari–Giraudon, Paris (46, 47, 186); Anderson, Rome (269); Anderson–Giraudon, Paris (53, 79, 86, 135, 139, 166, 167, 198, 199); Anderson-Viollet, Paris (85); Archives Photographiques, Paris (31, 89, 93, 94, 187, 188, 192, 252, 256, 258); Jean Arlaud (189); Ina Bandy (13); André Barry (210); Bibliothèque Nationale, Paris (65, 147, 170, 233, 301); Bibliothèque Royale, Brussels (72,73,74); L.Borel(149); H.Bouillière(154); Boudot-Lamotte (103); Braun & Cie, Paris (24, 241); Ann Bredol-Lepper, Aachen (131); British Council, London (283); Brogi, Florence (58); Bron (236); Bruckmann-Giraudon (200); J.-E. Bulloz, Paris (87, 191, 193); Calavas (140, 178); Carjat (259); Carles (34); Cinémathèque française, Paris (280); Coulet (260); Alfred Daber, Paris (262); A. Dingjan (299); Duprat (42); Edizione Artistiche Fiorentini, Venice (1, 2, 162, 173, 175); Flammarion, Paris (14, 17, 22, 33, 64, 83, 91, 99, 112, 125, 151, 152, 176, 185, 238, 245, 246, 247, 264, 266, 267, 281, 303); J. R. Freeman (12); A. Frequin (169, 171, 201); Giraudon, Paris (3, 5, 23, 44, 45, 54, 59, 70, 76, 78, 84, 104, 128, 146, 148, 153, 160, 161, 181, 182, 195, 204, 207, 209, 211, 212, 221, 234, 253, 274, 302, 306; Colorplate IV); Archives Musée Guimet, Paris (82); Carlfred Halbach (105); Lucien Hervé, Paris (41); Hinz, Basel (Colorplate XIII); Hgl.-Giraudon (232); Hurault (307); Jacomet (231); Galerie Maeght, Paris (295); Bildarchiv Foto Marburg, Marburg Kunstinstitut (98); Mas, Barcelona (235); Moreno (257); Sydney W. Newbevry (206, 215); Piaget (293); Copyright Editions Cercle d'Art, Paris (219); P.L. (106); Puytorac (6, 63, 174, 270, 287, 288, 289, 304; Colorplate VIII); R. Rémy (126); Rheinisches Bildarchiv (116, 202); Rodriguez (305); Rothier (92); Scala (Colorplates X, XV); S.N.C.F. (40); Sougez (237); Walter Steinkopf (10, 18, 220, 224, 229); Studios, Ltd. (48); Soichi Sunami (294); O. Vaering (108); Marc Vaux (communicated by "Art et Style," Paris: 25, 77, 109, 273, 291); André Vigneau (32); Roger Viollet (88); M. Wildenstein (180); Wilse (39).